T0344730

Make Way for Liberty

Make Way for Liberty

*Wisconsin African Americans
in the Civil War*

Jeff Kannel

WISCONSIN HISTORICAL SOCIETY PRESS

Published by the Wisconsin Historical Society Press
Publishers since 1855

The Wisconsin Historical Society helps people connect to the past by collecting, preserving, and sharing stories. Founded in 1846, the Society is one of the nation's finest historical institutions. Join the Wisconsin Historical Society: wisconsinhistory.org/membership

© 2020 by the State Historical Society of Wisconsin

For permission to reuse material from *Make Way for Liberty* (ISBN 978-0-87020-946-8; e-book ISBN 978-0-87020-947-5), please access www.copyright.com or contact the Copyright Clearance Center, Inc. (CCC), 222 Rosewood Drive, Danvers, MA 01923, 978-750-8400. CCC is a not-for-profit organization that provides licenses and registration for a variety of users.

Photographs identified with WHi or WHS are from the Society's collections; address requests to reproduce these photos to the Visual Materials Archivist at the Wisconsin Historical Society, 816 State Street, Madison, WI 53706.

Front cover images, from left to right: Benjamin "Benny" Butts (Fifth Wisconsin Infantry), UW Archives; Horace Artis, ca. 1900 (Thirty-First USCT), Wisconsin Veterans Museum; and Joseph M. Ellmore, ca. 1900 (USCI), Wisconsin Veterans Museum | Back cover images , from left to right: Thomas Greene (Thirteenth USCHA), Grant County Historical Museum; John J. Valentine (Seventeenth USCI), courtesy of Patricia J. Roberson; Henry Sink (Twenty-Ninth USCI), courtesy of the De Pere Historical Society

Printed in the United States of America
Designed by Sara DeHaan

24 23 22 21 20   1 2 3 4 5

Library of Congress Cataloging-in-Publication Data
Names: Kannel, Jeff, author.
Title: Make Way for Liberty : Wisconsin African Americans in the Civil War/ Jeff Kannel.
Other titles: Wisconsin African Americans in the Civil War
Description: [Madison] : Wisconsin Historical Society Press, [2020] | Includes bibliographical references and index.
Identifiers: LCCN 2020007880 (print) | LCCN 2020007881 (ebook) | ISBN 9780870209468 (paperback) | ISBN 9780870209475 (epub)
Subjects: LCSH: United States—History—Civil War, 1861–1865—Participation, African American. | Wisconsin—History—Civil War, 1861–1865—Participation, African American. | African American soldiers—Wisconsin—History—19th century. | African Americans—Wisconsin—History—19th century. | African Americans—Wisconsin—Biography.
Classification: LCC E540.N3 K275 2020 (print) | LCC E540.N3 (ebook) | DDC 973.7/475092396073—dc23
LC record available at https://lccn.loc.gov/2020007880
LC ebook record available at https://lccn.loc.gov/2020007881

♾ The paper used in this publication meets the minimum requirements of the American National Standard for Information Sciences—Permanence of Paper for Printed Library Materials, ANSI Z39.48-1992.

Publication of this book was made possible in part by a grant from the Amy Louise Hunter fellowship fund and by support from the Wisconsin Historical Society Press Readers Circle. For more information or to join the Reader's Circle, visit support.wisconsinhistory.org/readerscircle.

This book is dedicated to the African American soldiers and sailors who served from Wisconsin in the US Civil War, as well as their descendants. May their sacrifices, service, and contributions to the state and nation be respected and remembered.

CONTENTS

Preface   ix
Introduction   1

1   Arrival   7

2   Recruitment   21

3   On the Battlefield   53

4   Postwar Life   89

5   After Reconstruction   115

Epilogue: Legacy   155
Appendices
   Enlisted Men   163
   Employees   221
Acknowledgments   243
Notes   245
Index   289

PREFACE

The creation of this book began around 2009 at an event I attended at the Civil War Museum in Kenosha, Wisconsin. Present at the event was a group of African American Civil War reenactors portraying Company F, Twenty-Ninth United States Colored Infantry (USCI). They introduced me for the first time to the "Milwaukee Company": black soldiers from Wisconsin who fought in the Battle of the Crater during the Siege of Petersburg. I admitted with embarrassment that I knew nothing about black Civil War soldiers from Wisconsin. After all, my father, Wayne, was a retired high school history teacher with special interest in the Civil War. When I told him about meeting the reenactors, he said that he too was unaware that there had been African American soldiers from Wisconsin in the war. He may have been more surprised and embarrassed than I.

I decided on that day to learn what I could about this history and why it wasn't better known. During the past ten years, I have found that the story of these real-life soldiers and freedom fighters should occupy a prominent place in Wisconsin's Civil War history. Although the number of Wisconsin African Americans who served is quite small compared with the number of white soldiers, black men served in disproportionately high numbers relative to their population in the state. The core issue of the Civil War was slavery, and the presence of black men and women in the state and their part in the war effort brought the issue home, even to people who initially chose to believe that the war could be ended without addressing slavery.

Some of these individual stories are stories of achievement. These contrast with the lives of the majority of their comrades, who were less successful in overcoming racism, discrimination, poverty, disability, a lack of education, and a lack of opportunity. Together, the stories in this book reveal the complicated and often contradictory response of many white Americans to the African American men who helped save the Union: some black veterans were accepted and respected for their service, while others were rejected and sometimes assaulted because of their race.

The title of this book is taken from a hopeful and positive editorial that appeared in the *New York Anglo African* weekly newspaper in the first month of the war. In sections addressed to white Unionists, it said, "If you would restore the Union and maintain the government you so fondly cherish, make way for liberty, universal and complete. But the day of supplication is past—the hour of action is at hand. The black man, either with cooperation or without it, must be ready to strike for liberty whenever the auspicious moment comes." To black readers, it said, "Let us concentrate our energies and unite our hearts, by taking counsel with each other how slavery can most speedily be abolished."[1]

INTRODUCTION

In *Race and Reunion*, historian David W. Blight documents the systematic effort by southerners and many northerners to deny that slavery was the principal cause of the Civil War. Southern whites, including most Confederate veterans, began as soon as the war ended to create and promote the mythology of the "Lost Cause": that secession was a noble crusade for liberty that failed only because of the North's superior numbers and economic power. In the Lost Cause myth, the defeat of Reconstruction and triumph of white supremacy were portrayed as victories benefiting the whole nation. Sectional reconciliation was promoted by white Union and Confederate veterans, who together celebrated their previous suffering and valor while avoiding discussions of race.[1]

For African Americans, there would be no return to enslavement. However, the seemingly bright future when the war ended, and the progress made during Reconstruction, were wiped out by a combination of racist violence, legal backtracking, and eventual abandonment by the Republican Party. Black veterans watched from the sidelines as their role in winning the war and eliminating slavery was forgotten by the surrounding white society. For white veterans North and South to "clasp hands across the bloody chasm," black veterans had to be excluded.[2]

With few exceptions, writers of history and fiction followed this same path, glorifying the bravery and sacrifice of white soldiers on both sides and ignoring or glossing over issues of race and slavery. Even at the local level, African American participation in the war was erased. In the Civil War chapter in a 1912 history of Fond du Lac County, the author listed every white man who served from the county but included none of the black

1

men.[3] In the 1880s, *Century* magazine solicited articles from veterans on both sides, mostly officers, which were later compiled into a four-volume work, *Battles and Leaders of the Civil War*. One of the few to write about the black soldiers was General Henry Goddard Thomas, who commanded US Colored Troops (USCT) in the Battle of the Crater. The *Century* project was consciously trying to encourage sectional reconciliation and to sell books in the North and South and therefore rejected pieces that directly addressed the causes of the war—secession and slavery.[4]

In the late nineteenth century, a few African American veterans did write about the role that black soldiers played in the Civil War. George Washington Williams, a veteran of the USCT and the Buffalo Soldiers, and later a minister, Ohio legislator, and historian, wrote *A History of the Negro Troops in the War of the Rebellion, 1861–1865* (1888). His thorough work, however, was overwhelmed by the tide of reconciliationist history and literature at the end of the nineteenth century. Robert Beecham, a private from Sun Prairie in the Iron Brigade, became a captain in the Twenty-Third US Colored Infantry (USCI), which he led in the Battle of the Crater. While *Century* magazine was soliciting the memoirs of officers, Beecham wrote to the editors offering to write a narrative, but they did not accept his offer.[5] Beecham's serialized memoirs were instead published in 1902 in the *National Tribune*.[6] Like Williams's work, Beecham's memoir countered the prevailing narrative that was fueled by racism and beliefs about white supremacy. Indeed, he called the black troops in the Crater battle "the bravest and best soldiers who ever lived."[7]

Veterans of many white regiments and companies wrote and read histories of their units, and readings from these works were common at Grand Army of the Republic (GAR) meetings.[8] The only black regiments in which Wisconsin men served that had histories published during the veterans' lifetimes were the Fifty-Fourth and Fifty-Fifth Massachusetts. The scarcity of written remembrance of the war from the African American perspective made it easier for whites to ignore it altogether.

African American communities and veterans commemorated the war, emancipation, and their own service in other ways. Veterans took part in community celebrations of the most important outcome of the Civil War—emancipation. On January 1, 1867, the fourth anniversary of the Emancipation Proclamation was celebrated in Milwaukee with a supper and ball.[9] Emancipation Day celebrations in August began in the United States in 1834 in recognition of the date of the British Empire's Slavery Abolition Act, ending bondage in the British West Indies. This date continued to be celebrated after the Civil War, in part because it was easier to hold parades, picnics, and baseball games in August than in January. These events combined secular and spiritual aspects: invocations, church services, prayers of thanksgiving, reading of the Emancipation Proclamation, music, dancing, and speeches.[10]

Local Emancipation Day commemorations always involved black veterans and were held in many Wisconsin locations—Prescott, Oshkosh, Lake Mills, La Crosse, Cheyenne Valley, Fond du Lac, Beloit, Racine, and Madison. In 1888, Delavan's Emancipation Day was an all-day affair, with speeches, a reading of the Emancipation Proclamation, a picnic, boat rides, a dinner, a dance with live music, and a midnight supper. The three signers of a public card of thanks from the organizing committee were all veterans: Alfred Matson, Eli Harwell, and Oscar McClellan.[11] The Beloit celebration in 1889 was held on August 1 and included "a parade in the morning and a picnic, at which there were orations and other exercises."[12] Juneteenth Day, commemorating the month in 1865 when enslaved persons in Texas learned that they were free, is still celebrated in Milwaukee with a parade led by the Civil War reenactors portraying Company F of the Twenty-Ninth USCI.[13]

The Civil War monument on the courthouse lawn in Lancaster was one of the first in the nation to memorialize the Civil War dead. Dedicated in 1867, the engraved names include those of Charles and John Shepard, a father and son who died while in service. It is the only Civil War monument in the state to specifically include the names of African American soldiers.[14] In his 1888 history of black troops in the war, George Washington Williams tried to initiate a nationwide campaign to raise funds for a monument to the African American soldiers and sailors who had served the cause of liberty and union. Williams included a detailed description of the design and the inscriptions for the monument and hoped that Congress would choose a location and appropriate funds.[15] Congress took no action.

On Memorial Day 1897, the city of Boston dedicated a monument to honor Colonel Robert Shaw, the white commander of the Fifty-Fourth Massachusetts, and the black soldiers who served with him. Arthur B. Lee, a resident of Milton, Rock County, did not attend the event, but 140 of his former comrades from the Fifty-Fourth and Fifty-Fifth marched in the procession past the monument.[16]

In September 1908, the "Old Colored Soldiers Re-Union and Second Annual Encampment" took place at "Camp Frederick Douglass" in Warrensburg, Missouri. The three-day event included baseball in the afternoons, evening concerts, orations, and Emancipation Day recognition. Among the organizers of the event was Dr. Charles South Walden (Twenty-Ninth USCI, credited to Milwaukee): an African American physician from Sedalia, Missouri, and several times a resident of the Soldiers Home in Milwaukee.[17]

Because social events and commemorations were important to the African American population, the 1903 commemoration of the Battle of the Crater was a slap in the face for black veterans. White Union and Confederate veterans participated in a reenactment of the battle and listened to speeches from the participants. And yet, despite their central role in the battle, no African Americans were asked to participate in the reenactment and no USCT unit was represented.[18]

African American communities and soldiers kept alive the memory of their active participation and sacrifice in the war that ended their enslavement. This book documents African Americans' participation in Wisconsin's Civil War effort so that their involvement can no longer be ignored or erased. In the following chapters, I discuss the arrival of African Americans in Wisconsin (as enslaved lead miners, pioneers, lumberjacks, and as passengers on the Underground Railroad); black soldiers' service in the Civil War as enlisted men and employees of Wisconsin officers and regiments, and the sacrifices of their families while they served; and finally, how black veterans fared immediately after the war and how they fought for their economic survival at a time of growing racism.

—‖—

NOTE ON APPENDICES

Published histories of Wisconsin prior to this decade that cover the Civil War era mention only in passing the black servicemen from the state. Other works ignore them completely, even if they recognize the central role of slavery in the causes and outcomes of the war. Estimates of the number of African American soldiers from the state have ranged from 155 to 363 but do not explain the source or method for determining the numbers. As this book will show, the actual numbers are much higher than those cited in previous books.[19]

A majority of the African American men representing Wisconsin who enlisted in the army were enslaved prior to the war. Most of them were illiterate and had no documents from their prewar lives. Wisconsin had been a state for only thirteen years when war broke out, so no more than a few dozen soldiers of African ancestry were born here. Public records in the state were kept inconsistently before 1865, so many life events like births, marriages, and deaths were not recorded.

In this work, I have taken an inclusive view of who qualifies as a "Wisconsin African American serviceman." It includes the following groups:

1. Soldiers whose service was credited to a Wisconsin location, regardless of whether they ever lived in the state. After 1863, the service of each volunteer, draftee, or substitute was credited to a location (a city, village, or township), which reduced the number of additional men that the locality had to produce for the war effort.

2. Soldiers and sailors with documentary evidence of living in Wisconsin before or after their military service, regardless of where their service was credited. Before the state began to recruit African Americans in March 1864, Wisconsin men went to Illinois, Massachusetts, and other states to volunteer.

3. African American men and women who served as employees of Wisconsin officers and regiments. These individuals are usually not considered to have done military service, but more than 180 of them were listed on Wisconsin regimental rosters, and many more were not on rosters but served in various capacities: as servants, teamsters, blacksmiths, cooks, wagoners (teamsters), hostlers, and hospital stewards. Whether rostered or not, they were exposed to the same hardships and hazards as white soldiers and suffered disease and death along with them as they performed vital work. A

number of these men later joined the USCI as free men, while others went north with white soldiers and took up residence in Wisconsin after the war.

4. Men of mixed white, Native American, and African American ancestry were occasionally accepted into Wisconsin regiments early in the war, despite the state's ban on militia service by men with African ancestry. Later in the war, the need for manpower caused the color line to be ignored as black men were drafted into so-called "white" Wisconsin regiments.

A total of 677 individuals across these four groups appear in the tables in the appendices. Twelve are those of employees who later served as enlisted soldiers, so the unduplicated total of black soldiers and employees is 665; 461 of them were enlisted soldiers on muster rolls for regiments of the USCT, Wisconsin regiments, and the US Navy.

Future researchers may find more African American veterans who moved to Wisconsin after the war. There were many more nonrostered employees than those listed in this work, but finding them will be difficult because no single source for this information exists. It is also likely that more men of African ancestry served in Wisconsin regiments than I have been able to document here.

Note on Terms

In the text, I have used the terms *black, African American,* or *of African ancestry* in referring to soldiers' race. The excerpts from newspaper articles, letters, and government documents from the nineteenth and early twentieth centuries that appear throughout the text include terms that are racially derogatory and offensive. I have not changed these terms when they are quoted because they are important for understanding the environment in which the black servicemen and veterans lived and the ways in which white people viewed them.

CHAPTER ONE

ARRIVAL

On November 27, 1923, the last surviving Wisconsin veteran of Company F, Twenty-Ninth Regiment, United States Colored Infantry (USCI), was laid to rest in Walnut Hill Cemetery in Baraboo. Aaron Roberts's adult life began early when he lied about his age in order to volunteer to fight for the Union and against slavery in the Civil War. After his service, he was a farmer, husband, father and grandfather, carpenter, entrepreneur, minister, and a respected member of every community in which he lived. He was buried in the veterans' section of the cemetery by his white comrades of the local post of the Grand Army of the Republic and his black brothers of the Madison Masonic Lodge.[1]

Aaron Roberts came from a community of multiracial families with roots in northern North Carolina and southwestern Virginia. His great-grandfather, Ishmael Roberts, was free and served with whites in a North Carolina militia in the Revolutionary War. Ishmael may have been at Valley Forge with George Washington's army in early 1778.[2] After Nat Turner's slave rebellion in 1830, free blacks and their allies were no longer welcome along the Virginia/North Carolina border, despite generations of residence there. Over several years, the Robertses and other black and mixed-ancestry families and some white neighbors uprooted themselves and moved to Indiana, joining one of several multiracial farming communities.[3]

A generation later, some members of the Indiana communities moved again because of threats from the slave-owning South. The Fugitive Slave Act of 1850 allowed slave hunters to go anywhere within the United States to try to reclaim persons accused of running away from enslavement. The

Roberts family lived not far from the Ohio River and the slaveholding state of Kentucky, and there were documented cases in Illinois and Indiana of free persons being kidnapped and sold across the river into enslavement.[4]

This time, the group moved far from the Ohio River, resettling on the Wisconsin frontier during the 1850s and 1860s. Aaron Roberts, born in Indiana in 1848, moved to Wisconsin with his parents and siblings around 1856, where they joined free blacks from Illinois, including the Wesley Barton and Walden Stewart families. These were the pioneer families of Cheyenne Valley, Forest Township, in what became Vernon County. Another smaller community of African American farmers from Ohio formed nearby in western Sauk County.[5]

The arrival of other black future soldiers in Wisconsin is not as well documented as the arrival of Aaron Roberts. Few were born in Wisconsin. A number came from the North and had never been enslaved, but some of these men were born to parents who had escaped enslavement. The largest portion of future Wisconsin soldiers was born enslaved. A few were freed by their owners, and a few bought their freedom. Some made it to Wisconsin on the Underground Railroad, though most of them freed themselves after the Civil War began, when the presence of the Union army in the South provided an enhanced opportunity for self-liberation. A large contingent from the slaveholding state of Missouri braved threats and acts of violence to cross the Mississippi River during the war to find freedom in Illinois and Wisconsin.

Hundreds of African American men and women enslaved in Tennessee, Mississippi, Louisiana, Alabama, and Georgia began their connection to Wisconsin by seeking refuge with regiments serving in those states. Many of the men (and some women) were employed by Wisconsin regiments and officers and later came to the state with their employers. Some of them went back to the South as full-fledged soldiers when the federal government finally allowed them to volunteer to join the fight to end the South's system of slave labor. Several hundred people, mostly women and children but also some future soldiers, traveled by train to Wisconsin as part of a short-lived federal program from late 1862 to early 1863 to resettle black war refugees in the North and relieve the Union army of the responsibility of sheltering and protecting them.

Although their numbers were small, the formerly enslaved people who migrated to Wisconsin during the Civil War completely reshaped the small African American population and communities where they settled. The response of whites to these arrivals was a mix of acceptance and rejection, but by the late nineteenth century, rejection and restriction of the black population became the norm. Black Civil War veterans were paradoxically accepted and respected for their service but shunned because of their race.

The influx of black men into the Union army after the Emancipation Proclamation was crucial to the Union victory and the end of enslavement. The immediate postwar years were a time of hope for African Americans. Civil rights amendments were added to the Constitution, and black men became a permanent part of the nation's armed forces. African Americans had more freedom of movement than ever before. However, by the time of Aaron Roberts's death in 1923, the military service of nearly 200,000 African Americans in the Civil War had been ignored and largely forgotten by the mostly white public. At the end of the nineteenth century, white Union veterans began holding joint events with Confederate veterans to foster reconciliation between the regions, but they excluded the African Americans who fought and died beside them in the war.

The end of Reconstruction (1877) and the subsequent imposition of Jim Crow segregation in the South were only part of the story. In the North, African Americans retained their voting and property rights, but legal and extra-legal segregation increased and the rural and small-town black communities gradually shrank and many disappeared. Twentieth-century obituaries of black veterans in small towns or rural areas often included the line "the last colored man in town." Those who died in larger cities, where the black population was concentrated, died without obituaries. The week before Aaron Roberts died, the Ku Klux Klan burned crosses on the hilltops around Baraboo to announce its arrival in the area.[6] No record remains of what the old freedom fighter and self-made man thought about this as he lay dying.

AFRICAN AMERICANS IN WISCONSIN

The land that became the state of Wisconsin was part of the Northwest Territory, created by Congress in 1787. At that time, the area was inhabited almost exclusively by the Ho-Chunk, Menominee, Ojibwe, Meskwaki

(Fox), and Dakota; fur trappers and traders; and a few men of African ancestry. Congress declared it a free territory. However, documentation proves that there were black slaves in Wisconsin as far back as 1725.[7]

As white people moved into the territory, free and enslaved African Americans did as well. Army officers from the South who were stationed at Fort Crawford, near Prairie du Chien, brought enslaved people with them and took them back to the South when the officers' terms of service expired. Slaveholders from Virginia, Missouri, and other states brought enslaved persons with them to the farmland and lead mines in the southwestern part of the state. In 1827, future territorial governor and senator Henry Dodge brought enslaved persons with him when he settled in Iowa County. Five of them worked as slave labor in his home and his mining and smelting works for eleven years until he freed them in 1838. What happened to the other persons Dodge enslaved has not been documented.[8]

The 1840 Wisconsin Territorial Census counted 11 slaves and 185 "free colored persons."[9] By the time Wisconsin became a state in 1848, the pockets of enslaved African Americans were gone but free African Americans remained less than full citizens. Anti-black prejudice was common and strong throughout the Midwest.[10] The 1848 state constitution did not allow men of African ancestry to vote, but it did allow the legislature to authorize black suffrage if it was approved in a statewide referendum. In 1849, a referendum vote supported black suffrage, but the result was interpreted legally as a loss because the "yes" vote was not a majority of all votes cast in the general election. In addition to the ban on voting, African American men were not allowed to serve in the militia, though they were allowed to testify in court, serve on juries, and attend public schools.[11]

In 1850, 635 "free colored" persons were living in Wisconsin. That population was widely scattered over the settled parts of the state, primarily in small villages and rural areas, a pattern that continued through the 1850s.[12] In Grant County, a group of formerly enslaved persons from Virginia and Missouri formed the small farming community of Pleasant Ridge. Charles and Caroline Shepard and their three children came from Virginia with William Horner, the nephew of their former owner, who had freed them in her will. Horner bought three thousand acres in Beetown Township. Also arriving with them were Charles's brother Isaac, and Sarah Brown, who was still enslaved. Isaac later returned to Virginia and purchased Sarah's freedom, then married her. The Shepards worked for wages on Horn-

Formal studio portrait of Isaac Shepard and his daughters Ella, Eliza, and Emily. WHI IMAGE ID 45968

Ed Shepard, pictured here in the 1920s, became the oldest male in his family at age 13, when both his father Charles and brother John died while serving in the Union army. WHI IMAGE ID 45967

er's farm until they saved enough to buy their own farmland from him. They were soon joined by individuals and families escaping enslavement in Missouri.[13]

Just after the Civil War began, two more families—the Grimeses and the Greenes (sometimes spelled "Green")—moved to Pleasant Ridge. William Ross came to Wisconsin from Missouri with his former slaves, including the Grimes family—Nancy, her five children, and several grandchildren—whom he subsequently freed. The Thomas Greene extended family took the change they had saved from paid work while enslaved in Missouri, escaped to St. Louis, and then came north by train. On arrival in East Dubuque, Illinois, they discovered that all of their clothing had been stolen from their trunk. "We toted an empty trunk to Potosi and then to Pleasant Ridge," wrote granddaughter Lillie years later. They arrived in Grant County with no clothes but a small amount of cash, ready to start a new life as independent farmers.[14]

Thomas Greene (Thirteenth USCHA).
GRANT COUNTY HISTORICAL MUSEUM

Thomas and Harriet Greene's children:
William, Sarah, and Ollie, 1900.
WHI IMAGE ID 44861

Like their white contemporaries, the early black pioneers had difficult times in the beginning, especially during the winter, which some of them spent in tents or in dugouts carved into hillsides.[15] They needed multiple skills in order to succeed on the frontier. Families like those in Cheyenne Valley and Pleasant Ridge who were building farms needed to be lumberjacks to clear their forested land, masons and carpenters to build their homes and barns, caretakers of livestock, cultivators, cooks, tailors, and hunters, as well as parents.

Abolitionism was supported by a small minority of white Wisconsin residents, but support for it increased after the passage of the Fugitive Slave Act of 1850, which made it a federal crime to assist a fugitive or to refuse to assist slave catchers and owners in locating and returning fugitives to enslavement. Underground Railroad activism existed in Wisconsin, as shown in the 1842 escape of Caroline Quarlls, who was sheltered for a week in Milwaukee by black barber Robert Titball after a coach dropped her off in front of his shop. Titball was confronted by Quarlls's former owner and a slave hunter, who pressured and bribed him to reveal her hiding place. She was not found in the place to which he sent them. Abolitionists transported

John Greene, one of Pleasant Ridges's original settlers. WHI IMAGE ID 44800

Lewis Washington Sr. His son Lewis Jr. served in the Twenty-Ninth USCI.
WHI IMAGE ID 145964

her around Milwaukee and Chicago, eventually delivering her to freedom in Canada via Detroit.[16] Stockbridge in Calumet County included Mohican people, whites, and African Americans who often intermarried; it was also known for harboring fugitives from enslavement. Milton House, a hotel in the village of Milton, Rock County, was a way station on the Underground Railroad, one of the few places where the "railroad" actually ran underground, through a tunnel into the hotel basement from a nearby cabin.[17]

The small African American population living in the territory and then state of Wisconsin in the 1840s and 1850s was not far removed in place or time from enslavement. Individuals trying to escape it were not safe from the reach of slave hunters, and those who spoke out against enslavement did so at personal risk in some locations.

Lewis Washington Sr., born enslaved in Virginia, came to Wisconsin with his family in the late 1840s and made connections with abolitionists in Waukesha. He was an illiterate farmer but developed a gift for speaking, preaching, and singing. He did a three-week speaking tour on the evils of slavery around southeastern Wisconsin in 1847, a tour organized by Waukesha abolitionists. In the town of Raymond, he spoke in front of a

Milton House, 1900. WHI IMAGE ID 39828

supportive crowd but was refused lodging at a hotel owned by the town's namesake. He also spoke in Racine, Kenosha, Paris, Rochester, Burlington, and Bristol. Washington was said to be very effective in moving crowds and soliciting donations for the movement.[18] He also spoke on his own in other parts of the state. In October 1847, "a considerable excitement was caused by the lecture of a fugitive slave, named Lewis Washington, on the conditions of Negroes in the South. He was the first Negro to appear in public in Fond du Lac."[19] In the 1850s, Washington sold his Waukesha farm and purchased another in the town of Trimbelle in Pierce County, becoming part of a small black farming community. In 1860, Pierce County had an African American population of thirty-three, most of them from five farm households in Trimbelle.[20]

Unlike Washington, Joshua Glover was ultimately unable to remain in Wisconsin after escaping from slavery in Missouri. In Racine, he found support and work and decided to stay there in spite of the risk posed by the Fugitive Slave Act. In March 1854, his former owner hired slave catchers and a federal marshal broke into his cabin where he was playing cards with friends. They overpowered Glover and carried him to jail in Milwaukee to await a judge's order the next morning. A mob estimated at five thousand, led by friends from Racine and abolitionist editor Sherman Booth, surrounded the jail and broke Glover out. He spent forty days hiding in various safe houses until he was dispatched to freedom in Canada.[21]

On May 11, 1854, four men were charged for Glover's breakout, including one African American named Martin Smith. The accused whites were released on bail on May 15; bail was posted for Smith two days later. After much legal maneuvering, their trial began on March 9, 1855, before a jury that included one African American man. All of the defendants were found not guilty. However, fearing what had happened to Glover and feeling hostility from the whites who opposed abolitionism, many black people moved out of Milwaukee.[22]

As indicated by the Glover case and its aftermath, acceptance of African Americans in the state was mixed. Some states were even more hostile; Illinois, for instance, passed an exclusion law in 1853 that was designed to keep African Americans from migrating into the state. Violators of the law could be sold in a neighboring slave state if they could not post the required cash bond.[23] A similar exclusion law was proposed in the Wisconsin legislature in 1858 but did not pass. Around the same time, Wisconsin's Senator James Doolittle sponsored a bill to create a fund that would pay black people to leave the United States. Doolittle continued to support colonization proposals and encouraged Abraham Lincoln's interest in the idea until the Emancipation Proclamation was signed in 1863.[24]

A small percentage of the African American men who became Civil War soldiers was well established in Wisconsin before the war began, and only a handful of the soldiers and sailors of African descent were born in what became the state of Wisconsin. Most came to Wisconsin as adults to become farmers or as children with their pioneering parents. Some worked in small towns as barbers, day laborers, dock workers, millhands, and cooks. A few worked as lumberjacks in the northern part of the state and on riverboats on the Mississippi and its tributaries. Some of the early black residents of Wisconsin who later became Civil War soldiers are described in the following paragraphs.

One of Wisconsin's early black residents, Edward Hunter, who was born enslaved in Virginia, would go from town barber to private in the Twenty-Ninth USCI. The first documentation of his presence in Wisconsin is a fragile marriage certificate in his pension file at the National Archives. In Stockbridge, Calumet County, on February 17, 1854, Hunter married Nancy Ann Toucey, a woman of African and Stockbridge ancestry. By 1858, they were living in Waupaca with two children, where Hunter was the village barber. On the evening of July 3, Edward Hunter attempted to make a speech at an Independence Day event but was driven from the podium by a group of "*gentlemen*, who assaulted him with firecrackers, squibs, and other missiles," boasting that "if Hunter ever attempted to speak in Waupaca they would stop him." On July 5, with a large crowd committed to protecting Hunter and his right to speak, he succeeded in delivering the speech he could not make two evenings earlier. However, he was attacked after dark on his way home and his house was vandalized. The perpetrators were well known; one was a local teacher. They were charged, tried by a jury, convicted, and fined, and the teacher lost his job. The Hunters did not remain long in Waupaca, though, eventually moving to Markesan.[25]

Alfred Carroll, who would go on to serve in the Twenty-Ninth USCI, may have been born in Milwaukee, which would make him one of the first persons of African descent born in the city. His mother, Sarah Carroll, raised Alfred and his brother, Walter. Sarah ran a millinery shop from the early 1850s until after the Civil War. For a time, her shop was located in the same space where barber Robert Titball had harbored Caroline Quarlls in 1844. In 1862 and 1863, Alfred Carroll worked in the city as a paperhanger.[26]

Four men from the Valentine family would serve in the Civil War. Born in North Carolina, John J. and Julius Valentine moved with their parents to Ohio, and then, in 1846, their family and their uncle's family moved to Wisconsin. Julius, age around thirteen, lived on his parents' farm in Rutland Township, Dane County, in 1850. Nearby in Oregon, Dane County, their cousins Shadrach and John lived on their parents' farm, while John and his wife, Louisa, settled in Janesville. In 1860, he and Louisa had two daughters and shared a household with William McGraw and his wife, Lavinia,[27] Louisa's sister. Meanwhile, Shadrach moved to the black farming community in Trimbelle Township, Pierce County, to live among other future soldiers—Andrew Bennett, Charles Morgan, and Lewis Washington Jr., son of the abolitionist speaker. Julius's name appeared on the 1863 draft roster as a resident of Winneconne, Winnebago County.[28]

John Rosier was born in Virginia around 1825 and married Hannah Bruce in 1848 in Alexandria. They had three children in Virginia; their fourth child was born in 1855 in Wisconsin. By 1860, they had six children and owned a farm valued at $1,200 in Fort Winnebago Township, Columbia County, near Portage. Henry Rosier (spelled "Rusher" on the census), age thirty, and Maria, age twenty, who also lived with them, were probably John's brother and sister.[29]

John Sutfen (Sutphen) was born in 1839, and while his vital records give his birthplace as Oneida, New York, some later military and pension documents indicate that he was born in Milwaukee. His parents were Titus and Averline Sutfen. Titus first appears in public records in Wisconsin in 1860, farming in the town of Eagle, Waukesha County, with two children, John (age twenty-two) and Sarah (age sixteen). John was still a resident of Eagle when he enrolled in the draft in 1863.[30]

Henry Bostwick Sr. married Lucy Caesar Cochegan, a Brothertown Indian of Mohegan ancestry. Both of them were born in upstate New York, though their three sons, Henry Jr., Cyrenus, and Calvin, and a daughter, Rachel, were born in Brothertown, Calumet County, in the 1840s. The Brothertown Indian Nation lost federal recognition as a nation as a con-

John J. Valentine (Seventeenth USCI). His brother Julius served in the Twenty-Ninth USCI, and two nephews also served in the Union army. COURTESY OF PATRICIA J. ROBERSON

Lavinia McGraw and Louisa Valentine, sisters married to veterans of the 17th USCI. COURTESY OF PATRICIA J. ROBERSON

dition for being allowed to stay in their settlement in Calumet County. They were Christian, English-speaking farmers, and many Brothertown men served in Wisconsin Civil War regiments. Nevertheless, the Bostwick brothers, because of their father's race, were not accepted into the service until the creation of the USCT.[31]

Abram Thornton Sr. and his wife, Ellen, were born in Virginia and began their married life there. They had at least two children in Virginia and three more after they moved to Ohio around 1848. Their oldest daughter, Sarah Ann, married Reuben Thompson in Ohio. The Thornton family moved from Ohio to Westfield Township, Sauk County, around 1855 with four children. Ellen Thornton had another child within a year of their arrival. Reuben and Sarah Ann Thompson joined them in Sauk County. In 1860, the Thornton farm was valued at $900. Future soldier Abram Jr., age sixteen, and daughter (and future soldier's wife) Eliza, twelve, were the oldest children.[32]

The original settler in what became the Cheyenne Valley community was Walden Stewart, a free black man from Morgan County, Illinois, who filed the first land claim in Forest Township. His family joined him after 1855. In 1860, three of Walden and Hettie Stewart's six children were still alive and living with them on their frontier farm, including William P., age twenty, and Martha, age eighteen.[33]

Henry Sink was enslaved in Arkansas from his birth in 1830 until around thirty years of age. The details or date of his escape from bondage are not known. He appears on the draft list in the village of Rosendale, Fond du Lac County, in June 1863, along with Ebenezer Morgan, both listed as farmers. Neither one owned land.[34]

Born in the early 1820s in Richmond, Virginia, Cornelius Butler married Barbara Blankenheim, a German immigrant, in Kenosha in 1852. His various jobs in Wisconsin included cook,

Henry Sink (Twenty-Ninth USCI) wearing his GAR badge. COURTESY OF THE DE PERE HISTORICAL SOCIETY house painter, and barber. By 1860, they had seven children in their home in Kenosha's First Ward.[35]

Daniel Underhill was born free in Lancaster County, Pennsylvania. His wife, Mary Jane, bore their first child there. By 1855, though, they were living in the unincorporated village of Black River Falls. Another child was born around 1856. Prior to 1860, Underhill operated a barber shop and worked as a ferryman. The Underhills bought and sold several properties in town between 1856 and 1860. In February of 1860, their daughter Harriet died at less than one month of age from "inflammation of the brain." They remained in Black River Falls at least until June of 1860. Between then and the spring of 1864, they had two more sons and moved to Monroe County. On his enlistment form in 1864, Underhill gave his occupation as "lumberman." He may have worked winters in the pineries, on rafting crews, and in a mill during the summers.[36]

By 1860, the African American population in Wisconsin had reached 1,171. Racine County had 135 "free colored" residents, the largest county population in the state. Other counties with more than fifty black residents included Milwaukee, Rock, Dane, Walworth, Fond du Lac, and Winnebago.[37] The black population of Milwaukee suffered another exodus in 1861 following the lynching of Marshall Clark. Clark and James Shelton were walking with two white women when they were attacked by a band of Irish men. In the ensuing fight, Shelton stabbed George Carney, who later died. Clark and Shelton were arrested. A mob attacked the jail, knocked the sheriff unconscious, and hauled Clark out. Clark insisted that he had not stabbed Carney, but the crowd proceeded to hang him anyway. Shelton escaped from jail but was later captured. He was tried for Carney's murder but was found not guilty on the basis of self-defense.[38]

During these early years of Wisconsin's statehood, federal government policies favored Southern slaveholders. The Southern states controlled the federal government through their domination of the Senate. In addition to passing the Fugitive Slave Act, Southern senators prevented the admission of Minnesota into the Union for years in order to maintain their control of the Senate. The Supreme Court was also firmly on the side of slaveholders and white supremacists. The 1857 *Dred Scott* decision ruled that Scott, an enslaved man, was not entitled to freedom simply because his owner had taken him to live in Illinois and the Wisconsin Territory, where slavery was forbidden. The court ruled further that persons of African ancestry "had no rights which the white man was bound to respect."[39]

Enslaved persons in the South had no political or civil rights, but the rights of free African Americans were limited as well. At the time of the 1860 election, only five of the thirty-three states, all in the Northeast, allowed black men to vote. The election of Abraham Lincoln as the first Republican president set off the series of events that resulted in four years of civil war. The Republican campaign platform, which Lincoln supported, pledged to leave slavery untouched where it already existed but opposed its extension into new territories or states. This weak antislavery position was enough to attract the support of abolitionists and Free-Soilers but was an outrage to Democrats and slave owners. Three candidates ran against Lincoln, advocating various proslavery positions. Lincoln won only 39.8 percent of the popular vote but easily won the electoral vote by winning all of the free states. In Wisconsin, Lincoln won with 56.6 percent of the popular vote.[40]

Led by South Carolina, seven states seceded from the Union in the following months. When Lincoln was sworn in, four more states joined them and formed the Confederate States of America. After Lincoln announced his intention to resupply Fort Sumter in the harbor of Charleston, South Carolina, the state militia began bombarding the fort, marking the opening battle of the Civil War. The fort surrendered on April 13, 1861.

When war broke out, Wisconsin's Aaron Roberts, Edward Hunter, Alfred Carroll, John and Charles Shepard, the Valentines, the Bostwicks, Lewis Washington Jr., and Daniel Underhill, were barred from joining the Wisconsin militia or the federal army because of their race. All of them would go on to serve in the war that put an end to enslavement in the United States.

CHAPTER TWO

RECRUITMENT

When war broke out, the federal army and Northern state militias were small and untested, and African American men were not permitted to join. The few soldiers of African ancestry in the Union army in the first year of the war were men of mixed ancestry whom local recruiters did not recognize as black or whom they recognized as Native American. The Union's refusal to allow black men to serve gave a manpower advantage to the Confederate army, which used enslaved black men in large numbers as laborers, servants, and cooks.

NOT WANTED IN UNCLE SAM'S ARMY

The rival governments each believed it would win a quick military victory because the other side would not fight. President Lincoln's initial call for 75,000 volunteer soldiers met with enthusiasm across the Union, but men of African ancestry were not allowed to join. African Americans had never been accepted into the federal army and had been barred from the state militias since 1792.[1] Lincoln's goal in prosecuting the war was limited to preserving and restoring the Union, not abolishing slavery—a policy designed to keep the slaveholding Border States (Missouri, Kentucky, Maryland, and Delaware) in the Union.[2] Lincoln's call for the volunteers to serve for only ninety days reflected his view that the war would be over quickly.[3]

To enslaved and free African Americans, and to white and black abolitionists, the war was about slavery from the opening shot. Abolitionist leader and author Frederick Douglass saw the war as the pathway to freedom for enslaved people. He began agitating immediately to open the

Union army to black men.[4] Abolitionist, journalist, and physician Martin Delany had given up on white America ever accepting black people as equals and led a commission to investigate colonization on the West African coast. With the outbreak of war, Delany returned to the United States with renewed hope. He joined his former publishing partner Douglass in trying to open the way for black military service.[5]

Following the fall of Fort Sumter, letters poured into the office of Wisconsin governor Alexander Randall from men volunteering to serve in the militia. One of the first came from William H. Noland, an African American Madison resident who was also a barber, musician, and owner of a laundry business. He explained that he was "enquiring whether you would (if tendered) accept the Services of a Military Company of Colored Men, with a view of mustering them into the Service of the State or the United States upon Equal footing with other soldiers . . . I have no doubt but that thousands of brave hearts among them are burning with impatience for an opportunity to flock to the American Standard and prove to the world that they are alike brave, loyal, and reliable and to maintain these rights."[6] He identified himself as "a citizen of the State of Wisconsin" but was well aware that his citizenship was only partial. He linked the issue of voting rights to his plea to be allowed to engage in military service.

In the summer of 1862, two other black men wrote to recently installed Governor Salomon requesting the opportunity to serve. Cornelius Butler of Kenosha wrote on July 29, "I wish to lay before your excellency the hope and desire of the colored men of the state to do something to aid the government at this time. If it shall meet with your approbation and receive the cooperation of the public authorities we can raise a company perhaps two in the State to be joined to any regiment of our race to fight for the country. I look forward favorably upon this request."[7] There is no indication that Salomon responded directly to Butler, but he reportedly "forwarded these sentiments to (Secretary of War) Stanton . . . but neither Stanton nor Lincoln were willing to receive them."[8]

Two weeks later, a letter arrived from Ferdinand Shavers, an African American man living in Shullsburg. He asked "if a man is Black or a mulatto Can he inlist in the United States Servises or as a teamster . . . Or can he be taken in as a substitute in the place of eny one that is drafted[?]" In the letter, Shavers did not indicate his race. The governor did not reply. An aide to the governor wrote a comment on the back of Shavers's letter, "Relative to the enlistment of negroes or mulattos, that African extraction will exempt, but complexion, however dark, does not."[9] Shavers did not mention that he was employed by Abraham Lincoln as a valet prior to and during Lincoln's campaign for president. Lincoln reportedly wanted to take Shavers with him to work in the White House but decided not to out of concern for Shavers's safety.[10]

Letters also came from white soldiers advocating black recruitment. Thomas Holmes of Shopiere, Rock County, wrote to the governor in August 1862: "Our community were very much disappointed & displeased when the word came yesterday that the President refuses to arm the Negroes. We think that he should receive them for that, as well as any thing else it will make a very great difference about volunteering. A great many express the hope that the govs. of the North will refuse to send troops unless they receive all Black as well as White and force the Pres. to receive them or resign . . . The Negros freedom is what this war is for. Why not have them help in all ways possible?"[11]

In July 1862, African American men were invited to help with the war effort, but not as soldiers. At that time, Congress passed and Lincoln signed a bill authorizing the president "to accept persons of African descent for the purpose of constructing entrenchments or performing camp service or any war service for which they may be found competent," except as soldiers.[12] This tentative first step only matched the Confederacy's use of enslaved labor for the same tasks.

The initial enthusiasm for a quick and glorious war had already dissipated by mid-spring of 1862. There were Union victories in the Mississippi Valley but with high casualties, while Virginia saw high casualties but no progress toward taking the Confederate capital at Richmond. To meet military manpower needs, a draft was instituted. The first draft in Wisconsin occurred in November of 1862 in districts where volunteers had not filled the local manpower quotas. An antidraft riot took place in Ozaukee County in which draft records were burned, the draft commissioner was hurled down the courthouse stairs, and homes and businesses were vandalized. The Twenty-Eighth Wisconsin Infantry was sent to Port Washington to quell the disturbance.[13] The first draft in Fond du Lac was held around September 1, 1862, where "[f]or one whole week the draft commissioner's and surgeon's office in this city has been crowded with applications for exemption." In addition to medical exemptions, men could avoid service if they had been convicted of felonies, came from families with other members already serving, or were the sole support of children or elders. Men with resources could pay three hundred dollars to be exempted from the draft.[14]

LABORERS AND REFUGEES: THE "CONTRABANDS"

Almost as soon as the war began, enslaved men and women presented a challenge to the federal government. As they liberated themselves from their owners, they sought refuge with the Union army. With the Fugitive Slave Act still on the books, some army commanders sought out the owners or voluntarily gave the fugitives back if the owners came for them.[15] Other commanders put them to work as pioneers (construction workers), cooks, laundresses, and teamsters. In May 1861, Major General Benjamin Butler, commanding Fortress Monroe at Hampton, Virginia, refused to send three fugitives back into bondage, declaring them "contraband of war."[16] Since Southern slaveholders and the Confederate government considered enslaved people to be property, Butler reasoned that they could be confiscated like other enemy property or war materiel. On August 6, 1861, it became federal policy that fugitive slaves would be declared contraband and free.[17] Congress went even further on March 13, 1862, and forbade Union soldiers and sailors from returning freed people to their former owners, regardless of the latter's political loyalties.[18] While this policy was enthusiastically accepted and implemented by officers and soldiers with abolitionist sympathies, it was ignored or resisted by others well into 1863.

The Twenty-Second Wisconsin Infantry, known as the "abolition regiment," famously defied orders in helping a young fugitive woman escape enslavement.[19] While stationed in Kentucky in 1862, Commander (Colonel) William Utley received an order from his superior to "send at once to my headquarters the four contrabands John, Abe, George and Dock, known to belong to good, loyal citizens. They are in your regiment, or were this morning." Utley responded, "I recognize your authority to command me in all matters pertaining to the military movements of the army, but I do not look upon this as belonging to that department . . . I have not had anything to do with their coming into camp, and I shall have nothing to do with sending them out." Several other times while they served in Kentucky, the Twenty-Second was ordered to give up all contrabands except servants of officers but found ways of not complying with the orders.[20] Despite the abolitionist sympathies of the Twenty-Second, the protection they offered to refugees from enslavement was transitory. Hundreds of soldiers and officers were taken prisoner in March 1863, temporarily destroying the regiment.[21] Contrabands who were with them scattered or, if captured, were returned to enslavement on plantations or for the Confederate military.

Another dispute over contrabands involved General Thomas Williams and Colonel Halbert Paine, Fourth Wisconsin Infantry. Williams's brigade occupied Baton Rouge, Louisiana, in May 1862, with formerly enslaved people arriving at their camps soon after. General Williams issued orders for his officers to "expel fugitives in their camps or garrisons out beyond the limits of their respective guards and sentinels," where slave owners and bounty hunters lay in wait. Some officers complied with the order, pushing the contrabands out of camp and telling them to return to their masters. Colonel Paine defied the order and defended his actions before Williams by quoting the law recently passed by Congress. Paine valued the labor of the refugees and the military intelligence that they provided. Williams had Paine arrested and confined, but it did not stop the fugitives from flowing into camps seeking protection. By late June, hundreds of fugitives were living and working with the Union army.[22] Williams released Paine from confinement when he was needed for battle, but re-arrested him when the fighting stopped. This continued until Williams was killed in battle in August. Paine was then released and replaced Williams as military commander of Baton Rouge.[23]

Escaping enslavement and arriving at Union army lines, however, was no guarantee of safety and security. Contrabands with the Eleventh Wisconsin Infantry were employed in some dangerous tasks, including digging trenches near the front line during daylight in the siege of Vicksburg.[24] William McKenney and Isaac Smith were employed as servants by officers of the Eleventh Wisconsin, and Ansel Clark was a nurse in the field hospital. In addition to working under fire, these men witnessed the corrupt business of brigade commander Colonel Charles E. Hovey, Thirty-Third Illinois, who used his troops to seize or buy cotton from captured plantations and then sold it in the North for personal profit. Hovey is reported to have exchanged black refugees for bales of cotton, in one case fifteen contrabands for thirty-three bales of cotton. Jesse Mather, a white private from Sauk County in Company F, Eleventh Wisconsin Infantry, wrote in a letter to his sister, "The transaction has made the whole camp indignant, and the soldiers ask how many bales of cotton a soldier is worth if a Negro is sold for two bales."[25]

In places like Helena, Arkansas; Cairo, Illinois; and Island No. 10 on the Mississippi River, camps were set up to shelter the contrabands. The camps provided food and temporary housing, and some had schools to teach the free persons to read and write. Because the army took in able-bodied males as employees, the residents of the camps were mostly women, children, the elderly, and people with disabilities.[26] Reverend James B. Rogers, who had served as pastor of Fond du Lac Baptist Church before becoming chaplain of the Fourteenth Wisconsin Infantry, was reassigned to supervise the contraband camp at Cairo, where conditions were desperate, with mud, disease, rats, limited food, and limited productive activity. Rogers sympathized with the sufferings of the contrabands. Over time, barracks, a hospital, and a school with four hundred students were built.[27]

In late 1862, the end of the war was nowhere in sight and labor shortages plagued the North. Thousands of men were away from home serving in the army, farm labor was in short supply, and families were losing their farms. For six months in 1862 and 1863, the federal government began transporting groups of contrabands north to free the army of responsibility for them, to relieve the squalid conditions in the camps, and to ease the Northern labor shortage.[28] At least three groups of freepersons were shipped to Wisconsin under this policy.

Some Wisconsin residents strongly opposed black migration from the South. While Democrat newspapers warned of an invasion of fugitives into the Midwest, Republican papers argued that, with emancipation, Northern blacks would move south because the climate was more agreeable to them.[29] Dodge County state senator Satterlee Clark, a vigorous opponent of the war, introduced a state senate resolution to deny blacks the right to enter Wisconsin after August 1, 1862. His resolution was voted down.[30] Another exclusion resolution was proposed in the state assembly in January 1863, with the support of such Democrat newspapers as the *Manitowoc Pilot*, *Milwaukee See Bote*, and *Beaver Dam Argus*. When it came to a vote, opponents proposed a substitute calling for black male suffrage. Both bills were voted down.[31]

In October 1862, between seventy-five and one hundred contrabands came to Fond du Lac by train from the Cairo camp, accompanied by Reverend Rogers. The *Fond du Lac Commonwealth* was supportive of the arrival of the African American refugees, noting that "[a] great crowd of curiosity seekers, swarmed at the Depot to gaze at the great Southern Idol . . . Some most excitedly deprecate the bringing of these unfortunate waifs that are thrown to us from the surges of the great sea of rebellion. We beg of such timid folks not to be alarmed . . . Their coming is only an incident of the strife; and they come to stay no longer than it takes to subdue their rebellious masters, and make peace and freedom for them in their own more genial clime." Contrary to this last sentiment, the refugees stayed and became the core of the largest African American community in Wisconsin for the next twenty years. Most of the adults among the contrabands found employment and shelter within their first week in town.[32]

The majority of the opposition to the presence of the freepersons came from Democrat newspapers, which feared that emancipation would create competition for white jobs. Hostility to the new African American residents was not limited to words and paper. Frances Shirley, one of the contrabands, was interviewed in 1933 by Zona Gale Breese, Wisconsin author and great-niece of Reverend Rogers. Shirley, nearly ninety years old, recalled "how they threw a rock through the window of his (Rogers') house and it fell between their heads as they lay asleep and did them no harm."[33]

Another group of contrabands arrived in Racine and was welcomed by the *Racine Weekly Advocate*, which noted that "It gives us pleasure to say that the men are a very worthy class, industrious and well behaved. They come among us in good time as laboring men are very scarce, and ask from two to three dollars a day for their labor . . . We bespeak for these colored men from Dixie a kind word and a fair field. There is room for five thousand more in this county."[34] The *Milwaukee See Bote* saw otherwise: "About 150 negroes have been brought to Racine last week . . . The abolitionists have distributed the quota for the different counties, and, in order not to make too much of a show, the imported negroes will be unloaded now in one county, and then in another. That is the 'free labor' that John F. Potter and Doolittle have fought for in Congress."[35]

The arrival of the contrabands had immediate negative political consequences for Republican office holders. John F. Potter, Republican congressman from Racine, lost his reelection bid a few weeks after the arrival of the contrabands. Fond du Lac's Republican congressman did not run for re-election in 1862 and was replaced by a Democrat.[36] This contributed to Democrats winning a majority of Midwestern seats in Congress in the November 1862 elections.

Another group of contrabands arrived in Satterlee Clark's state senate district of Beaver Dam on April 8, 1863. Their sponsors included Edson P. Cady, a Baptist deacon, and Assemblyman Quartus H. Barron. The *Dodge County Citizen* supported the effort: "A few weeks ago a number of farmers in the town of Trenton, finding great difficulty in securing farm help for the season, clubbed together and sent Elder Cady to Cairo to bring up a lot of Emancipated negroes; and he returned last Wednesday, bringing some thirty-three with him, who are already domiciliated and at work."[37] Vehemently opposing the experiment was the *Beaver Dam Argus*: "These negroes work for very low wages and consequently farms can be worked by them cheaper than by hiring white labor . . . there is an 'irrepressible conflict' between free white labor and free black labor and one or the other must triumph, consequently white laborers may as well prepare to take a 'back seat.' "[38]

The shipment of contrabands aroused such controversy and opposition that the program ended in the spring of 1863.[39] The three groups whose arrivals in Wisconsin have been documented became the foundations of the African American communities in Fond du Lac, Racine, and Fox Lake, among the largest in the state in the latter half of the nineteenth century. From these groups came men who returned to the South in 1864 and 1865 as Union soldiers—Lewis Gaines and Van Spence from Fond du Lac and Hayden Netter (Johnson) and Wesley Walter (Walton) from Dodge County.

African Americans Employed by Wisconsin Regiments

Though barred from enlisting, African American men and women worked for Wisconsin regiments from the earliest months of the war. William Cleggett, a barber from Plover, served as a cook for the Eighth Wisconsin Light Artillery at their camp in Racine in the early months of the war, but his name was never placed on the regimental roster.[40] Mickey Sullivan, Sixth Wisconsin Infantry (part of the Iron Brigade), mentioned a barber from Fond du Lac who was with the regiment and "was as well known through the brigade as was General Gibbon." This may have been John Riley, who had been cutting hair in Fond du Lac since the late 1840s.[41] Hundreds, perhaps thousands, of African American men and women in the South escaped enslavement, fled to the camps of Wisconsin regiments, and found employment. The vast majority of these persons were never listed on army rosters. Some regiments employed few or no contrabands. Others that hired contrabands did not document their service because officers did not consider them to be enlisted military personnel.

Corporal William Ray, Seventh Wisconsin Infantry, noted in his journal the arrival of twenty-five to thirty contrabands at the camp of the Iron Brigade in March 1862, in Virginia: "A great many of the officers got a male contraband (black servant) to carry their things and be waiters for them thereby giving the most or all of them work."[42] Rufus Dawes, commander of the Sixth Wisconsin, mentions by name six contraband employees in his memoir. One of them was William Jackson, who remained with Dawes from 1862 until Dawes resigned in August 1864. Dawes described several acts of bravery and dedication by Jackson during his service.[43] Jackson and the other African Americans employed by the Sixth and Seventh Wisconsin were never listed on the muster rolls. Men who worked as valets or servants for officers were never included in company or regimental rosters.

The scale of black employment by Wisconsin regiments can be guessed by those who *were* listed on official rosters—nearly two hundred. The earliest rostered black employee was William P. McAlroy, a cook with Company H, Twenty-Seventh Wisconsin. He joined on March 20, 1862, and served until he was mustered out on August 29, 1865.[44] Halbert Paine's Fourth Wisconsin participated in the capture of New Orleans in April

Officers of Company I, Seventh Wisconsin Infantry. Alonzo Gambel, their African American servant, stands in the shadow of the tent. Taken in the summer of 1862 near Fredericksburg, Virginia. WHI IMAGE ID 25588

1862. They fought up and down the lower Mississippi Valley, seeing heavy combat in May and June of 1863 at Port Hudson, Louisiana.[45] Paine noted in mid-June 1862 that there were "Forty-Eight Negroes belonging to the Fourth Wisconsin" onboard a steamer with his regiment, but not one of them appeared on muster rolls. The first rostered black man in the Fourth was "Archie" Blue, "colored cook," enrolled August 1, 1862.[46]

Private Leon C. Bartlett, Fourth Wisconsin, wrote a letter to the *Sheboygan Times* dated June 16, 1863, detailing acts of bravery during the Siege of Port Hudson. Halbert Paine, now Brigadier General, was shot in the leg and severely wounded, stranded between the lines with only a shallow gulley to shield him: "Two faithful negroes belonging to the Fourth, volunteered to go and bring him off, but were killed in the attempt." These men were not on the muster rolls of the Fourth. A letter to the *Madison Journal* from "V.W.R.," also of the Fourth Wisconsin, continued the story: "Four negro soldiers volunteered to bring him on a stretcher.—When they came within a short distance of the General they were shot dead. Several attempts were made, and fourteen negroes were killed before the General was relieved. It is universally conceded that the negroes make capital soldiers; and at Port Hudson, so far, they have fought as well as any soldiers in the United States Army." Versions of this story were reprinted in other Wisconsin newspapers.[47] Paine lost his leg but survived and remained in the service.

In the early summer of 1863, with the ranks of enlisted soldiers in the Fourth Wisconsin Infantry severely depleted, the number of black cooks increased. On September 1, the day the Fourth was officially converted from infantry to cavalry, four more black cooks were added, bringing the total on the rosters to twenty.[48] By war's end, at least forty-nine African American men were on company rosters as cooks with the Fourth, the most black employees in any Wisconsin regiment, though they represent a minority of the freedmen who worked for the Fourth. Five of the African American cooks died from disease during their service. Twenty, including "Archie" Blue, were still with the regiment at muster out in Texas on May 28, 1866.[49]

Other Wisconsin units with African American employees on their rosters were the Thirty-First Infantry (twenty-seven men), Thirteenth Infantry (twenty-five), Twenty-Seventh Infantry (fourteen), Seventeenth Infantry (seventeen), and Thirty-Fifth Infantry (eleven). These men ran the same risks from disease and battle as the white soldiers with whom they served. At least sixteen African American cooks on Wisconsin rosters died while in service. Though some women worked for Wisconsin officers and regiments as cooks, nurses, and laundresses, none was entered onto the rolls.[50] Despite its early fame in protecting contrabands, the Twenty-Second Wisconsin Infantry had no rostered black employees,[51] though Alfred Matson, postwar resident of Delavan, stated that he served a stint with the Twenty-Second in between times with the Eighth and Forty-Second.[52]

The Thirty-Eighth Wisconsin Infantry, formed in the summer of 1864, had five "colored undercooks" on its rosters who volunteered in Wisconsin. John Valentine, Lemuel Manley, Isaac Collins, and John Joiner all lived in Adams County, the commander's own home county. Matt James came from Madison.[53]

Henry Ashby worked for Lieutenant Colonel Samuel Clark of the Sixth Independent Wisconsin Light Artillery from July 1862 until Clark left the service in October 1864. Clark stated that Ashby sometimes went into battle carrying a musket and knew how to use it. He was wounded in battle around Corinth, Mississippi, the site of frequent skirmishes from 1862–1864. Ashby returned with Clark to Wisconsin after his service. His name was never entered on a muster roll.[54] Ashby's sister may have also worked for the battery. As Clark wrote in 1893, "Tell Henry I have not forgotten him or his kind gentle sister who died at Rienzi," near Corinth.[55]

An unknown number of black men, rostered and not, served with Wisconsin officers and regiments and came to the state with them. Later, some of these men returned to the South as soldiers with the US Colored Troops (USCT). They had freed themselves by going to army camps and left the slaveholding South with the Wisconsin soldiers. But when the opportunity came later in the war, they gave up the relative security of life in Wisconsin to return to the South as soldiers and fight to end slavery. Following are the stories of a few of these men.

Albert Hamlet was born in Mississippi, the son of an enslaved woman named Jane and the white man who owned them both. He was the servant of the same-aged white son of his father. When the war reached him, he escaped to the Second Wisconsin Cavalry and worked as a servant to Lieutenant John Showalter. In 1863, Showalter sent Hamlet to Grant County to work for Showalter's father-in-law, who had two sons in the army and needed a laborer. When Wisconsin began recruiting black soldiers, Hamlet enlisted at Ellenboro, joining the Forty-Ninth USCI.[56]

William "Pitt" McKenney and Isaac Smith were born enslaved, Smith in Kentucky and McKenney in Mississippi. In 1862, the Eleventh Wisconsin was posted at Helena, Arkansas, a location that became a magnet for contrabands. In 1883, Smith said, "I first got acquainted with him (McKenney) at Helena . . . We have been together ever since and will probably stay together 'til death."[57] Both men found work with the Eleventh Wisconsin as servants for officers. When Lieutenant Colonel Charles Wood's term of service ended, he returned to Madison accompanied by McKenney, who was employed in Wood's home. Smith remained with Colonel Charles Harris through the siege of Vicksburg and went to Madison with Harris when he was furloughed in March 1864. Weeks later in Madison, McKenney and Smith volunteered, assigned to Company F, Twenty-Ninth USCI. They were tentmates throughout the war.[58]

Dennis Hughes, born in Alabama, worked for Lieutenant Lafayette Munsel of the Eighth Wisconsin Infantry. The regiment received a veteran furlough in June 1864, and Hughes came to Wisconsin with them. When the regiment went back south, Hughes left them at Chicago to join the army as a soldier. He was assigned to Company D, Twenty-Ninth USCI.[59]

Peter Dabney escaped enslavement in western Tennessee and was hired as a body servant by Lieutenant Charles Nelson, Fifteenth Wisconsin Infantry. Nelson was wounded in battle in the spring of 1864. Dabney brought Nelson home to his farm near Beloit and worked for Nelson until he enlisted in Janesville in August 1864, assigned to the Eighteenth USCI. He later changed his last name from Dabney to Thomas.[60]

BLACK ENLISTMENT IN WISCONSIN

From July to October 1863, Governor Salomon received more letters about black enlistment than the governor's office had received in the previous two years. A man named James Perine wrote to the governor on behalf of Josephus Heuston (Houstin), who carried the letter personally when he went to see the governor in Madison. The letter stated that Heuston was "desirous of raising a company of colored soldiers in this state . . . He seems to be possessed of a good degree of zeal to serve the country + I hope he may be favored with an opportunity to do so." There is no indication of a response from the governor.[61]

Others, like Captain Orrin T. Maxson of the Twelfth Wisconsin Infantry, believed that the black men they could recruit would make better soldiers than the white men being drafted into the army. Maxson wrote from Vicksburg on July 29 with a proposal to organize a regiment of the USCT and requested a commission to recruit Wisconsin black men to serve as noncommissioned officers. He would "take these recruits to such point on the Mississippi River or elsewhere in the rebellious states and fill up the regiment. I feel sanguine with such an order I could soon offer to the service a regiment that, if properly officered, would compare favorably with the new men being forced into the service, so far as good fighting material is concerned."[62]

Maxson's letter arrived in Madison at almost the same time as a letter

from the Adjutant General's office in Washington, authorizing Governor
Salomon to initiate the recruitment of black men: "If you should find it
impracticable to raise a full regiment, any number of companies less than
that required for a regimental organization will be accepted."[63] The governor met personally with Maxson on August 25 and asked Federal Adjutant
General Lorenzo Thomas to release Maxson and other white officers so
they could begin recruiting. Thomas responded in mid-October that he
would not release Maxson or the others, so the plan died.[64]

In the fall, Wisconsin authorities publicly announced that they would
authorize raising "a regiment, battalion, or company of colored troops."[65]
On October 29, John W. Birney, a black barber in La Crosse since 1857, saw
the announcement and wrote to Gysbert van Steenwyk, a bank president in

John W. Birney. COURTESY OF THE LA CROSSE
PUBLIC LIBRARY ARCHIVES

La Crosse, asking to participate:
"Having noticed in the *Tribune*
of yesterday that Gen. Gaylord,
Adjutant Gen. of Wis. has authorized the raising and organization
of a Colored Company in this
state, I desire to have a Commission in it." He asked the banker
to intervene on his behalf for an
appointment as an officer and
recruiter. Van Steenwyk wrote
to the governor the same day, including Birney's letter, asking the
governor to grant a commission
to Birney: "I have held several
conversations with him about
the rebellion and I have no doubt
but he can enlist almost all of the
steamboat colored men in this
section . . . I think he will make an
excellent recruiting officer." An
unsigned note on the back of van
Steenwyk's letter by an aide to the
governor said in part, "there ex-

ists no authority to appt. colored men to commissions in the army. They can only be non-comm. officers." The note made no comment regarding whether or when the state might begin recruiting.[66]

THE EMANCIPATION PROCLAMATION

In the summer of 1862, President Lincoln concluded that the end of enslavement was necessary in order for the Union to win the war. Abolition would reduce foreign support for the Confederacy and would weaken the Southern economy and war work by increasing the flood of enslaved persons fleeing their owners. Finally, it would allow African Americans to help meet the manpower needs of the army. Lincoln told his cabinet that he was preparing to issue an emancipation proclamation, but invited their comments. They convinced him to hold off until after a Union victory on the battlefield, so that it would not appear to be an act of desperation.[67] Meanwhile, Lincoln continued to publicly indicate willingness to preserve the Union without regard to slavery. On August 19, Horace Greeley, editor of the *New York Tribune*, wrote a letter and editorial urging emancipation. Three days later, Lincoln responded in an open letter: "If I could save the Union without freeing any slave, I would do it; and if I could save it by freeing all the slaves, I would do it; and if I could save it by freeing some and leaving others alone, I would also do that. What I do about slavery and the colored race, I do because I believe it helps to save the Union."[68]

A month later, the bloodiest single day in United States history occurred along Antietam Creek in Maryland. The battle was inconclusive, but the Confederate Army withdrew back into Virginia and abandoned its campaign into Union territory. It gave Lincoln the battlefield success he was waiting for. On September 22, the president issued the provisional proclamation, giving the states in rebellion until January 1 to return to the Union or their slaves would be declared forever free. None of the Rebel states accepted the offer so, on January 1, 1863, Lincoln signed the Emancipation Proclamation.[69]

The document proclaimed freedom only for enslaved people under control of the Confederate government. It did not give freedom to persons still enslaved in Missouri, Kentucky, Maryland, and Delaware; Lincoln was still making concessions to Border State slaveholders in order to keep those states in the Union. Lincoln justified the proclamation as a military necessity, but its effect was clear. If the North won the war, there would be no more slavery, and there was no more possibility of restoring the Union with slavery intact. In response to the proclamation, Frederick Douglass wrote in his *Monthly*, "We shout for joy that we live to record this righteous decree."[70] The lesser known part of the proclamation declared that African Americans "will be received into the armed service of the United States."[71] What Lincoln had refused to do in 1861 and 1862 now became reality—black men, enslaved and free, could join the army. Lincoln was not alone in changing his thinking. According to historian Chandra Manning, a shift toward acceptance by white soldiers of black enlistment began before Lincoln's proclamation and increased after it.[72]

African American men became a major source of manpower for the Union army for the rest of the war. Here was the moment that Douglass had worked and hoped for: "Once let the black man get upon his person the brass letters U.S., let him get an eagle on his button, and a musket on his shoulder, and bullets in his pocket, and there is no power on the earth or under the earth that can deny that he has earned the right to citizenship."[73] Recruitment posters appeared in the North encouraging black men to join the army. Black volunteers came forward quickly, but it took federal and state officials months to organize the new recruits into a fighting force.

In May 1863, the Bureau of Colored Troops was formed to coordinate recruitment, eventually resulting in the creation of 175 regiments of infantry, cavalry, engineers, and artillery. Martin Delany and his son and two of Douglass's sons were among the more than 180,000 African American men who served in the USCT and the Union Navy. Douglass and Delany enthusiastically threw themselves into recruiting black troops.[74]

Nonetheless, the USCT incorporated the deeply held white prejudices against African Americans as people and soldiers. Lincoln's proclamation envisioned assigning black troops "to garrison forts, positions, stations, and other places" but did not mention combat. Pay for USCT soldiers would be ten dollars per month, minus a deduction of up to three dollars per month for clothing. Pay for white soldiers was thirteen dollars per month with no clothing deduction. The pay for black soldiers was equal to the pay authorized by the War Department for black laborers (like cooks), but cooks did not have to pay for uniforms.[75]

MEN OF COLOR!
TO ARMS! TO ARMS!
NOW OR NEVER

This is our Golden Moment. The Government of the United States calls for every Able-Bodied Colored Man to enter the Army

For Three Years' Service

And join in Fighting the Battles of Liberty and Union.

A MASS MEETING

Of Colored Men, will be held on

FRIDAY, JULY 17,

AT 8 O'CLOCK, P. M., AT

WASHINGTON HALL

SOUTH CAMDEN, N. J.,

To Promote Recruiting Colored Troops for Three Years or the War.

FREDERICK DOUGLASS

And other Distinguished Speakers, will Address the Meeting.

U. S Steam-power Job Printing Establishment, S. W. Corner of Third and Chestnut Streets, Philada.

Recruitment poster distributed after the Union army began accepting African Americans as soldiers in 1863. COURTESY OF THE LIBRARY COMPANY OF PHILADELPHIA

Photographic print showing the regimental flag and motto of the
Twenty-Fourth Infantry Regiment, USCT. The banner text reads "24th
Regt. U.S. Colored Troops. Let Soldiers in War, Be Citizens in Peace,"
ca. 1865. LIBRARY OF CONGRESS, LC-DIG-PPMSCA-11274

All commissioned officers in the USCT were white, accepting the false
assumption that black men could be controlled only under white leadership and the correct assumption that most white enlisted men would not
tolerate black officers of higher rank. Black enlisted men could rise no
higher than sergeant. Regiments already fighting in Louisiana had black
captains and lieutenants, but these officers were demoted or forced out of
service when their units became part of the USCT.[76]

The offers and promises made to the African American recruits North
and South were not matched by their treatment in the army. Recruiters
promised fair and equal treatment to the black recruits, but they found that
life in the army mirrored the restrictions and limitations they confronted
in civilian life in the North. As historian John David Smith explains, "The

twin forces of white racism and military necessity converged on the men of the USCT, and throughout their service black soldiers received discriminatory duties, inferior assignments, inadequate care, insufficient training, and insults from white soldiers."[77]

African American historian George Washington Williams notes that the black soldier "had enemies in his rear and enemies in his front."[78] Though white attitudes toward African Americans had softened, there were still officers and soldiers who did not want to serve alongside them and who did not believe that they were capable of being soldiers. For their part, the Confederate soldiers viewed formerly enslaved men in uniform as offensive, and official Confederate policy was to kill black captives rather than hold them as prisoners of war: "When Confederate troops overran positions held by black soldiers, the number of prisoners they took (alive) was usually far less than when the defenders were white."[79]

In spite of undesirable assignments, unequal pay, second-rate equipment, inferior rations and medical care, and higher death rates from disease, the desertion rate among black troops was 67 per 1,000 soldiers, only slightly above the 62.5 per 1,000 rate for all volunteers.[80] African American soldiers stayed in the army and struggled actively against racism and discrimination, at times successfully and at times with the support of their white officers.

SECOND DRAFT: NOVEMBER 1863

Statewide draft registration was conducted in June 1863, this time including African Americans. Compiled registration books still exist for four of the six congressional districts, and nearly complete original registration sheets for the other two districts are held in the National Archives in Washington. There were approximately three hundred black men on the complete lists, spread across all six districts, noted as "black," "colored," "Mulatto," "mixed," "Creole," "yellow," or "dark." Calvin Russell, from the town of Avon in Rock County, was noted to have "deserted from the Rebels," while Bank Craven, a shoemaker from Boscobel, and Charles Harris of Johnstown in Rock County were listed as "contrabands." Previous experience as servants to Wisconsin officers was noted for Jessie Harris of Watertown, Samuel Holsey of Rock County, and George Fortune of

Madison.[81] On the draft register for Grant County were Henry Donaldson, Joseph and Thomas Grimes, Charles and Isaac Shepard, William Spillers, and Chesley and Henry Taylor. On the Lafayette County draft rolls were William P. Stewart, son of pioneer farmers in Vernon County, and Ferdinand Shavers, President Lincoln's former servant.[82]

Draft resistance and evasion increased with each draft call. This was particularly true among immigrant groups, many of whom had fled Europe to get away from compulsory military service. Beginning with the draft of 1862, many Wisconsin men fled to Canada to avoid being drafted.[83] White men could avoid the draft in several ways: have a disability verified by the examining physician, claim allegiance to another country, pay a commutation fee of three hundred dollars, find a substitute to serve in place of a drafted man (in this draft, black men could not be substitutes for white men), leave home when it came time to report, or volunteer before being drafted.[84]

A new development among draft-eligible whites was the formation of draft associations. In Fond du Lac, each member paid a fee to join, and their pooled funds were used to pay the three-hundred-dollar commutation fee for each drafted member. Additional funds were contributed in case the pool ran short.[85] Similar associations formed in other larger towns. The draft quota for Milwaukee County was 4,712 men: 1,164 men, most members of draft associations, paid the commutation fee; 1,787 men were discharged on examination for some type of disability; 1,047 drafted men failed to report; and 140 men were enrolled as substitutes for drafted men. Only 34 of the drafted men, less than one percent, actually mustered in.[86]

In late 1863, Wisconsin African American men found themselves in a catch-22 situation. They were subject to the draft but were not allowed to volunteer for white Wisconsin regiments or for the USCT. Volunteers qualified for bounties, but draftees did not. This unfair situation led one man in particular to protest such treatment. An escapee via the Underground Railroad, Andrew Pratt arrived in Milton in 1861 and decided to stay. Pratt's name appeared on the June 1863 draft register. In response, he went to Madison and met personally with Governor Salomon, asking how he could be drafted but not allowed to volunteer and receive a bounty. After the visit, he wrote to the governor: "I have been notified that I am drafted to serve in the army for three years . . . I am willing and anxious to serve my country but it would seem to me more like being a man were I allowed to do it voluntarily. I have served faithfuly in the House of Bondage all my Life until within 18 months and I hope you will not blame me for desireing to be counted a Man."[87] The governor responded, "You are quite mistaken when you suppose that the laws of the country do not recognize you as a man. You are recognized as a man by the laws of this state equally with others enjoying full protections of your person or property under those laws." Salomon's answer was silent on Pratt's main point—that as a black man, he could be drafted but he could not volunteer.[88]

African American men called in this draft were assigned to white Wisconsin regiments. The ban on black men in the militia was now ignored, overcome by expediency. Henry Roseman of Beaver Dam, for instance, was drafted in Fond du Lac and assigned to the Thirty-Seventh Wisconsin Infantry. At least five other drafted men of African ancestry joined Wisconsin regiments at this time: Andrew Bennett of Trimbelle, Pierce County (First Infantry); Anderson Reese (Nash) of Rock County (Thirty-Seventh Infantry); Henry Donaldson (Thirty-Seventh Infantry) and William Spillers (First Cavalry), both from Grant County; and Hayden Netter (Johnson) of Trenton, Dodge County (First Infantry).[89]

These were not the first men of African ancestry in white Wisconsin regiments. The color line was in the eye of the recruiter. Native American men were accepted into Wisconsin regiments, and local recruiters made their own decisions about enrolling men of mixed African and Native American ancestry. Jerome and John Pendleton, grandsons of mixed-race Fox Valley pioneer Peter Pendleton, served in the Wisconsin infantry. Other examples include the sons of Moses Stanton, who was the African American founder of the Calumet County village of Stantonville, later changed to Chilton. Stanton's first wife, Maria, and second wife, Catherine, were Narragansett. Three sons—Cato, Zack, and William—served in white regiments from Wisconsin. Cato enlisted in 1861 and served in the Fourteenth Wisconsin Infantry.[90] In the same county were the Brothertown Indians and a community of nonreservation Stockbridge Indians. Both groups had a history of intermarriage with persons of European and African ancestry while living in the East and after they came to Wisconsin. The Brothertown Indians were Christian, English-speaking farmers who gave up their tribal recognition in the 1830s so that they could remain on their lands east of Lake Winnebago undisturbed. A high percentage of young Brothertown men served in the Civil War, almost all with Wisconsin regiments. Some Stockbridge Indians served with Wisconsin units, but others were denied the right to enlist until recruitment opened for the USCT.[91]

In Cheyenne Valley, Vernon County, young men presumed to be at least part black served in white units. Brothers Aaron, Henry, John, and William Revels, mixed-race men whose genetic background was mainly white and Cherokee, served in the Wisconsin infantry and cavalry. The 1860 and 1870 US Census listed them as "Mulatto." Local recruiters knew the Revels brothers and accepted them all into Wisconsin units, while other local mixed-race and black men were barred. Henry and William Revels served in the Sixth Wisconsin Infantry, part of the Iron Brigade, and fought at Gettysburg. William was killed in action at Weldon Railroad, Virginia, in August 1864.[92]

In the first months of the war, two Madison brothers, grandsons of President Thomas Jefferson, volunteered for the army. Beverly Jefferson served from April through August of 1861 in the First Wisconsin Infantry, after which he returned to his hotel business. His brother John Wayles Jefferson enlisted in the Eighth Wisconsin Infantry in August, serving until the war ended and rising to the rank of colonel. He was wounded twice during his service. After the war, John Wayles became a Memphis cotton broker and breeder of thoroughbred horses.[93]

In 1998, a descendant of Beverly Jefferson volunteered for genetic testing, which proved that Beverly and John Wayles Jefferson were not only grandsons of the former president but also of Sally Hemings, an enslaved woman at Jefferson's home at Monticello, where Hemings lived from her birth until after Jefferson's death. All of Sally's children went by the last name "Hemings." Two sons, Eston and Madison, were freed in Jefferson's will, and moved to Chillicothe, Ohio, in the 1820s, where they were known as "mulatto" and raised their families. Around 1852, Eston and Julia Isaacs Hemings decided to move to Wisconsin, adopted the name Jefferson, and passed as white. In Madison, they were known as relatives of Thomas Jefferson but not of Sally Hemings.[94] By the norms of the time, John Wayles Jefferson would not have been allowed to serve or become an officer if his racial identity had been known.

The Door Opens: The USCT

Illinois delayed in organizing a USCT regiment, in part because of fear that white soldiers would refuse to serve alongside black soldiers, even in separate regiments. There were large-scale desertions from some downstate white regiments when the Union army was opened up to African Americans.[95] Illinois officials watched as more than seven hundred black men from the state joined Massachusetts regiments and USCT regiments from other states. In November 1863, Illinois officials relented and recruitment began for what became the Twenty-Ninth US Colored Infantry (USCI).[96] In early 1864, black men started traveling to Illinois to enlist in the new regiment.

Even after drafting black men into Wisconsin infantry units in November 1863, the state still did not open recruiting for the USCT. Streams of black men of military age were entering the state. They arrived after being employed by Wisconsin officers and regiments in the South. They liberated themselves from owners and plantations and came to Janesville, Grant County, Prairie du Chien, La Crosse, and Prescott, entering the state by train with groups of other contrabands. In the spring of 1864, the state hired Chicago barber Lewis Isbell to head African American recruitment into the USCT.[97] On March 25, 1864, Alfred Weaver, a thirty-three-year-old farmer from Sauk and later Vernon County, became the first volunteer enrolled by Isbell.[98]

Weaver was not, however, the first African American to enlist in the USCT in Wisconsin. Documented enlistments began on March 16 when the provost marshal in Green Bay began signing up black men. Alexander Bell (born in Michigan), Charles Rollins (born in Racine), William R. Thomas (born in Ohio), and sixteen other men enlisted in March and early April. They were with the Sixty-Eighth USCT at Benton Barracks near St. Louis when the regiment mustered in on April 12. Six of the Green Bay recruits were listed in the Wisconsin Census of 1860 or the 1863 Wisconsin draft registers. It is likely that almost all of these men were Wisconsin residents at enlistment.[99] The answer to why they were in Green Bay and enlisted during a four-week period may be found in the pension file of Alexander Bell, who stated that prior to enlistment he was "working in pinery." He and other lumberjacks would have been coming out of the forests right at this time of year.[100]

RECRUITMENT FOR COMPANY F, TWENTY-NINTH USCI

The only unit of black troops officially credited to Wisconsin by the War Department was Company F, Twenty-Ninth Regiment, USCI. The Twenty-Ninth was organized and trained at Quincy, Illinois, a strategic location for recruitment, across the Mississippi from slaveholding Missouri. Alfred Weaver and all Wisconsin black volunteers from late March until late June 1864 were sent to Company F: a total of nineteen men. Among them were Aaron Roberts and Charles Allen from Cheyenne Valley, Henry Sink and Lewis Gaines of Fond du Lac, Daniel Underhill of Sparta, Jonathan Carter of Stockbridge, Lloyd Bryon of Berlin, and Benjamin Colder of Elkhorn. William McKenney, Isaac Smith, and Lewis Paten (Payton),[101] residents of Madison after working for a Wisconsin officer, signed up to go back to war as soldiers. Perhaps unaware that Wisconsin had begun recruiting, John Briggs journeyed from Racine to Chicago to enlist in late March.[102]

Little is known about some Wisconsin volunteers. Richard Robinson and William Ross both enlisted in Wisconsin, but no evidence exists of where they lived before that. Service documents of the soldiers do not provide information on their preservice residences other

Company muster roll of Lewis Paten (Twenty-Ninth USCI) stating that he was "free before Apr 19, '61." Paten was enslaved well into 1862 before freeing himself and reaching Union lines. This statement was added to the records of soldiers, whether true or not, in order for them to receive full pay. NATIONAL ARCHIVES AND RECORDS ADMINISTRATION

VOLUNTEER ENLISTMENT.

STATE OF Wisconsin ~~TOWN~~ City OF Madison

I, Henry Sink born in ...... in the State of Arkansas aged 25 years, and by occupation a Labourer Do hereby acknowledge to have volunteered this 16th day of April 1864, to serve as a **Soldier** in the Army of the United States of America, for the period of *THREE YEARS*, unless sooner discharged by proper authority: Do also agree to accept such bounty, pay, rations, and clothing, as are, or may be, established by law for volunteers. And I, Henry Sink do solemnly swear, that I will bear true faith and allegiance to the **United States of America**, and that I will serve them honestly and faithfully against all their enemies or opposers whomsoever; and that I will observe and obey the orders of the President of the United States, and the orders of the officers appointed over me, according to the Rules and Articles of War.

Sworn and Subscribed to, at Madison Wis.
this 16th day of April 1864
Before B. F. McCormack
Notary Public Wis.

Henry his mark Sink

I CERTIFY, ON HONOR, That I have carefully examined the above named Volunteer, agreeably to the General Regulations of the Army, and that, in my opinion, he is free from all bodily defects and mental infirmity, which would in any way disqualify him from performing the duties of a soldier.

Otto Hoyt
Examining Surgeon.

I CERTIFY, ON HONOR, That I have minutely inspected the Volunteer, H. Sink previously to his enlistment, and that he was entirely sober when enlisted; that, to the best of my judgment and belief, he is of lawful age; and that, in accepting him as duly qualified to perform the duties of an able-bodied soldier, I have strictly observed the regulations which govern the recruiting service.

This soldier has Brown *eyes,* Brown *hair,* Brown *complexion,* is 5 *feet* 4 *inches* high.

L. Isbell
29th *Regiment of* U. S. C. T. *Volunteers.*
Recruiting Officer.

(A. G. O. No. 74 & 76.)

Mustered into the service of the United States, in Company ......, Regiment of ...... Volunteers, on the ...... day of ......, 186 , at ......

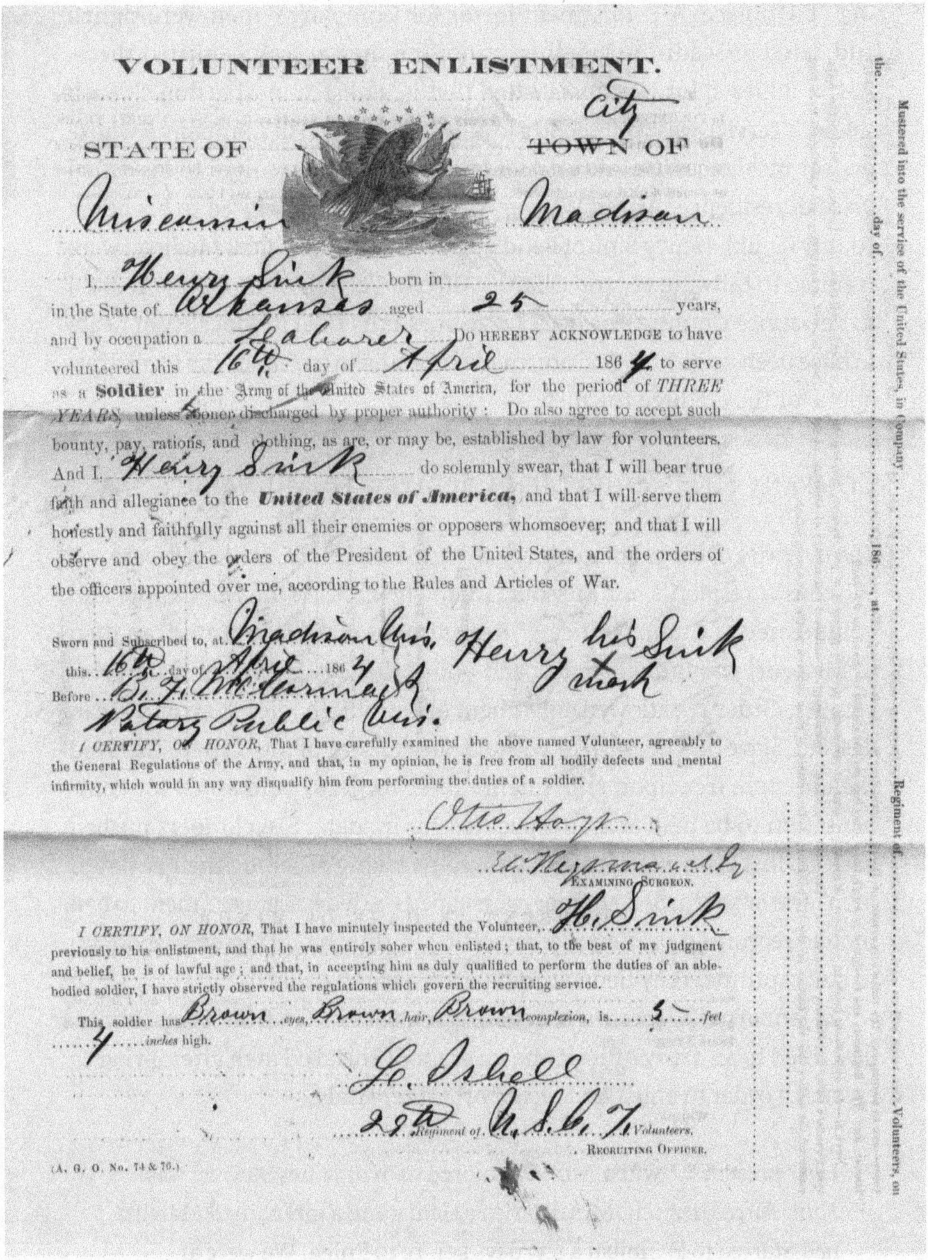

Henry Sink's 1864 Civil War enlistment form. Sink probably signed up in Fond du Lac, though the location was listed as Madison. Lewis Isbell, an African American barber and anti-slavery activist from Chicago whose signature appears here, was Wisconsin's African American recruiter. NATIONAL ARCHIVES AND RECORDS ADMINISTRATION than birthplace. All enlistment forms for Company F men were signed and dated in Madison, whether or not the men actually enlisted there. Aaron Roberts, for example, stated that he enlisted in Mauston.[103] Each soldier's service was credited to a locality. Of the men in Company F whose prewar residences are known, not one of them was credited to his actual place of residence. Alfred Weaver was the only one credited to his home county (Sauk), Henry Sink of Fond du Lac and Isaac Smith of Madison were credited to Milwaukee, and Charles Allen of Vernon County was credited to Kewaunee County. The decision to credit the men to a locality appears to have been a political decision made in Madison to reduce the local draft quota for the credited town.[104]

COMPANY F MISSOURI MEN CREDITED TO MILWAUKEE

The majority of the original ninety-three members of Company F were not Wisconsin residents but Missouri men who crossed the Mississippi and volunteered at Camp Quincy.[105] Recruitment of African American men in Missouri was limited by law and policy through most of 1863. In November, Order 135 allowed enlistment of any able-bodied man of African descent, slave or free, with or without the consent of the owner. Enslaved men became free upon enlistment. Their owners could apply for compensation to be paid at an unspecified future date. Slaveholders pushed back against army recruitment, with some taking or selling their enslaved men farther south. Slaveholders persuaded the federal government to ban mobile recruiting parties of army officials, thus requiring enslaved men to risk capture if they fled without permission to enlist.[106]

In January 1864, Aaron Mitchell, an enslaved man from Pike County, described to an army official one incident of enslaved men attempting to escape in order to enlist and facing brutal reprisals:

> I was present . . . when Alfred a colored man of James Stewart was Shot. Alfred, myself, Mrs. Beasley's Henry and a girl named Malvina had Started to Hannibal a few days before to Enlist. We were arrested . . . taken to Frankford, kept there all night, and the next day we were taken back to our homes near Prairieville. They took Henry

home to Mrs. Beasley and whipped him. They then took me and
Alfred to Stewart's, and whipped us both. I was first taken home to
Mr. Waugh's & learning that Mr. Waugh was at Stewart's they took
me there. Just before we got to the house I heard a pistol fired. I was
about 200 yards off when I heard it. When I got there, I saw Alfred
lying in a little ice house in the yard. He was dead. He had been Shot
through the heart.[107]

In an earlier investigation, another army official learned that Alfred's
owner offered five dollars to the man who would kill him. One of the party
stepped forward and shot him in the heart.

The still-enslaved wives of the enlisted men were forced to perform
outdoor work that their absent husbands had done, like chopping wood
and splitting rails. Owners confiscated the money that the soldiers sent
home to their families. Slave owners even took away clothing from families to prevent enlistment. Some women and children escaped their owners and arrived at the provost marshal's office in Louisiana, the county
seat of Pike County, in a state of near nudity. In February 1864, a petition
signed by 132 Pike County residents was presented to General Rosecrans,
the Union Commander, that stated: "We earnestly desire the Enlistment of
all of them that will do so, but they will not do so if their families are to be
abused, beaten, seized and driven to their former homes in the night and
deprived of reasonable food & clothing because of their enlistment. These
sceines [sic] have been enacted here in our streets by day and night during
the past two weeks by the owners of the women and children, families of
recruits."[108]

Hundreds of men from Pike and neighboring counties braved these
dangers and joined the Twenty-Ninth USCI at Quincy, forty-five river
miles upstream. Acceptance into the army meant freedom and respect
to the formerly enslaved men. One such enlistee, Matthew Griffith of
Pike County, credited to Milwaukee, sent a letter to his wife, Mathilda,
while he was hospitalized about his improved situation: "I have had a hard
time an or from Sickness but have had good car. So far as I have bin the
yankeys treat me wel. I am looked apon as a man and not as a muel and
a dog."[109]

100-DAY REGIMENTS

To address the severe manpower shortage, the War Department authorized states to recruit "100-day regiments" starting in the spring of 1864. It believed that the short enlistment period would attract additional volunteers to fill the immediate need for more men. The Thirty-Ninth Wisconsin Infantry, a 100-day regiment, accepted African American men as volunteers for the first time. Among them was Cornelius Butler of Kenosha, who wrote to the governor in 1862 pleading for the opportunity to serve. John Bowman, from the Green Bay area, served in the Thirty-Ninth and, after his discharge, served in the Sixty-Seventh USCI. Since race was not a reason for exclusion from the Thirty-Ninth (or the Fortieth, another 100-day regiment), there may have been more men of African ancestry in these units. The Thirty-Ninth saw combat when it helped to repel an attack by Confederate cavalry under Nathan Bedford Forrest, the perpetrator of the Fort Pillow massacre. Forrest had attacked Memphis to try to kidnap Union generals, to free Rebel prisoners, and to draw Union forces out of northern Mississippi.[110] One of Forrest's targets was Major General Cadwallader Washburn of La Crosse, a future governor of Wisconsin. With Washburn was Nathan Smith, a refugee from enslavement employed as his valet and hostler. He returned to Wisconsin with Washburn after the war.[111]

SUBSTITUTES

The rule allowing men to pay a three-hundred-dollar commutation fee to be exempted from the draft was dropped for the draft of July 1864 because of the army's desperate need for manpower. The army needed men more than money. A drafted man would now have to serve or find a substitute to take his place. Another rule change occurred on July 20, which stimulated African American service from Wisconsin. Until that date, "a Negro could be a replacement for a Negro," but thereafter, he could also substitute for a white man.[112] Many of the African American enlistees after August 1, 1864, were such substitutes.

The principal locations for later black enlistments in Wisconsin were Janesville, Milwaukee, La Crosse, Fond du Lac, and Prairie du Chien. Many of these men spent brief times in Wisconsin before enlisting. They left little documentation of their presence other than their enlistment papers. The service of substitutes was credited to the residence of the men for whom they substituted. Of the thirty-three Wisconsin men who served in the Third US Colored Heavy Infantry, seventeen were substitutes, credited to ten different counties.[113]

THIRD DRAFT: SEPTEMBER–OCTOBER 1864

There was little enthusiasm for the third draft, scheduled for October 1864. With the War Department's decision to allow white men to pay black substitutes, local governments and draft associations in Wisconsin saw a new option to reduce the local draft quota. Many individuals wrote to the governor requesting authorization to recruit substitutes in the South, most specifying that they would try to enroll black substitutes. Requests came from officers in the field and from citizens and elected officials from all corners of the state: West Bend, Portage, Hartford, Beloit, Prairie du Chien, Darlington, Reedsburg, Milwaukee, Eau Claire, and Black River Falls.[114]

An unknown number of individuals and local governments received authorization to send agents south to recruit substitutes, most seeking African American men. Among those who actually went were Eau Claire agents sent to Virginia and E. L. Brockway of Black River Falls, who traveled to Georgia. Brockway reportedly found some recruits, but the train on which they were riding toward Wisconsin was attacked by Confederate cavalry. According to a news report, "He escaped, and so did most of the negroes, they taking to the woods. He got five negroes as far as Nashville, when the Provost Marshal impressed them and Brock was left without a nigger to his back . . . We had invested in the enterprise, and the nigger that we had hoped to 'fondly call our own,' is now, peradventure, rooting for a living in the woods of Georgia."[115] No African American soldier was credited to Black River Falls.

The third draft was even less popular than the previous two. Bounties of one hundred dollars per year of enlistment attracted volunteers, but not enough to cover the call for half a million more men. Drafted men received no state or federal bounty, though some received small local bounties. Furthermore, draft associations became more widespread. Republican newspapers, which had criticized the associations as unpatriotic a year earlier, now published their meeting announcements without comment. Money previously used for commutation fees now went to pay a substitute. In July, recruiting agents were charging one hundred dollars per year of enrollment to find substitutes. By August, on the last day of medical exams, the rate had doubled. As draft day approached, the actual price to secure a substitute reached as high as eight hundred dollars for a three-year man.[116] It is not known how much money actually reached the substitutes, black or white. Recruiting agents were notorious for skimming excessively from the substitutes' compensation.

At the same time as the approaching draft, the labor shortage in the North was critical. As they arrived in town, African American men were hired to work on the docks in La Crosse and Prescott, in the tanneries of Milwaukee, in the pineries up north, and on farms in the south. Corruption became a problem, as seen in one blatant case involving a recruiting agent and three African American men credited to Milwaukee. In 1864, Robert Graham, Dick Kane, and Will Paine were recruited in Nashville to come to Milwaukee to work in a tannery for forty dollars per month. Once in Milwaukee, they were taken to an office where they touched their pens to documents that they could not read. The documents were not employment contracts but army enlistment papers, enrolling them for three years as substitutes for white men. The going rate of six hundred dollars for a three-year enlistment was supposed to go to the substitutes, minus the expenses of the recruiter. As in many other cases, the recruiter kept the substitute compensation, spending only a fraction of this sum in transporting the men for fraudulent purposes to Milwaukee.[117]

Graham, Kane, and Paine never saw a Milwaukee tannery. They were shipped to Missouri and joined the Eighteenth USCI. They told other soldiers and their officers that they were not volunteers but had been kidnapped under false pretenses. By chance, when their company was first deployed, it was to Nashville. Knowing exactly where they were, Graham, Kane, and Paine deserted and never returned to the regiment. Their story was apparently believed by their superiors because it was transcribed on the descriptive list of deserters for each of the men.[118] While the Union army did force black men into service as laborers and soldiers against their will, it did so on a lesser scale than the Confederate army, which notoriously used impressment to force enslaved men to perform manual labor.[119]

Among the men who paid for African American substitutes were some pillars of their communities. Charles and Frederick Ilsley, Milwaukee bankers, paid for substitutes Henry Loyd Johnson and William Riley; Edmund Burrell substituted for Henry M. Frame of Waukesha; Warrick Price, a railroad company official, was replaced by Henry Howard; and William H. Turner served in place of brewer Joseph Schlitz. All five served with the USCI.[120]

In this draft, more men of African ancestry were assigned to Wisconsin regiments. John Rosier, living near Portage, Anthony Richardson and John Shepard of Grant County, and two Stanton brothers from Chilton served with Wisconsin regiments for the duration of the war.

Fourth Draft: March 1865

The 1864 report of Wisconsin adjutant general Augustus Gaylord painted a positive picture of the African American troops and Wisconsin's role in bringing them into the service. "Whatever prejudice may have existed in the minds of the people against the employment of colored troops," the report noted, "it has fast given way if it be not now everywhere extinct. Aside from arguments of expediency and necessity, the exhibitions of moral courage and heroic devotion, forgetful of the wrongs and obloquy of the past . . . have compelled the admiration of their fiercest opponents."[121]

By the time of the third draft, the end of the war appeared just over the horizon. Statewide, 1,325 men were drafted, only one of whom went into the USCT. At least 46 other African American men in Wisconsin were volunteers, draftees, or substitutes in 1865. For example, Johnson Neal was drafted at Columbus into the Fifty-First Wisconsin Infantry. The last USCT recruit was Manuel Reynolds, who enrolled as a substitute in Fond du Lac on April 10, the day after Lee's Army of Northern Virginia surrendered. At Benton Barracks, Missouri, he was assigned to the Third USCHA but was mustered out in late May without ever being deployed.[122]

The Civil War began with African American men barred from service in the federal army or the state militia. By its end, more than 450 black men, residents of or credited to the state, had served in the USCT, and several dozen had served as volunteers or draftees in Wisconsin regiments. Many hundreds, perhaps thousands, had been employed by Wisconsin officers and regiments during their service in war zones in the South.

CHAPTER THREE

ON THE BATTLEFIELD

FIFTY-FOURTH AND FIFTY-FIFTH MASSACHUSETTS[1]

The Fifty-Fourth Massachusetts, the most famous African American regiment of the Civil War, was the second to be organized in the North and one of the first to see combat. The Fifty-Fourth and Fifty-Fifth Massachusetts were among a handful of black infantry regiments that remained state regiments and were not incorporated into the US Colored Troops (USCT).

Massachusetts began recruiting and organizing for the Fifty-Fourth in late February 1863 at Fort Meigs in Readville. Recruiters traveled across the Union to sign up volunteers; Martin Delany, for instance, recruited for the Fifty-Fourth in Cleveland and Chicago. Two Wisconsin men served with this pioneer regiment: John Tucker from Racine joined in April, possibly recruited by Delany; and Commissary Sergeant Arthur B. Lee, who moved to Wisconsin after the war. Following mustering in on May 11, 1863, ten companies were shipped to South Carolina. After the Fifty-Fourth's ranks were filled, the Fifty-Fifth was formed from the continued influx of recruits.[2] Only 22 of the 880 men who joined the Fifty-Fifth were natives of Massachusetts. The largest contingents came from Ohio, Pennsylvania, and Virginia, while at least nine men in the Fifty-Fifth came from Wisconsin. The Fifty-Fifth mustered in on June 16, 1863, marched to Boston on July 21, and boarded steamers that delivered them four days later to North Carolina.[3] One of the Wisconsin men, Edward Diggs of Racine, never saw combat. He was hospitalized throughout August and was then delegated to service in the hospital. The regimental history lists him as a prisoner of war who never returned.[4]

On July 18, the Fifty-Fourth led the late afternoon assault on Fort Wagner, which defended the entrance to Charleston harbor, suffering heavy casualties when the attack was unable to overcome the fort's defenses. John Tucker was wounded in the battle, though he was able to return to duty in August.[5] Despite the defeat and casualties, the news of Fort Wagner spurred the enlistment of black soldiers.[6]

After recruiting more troops and officers to replace casualties from Fort Wagner, the Fifty-Fourth engaged in combat again in February 1864 in an effort to break Florida away from the Confederacy. Union forces, including the Fifty-Fourth, occupied the city of Jacksonville on February 7 with little opposition. The Fifty-Fifth Massachusetts joined them in Jacksonville on February 15.[7] They remained behind on garrison duty as a Union force of 5,500 men, including most of the Fifty-Fourth, moving out along the St. John River.[8] On February 20, they encountered a Rebel force near the town of Olustee. The Rebels blocked the federal advance and forced a retreat at the end of the day. The Fifty-Fourth Massachusetts held its own against the entrenched Rebels and their artillery and needed to be ordered three times to give up the fight and retreat. Its rearguard action was credited with saving the entire Union force.[9] The regiment had thirteen men killed, eight missing, and sixty-five wounded.[10] John Tucker of Racine suffered a gunshot wound to the ankle. He was hospitalized again, returning to duty in May.[11]

The men of the Fifty-Fourth and Fifty-Fifth, including Tucker and Lee, refused all pay until it was made equal to that of white soldiers.[12] They further refused an offer from the governor of Massachusetts to make up the pay difference with state funds. Men from Companies C and D of the Fifty-Fifth signed and sent a petition to President Lincoln about the continued unequal pay.[13] Soldiers of the Fifty-Fifth stacked arms and refused duty at least twice during 1864 to protest the inequality, but their officers supported the protest and took no action against the leaders.[14] This was in contrast to the Third South Carolina Colored Infantry, where Sergeant William Walker was executed for mutiny for leading a protest in which the black soldiers stacked weapons because of unequal pay.[15]

These protests prompted Congress, on June 15, 1864, to pass an act equalizing pay for black and white soldiers, but with a catch. Black soldiers would receive retroactive pay for 1862 and 1863 only if they had been free when the war began. This stipulation denied back pay to men enslaved at any time during the war. In the Fifty-Fifth, 247 men on the original muster had been enslaved.[16] There was anger at this, but officers of both regiments told their men to take an oath that they had been free on April 12, 1861. The same tactic was used in the Twenty-Ninth US Colored Infantry (USCI), including more than one hundred Wisconsin men, most of whom were enslaved when the war began.[17] On October 4, the men of the Fifty-Fourth and Fifty-Fifth finally began receiving their pay, more than eighteen months after enlistment. One member of the Fifty-Fifth said that it felt "like the loosening of a cord, long drawn to extreme tension."[18]

The Fifty-Fourth was frequently in combat due to its earned reputation, but the Fifty-Fifth saw very little combat. The two regiments were in battle together at Honey Hill, South Carolina, in November 1864. The Union army was trying to block a flank attack on Sherman's army and cut a rail line that would allow Confederate soldiers to escape from Savannah. Honey Hill was a loss for the Union, the result of "poor generalship." The Confederates kept control of the rail line and used it weeks later to evacuate troops from Savannah ahead of Sherman's arrival.[19] Among the casualties were William Bowdry of Milwaukee, who lost the middle finger of his left hand from a gunshot wound, and Edwin Cross of Rock County, who took a rifle ball in the arm. Cross served out the remainder of the war with the regiment. Bowdry was hospitalized for three months and returned to duty in January.[20]

The soldiers of the Fifty-Fourth and Fifty-Fifth Massachusetts were among the thousands who fought their way toward Charleston, South Carolina, from different directions. They helped to conquer the "Cradle of Secession" in late February 1865.[21]

Sixty-Eighth USCI

The black soldiers in the Sixty-Eighth had a very different military experience from most others credited to Wisconsin. They saw duty, including combat, in Missouri, Tennessee, Mississippi, Florida, Alabama, Louisiana, and Texas. All of them were three-year recruits, none were substitutes, and all but one of them belonged to Company I.[22] Seven of the Wisconsin men served as noncommissioned officers: First Sergeant William R. Thomas, Sergeant William Babcock, Corporal Alexander Bell, Corporal Major Flows, Corporal Albert Grace, Corporal John Q. Nusom (Newsom), and Corporal Charles Rollins. All but Grace were born in the North. It was common for men who had lived in the North to serve as noncommissioned officers because they were more likely to be literate than the men who had recently escaped enslavement.[23]

From July 5 through 21, 1864, the Sixty-Eighth was in battle at Tupelo, Mississippi, with a federal force of fourteen thousand. Their purpose was to protect Sherman's rail supply line from Nashville during the Atlanta campaign. The USCI brigade, which included the Sixty-Eighth, was under attack while protecting the rear of the column on July 13. The Confederates attacked again the next morning and several more times that day and the next but were repulsed by the Union army. Casualties for the Sixty-Eighth in the four days of fighting were four killed and three wounded (none was from Wisconsin).[24]

After Tupelo, they returned to the defense of Memphis. Two Wisconsin men died of disease during this time and another deserted. The regiment was sent to New Orleans in February and then to Fort Barrancas, Florida, near Pensacola. The Sixty-Eighth was one of nine USCT regiments that set off on a march from Pensacola to Fort Blakeley, Alabama, on March 20. Only ten of the original eighteen from Wisconsin were present. William Babcock and Henry Phillips were left behind in a hospital in Florida, Charles Rollins was on the march as part of an ambulance detail.[25]

The eleven-day march was described by their division commander as "a severe one on the men, being attended with constant labor, making corduroy roads to get the wagons through the almost impassable swamps." They participated in the nine-day siege, assault, and capture of Fort Blakeley. The division occupied low ground, with the fort's artillery and snipers before them and Confederate gunboats behind them on the river. A Confederate commander stated that he ordered his best troops to oppose the African American division. The final charge on the fort was April 9. When the fort fell, the USCI division captured twenty-three officers and two hundred men—"a small number, owing to the fact that when we entered, many of the enemy, fearing the conduct of my troops, ran over to where the white troops were entering" to surrender. The fort was captured only hours after Lee's surrender in Virginia. The nearby city of Mobile was occupied on April 12.[26]

In the final charge on Fort Blakeley, Private Jasper McDonald of Oshkosh suffered a severe gunshot wound to his left shoulder; he was discharged for disability on August 1, 1865.[27] In addition to the men of the Sixty-Eighth, three other African American soldiers from Wisconsin fought at Fort Blakeley: Wesley Walter with the Forty-Seventh USCI and Charles Shepard and Henry Ford with the Fiftieth USCI. All three survived the battle without injury, but Charles Shepard would never see his family or farm on Pleasant Ridge in Grant County again. He died from anemia at Vicksburg General Hospital in August.[28]

Simultaneous with the siege of Fort Blakeley was the siege of Spanish Fort a few miles to the south, lasting from March 28 until the fort fell on April 8. Present during the siege was the Thirty-First Wisconsin, which included at least twenty-two African American cooks. The Thirty-Third Wisconsin Infantry fought at Spanish Fort, with at least six African American male cooks during the siege. One of them, whose name was listed only as "Henry . . . Colored Cook" was severely wounded—"both legs shot off, Mar. 30, '65, Spanish Fort, Ala."[29] At least eleven other Wisconsin regiments that employed African Americans were involved in the two final battles around Mobile.

Twenty-Ninth USCI

Missouri men made up a large portion of Companies A through E of the Twenty-Ninth USCI at Camp Quincy, Illinois. In these companies were thirteen men from Wisconsin, only three of whom were credited to the state, and seven men credited to Wisconsin who were not state residents. One other man, George Roberts, who enlisted in Madison and was credited to Milwaukee, died at the base hospital before deployment. Corporal Thomas Burnett was a waiter from Oshkosh, First Sergeant Alfred Carroll a paperhanger from Milwaukee, and Henry Rosier a Columbia County farmer. All three men were in Company D.[30] Julius Valentine of Company E came from a family that had been farming in Wisconsin since 1846. By war's end, his brother John and nephews John and Shadrach Valentine would also serve from Wisconsin in the Union army.[31] During their training at Camp Quincy, the recruits had no hands-on training with weapons.[32]

On April 25, 1864, Companies A through E mustered in at Quincy and boarded trains heading east. This came just after the Confederate massacre of surrendered black and white troops by General Nathan Bedford Forrest at Fort Pillow, carrying out the Rebel promise to offer no quarter to black soldiers or their white officers. Cries of "Remember Fort Pillow" were heard during speeches at a send-off dinner for the regiment during a stop in Chicago. Colonel John Bross, the Chicago man who commanded the Twenty-Ninth, said, "When I lead these men into battle, we shall remember Fort Pillow, and shall not ask for quarter . . . if it is the will of Providence that I do not return, I ask no nobler epitaph, than I fell for my country at the head of this black and blue regiment."[33]

Bombproof tents occupied by USCT soldiers, Petersburg, VA, August 7, 1864.
LIBRARY OF CONGRESS, LC-DIG-STEREO-1S02899

They arrived in Washington, DC, on May 1 and spent nearly a month training at Camp Casey, near the present-day Pentagon and Arlington National Cemetery. Here they finally were issued weapons but did minimal practicing "to conserve ammunition." They moved down to Alexandria and joined the Army of the Potomac, guarding supply trains and building fortifications. USCT troops and commanders complained that they were relegated to menial tasks and support functions, but this would not be the permanent fate of the Twenty-Ninth. They arrived at the Petersburg front, south of Richmond, on June 19.[34] During their training in Virginia, the ranks were increased by formerly enslaved men who arrived at camp and volunteered, including five men credited to Madison.[35]

The first death in Virginia occurred while the regiments marched toward Petersburg. Edward Hunter, who was attacked years before while trying to make an Independence Day speech in Waupaca, died from an unknown disease while being transported by ambulance, near where he was born. He was survived by a widow and three children in Wisconsin.[36] Twelve days later, Wade Hampton, credited to Wisconsin and possibly a state resident, died at L'Ouverture Hospital in Alexandria of a lung infection.[37]

Meanwhile, back at Camp Quincy, Company F's enlistment of Missouri men was Wisconsin's only success in recruiting African American soldiers outside of the state. Neither Illinois nor Wisconsin paid state bonuses to volunteers. Wisconsin recruiting agents paid enlistment bounties to the volunteers from funds collected by the Milwaukee draft associations. The soldiers' service was credited to the city ward providing the funds. One of the most effective and bold recruiters was Lieutenant Nimrod Ferguson, a white attorney and resident of Louisiana, Pike County, Missouri. In late May and early June of 1864, he signed up at least eight men on the streets of his hometown.[38] Two of them, Lewis and James Orr, were eighteen and twenty-five years old, respectively, and credited to Milwaukee. Their owner, Lucy Orr, came to Camp Quincy and demanded the return of her property. Summoned by an officer, Lewis and James acknowledged Orr as their former owner. She wanted them returned to her, but the officer refused because they were now free men and soldiers.[39]

Lucy Orr filed compensation claims for three formerly enslaved men who served in Company F, all credited to Milwaukee, and signed the loyalty oath, which was part of the compensation form. During the war, compensation to slave owners was offered for the service of enslaved men from Border States. At least sixteen claims were filed in Missouri for the service of the volunteers of Company F and eleven for men of Company D. In the military files of Henry Hill, credited to Milwaukee, is a compensation claim by his former owner. Included with it is a copy of an 1848 bill of sale for $450 for "a negro woman named Rachael, about thirty-three years old, and her two infant male children, each about fifteen months of age," one of whom was Henry.[40] None of the compensation claims was ever paid. By the time they were submitted in 1867, Congress had suspended the program.[41]

Five of the twelve noncommissioned officers of Company F were Wisconsin men: First Sergeant Lloyd Bryon of Berlin, Sergeant Alfred Weaver of Sauk County, and Corporals Lewis Paten, Isaac Smith, and William McKenney, all of Madison.[42] The company mustered in on July 8 and arrived at Petersburg on July 15. They were incorporated, along with the other companies of the Twenty-Ninth, into the all-black IV Division, Army of the Potomac.[43] Of the ninety-three enlisted men who left Quincy with Company F, eleven were credited to Chicago (one of them a Racine resident); sixty-four from Missouri were credited to Milwaukee or other Wisconsin locations; and eighteen men enlisted in Wisconsin, credited to various Wisconsin localities. Including other companies and later recruits, a total of 127 enlisted men who served in the Twenty-Ninth USCI were credited to Wisconsin and/or were residents of the state.[44]

TWENTY-NINTH USCI (AT THE BATTLE OF THE CRATER)

The siege of Petersburg was underway in 1864 when Company F arrived. To try to break the deadlock, Pennsylvania soldiers, who had been coal miners before the war, dug a tunnel five hundred feet long, reaching from behind Union lines to a key point beneath the Confederate entrenchments. It was packed with explosives to be detonated in the early morning. Taking advantage of damage and confusion along Confederate lines, Union troops were to attack immediately after the explosion and try to capture Cemetery Hill. If successful, Petersburg would have fallen, cutting off rail connections from Richmond to the rest of the South.[45] General Burnside chose the Fourth Division to lead the assault because the black troops were fresh and motivated. In the days before the explosion, some units practiced maneuvers they would follow during the attack.[46] The men in the Twenty-Ninth were not the only black soldiers from Wisconsin awaiting the mine explosion, however. Anthony Diggs, a prewar resident of Racine, waited with his comrades in the Twenty-Third USCI. Also present were Henry Roseman, Anderson Reese, and Henry Donaldson, black draftees in the Thirty-Seventh Wisconsin, whose Company K included dozens of Menominee men.[47]

Surgeon David Mackay recalled that "the [Twenty-Ninth] regiment was camped in a pine forest" on the night of July 28. Around their fires, soldiers sang a song so well remembered by their brigade commander that, decades later, he transcribed the words and music in a memoir. The lyrics were simple and repeated, with harmony: "We looks like men a-marchin', we looks like men of war."[48] The next day, less than twenty-four hours before the mine was to explode, the plan changed. General Meade overruled Burnside, deciding that the black Fourth Division should not lead the assault because the soldiers were untested. General Grant concurred, not wanting to be accused of sacrificing black soldiers if casualties were high. The lead in the attack was reassigned, by drawing straws, to the division lead by General Ledlie, a weak leader with tired troops who had not prepared for the assault.[49]

The mine exploded just before sunrise on July 30, more than an hour later than planned. Ledlie's division did not advance. Instead, his soldiers stayed put in the covered walkways between the trenches or descended into the huge crater left by the explosion. Ledlie was drunk throughout the day in a bombproof shelter well behind the line of battle. The disorganized division blocked other units from moving forward. The element of surprise was lost.[50]

More than three hours after the explosion, the Fourth Division was finally able to climb out of the trenches and advance, passing over and around the white troops who had never moved forward. By this time, the Confederates had reorganized. Sergeant Henry Reese, one of the Pennsylvania men who dug the mine, later told a congressional inquiry, "It made me frantic to see the useless destruction; and when the assault failed, it made me still more furious to see a division of colored soldiers rushed into the jaws of death with no prospect of success; but they went in cheering as though they didn't mind it and a great many of them never came back."[51] They advanced farther than any other Union troops and captured more Rebel prisoners than all other Union units combined. They were driven back by reorganized and enraged Southern troops.[52] When they reached the crater, Confederates shot down into the pit and killed large numbers of Union soldiers, white and black. The recollections of some of the Confederate soldiers revealed their intense, racially fueled animosity toward black troops. Some white Union soldiers in the crater bayoneted their black comrades in an attempt to convince the Rebels above to spare them.[53]

The battle was a devastating loss for the Union. Seven of the ten regiments with the highest casualties (men killed or wounded) were USCT regiments, including the Twenty-Ninth, whose six companies suffered 124 casualties. Participating in the battle were eighty-eight enlisted men of Company F; ten were killed or died shortly afterwards, and at least twenty-three others were wounded.[54] The following Wisconsin men lost their lives:

Joseph Jordan, Company D, credited to Madison (MIA)

Jefferson Allen, Company F, credited to Milwaukee

John Jackson, Company F, credited to Milwaukee

Jackson Mackay, Company F, credited to Milwaukee (died August 14 from Crater wounds)

Benjamin Price, Company F, credited to Milwaukee

Richard Robinson, Company F, credited to Brighton, Kenosha County; enlisted in Wisconsin

William C. Ross, Company F, credited to Carlton, Kewaunee County; enlisted in Wisconsin

Peter Stark, Company F, credited to Milwaukee

Sanford Strauder, Company F, credited to Milwaukee

Charles Tinsley, Company F, credited to Milwaukee

Anthony Diggs, Company I, Twenty-Third USCI; prewar resident of Racine.[55]

In an address to the Circuit Court of Cook County, Illinois, H. G. Spafford dramatically named the soldiers who carried the colors of the Twenty-Ninth Regiment during the Crater battle: "Corporal Maxwell, carrying the colors, was at once wounded and fell. Corporal Stevens caught them, bore them to the parapet, and was cut down. Corporal Bailey, who next held them, was instantly either captured or killed. Thomas Barnett, a colored private, seized them from Bailey, bore them a few steps onward, and fell mortally wounded. Captain Brockway carried them a like distance further, and met the same fate. They then fell into the hands of Colonel Bross."[56]

Spafford's oration captured the danger in carrying the colors, even if some details were inaccurate. Maxwell was probably Corporal John Maxon, Company C; he suffered a gunshot wound to the neck but survived. Corporal Isaac Stevens, Company B, was wounded and taken prisoner. He was paroled in March 1865 directly to a hospital, where he died in April. Corporal Frederick Bailey, Company C, died on the battlefield. Barnett was probably Corporal Thomas Burnett, Company D, a Wisconsin soldier. He was shot in the left shoulder and captured and held as a POW at the notorious Libby Prison in Richmond after some time in a hospital. Later he was transferred to two prison camps in North Carolina and was paroled March 4, 1865. All four of these men were African American. Company C's Captain James Brockway was shot in the left ankle, requiring amputation of the left leg. He was discharged for disability in March 1865.[57]

After Brockway fell, Colonel John Bross, the commander of the Twenty-Ninth, held the colors for a matter of seconds, exhorting his troops to go forward. He was shot and died on the spot.[58] A seventh soldier picked up the colors from their fallen commander. The fate of this unnamed soldier and the colors is unknown.[59]

For the men of Company F and the Twenty-Ninth Regiment, the glory of warfare had been replaced with its brutality. The song "We Look Like Men of War," which they sang every night before the battle, was sung no more.[60] The congressional inquiry into the battle found that command decisions doomed the Union army that day. General Grant admitted to the inquiry that "if they (the Colored Troops) had been placed in advance, as General Burnside desired, the assault would have been successful."[61]

Several Wisconsin men were taken prisoner but survived. In addition to Corporal Thomas Burnett, Private James Bibb (credited to the Town of Black Wolf in Winnebago County) was held six months as a POW. Paroled in February 1865, he spent a month on furlough, a month on duty in Virginia, and six months hospitalized at Fort Monroe, Virginia. Frank Oden, Company F, credited to Milwaukee, was wounded at the Crater and held as a POW until exchanged in January 1865. He returned to the regiment and served until muster out.[62]

Richard Carey of Palmyra and John Christine, Anderson McCann, and Phillip Smith (all three credited to Milwaukee) were wounded and hospitalized. Among the most severely wounded were Henry Sink, Charles Walden, and Alfred Weaver. Sink, from Fond du Lac, was shot in the left arm. The bones around his elbow were shattered. Miraculously, he did not lose the arm, but it was essentially useless for the rest of his life. After healing, his elbow was ankylosed (fused) in a slightly flexed position, which prevented him from reaching his head or face or from turning his left hand palm-up. Charles Walden, formerly enslaved in Missouri and credited to Milwaukee, had a very similar wound, leaving his right arm "all but useless" in the opinion of a surgeon who examined him later in life. The elbow moved little, and he was unable to turn his palm up or down. Months later, both men were discharged from the service for disability.[63]

Sergeant Weaver suffered injuries that plagued him for life. Regimental surgeon Mackay recalled that Weaver was carried to him from the battlefield "in a comatose condition with contused wounds on head and back." Comrades Aaron Roberts and William Reed said that they saw him fall into a ditch when he was hit in the head by a piece of shell or other object as they were climbing over the enemy breastworks. Weaver had lifelong back problems, limiting his ability to work, and also displayed long-term effects consistent with concussion or traumatic brain injury. Weaver remained a patient at the divisional hospital until November and was a hospital attendant for another month. When he returned to duty, he was detailed as a cook. William Reed said of Weaver that "after that day he was never the same man for any physical duty that he was before." In spite of his injuries, Weaver remained with his company for the duration of its service.[64]

Wounded and sick black soldiers were treated in segregated hospitals. While the regimental hospital was in the field, the division hospital, where Weaver stayed for months, was at City Point, Virginia, near General Grant's headquarters. Sink and South both spent months at Summit General Hospital in Philadelphia.[65] Many African American wounded and sick soldiers were taken to L'Ouverture Hospital in Alexandria, Virginia. The hospital

Henry Sink's Surgeon's Certificate of Disability, which discharged him from service because of the wound to his left arm suffered in the Battle of the Crater. NATIONAL ARCHIVES AND RECORDS ADMINISTRATION complex included a building that housed a slavetrading business, which operated until the Union army captured Alexandria in 1861. L'Ouverture patients who died were not buried in the nearby Alexandria National Military Cemetery but in an untended Freedmen's Cemetery more than a mile away. In December 1864, four hundred hospital patients signed or put their "X" on a petition demanding the right to be buried in the military cemetery. The petition said, in part:

> As American citizens, we have a right to fight for the protection of her flag, that right is granted, and we are now sharing equally the dangers and hardships in this mighty contest, and should shair the same privileges and rights of burial in every way with our fellow soldiers, who only differ from us in color. . . . We ask that our bodies may find a resting place in the ground designated for the burial of the brave defenders, of our countries flag.[66]

One of the leaders of the petition campaign was Company D's First Sergeant Alfred Carroll, of Milwaukee. Private John Christian (Christine) of Company F was among the signers. Their petition succeeded in changing burial policy. Soldiers who died subsequently were buried in the military cemetery, and those already buried in Freedmen's Cemetery were reburied at Alexandria National. Twelve veterans of the Twenty-Ninth are buried there, including Wade Hampton, who was among the soldiers reinterred after being initially buried in the Freedmen's Cemetery. Private Christian remained hospitalized with a right hip injury until his discharge for disability in August of 1865. Sergeant Carroll, hospitalized for respiratory problems, returned to duty with the regiment.[67]

The nation's most famous cemetery, Arlington National, opened on May 13, 1864, on land that was previously part of the plantation of Confederate General Robert E. Lee. Two early burials at Arlington were Wisconsin African American soldiers. Martin Lyons of Company F, credited to Milwaukee, fought at the Crater and survived but died a month later from typhoid and pneumonia.[68] Shadrach Valentine, who lived on his parents' farms in Dane and Adams Counties and was on the 1863 Pierce County draft roll, died from typhoid fever while serving in the One Hundred Second USCI and was buried at Arlington in late 1864.[69]

Due to casualties from the Crater battle, new noncommissioned officers were needed in Company F. Daniel Underhill of Sparta was promoted
to sergeant. Jonathan Carter of Stockbridge became a corporal but was
reduced to ranks a month later. Benjamin Colder of Elkhorn became a
corporal January 1, 1865.[70] The regiment spent the fall under the constant
stress of trench warfare but wasn't involved in any battles. They were limited to building fortifications and other noncombat duties. By January 1,
1865, new recruits from the Midwest and from Maryland and Virginia
filled the gaps in Companies A through F and allowed the formation of six
more companies. For the first time, the Twenty-Ninth was at full strength.
Among the new recruits were thirty-three men credited to Wisconsin, the
majority of them state residents. They included Lewis Washington Jr.,
William Albare, Isaac Crawford (and three other men from Pierce County)
William Lumpkin of Menomonee, Howard Brooks of Madison, Stephen
Burrell of Jefferson County, and John Cosley of Walworth County.[71] Wil-
liam P. Stewart from Cheyenne Valley and Abram Thornton from nearby
Sauk County went to Chicago to enlist rather than to Madison. Enlisting in
Chicago allowed them to be assigned to Company F with their neighbors.
Stewart and Thornton joined Company F in Virginia on March 14, 1865.[72]

The siege of Petersburg continued through the rain, snow, and cold of
winter. In late March 1865, the full Army of the Potomac moved against
Petersburg and Richmond. Daniel Underhill, William Lumpkin, and Lewis
Paten were put on detached service with the Division Sharpshooters (snipers).[73] Sergeant Lloyd Bryon noted in Company F's morning reports, "Left
camp on the Twenty-seventh inst. Crossing the James and Appomattox to
join the Army of the Potomac South of Petersburg."[74] The Twenty-Ninth
was involved in combat almost daily at the Bermuda Hundred, Hatcher's
Run, and the captures of Petersburg and Richmond.[75] They continued the
pursuit of Lee's Army of Northern Virginia. When Lee tried to break out
from Appomattox Court House, the Twenty-Ninth Regiment, after an
all-night march, was among the troops who moved into position just in
time to block Lee's escape on April 9. "The last guns fired at Lee's army at
Appomattox were in the hands of Negro soldiers," wrote George Washington Williams, and many of those hands belonged to Wisconsin soldiers.[76]
After Lee's surrender, the Twenty-Ninth marched back to Petersburg.
From March 27 through April 17, they had only one day of rest. As Ser-

geant Bryon wrote on April 30, "This Company...shared in the memorable campaign which resulted in the fall of Richmond and surrender of General Lee with the Army of Northern Virginia. The Company marched in the aggregate 250 miles and is now encamped near Petersburg, Va."[77]

No combats deaths occurred among the Wisconsin men of the Twenty-Ninth between the Crater and Appomattox, but fifteen died from diseases like typhoid fever, chronic diarrhea, dysentery, pneumonia, and tuberculosis. Many more acquired permanently disabling conditions from disease or injury.[78]

Eighteenth USCI

The Eighteenth USCI was organized in Missouri beginning in February 1864 and remained there until November of 1864. This regiment had sixty-seven men from Wisconsin, second in number only to the Twenty-Ninth. All but one of the men enlisted in the state; Thomas Willis volunteered in Shakopee, Minnesota, but lived most of his postwar life in Prescott. Almost all of them enlisted in August 1864, most in La Crosse, Green Bay, Fond du Lac, Milwaukee, and Janesville. One of the enlistees, Shepard Sheldon, said, "For a year or so before enlistment I lived at Rippon Wis. Was 'steamboating.'" William Ousley was a pre-enlistment resident of Darien, Walworth County, who gave his occupation as laborer and farmer. Cyrenus Bostwick, born in Wisconsin to an African American father and Native American (Brothertown) mother, was a farmer near Brothertown.[79] They were shipped by train in small groups to Benton Barracks, Missouri, beginning August 10 and ending on October 1. Once they arrived, the conditions in the camp decimated their ranks. Thirty-one of the Wisconsin men were "absent, sick" at some time between October and December, the majority at Benton Barracks. Five men deserted before the regiment left Missouri. None of the Wisconsin men died while in St. Louis, but several died later from conditions they acquired while at the base.[80] One man who was not hospitalized in St. Louis was Caleb Hudson. Born enslaved in Kentucky, he never knew his father, and his mother was sold away from him when he was a child. He gave no details of how he escaped enslavement. Hudson wound up working on Mississippi River steamboats, which is how he came to La Crosse, where he enlisted. Although he was only 5'8", comrades spoke in awe of his size and strength. He was reported to have punched a sergeant and broken his jaw but was not disciplined for his action.[81]

Through the fall, the Eighteenth was frequently on the move between St. Louis and various locations in eastern Missouri. A note in the Company D morning reports indicates that their purpose was recruitment.[82] In November, the entire regiment went to Paducah, Kentucky, by steamer and on the 26th left by steamer up the Cumberland River to Nashville. Here the regiment was split; four companies stayed in Nashville, and the others continued on to Chattanooga and Bridgeport, Alabama.[83] Shepard Sheldon, Company D, later stated, "When we got to Chattanooga we had no quarters and had to lay out, and it was raining and cold and sleety. . . . The second or third day after we got to Chattanooga I was sent to the hospital at Chattanooga . . . the measles broke out on me after I was taken to the hospital."[84]

The Battle of Nashville, December 15–16, 1864, was the last major battle away from the coasts. The Confederates tried to recapture Nashville, hoping it would draw Sherman's army out of the Deep South. The outcome was a decisive Union victory and left the Confederate Army of Tennessee nearly destroyed. African American soldiers from Tennessee were a major part of the Union army's manpower under General George Thomas. Surveying the battlefield on December 17, Thomas saw many black soldiers among the dead. The son of a slaveholding family from Virginia, Thomas commented to his subordinates, "Gentlemen, the question is settled; Negroes will fight."[85]

The Eighteenth USCI was listed in the Union's order of battle at Nashville, but few Wisconsin black soldiers participated. Based on the company morning reports, only Companies B, G, and K were present during the battle. Company D's morning reports indicate that they were at Bridgeport, Alabama.[86] However, Caleb Hudson's pension files note that he and five comrades of Company D stated that they were present at the battle.[87] The casualties did not include Wisconsin men.

The Eighteenth Regiment spent the rest of its wartime service in eastern Tennessee and northern Alabama on garrison duty or guarding railroad lines. By muster out on February 21, 1866, at Huntsville, Alabama, only eighteen of the original sixty-seven Wisconsin men were still with the regiment. Many had been discharged in August 1865 because their one-year enlistments had expired. Seven men died from disease and one, John Ron, who enlisted in La Crosse, died from an unexplained gunshot wound to the abdomen ten days before muster out. A total of eleven Wisconsin men (16.4 percent) in this unit deserted.[88]

SHERMAN'S MARCH TO THE SEA (NOVEMBER–DECEMBER 1864)

General Thomas had thousands of USCT soldiers at his disposal for the Battle of Nashville because Sherman left them all behind when he began his Atlanta campaign. Although most of Sherman's peers gradually changed their attitudes toward African American as soldiers, Sherman never budged, even under direct pressure from the president. Sherman only gradually introduced them to "the art of the Soldier, beginning with the duties of the local garrison."[89] As he wrote to his wife, "I would prefer to have this a white man's war, and provide for the Negroes after the time has passed. . . . With my opinions of Negroes and my experience, yea, prejudice, I cannot trust them yet."[90] With his military peers, his language was not so clean. During the Atlanta Campaign and the March to the Sea, no USCT regiments were included in Sherman's army.

In spite of his attitude, the success of Sherman's March depended on the work of African American men. Sherman issued Special Field Order No. 16, which forbade recruiting officers from enrolling black men as soldiers. Sherman wanted all able-bodied black men to be employed as pioneers, cooks, teamsters, servants, blacksmiths, and musicians to relieve his white troops from those duties. Pioneers were essential to the March, working under the engineers to clear paths, set up and tear down bridges, build or tear down fortifications, and build corduroy roads over swampy areas. They were out in front of and behind the army, taking casualties as they performed their high-risk tasks.[91] The March also depended on coordinated Union attacks on Rebel installations to prevent them from joining Confederate forces opposing Sherman. Wisconsin black soldiers in the Sixty-Eighth USCI and the Fifty-Fourth and Fifty-Fifth Massachusetts defended Sherman's flanks.

Although Sherman kept the USCT out of his army, African American soldiers were still with him, including in "white" units from Wisconsin.

Leonard Barton and Samuel Waldron (Waldon) of Cheyenne Valley and Hayden Netter (Johnson) of Dodge County were in the Thirty-Second Wisconsin. Andrew Bennett of Pierce County transferred into the Twenty-First Wisconsin Infantry and marched with Sherman to Savannah. Half-brothers William and Cato Stanton of Chilton served in the Sixteenth and Twenty-First Wisconsin Infantries, respectively.[92] In addition to enlisted soldiers, hundreds of other African American men marched with Wisconsin units. At least twenty-two served with the Thirty-First Wisconsin Infantry as cooks and musicians through the conquest of Atlanta and the march to Savannah. George Washington, a cook with Company A, only made it as far as Atlanta, where he died from disease. Samuel Ewing (Bowden) served as a cook with Company C for twenty months. Other Wisconsin units with men of African ancestry included the Third Infantry (enlisted soldier Jefferson Fiddler), Sixth Light Artillery (Henry Ashby and Anthony Parks, cooks), Twenty-First Infantry (Gus Cowen, Captain Randall's servant), and Seventeenth Infantry (at least thirteen men).

As Sherman's army cut across Georgia, an ever-growing mass of formerly enslaved people followed. They viewed it as an army of liberation, but they also followed because that army left no means of subsistence in its wake.[93] Sherman took able-bodied men from among the contrabands into his pioneer corps and left the rest to fend for themselves in the rear. His army numbered sixty thousand soldiers and thousands of African American workers, with thousands of refugees bringing up the rear.[94]

About twenty miles from Savannah, one of Sherman's subordinates pulled up the pontoon bridges over swollen Ebenezer Creek after his troops had finished crossing, leaving five thousand black refugees abandoned on the other side. With a Confederate cavalry unit close behind them, hundreds of the refugees drowned trying to ford the river. Those who remained on the shore were captured by the Rebel cavalry and killed or re-enslaved. Sherman did not order this action, but he defended it. Later, his Special Order No. 15, one of the origins of the "forty acres and a mule" idea, was issued as damage control for the public outcry against what happened at Ebenezer Creek.[95]

Among the African Americans who marched with Sherman's army through Georgia and the Carolinas was a twelve-year-old enslaved youth who ran away from his owner after fighting back when the owner's daughter whipped him. Samuel Arms sought refuge in the camp of a Pennsylvania regiment. He was hired as a servant to an officer and helped take care of horses. Eventually, he became the drummer for the regiment for the remainder of the war and returned to Pennsylvania with the officer, taking his drum with him. Eventually, Samuel Arms and his drum settled in the Cheyenne Valley community in Vernon County.[96]

FORTY-NINTH USCI

The Forty-Ninth USCI began as the Eleventh Louisiana Infantry (African Descent) in May 1863, the first black regiment to see combat. At the battle of Milliken's Bend on June 7, with support from Union gunboats in the Mississippi River, they fought off a Confederate attack and protected supply lines supporting the Union siege of Vicksburg. It was the first proof that African American troops could and would fight effectively.[97]

On March 11, 1864, the regiment became the Forty-Ninth USCI, which was relegated to post and guard duty at Vicksburg. Wisconsin men joined the regiment beginning in November 1864. After assembling and training at Camp Randall in Madison and at St. Louis, forty-two men joined this regiment.[98] One volunteer was Martin Smith of Milwaukee, a leader of the crowd that freed fugitive slave Joshua Glover from jail in 1854. Other soldiers included Edward Hall of Ripon, Leroy Ironmonger (later Leroy Jackson) and four Taylors from Grant County, Charles Marion Hines of La Crosse, and Albert Milum of Rock County. Nearly half of the men were substitutes for white men from sixteen different Wisconsin counties. One Freeman Richards, from Brothertown, Calumet County, married Charlotte Simons on August 26, 1864, and went to Fond du Lac the following day to volunteer.[99] During their time with the Forty-Ninth, they were not involved in combat. Muster out was March 27, 1866. Seven Wisconsin men died in service, all from disease, including Albert Milum (smallpox), Iverson Hicks (smallpox), and Edward Foster (consumption).[100]

The morning reports and the service records of this regiment contain rare documentation of women's service. From late 1863 on, the morning report sheets of every company counted the number of women in camp working for the regiment as cooks and laundresses. Companies F and K included thirty Wisconsin men; at most times there were three or four women working in each company.[101] In December 1864, company muster rolls included the names of twenty-six women, the dates and locations when they joined the company, and comments such as: "Pay due from enrollment as company cook" and "Detailed as company cook Nov. 2 1863 . . . for three years." The three-year "enlistment" was the same for the men, and a few of the women served nearly that long.[102] Some of them were sisters or wives of soldiers. Lucinda Beard was a cook for Company K; her husband, Adam, was First Sergeant of the company; Lucinda and Adam were married in camp on October 12, 1863, by a white chaplain. As Lucinda remembered, "After we got married I stayed in the army there at Vicksburg and cooked and washed for him and some of the other soldiers so long as my husband was in the army."[103]

The women's names never appeared again on the bimonthly rolls, but the daily count of women in the companies continued until the regiment mustered out in March 1866. There is no indication in regimental records of sickness and deaths among the women. If one-sixth of the Wisconsin men in the Forty-Ninth died from disease during their service, it is likely that women living and working in the same conditions, and for a longer time, also suffered and died while in service.[104]

SIXTY-FIFTH AND SIXTY-SEVENTH USCI

Benton Barracks near St. Louis was a major assembly point and training facility for western regiments of the Union army. It housed as many as thirty thousand soldiers at a time and was known for unsanitary conditions, resulting in high casualty rates among troops who stayed there. The Eighteenth, Sixty-Fifth, Sixty-Seventh, and Sixty-Eighth USCI, which included Wisconsin men, trained at Benton Barracks. A researcher at the University of Virginia found a high mortality rate for African American soldiers born in Albemarle County, Virginia, because forty of them served in the Sixty-Fifth and Sixty-Seventh USCI and spent time at Benton Barracks.[105]

Thomas Grimes was on the draft rolls for Beetown, Grant County. He walked to Prairie du Chien to enlist in the USCT in late August 1864, as did a number of other men from the Pleasant Ridge farm community. When he arrived at Benton Barracks at St. Louis in early October, Grimes was assigned to Company H, Forty-Second USCI, but he never actually joined the company. On his second evening in camp, Grimes stood in front of his barracks along with fellow Grant County volunteer Jerry Taylor. Taylor recalled, "One of the guards came out of the barracks with the gun in his hand. The gun of the other soldier went off and shot Thomas Grimes through the right leg." The ball passed through the right thigh but did not touch the femur. Grimes said that two other Grant County black soldiers were witnesses: Charles Shepard and Albert Hamlet. The white soldier who accidentally shot him was never identified. Grimes spent the rest of his service time hospitalized for the wound.[106] Grimes's army comrades were other hospitalized black Wisconsin soldiers: Reuben Thompson, Jackson Hill, Thomas Hillman, John H. Brown (formerly William Wilson), Thomas Richmond, and Jerry Taylor.[107] Among those who died in the St. Louis hospitals were William N. Jones (smallpox) and William Thomas (pneumonia) of the Sixty-Eighth, and Bill Williams (measles), unassigned.[108]

At least twenty-one men from Wisconsin served in the Sixty-Seventh, joining in late 1864 or early 1865; all were one-year enlistments. Among them were George Adams, a butcher who enlisted in Boscobel; Antoine Dodge, a Kenosha laborer; George Newsom, a farmer from Dodge County; Abraham Jackson, a Sauk County farmer; William J. Campbell and John Battise from the Fond du Lac area; and William Kneley from Milwaukee. They trained at Camp Randall and were shipped to Benton Barracks by train.[109]

The Sixty-Seventh was deployed to Port Hudson, Louisiana, arriving on March 19, 1864, and served there and at Morganza and Bayou Sara, Louisiana. According to historian John David Smith, disease killed many of the men stationed at Morganza: "In October 1864 a military medical board reported that an undiagnosed disease had ravaged three Missouri black regiments—the Sixty-Second, Sixty-Fifth, and Sixty-Seventh USCT—units subjected to continuous labor at Morganza, Louisiana. Sickness wiped out one-third of the enlistees."[110] The Wisconsin men began arriving just after this, replacing the men who had died from disease.

As many men with one-year enlistment terms were being discharged, the remaining men of the Sixty-Seventh were consolidated into the Sixty-Fifth Regiment, also stationed at Morganza. The Sixty-Fifth and Sixty-Seventh did only garrison duty and were not involved in combat.[111] When the Sixty-Seventh disbanded, eight Wisconsin men remained and were transferred to the Sixty-Fifth, including Thompson and Battise. Muster out was January 8, 1867.[112]

The Sixty-Fifth and Sixty-Seventh Regiments had no combat deaths but had extremely high death rates from disease. This reflected the woeful conditions at Benton Barracks and in the Delta. Among the dead were five Wisconsin men: Milton Crawford (malaria), Abraham Jackson (dysentery), David Newsom (typho-malarial fever), Samuel Lackey (pneumonia), and William Kneley (consumption). Jackson left behind a widow named Susan and at least four children on their Sauk County farm. They lost the farm, and Susan moved back to Ohio with their children.[113]

Lily Greene was the daughter of Thomas Greene (Thirteenth USCHA). She later sang African American spirituals for song collector Helene Stratman-Thomas. August 23, 1946. WHI IMAGE ID 25305

Seventeenth USCI

Fifteen Wisconsin men, all residents of the state, served in the Seventeenth USCI. Reflecting the scarcity of manpower, seven of the Wisconsin recruits were thirty-five or older. John J. Valentine, a cook from Janesville, was forty-two years old at enlistment. At the other extreme, Charles Morgan from the town of Trimbelle, Pierce County, was only sixteen; his father Moses gave signed permission allowing him to enlist.[114]

Four men enlisted in late summer and early fall of 1864 but were not forwarded from Camp Randall to St. Louis until April 1865, along with the other men who enlisted in early 1865. They joined the regiment four months after it fought in the Battle of Nashville. Michael Brady of La Crosse (and Prescott after the war) rose to the rank of corporal. During their service with the Seventeenth, the Wisconsin men saw no combat, and none died while in service. They did garrison duty in Nashville and other locations in Tennessee. All were discharged when their terms of service expired. Two late enlistees, Alexander Webb and George Thompson (Thomas), both of Janesville, served out their terms with the Forty-Second USCI, doing garrison duty until January 1866.[115]

Noncommissioned officers of Company C of the Second Wisconsin with their African American servant or employee, identified only as "Josh," 1862. WHI IMAGE ID 41937

THE UNION NAVY

The story of black men in the Union Navy is not as well-known and was very different from their history in the army. African Americans had a long history in the US maritime industry and the navy. From the beginning of the war, free black men were accepted into the navy, serving on ships and at bases with racially integrated crews. Like the USCT, all commissioned naval officers were white, and discrimination influenced job assignments, but the integration in the Civil War navy was not equaled again in the US military until after World War II.[116] Nevertheless, racial conflict did flare up between white and black sailors, particularly on the inland ships. For its part, the navy had only one set of rules for handling misconduct, unlike the army's separate and unequal branches of service and sets of rules.[117]

Early on, the navy also faced the problem of what to do with "contrabands" who arrived at ships or in navy yards asking for protection. Secretary of the Navy Gideon Welles was aware that the Confederacy was using slave labor to build fortifications and to man ships. On September 25, fifteen months before the Emancipation Proclamation, Welles issued a directive "with respect to the increasing number of persons of color . . . can neither be expelled nor can they be maintained unemployed; . . . you are therefore authorized, when their services can be useful, to enlist them for naval service under the same forms and regulations as apply to other enlistments."[118] The contrabands were paid less than free blacks and were limited to the lowest ranks and pay, but they nonetheless became free men and sailors.[119]

The Union navy engaged in warfare at sea, blockading Confederate coast and ports and transporting troops and materiel to war zones. The "Brown-water Navy" was the name for boats that patrolled and fought on inland waterways like the Mississippi, Ohio, Tennessee, and Red Rivers. Around ten thousand African American men served in the US Navy during the war, about 8 percent of all Union sailors.[120] The Great Lakes were relatively peaceful, so there were no bases or recruitment centers in Wisconsin. However, at least four black men from the state served in the navy: James K. Mitchell, Jonathan Barber, Major Lewis, and Henry Mason. All of them served as landsmen, the second-lowest rank, performing menial tasks on ships.

Mitchell, from Milwaukee, was a painter before enlisting and served on the USS *Lackawanna*, a steam-powered sloop that blockaded ports on the Gulf of Mexico. Mitchell appears to have been on board throughout the ship's three years, including the Battle of Mobile Bay in the summer of 1864, which closed the last Confederate port on the Gulf. Jonathan Barber, a waiter from Columbus, enlisted at Cairo, Illinois, in October 1864; no record was found of service on a named ship. Major Lewis, a farmer whose origin was listed only as "Wisconsin," volunteered at Chicago in September 1864. He served on the *General Lyon*, a transport and storeship on the lower Mississippi. Finally, Henry Mason of Milwaukee, an eighteen-year-old who was a boatman before the war, served on the *Forest Rose* (a tin-clad transport steamer armed with artillery, supporting army operations along the Lower Mississippi and tributaries) and the *Huntress* (a steamer gunship that patrolled between Memphis, Tennessee and Columbus, Kentucky).[121]

US Colored Heavy Artillery

The largest contingent of Wisconsin black artillerymen was in the Third US Colored Heavy Artillery (USCHA). Its entire service time was in Tennessee at Fort Pickering at the south end of Memphis, and it never saw combat. Although designated as an artillery regiment, it was equipped as infantry throughout its service.[122] Thirty-three Wisconsin men were assigned, but sixteen got no farther than Benton Barracks. These men were not shipped from Camp Randall until mid- or late April 1865. All were discharged from service at Benton Barracks and never made it to Memphis. An unknown number of them spent time in St. Louis hospitals, including William (Billy) Brookfield, a pre- and postwar resident of Rock County.[123]

Joseph Williams, who enlisted in Fond du Lac, joined the regiment at Memphis in December 1864. He was erroneously reported dead in April 1865 but in reality served out his one-year term and did not return to Wisconsin after the war. All of the others reached Memphis in March or April 1865. John Douglass and William Yates, both of whom enlisted in Milwaukee, deserted from Memphis. Douglass was the only man who enlisted for a three-year term.[124] Others who served out their terms at Fort Pickering were Alfred Greene, Henry Johnson, James Lay, Jerret Nelson, William Riley, Van Spence, Pinckney Taylor, John Thomas, and Monroe Wayne.[125]

Horace Dangerfield, a railroad porter from Milwaukee, was drafted on September 21, 1864. He was promoted to sergeant in the Thirteenth USCHA in May 1865 and served with Thomas Greene, a farmer from Pleasant Ridge, Grant County, who was drafted October 1, 1864. The Thirteenth USCHA did garrison duty at Fort Nelson and other points in Kentucky until muster out on November 18, 1865. Both Dangerfield and Greene were discharged a few weeks earlier when their one-year terms of service expired. John H. Brown, a private and fifer, enlisted in Chicago. After his service, he lived in Janesville, Columbus, and Waukesha.[126]

Two other artillerymen moved to Wisconsin after the war. Charles Branum served twenty months with the Twelfth USCHA in Kentucky. He later lived in Fox Lake. Isaac Holden served for more than two years with the Sixth USCHA in Mississippi and Louisiana and was the only Wisconsin artilleryman to experience combat. He moved to Wisconsin in the 1880s, residing briefly in Oshkosh and at the Soldiers' Home in Milwaukee before settling in the La Crosse area.[127]

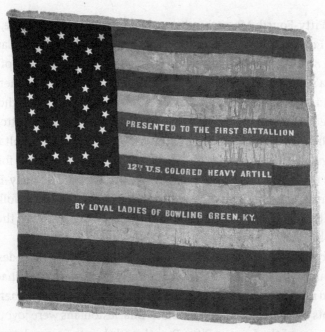

The battle flag of the Twelfth USCHA. DIVISION OF POLITICAL & MILITARY HISTORY, NATIONAL MUSEUM OF AMERICAN HISTORY, SMITHSONIAN INSTITUTION

AFTER APPOMATTOX

President Lincoln later summed up the results of his decision to issue the Emancipation Proclamation and accept African Americans in the Union Army: "Without the military help of the black freedmen, the war against the South could not have been won."[128] Less than a week after Lee's surrender at Appomattox, Lincoln was assassinated in Washington, DC. Many of the African American veterans and men still in uniform expressed shock and grief at the death of the president.

Because they had been serving longer than the USCT regiments, most white regiments were disbanded first. The USCT regiments remained in service to keep the peace and were stationed in most of the capital cities of the former Confederate states and other large cities and ports.[129] Their presence was welcomed by black southerners but was resented and opposed by most white southerners. In Charleston, South Carolina, and Memphis, Tennessee, violent conflict between black troops and white citizens led eventually to the removal of the USCT soldiers from Southern cities.

The Fifty-Fourth Massachusetts was included in a Union force, led by General Edward E. Potter, which set out from Georgetown, South Carolina, on April 8. Potter's Raid was intended to destroy what remained of South Carolina's railroad infrastructure and other resources that Sherman's army had not destroyed. The raid encountered resistance throughout but succeeded in destroying locomotives, rails, rail cars, bridges, cotton, and mills. Their mission was aided by contraband scouts and simultaneous uprisings of enslaved people. Twenty-five hundred contrabands followed them as they returned to Georgetown on April 25.[130] The Fifty-Fourth Massachusetts did not hear of Lee's surrender until April 22. The following day, while still on the march back to Georgetown, they received the news of Lincoln's assassination.[131]

After Potter's Raid, Arthur B. Lee found himself and his comrades of the Fifty-Fourth and Fifty-Fifth Massachusetts in the city where he had been born and raised—Charleston, South Carolina, along with two other USCT regiments recruited in the North. Black Charlestonians were joyous over the presence of the famous Fifty-Fourth and the men were determined to assert their hard-won victory over enslavement and white oppression.

White Charlestonians and white soldiers from New York, however, were not so welcoming. A series of fights broke out, with white troops pushing back, sometimes with force, against black soldiers and freedpeople who were asserting their newfound rights. These tensions finally erupted in three days of deadly riots in July. Regional military commanders decided, in consultation with General Grant, to remove the New York regiments and to send home the USCT regiments from the North, including the Fifty-Fourth and Fifty-Fifth.[132]

It was during this difficult time in Charleston, with no date yet set for discharge, that John Tucker, the Racine native who was twice wounded with the Fifty-Fourth, deserted on July 21, 1865, shortly after the riot and only a month before the regiment was discharged.[133] The Fifty-Fifth Massachusetts was mustered out on August 29, with five Wisconsin men still active: Edwin and David Cross, Henry Dodge, Augustus Golden, and John Sutfen. William Bowdry, William Caldwell, and Richard Thomas were discharged separately from hospitals.[134]

President Andrew Johnson planned with military leaders and his cabinet to hold a military parade in Washington, DC, to commemorate the end of the war and to raise spirits after Lincoln's assassination before all of the troops returned to their homes. On May 23 and 24, 1865, the Grand Review of the Armies took place in Washington. On the first day, General Meade's Army of the Potomac, eighty thousand strong, marched down Pennsylvania Avenue, past President Johnson, General Grant, Secretary of War Stanton, and other officials. Absent from the ranks were the thousands of African American men who had fought in Meade's army, including the Twenty-Ninth. The following day, General Sherman's army, which had no USCT soldiers, followed the same route. Mixed within and following Sherman's army were thousands of African American civilians who had been his pioneer battalions, carrying their shovels and axes rather than weapons. Among the soldiers may have been Samuel Arms, the young drummer, and Wisconsin black men who marched with state regiments.[135]

During the Grand Review, the Twenty-Ninth Regiment USCI and the rest of the Twenty-Fourth Corps were in Virginia amid rumors of what was to come next for them.[136] The Twenty-Ninth was among more than forty USCT regiments sent to Texas, along with some white regiments. Their tasks included protecting the border from the French puppet government in Mexico and eliminating Confederate power west of the Mississippi. On the page with May morning reports, First Sergeant Lloyd Bryon noted for Company F, "Embarked on board Steamer Wilmington on the 25th inst. bound for Fortress Monroe where we arrived on the morning of the 26th, then came to anchor awaiting orders which were received on the Thirty-first."[137] The remainder of the Twenty-Ninth Regiment was aboard the steamer *Kennedy*. The same steamers carried them down the Atlantic Coast and eventually to Brazos de Santiago, Texas, where the Rio Grande enters the Gulf of Mexico. When they arrived on the Texas coast, they had to remain on board several extra days because rough seas prevented them from landing. Regimental Surgeon David Mackay wrote that during the voyage the men were "subjected to an ordeal that resulted fatally to many on a crowded steamer . . . furnished with bad water and worse food— under a sweltering atmosphere."[138] The landing of federal troops, however, brought the first news of emancipation to the enslaved people of Texas. As troops spread across the state, Union officers announced that the war was over and slavery had been abolished. This is the origin of Juneteenth Day.[139]

Albert Wilson of Company D, credited to Milwaukee, contracted scurvy during the voyage and died at Corps d'Afrique Hospital in New Orleans. Jaundice, malaria, chills, dysentery, and fevers were also common, and the hospitals in Texas and Louisiana were worse than those in Virginia. Three other Company F men credited to Milwaukee died from disease in Texas: Joseph Summers, John Norton, and Perry Mackay. Among those hospitalized was Lloyd Bryon, whose last entry in the morning reports was June 27. He was reduced to ranks and was hospitalized for most of the regiment's time in Texas.[140]

In an 1886 affidavit supporting the pension claim of Charles Henry Taylor (Company D, Twenty-Ninth USCI), William Reed of Company F described the horrific conditions in Texas: "The only water we could get for use was at the Rio Grande River, to reach which it was necessary to go along the shore and wade a number of miles when the tide was out. We used to go through this water up to our armpits for over half a mile, every day for about ten days in a row."[141] The Twenty-Ninth regiment faced no combat in Texas. The seven men from northwestern Wisconsin in Companies B and D were discharged in August and September because their one-year enlistments expired. Muster out for the rest of the regiment was November 6 at Brownsville. The men could keep their muskets for a charge of six dollars, which almost all of them did. They sailed for New Orleans by steamer and there boarded a riverboat for Cairo and then to Springfield, where they were paid and discharged. One hundred sixty members of the regiment were left behind in hospitals in Texas and Louisiana.[142]

Also serving in Texas was the Sixty-Eighth USCI. When they mustered out in February 1866, ten of the eighteen Wisconsin men were still with the regiment.[143] The Seventeenth and Eighteenth USCI remained in Tennessee until muster out. By that time, most of the Wisconsin men had already been discharged because their terms of service had expired.[144] When the Forty-Ninth USCI mustered out at Vicksburg on March 22, 1866, Harrison Freeman from Racine and Abraham Tillman, credited to the Town of Sharon, Walworth County, were the only Wisconsin men still with the regiment.[145]

In late winter and early spring of 1866, members of the Third USCHA were assigned a gruesome task. They were sent with picks and shovels to the site of the Fort Pillow Massacre, thirty miles north of Memphis, to reinter the remains of the victims.[146] The regiment mustered out on April 30, 1866, but most soldiers were still around Fort Pickering on the following day, waiting for the paymaster to arrive with their back pay.[147] This probably included Jerret Nelson, who enlisted at Janesville and remained with the regiment beyond his one-year term. Armed white mobs, including city policemen, attacked and murdered black men and women in their homes and on the streets of South Memphis. They especially targeted black men in uniform, most of whom were unarmed because they had just mustered out. The rioting lasted for three days. At least forty-six persons, forty-four of them black, were killed, among them six named veterans of the Third USCHA and eight other unnamed black soldiers. One of the white men was killed by a self-inflicted wound, and the other was shot "by accident" by another white man. The riot showed convincingly that white southerners would not tolerate or respect black federal troops and that President Johnson's lenient policies toward the ex-Confederates, including officeholders and military officers, were encouraging violence against African Americans, particularly soldiers. The federal response

was to remove black regiments from Southern cities and replace them
with white troops.[148]

The last black soldier from Wisconsin to return home was John Allen,
who started his service in the Sixty-Seventh USCI and transferred to the
Sixty-Fifth. He was mustered out with the rest of the Sixty-Fifth regiment
at Baton Rouge, Louisiana, on January 8, 1867, over twenty months after
Appomattox.[149]

Part of a series of small lithographed cards depicting an imagined African American
man moving from slavery to freedom and death on the battlefield, ca. 1863.
LIBRARY OF CONGRESS, LC-USZC4-2519

THE HOMEFRONT

Families of all Civil War soldiers and sailors suffered economically and personally from the absence and loss of sons and husbands. Many of those families were subsequently unable to retain ownership of their homes and farms. For the Wisconsin African American servicemen and families, problems on the home front were often more dire. Wisconsin black soldiers were more likely to be single and childless, and many of those who had been enslaved before or during the war had already suffered dislocation from their families. For those with wives and children, their worries were great because they would be far away and would be unable to help if the family fell into financial straits. An additional problem was the lack of support for black families from state and local government agencies. What would happen to their precarious existence in Wisconsin if they were gone for the full term of enlistment, or returned disabled, or did not return at all? Men who volunteered were entitled to a bounty, but most of that was paid at the end of their service. Once in service, many black soldiers went months without pay to send home.

Some black farmers had a great deal to lose but enlisted in the Union army anyway. In Cheyenne Valley and its vicinity, Alfred Weaver and Charles Allen left their families and farms in order to serve the Union cause. The Barton, Stewart, Roberts, and Thornton families gave up their sons for the war. In Columbia County, John Rosier left his wife, Hannah, and children in September 1864 for a second term of service. He owned a farm valued at $1,200. Titus Sutfen owned a farm worth $800 in the town of Eagle, Waukesha County; his twenty-three-year-old son, John, volunteered for the Fifty-Fifth Massachusetts.[150] As landowners, these families were the exceptions. Most parents and siblings, wives, and children would have to struggle to hold onto their farms and homes and to keep themselves sheltered and fed.

The Bartons, a black family living in Cheyenne Valley, had a great deal to lose when Leonard, age twenty, and his father Wesley, age about thirty-nine, received draft notices in September 1864. Leonard was enrolled that month and served in a white regiment, the Thirty-Second Wisconsin Infantry, along with his mixed-race neighbor Samuel Waldron. Wesley and Martha Barton had six other children ranging in age from two to eighteen living at home, with another on the way. The Bartons owned their farm and feared losing it if Wesley went into the army, even if he did return. Their next-oldest son, Felix, was eighteen, old enough to enlist but below draft age. The family arrived at a difficult decision—young Felix would serve as a substitute for his father. Martha and Wesley must have felt regret for the remainder of their lives for this hard decision.[151] Felix Barton enlisted at La Crosse on October 4, signing his name in clear cursive script. After training in Madison, he was shipped to St. Louis, designated for the USCT but never assigned to a company or regiment. The only other paper in his service records is a casualty sheet documenting his death at Webster Hospital in Memphis on February 4, 1865, from lung inflammation.[152] The Bartons were able to hold onto their farm, but their decision cost the life of their son.

The vast majority of the African American soldiers from Wisconsin did not own property. Henry Sink, Ebenezer Morgan, and Lewis Gaines in Fond du Lac County owned no real or personal property, but all three of them had children. Many of the black men who enlisted in Wisconsin were young, single, owned nothing, and worked in menial jobs during their usually brief times in the state. The men from Missouri who were credited to Wisconsin had recently escaped enslavement, owning little more than the clothes on their backs. They risked their lives and left loved ones behind in Missouri but had little or no material wealth at stake when they joined the army.

Some black soldiers' wives were forced to write to their state officials to ask for financial support, the money they had expected to get never materializing. Such was the case with Josephus and Anna Heuston. Josephus married Anna Hanson in 1853 in Waukesha County; they owned no real estate and had personal property valued at just $50. Josephus was thirty-eight years old when he volunteered in August 1864 and was assigned to the Seventeenth USCI. He left behind Anna and at least three children under the age of ten. In the spring of 1865, Anna sent a plea to the Wisconsin adjutant general for subsistence. Many African American volunteers from Wisconsin, including her husband, had notations on their enlistment forms suggesting that they were in the Twenty-Ninth USCI, though most of them were not. The provost marshal's office wrote to the commander of the Twenty-Ninth to confirm that Private Heuston was in service but would have received a negative answer. Anna Heuston's petition for aid was still languishing in the bureaucracy when Josephus was discharged in August 1865 and returned home.[153]

Hannah Rosier, whose husband was serving in the Fifth Wisconsin Infantry, wrote to Governor Lewis in February 1865, asking for relief:

> Sir, my Husband (John) enlisted in the Fifth Reg. Wis. Vol. Infantry the 19th of last Sep. and he was assured that his family would get $5 per month from the state while he was gone. Now, sir, my family are sick and suffering. My Husband has not been paid any money so that he could send me any and I am told in Portage by the man that pays the money out to the women that there is none for me. . . . If you tell me that there is no help for me I will not trouble further. My Husband is John W. Rosier, Company D, under Col. Allen. He enlisted in the 2nd Reg in /61 and I was treated in the same way. But he was assured this time that I should get the money. Please answer soon and oblige your most humble servant, Hannah A. Rosier.[154]

No reply exists in the Governor's Correspondence Books. John was discharged on June 20, 1865.[155]

Some townships and cities provided aid to struggling families of soldiers, and the state offered five dollars per month to families of soldiers during the war. In January 1864, the legislature inquired as to whether additional legislation was needed "to secure to the families of colored soldiers in said volunteer service, the payments authorized by said laws." The Judiciary Committee determined that they were entitled to aid and no change in the law was needed. However, the first black family actually granted state aid did not receive it until 1866—after the war was over and most soldiers had already returned home.[156]

CHAPTER FOUR

POSTWAR LIFE

NOT WELCOME BACK HOME

Most of the Missouri men credited to Milwaukee who served in Company F, Twenty-Ninth USCI, returned to Missouri, while a few settled in Quincy, Illinois. Veterans who were Wisconsin residents when they enlisted returned to live in the state after discharge or muster out. As before the war, they scattered across the settled parts of the state, primarily on farms and in small towns. Some men who worked for Wisconsin regiments during the war came to the state with the men with whom they had served, but the majority returned to the Southern locations where they had lived while enslaved. Many of these men had left behind parents, wives, children, and friends, so they chose to return to familiar surroundings or to search for relatives from whom they had been separated during enslavement.

When African American veterans returned to or settled for the first time in Wisconsin, they were given a mixed reception by their white neighbors. In some communities, there was initial acceptance and tolerance, but in other towns and villages the veterans were either avoided altogether or subject to open hostility and violence. The experience of three men— Andrew Pratt, Arthur B. Lee, and Henry H. Roseman—demonstrates this mixed reaction that African American communities and veterans encountered in postwar Wisconsin.

Andrew Pratt came to Wisconsin on the Underground Railroad in 1861, having passed through Illinois and eventually arriving at Milton House.

At this hotel, the Underground Railroad actually did run underground, through a tunnel from a nearby cabin into the hotel basement.[1] After a period hiding in that basement, Pratt decided to stay in Milton and was accepted into some aspects of community life, including membership in the Knights Templar (the temperance organization). When he was enrolled on the list of draft-eligible men, Pratt visited the governor in Madison to request permission to volunteer for the army rather than be drafted. Pratt was not allowed to volunteer and ended up not serving in the army.[2]

A white army officer about to return to Milton at war's end asked relatives at home to see if they could get Andrew Pratt expelled from the Knights Templar. He would not join if Pratt were a member, he explained, because while in the army, "he was not fighting for Negro equality." His relatives started a petition for Pratt's removal, and Pratt was told that a majority of the members wanted him out. Believing that to be true, Pratt submitted a withdrawal card. However, upon learning that, in fact, a majority of the members wanted him to *stay*, he asked for the return of his withdrawal card. At a sparsely attended meeting, a motion was rammed through to accept his withdrawal card and ignore his request to retract it. Ezra Goodrich, who with his father had aided Pratt's escape from enslavement, carried out his threat to resign from the Knights Templar if they expelled Pratt. He published a sixteen-page diatribe chastising by name those neighbors who expelled Pratt and the methods they used. Although the expulsion was officially rescinded, Pratt left Milton shortly after the uproar, settling in Wells, Minnesota, where he worked as a barber and owned property, married, and raised a family.[3]

Veteran Arthur B. Lee encountered rejection in Janesville but later found acceptance in nearby Milton. Lee did not return to Massachusetts or South Carolina after serving in the Fifty-Fourth Massachusetts. He, his wife, Rose, and two young children moved to St. Louis, Chicago, and eventually to Janesville. There, he was unable to find work as a journeyman harness maker "as white men objected to working with him. . . . At Janesville his resources were entirely exhausted and want was staring him in the face."[4] He was brought to Milton by Ezra Goodrich, who helped establish him in the harness-making business. In Milton, he found acceptance, respect, and a stable economic life. His early years in Milton were difficult. Rose and both children died in 1869 or 1870.[5] Lee remar-

Arthur B. Lee (Fifty-Fourth Massachusetts), ca. 1891. WHI IMAGE ID 145456

ried in 1872 to Mary Hagney, a white woman.[6] They had one son, Arthur Jr., but Mary died six days after the child's birth. In 1876, he married Amanda Jane Barker, a light-skinned African American widow who came to Wisconsin as a contraband with an army surgeon. The couple lived in Milton for most of the next thirty years and raised Arthur Jr.[7]

Overt racial hostility and violence from white veterans greeted one black veteran in particular only weeks after he was discharged from the army. Henry Roseman, a veteran of the Thirty-Seventh Wisconsin Infantry, returned to his prewar residence of Beaver Dam. As Roseman was returning home one day from the post office, one of a group of white veterans who had been drinking together crossed the street to confront him, for no reason other than his color. The ringleader blocked Roseman's way on the sidewalk and pushed him into the street. Roseman "remonstrated, in a firm but reasonable manner, against such treatment, and was met with insult, curses, and finally blows, upon which the rest of the drunken gang were promptly on hand, blustering, swearing, threatening, and striking."[8]

Three men from this group were arrested, taken before a judge, and charged with assault and battery. They pleaded guilty and paid small fines. Immediately after their release, a group followed Roseman from the courtroom "and renewed the assault, dragged him into the street, and beat him severely." Four men were arrested this time, including two of the same men who beat him the first time. One of the arrested men was released because he had supposedly not struck Roseman, although he had encouraged the rest of the attackers by offering one hundred dollars "if they'd kill the nigger." The others were taken before the same judge and again pleaded guilty. This time, two of them were sent to county jail for thirty days, and the third paid a fine and was freed on the condition that he leave town.

The *Dodge County Citizen*—the local Republican newspaper—was sympathetic to Roseman. After noting his name and his military service, the article also named the attackers, calling them "cowardly, ruffianly and drunken sots." They said of Roseman that "he has shown himself honest, industrious, and gentlemanly, with high aims and aspirations" and accused the co-editors of the rival *Beaver Dam Argus* of egging on the assailants. The *Argus* also covered the incident, though very differently. In an article entitled "An Exciting Time," the names of the victim and the attackers were not mentioned. The attackers were described as "a party of returning soldiers" while only Henry Roseman's race, and not his veteran status, was mentioned. The article concluded, "of course, the soldiers cannot be justified in pounding the negro, but it would have been infinitely better for the peace of the city, and for his own safety, had the negro taken good advice, and got out of the way, instead of remaining to provoke an assault."[9] Roseman filed a civil suit for damages against one of the attackers, but the jury ruled against him.[10] Henry Roseman did not remain long in Beaver Dam, nor did any other black veteran.[11]

A further disturbing incident occurred in Brothertown in July 1865. Freeman Richards, Forty-Ninth USCI, returned after the war to Calumet County, where his wife, Charlotte, and their children lived. On August 26, he was serving as the fiddle player for a dance in Chilton. A fight occurred, resulting in the death of a white veteran from a stab wound. Richards was arrested and charged with the crime by a grand jury. Newspaper accounts emphasized that the victim was a veteran and a father, but Richards's status as veteran and father was not mentioned. In May 1866, Richards escaped from the Manitowoc jail where he was held for nearly nine months awaiting trial. News came a few weeks later that he had been captured in Ontonagon, Michigan. The sheriff there reported that on June 27, Richards hanged himself in his jail cell, leaving a long suicide note denying that he was the murderer. The note said that Richards knew who stabbed the victim, but no name was given. The letter was published in various newspapers, taking up a column and a half, supposedly from a man who could not sign his own name to his enlistment papers less than two years earlier.[12]

Disease, as well as violence, plagued some returning veterans. Richard Thomas, for example, spent much of his time in the Fifty-Fifth Massachusetts in hospitals for an unspecified disease. He was discharged from a hospital in New York City on September 1, 1865. Thomas returned to

Evansville, Rock County, briefly, and then lived for a short time in Brodhead. His wife had abandoned him, allegedly because of the "mysterious illness" he had when he came home. By May 1866, he was a resident of the Green County Poor House in Monroe, where he died on June 24, 1866.[13]

Gus Cowen, too, fell victim to an unknown illness. He was about twenty years old when he fled enslavement and joined the Twenty-First Wisconsin Infantry during Sherman's March through Georgia, employed by Captain J. M. Randall. Cowen came to Wisconsin after the war and settled in Mukwonago, where he found work caring for and training horses. In 1870, he rescued two boys from drowning in Phantom Lake, making him a local hero. Three years later, he died suddenly from an unknown illness. His tombstone inscription reads in part: "He gained the confidence and regard of all who knew him."[14]

POLITICAL ACTIVITY

Black Civil War veterans started engaging in political activism before the war ended. A petition was submitted to the Wisconsin legislature in March 1865 requesting a referendum to amend the state constitution to allow black men to vote. It read, in part, "We respectfully submit that by Law we are taxed and liable to Military Duty as other men. It seems to us but justice that we should have a voice in determining how the taxes should be expended, and how and when our services shall be rendered."[15] One hundred two African American men signed the petition, including the following seven soldiers: Michael Brady, La Crosse; Horace Dangerfield, Milwaukee; Robert Edmunds, La Crosse; Augustus Golden, Milwaukee; Joseph Holstein (Holster), Milwaukee; John Sutfen, Eagle; and Samuel Thompson, La Crosse. A mass meeting was held in Milwaukee on October 9, 1865 to support a yes vote on the referendum. John W. Birney was elected president of the meeting and Charles F. Wilkins secretary; both men were from La Crosse. Ezekiel Gillespie of Milwaukee served as a member of the committee that drafted resolutions. Reverend Henry Hyland Garnett, a nationally known abolitionist, delivered the keynote speech.[16]

The Republican Party officially supported the referendum but did not campaign vigorously for it, and many Republican candidates distanced themselves from it. The Republican ticket swept all of the statewide contests, but the vote in favor of black suffrage was just 45.6 percent, so the referendum failed.[17] On Election Day, Ezekiel Gillespie tried to vote in Milwaukee and was refused. He sued the official who denied him a ballot, and his case went to the Wisconsin Supreme Court.[18]

More veterans returned home after the referendum failed and became involved in agitation for the right to vote. In Prescott, a public meeting was held on the suffrage issue on March 8. Lewis Washington Sr. chaired the meeting, and Moses Morgan acted as vice president—both of them were fathers of Civil War veterans. Michael Brown and Charles Morgan, recently returned soldiers, served as secretaries. The resolutions of the day were quite radical and expressed optimism for a better future for African Americans.

> We believe the American system of Government rests on the great principle of equal rights to every man, irrespective of color . . . we are convinced that the spirit of slavery still exists in a great measure, and that constant effort is necessary to stay its influence . . . when we consider the beneficial results of the late war, how the nation has been awakened to a more realizing sense of the brotherhood of man, we would express our deep gratitude to the United States, and we cannot but look upon the future as full of promise, since the war for universal freedom and human rights is over, the battle fought, and the victory won, as we hope, for all succeeding time. Resolved: That inasmuch as Wisconsin has called upon us for the discharge of the duties of citizen soldiers, and has found us truly loyal, we hope to see her grant to us the rights of citizens to the elective franchise.[19]

The newspaper reprint of the resolutions was followed by a poem by Nancy Morgan, mother of veteran Charles Morgan, honoring President Lincoln.[20] Their resolutions were forwarded to Madison shortly before the Wisconsin State Supreme Court ruled on Ezekiel Gillespie's lawsuit. The court reinterpreted the 1849 referendum that supported black male suffrage, deciding that it should have been interpreted as granting the franchise at that time. Governor Fairchild issued a proclamation on April 2, 1866, which read, in part, "no citizen of this state is now debarred the privilege of the ballot box by reason of the color of his skin."

The *Dodge County Citizen* reported that Andrew Taylor, a black man, voted in the April 1866 election in Beaver Dam and remarked that "the country still survives. This was the first instance in this city of a colored man voting, and he was, four years ago a Southern slave."[21] The *Milwaukee Sentinel*, reporting on the first black voters, said "we were glad to see that no attempt was made to disturb them," but in the next sentence noted that "a few curses followed several of them as they marched up to the polls."[22] In the fourth and seventh wards, the sheriff summoned several African American voters to report for jury duty. The following day, Judge Smith, contrary to state law, discharged all of the black potential jurors and told the deputy sheriff to bring in only white jurors. One of the few poll lists still in existence from this period is from La Crosse. Among the men registered to vote in the city in November 1868 were John W. Birney, Charles F. Wilkins, and veterans Robert Edmunds and Samuel Thompson.[23]

African American veterans not only voted but engaged in political activism in support of the party of Lincoln. Grant, the Republican candidate for president in 1868, was ridiculed by his opponents for his humble background as a tanner. Supporters embraced the intended insult and formed grassroots pro-Grant organizations called the "Tanners," holding rallies and torchlight parades. Many Union veterans participated in the Tanners, which were organized along military lines. In Fond du Lac, one of four companies of Tanners was Company D, or what the newspapers dubbed the "Colored Company." The opposing group supporting the Democrat Seymour called itself the "White Boys in Blue," making clear that African Americans were not welcome.[24]

Henry Sink, a partially disabled veteran of Company F, Twenty-Ninth USCI, was involved with the Tanners for Grant's reelection in 1872 and paid a price for it. The 1872 Fond du Lac Tanner regiment had companies based on place of employment, ward, and race. They again held rallies, marches, and parades in Fond du Lac and traveled to Milwaukee by train and Oshkosh by boat to take part in pro-Grant rallies.[25] Following a Tanners meeting the night of September 3, Henry Sink was walking home when he was attacked on the street by unknown assailants, who shot him in the leg. The wound was described as "not dangerous." No one was ever arrested for the crime.[26]

William McKenney, another veteran of Company F, Twenty-Ninth USCI, wrote a letter to the editor of the *Janesville Gazette* that said, in part, "I, as an old soldier and a true friend of my country's right, will positively cast my vote at the coming election for US Grant; for in justice to the Republican party and to myself, I must give him my hearty support."[27] Hayden Netter (First Wisconsin Infantry) was among at least three African American residents and voters who were members of the Fox Lake Grant and Wilson Club.[28]

Arthur B. Lee, formerly of Company A, Fifty-Fourth Massachusetts, frequently wrote letters to the editor of his hometown *Milton Journal*, the *Janesville Gazette*, and the *Milwaukee Sentinel* about political and racial issues of the day. In 1872, he gave his first-ever public speech in support of Grant's reelection. In October, he wrote to the *Gazette*, "[W]e, their descendants, remained slaves, and now, that we have by fighting to sustain this government *earned* our liberty and enfranchisement we are determined that if our children should become slaves it will be by no fault of ours, and hence we are united and organized from the lakes to the gulf in support of Grant and Wilson and against the party whose rallying cry is 'down with Negro supremacy.'"[29]

EARNING A LIVING

With some notable exceptions, a majority of the black veterans in Wisconsin lived their entire postwar lives in poverty, never owned property, and never received an education sufficient enough to open doors to higher income or status. A few became farm owners or tradesmen, but most worked in low-paying, menial jobs that were often temporary or seasonal. Rural and small-town men were farm laborers and city men were day laborers. Even fewer options were open to women. As a result, many veterans, including those with families, moved often in search of work and opportunity. Of the six men confirmed to be USCT veterans living in Fond du Lac County in 1870, only one, Lewis Gaines (Company F, Twenty-Ninth USCI), owned real estate. Their occupations were millhands (two), farm laborers (two), laborer (one), and unemployed (one).[30] By the time of the 1880 census, Gaines had died and only one of the other five, Alfred Patterson, was still living in the county.[31]

Veterans in other parts of the state worked in similar jobs. A sampling of veterans and their occupations noted in the 1870 US Census include Horace Dangerfield (Milwaukee, porter), Cyrenus Bostwick (Oshkosh, laborer),

William Brookfield (Janesville, cook), Howard Brooks (Madison, laborer), Robert Edmunds (La Crosse, stone mason), Louis Brown (Salem Township, Kenosha County, farm laborer), Michael Brown (Prescott, stone mason), Thomas Nelson (Union Township, laborer), Hayden Netter (Fox Lake, day laborer), Thomas Spite (Hudson, farm laborer), Alexander Stamper (Union Township, grubbing), John Sutfen (Portage, laborer), Enoch Taylor (Janesville, laborer), and William R. Thomas (Oshkosh, cook). Among these men, only Edmunds and Netter reported owning real estate.[32]

William Brown of Eau Claire had resumed his prewar work as a steamboat cook. He and his wife, Eliza, an English-born white woman, owned $800 in real estate.[33] John Briggs had lived in Racine since the 1850s. In the 1860 census, John and Charity Briggs and their family were noted as "paupers" and owned no property. In 1870, John's occupation was given as "day laborer" and they owned $300 worth of real estate. John Davis lived in Union Township, Rock County, with $375 in real estate. His Eighteenth USCI comrade Thomas Nelson lived in the same household.[34]

After his discharge, Isaac Smith, Company F, Twenty-Ninth USCI, worked as a gardener and caretaker in a private home in Madison. His tentmate William McKenney worked briefly in Madison for Samuel Hastings, the state treasurer, until Hastings left office in early 1866. McKenney moved to Milwaukee, working as the cook and steward on a Great Lakes wrecking tug, the *Leviathan*. The ship's owner Lemuel Ellsworth, wrote, "I paid him 50 dollars per month, and think that if he had not been hard of hearing he would have been worth all of 60 dollars. . . . His character was first rate. I could always rely upon his truthfulness." At that rate of pay, he was one of the best-paid black veterans. In the winter, he worked in the city as a cook. McKenney had two children in Milwaukee with a black woman to whom he was not married; he then married a white woman, with whom he had a daughter. In 1872, Isaac Smith moved to Chicago and found work as a janitor. Four years later, William McKenney separated from his wife, left his daughters in Milwaukee, and moved to Chicago. He continued to work on the lakes during the season and as a waiter at the elegant Palmer House Hotel in winters.[35]

While Wisconsin was primarily an agricultural state, industrialization rapidly progressed in larger cities at this time. In general, African Americans were excluded from this employment sector. In La Crosse

The wrecking tug *Leviathan* was a well-known rescue and salvage boat on the Great Lakes. William McKenney (Twenty-Ninth USCI) worked as a steward and cook on the boat for many seasons following his service. COURTESY OF HISTORICAL COLLECTIONS OF THE GREAT LAKES, BOWLING GREEN STATE UNIVERSITY

Plankinton House (shown here, ca. 1880) was one of the premier hotels in Milwaukee in the late nineteenth century. All of the waiters there were black men, headed by John J. Miles (Thirty-Second USCI). William Reed (Twenty-Ninth USCI) also worked there. WHI IMAGE ID 54451

and Milwaukee, there is no evidence that any veterans found steady work in factories. In the early postwar years, African Americans were used as strikebreakers, as in a lumberman's strike in La Crosse in 1873.[36] Black men and women in cities were limited to service occupations or small businesses or trades. In 1872, the Plankinton House in Milwaukee hired twenty experienced black waiters, beginning many decades of relatively stable and high-paid employment.[37]

POPULATION

The African American population in Wisconsin rose from 1,171 in 1860 to 2,113 in 1870, mostly due to migration from the South during and after the war. In every county that had at least ten African Americans in 1860 (with the exception of Walworth), the 1870 population went up. Fond du Lac had the largest black community of any city or county in 1870. The statewide black population rose again in the 1880 US Census and was the same or higher in all cities and counties except for La Crosse and Racine County.

African American Population[38]	1860	1870	1880
Statewide	1,171	2,113	2,702
CITIES			
Fond du Lac	19	179	178
Milwaukee	106	176	304
Racine	71	141	142
La Crosse	36	101	55
COUNTIES			
Fond du Lac	59	209	206
Rock	93	194	203
Milwaukee	107	185	320
Racine	135	194	159
Winnebago	52	113	115
Vernon	69	71	130
Brown	20	67	116

One factor that limited the growth of the African American population was infant mortality, a scourge throughout the postwar decades.
Poverty was a major factor in infant deaths because parents could not af-
ford medicines or professional care. Contagious diseases like diphtheria,
cholera, and tuberculosis (called "consumption" at this time) were com-
mon. High infant mortality is mentioned in written and oral histories of
African American communities in Grant, Vernon, Pierce, Fond du Lac, and
Milwaukee Counties.[39] Nora Thomas and her veteran husband, William
(Sixty-Eighth USCI), lived in Green Bay and had five children, all of whom
were dead by 1895. Their last-born, William, died at the age of nine.[40]
Young wives of several of the veterans, such as Mary Lee (Arthur) and
Maria Rosier Jones (Alex), died from complications following childbirth.[41]

COMMUNITY INSTITUTIONS AND SOCIAL CONNECTIONS

A consistent development in rural and urban postwar black communities
was the creation and construction of churches. Milwaukee's St. Mark's
African Methodist Episcopal (AME) church was built in 1869, with suffrage
pioneer Ezekiel Gillespie among the founders.[42] The Zion African Methodist Episcopal Church of Fond du Lac was built in 1869, and the Fox Lake
Zion Methodist Church was built in 1872.[43] In all three locations, black
Civil War veterans and their families were involved. The multiracial community of Cheyenne Valley created a Wesleyan Methodist congregation
and built a log church. Land for the church was donated by Mark Revels,
a mixed-race man, and land for a log schoolhouse was donated by John
Eastman, a white man.[44] In Grant County, the black settlers on Pleasant
Ridge first built a school cooperatively with their white neighbors, which
children of both races attended and where church services were held. An
exception to this pattern was Prescott in Pierce County. While there were
enough African Americans in the town and surrounding countryside to
support a church, two white churches, Baptist and Methodist, invited
newly arrived blacks to join their congregations in the 1860s.[45]

These religious communities were just one aspect of the strengthen-
ing bonds between black veterans. While Wisconsin's black veterans did
not form regimental associations or produce books about their service,
they were connected by ties of comradeship, blood, and marriage. At least

twenty-seven marriages occurred between black Wisconsin Civil War veterans and the sisters, mothers, daughters, and widows of their comrades.

Veteran	Married	Relation	Veteran	Date and Location
Aaron Roberts	Martha Stewart	sister of	William P. Stewart	1866, Forest, Vernon Co.
William P. Stewart	Eliza Thornton	sister of	Abram Thornton	1868, Loganville, Sauk Co.
Aaron Roberts	Rachel Bostwick	sister of	Henry and Cyrenus Bostwick	1888, Oshkosh, Winnebago Co.
Benny Butts	Amy (Anna) Roberts	daughter of	Aaron Roberts	1888
Reuben Thompson	Sarah Ann Thornton	sister of	Abram Thornton	Before 1860, Ohio
Reuben Thompson	Delany Revels Roberts	mother of	Aaron Roberts	1877, Sauk Co.
Henry Sink	Charlotte Simmons Richards	widow of	Freeman Richards	1882, Green Bay, Brown Co.
Henry Sink	Amanda Bostwick	ex-wife of	Henry Bostwick	1897, Green Bay, Brown Co.
Samuel Arms	Mary Ellen Roberts	sister of	Aaron Roberts	Forest, Vernon Co.
John Sutfen	Maria Rosier	daughter of niece of	John Rosier Henry Rosier	1868, Columbia Co.
Alfred Weaver	Charity Revels	sister of aunt of	John, Aaron, William, & Henry Revels Aaron Roberts	1852, Indiana
Jonathan Carter	Aurora Fiddler	sister of	Jefferson Fiddler	1860, Calumet Co.

Veteran	Married	Relation	Veteran	Date and Location
Leonard Barton	Candace Revels	daughter of	Aaron Revels	1875, Forest, Vernon Co.
Richard Bradick	Anna Tousey Hunter	widow of	Edward Hunter	1864, Chicago, Illinois
Isaac Crawford	Ida Morgan	sister of	Charles Morgan	1869, Pierce Co.
Henry Donaldson	Martha Grimes	sister of	Thomas Grimes	1865, Grant Co.
Thomas Greene	Hattie Shepard	daughter of	Charles Shepard	1869, Grant Co.
Samuel Gadlin	Caroline Shepard	daughter of	Charles Shepard	1874, Grant Co.
Thomas Grimes	Amy Greene	sister of	Thomas Greene	1867, Grant Co.
Abraham Jackson	Susan Thompson	sister of	Reuben Thompson	1849, Ohio
Richard Burton (John Smith)	Julia Cattron	widow of	Richard Thomas	1896, Delavan, Walworth Co.
Hayden Netter (Johnson)	Seressa Newsom	widow of	George Newsom	1865, Dodge Co.
Samuel Waldron	Elizabeth Revels	sister of	John, Aaron, William, & Henry Revels	1854, Indiana
		aunt of	Aaron Roberts	
Wesley Walter	Susan Jane Branum	possibly sister of	Charles Branum	1878, Dodge Co.
Lewis Washington Jr.	Mary Jane Underhill	widow of	Daniel Underhill	1868, Pierce Co.
Alexander Jones	Maria Rosier	sister of	Henry & John Rosier	1865–70, Columbia Co.
Arthur Arlington Reese	Orcia Valentine	daughter of	John J. Valentine	1875, Waukesha Co.

In addition, veterans William McGraw and John J. Valentine were married to sisters, as were William Reed and Louis Brown. A generation later, Carrie Reese, daughter of Anderson Reese, married Oliver Artis, son of Horace Artis,[46] and Delbert Allen, son of Charles Allen, married Lizzie Arms, daughter of Samuel Arms.

Another indication of contact between the veterans was where they chose to live. Those who moved within the state of Wisconsin often settled near other veterans. For example, Anthony Richardson moved from Grant County to Janesville, while Michael Brady left La Crosse two years after war's end and settled in Prescott.

A cabinet card bust portrait photograph of Horace Artis (Thirty-First USCT) from Norfolk, Virginia. He is wearing a Grand Army of the Republic medal and lapel pin, ca. 1900. WISCONSIN VETERANS MUSEUM

After ten years in Fond du Lac, William and Nancy Reed resided in Beloit, Madison, and Milwaukee and left evidence of interactions with other veterans in each location.

Veterans supported each other when they or their widows applied for pensions. Those who lived in the same communities—Racine, Green Bay, Fond du Lac, Janesville, Cheyenne Valley—provided affidavits in support of their comrades' applications. There were a few cases of veterans providing support for pension claims for ex-comrades who did not live nearby. In 1872, John Davis and William Ousley, both living in Rock County, provided a statement in support of the pension claim of Peter Parsons, living in Quincy, Illinois.[47]

MAJOR POSTWAR AFRICAN AMERICAN COMMUNITIES IN WISCONSIN

In the immediate postwar years, rural, small town, and city communities of African Americans formed across the settled portions of the state. Civil War veterans were often among the leaders in these communities.

Cheyenne Valley, Vernon County

The mixed-race and African American veterans who served in the war from the Cheyenne Valley community took up farming in the immediate postwar years. The exceptions were Felix Barton and William J. Revels, who died during their service. Some of these men enlisted for three years and so had larger bounties to invest in purchasing farmland. The area was heavily forested when the pioneering families arrived, and the hard work of clearing the dense forest for cultivation took decades. Three Revels brothers who survived their service with Wisconsin regiments became farm owners in the Town of Forest, Vernon County: Aaron acquired 120 acres; John, 48 acres; and Henry, 72 acres.[48]

For his three-year enlistment, Charles Allen (Company F, Twenty-Ninth USCI) should have received a bounty of three hundred dollars along with his pay when he was discharged. On May 9, 1866, he paid three hundred dollars for 120 acres in the town of Forest, Vernon County. In 1870, his property was valued at five hundred dollars in real estate and two hundred dollars in personal property. Charles and Lydia had six children living with them on the farm.[49] In 1870, they had one milk cow, eight sheep, and four pigs. Farm production in 1869 included ten bushels of wheat, forty bushels of corn, twelve pounds of wool, thirty bushels of potatoes, one hundred pounds of butter, and two tons of hay. While a majority of their neighbors had switched over to horses, the Allens and a few other families still used oxen.[50]

The younger veterans married and started farms and families in the years just after the war. Aaron Roberts married Martha Stewart, sister of Company F comrade William P. Stewart in June 1866. By 1870, they had three hundred dollars in real estate and two daughters.[51] William P. Stewart married Eliza, the sister of Company F comrade Abram Thornton; they had one son. Stewart was a farm laborer in Westfield Township, Sauk County.[52] In the same township were Abram and Sarah Thornton, owners of a five-hundred-dollar farm. Sarah was veteran Reuben Thompson's wife.[53] Alfred and Charity Revels Weaver owned a seven-hundred-dollar farm in Woodland Township, Sauk County, with nine children, four born in Wisconsin.[54] In the early 1870s, Charity left Alfred and took the children with her to Indiana. A divorce was granted to her in 1875. Alfred remarried in Indiana in 1876 to Mary Serton, after which they moved back to Cheyenne Valley and he returned to farming.[55] Leonard Barton, veteran of the Thirty-Second Wisconsin, returned to his parents' two-hundred-acre farm. He served as the postmaster at Burr in the Town of Forest, a post his father held before him. In 1875, he married Candace Revels.[56]

The children of the veterans attended racially integrated rural schools and churches. There was cooperation among the families of this multiracial settlement and intermarriage among the residents.[57] The remoteness of their location facilitated cooperation and provided a degree of insulation from the racial prejudices of the outside world.

Fond du Lac, Fond du Lac County

The contrabands who arrived in 1862 formed the core of Fond du Lac's black community and attracted other African Americans to move into town. Veterans Henry Sink and Lewis Gaines (Twenty-Ninth USCI) returned to live in the city following the war. Over the next ten years, they were joined by newcomers Louis Brown (Eighteenth USCI), Van Spence (Third USCHA), Jackson Hill (Eighteenth USCI), Anderson Reese (Thirty-Seventh Wisconsin Infantry), David Newsom and Alfred Patterson (Fifty-Fifth USCI), and William Reed (Twenty-Ninth USCI). Ebenezer Morgan (Forty-Ninth USCI), who was of African and Stockbridge ancestry, returned to his prewar residence in Rosendale with his Brothertown wife, Nancy. They had seven children. During the 1870s, this family also moved to Fond du Lac.[58] As one of the larger cities in the state and with a strong industrial base, it offered more employment opportunities for the veterans, especially those who were kept illiterate during their years of enslavement. Henry Sink and William Reed worked as millhands for the J. G. Griffith Company, a factory producing wood products. Griffith was supportive of the families of employees who served during the war and employed veterans afterward. Sink, with only one good arm for manual labor, tended the fires in the mill.[59]

One of the contrabands and a veteran of Company F, Twenty-Ninth USCI, Lewis Gaines and his wife, America (Mary), had five children living at home with them.[60] Gaines died between 1872 and 1875. There was no death certificate, and all of the old records of the Estabrook Cemetery, his most likely place of burial, were lost in a fire. In March 1875, America Gaines married Lindsley Burks, a widower with young children. From the birthdates and places of his children, it is possible that he also was among the 1862 contrabands.[61]

In 1868, a piece of land was purchased for the construction of the Zion African Methodist Episcopal church. The land was situated near the homes of many African American families. The swampy location west of the Fond du Lac River could be reached only by footbridge from the east side of the river. Because of annual spring flooding, the wooden church building was on stilts, though flooding often still wiped out the footbridge. The first time the bridge was washed away, the city government donated forty dollars to rebuild it. The next time it happened, though, no city money was offered.[62]

Fox Lake, Dodge County

The group of contrabands that originally came to Trenton Township in Dodge County did not stay there for long. When the first winter came, the cold weather was reported to have driven most of the black refugees to leave the farms and move into the nearby village of Fox Lake.[63] In 1870, the village and town had a combined population of nearly three thousand, of whom seventy-one were black, while only two black residents were counted in Trenton.[64] None of the veterans became farm owners, but some eventually owned homes in the village. Their children attended school with white children, usually up through fifth or sixth grade.[65] The men worked as day laborers in town or as farm laborers, and the women cleaned and took in laundry.[66]

A Methodist congregation was organized in the Fox Lake African American community; they built the Zion Methodist Church in 1872. It had a resident pastor for twenty years.[67]

La Crosse, La Crosse County

When the Civil War began, La Crosse was a boomtown based on rail and river shipping, lumbering, and grain milling. Most of the residents in 1860 had already moved on by 1870, including the African Americans who had lived there. At least thirty-five men enlisted or were drafted into the US Colored Troops at La Crosse, but only a handful of them left any evidence of postwar residence in the city. Almost all of the veterans were single men with no roots or family in La Crosse. Michael Brady (Seventeenth USCI) returned to the city and resumed work as a butcher. Boarding with him was veteran Joseph Ellmore. Both of them left La Crosse around 1867.[68]

Veteran Samuel Thompson, however, worked as a barber, married and had children, and owned four hundred dollars in real estate in the city. He continued barbering into the 1880s, when he disappeared from the local public record.[69] Nathan and Sarah Smith prospered in La Crosse. They

A cabinet card bust portrait photograph of Joseph M. Ellmore, who served in the USCI. He is wearing a GAR lapel pin, ca. 1900. WISCONSIN VETERANS MUSEUM

owned two thousand dollars worth of real estate in the town of Campbell (French Island) and eight hundred dollars in personal property by 1870.[70] They came to La Crosse after Nathan had worked for General Cadwallader Washburn during the war.[71] The Smiths moved to a farm near West Salem where, as in La Crosse, they took in and raised both black and white foster children. One of them was a seven-year-old black orphaned boy named George Edwin Taylor, who arrived by steamboat at La Crosse, alone, in 1865. He was eventually placed as a foster child with the Smith family. Under their guidance, young Taylor would get a quality education and became an important figure in state and national politics.[72]

Pleasant Ridge, Grant County

Three families formed the core of the postwar Pleasant Ridge community: the Shepards (Isaac and Charles); the Thomas Grimes family; and the Greene family. Charles Shepard and his son John died while in the army. The Grant County veterans who returned home were Thomas Grimes, Thomas Greene, Albert Hamlet, Chesley Taylor, Henry Donaldson, Anthony Richardson, Pinkney Taylor, and William Spiller. Others may have returned but moved on before leaving any record of their postwar presence. Thomas Richmond, a veteran of the Sixty-Seventh USCI, arrived in 1867. Later, Richmond's parents and other family members moved to Pleasant Ridge, as well.[73] Samuel Gadlin, who came from Tennessee, was often described as a Civil War veteran. No record of his service has been found, so he may have been a nonrostered employee.[74]

These families became tightly interconnected by marriage. Almost all of the returning veterans married women from the Greene, Grimes, and Shepard families.[75] Chesley Taylor moved to Iowa and Anthony Richardson to Janesville within several years of the end of the war.[76] Almost all of the African American men at Pleasant Ridge, including the veterans, were farm owners or farm laborers. In 1868, 360 acres of farmland in Beetown Township were black-owned, a total which rose to nearly 600 acres by 1877. This included farms owned by veterans Thomas Grimes (143 acres) and Samuel Gadlin (37 acres). Henry Donaldson farmed in nearby Lancaster, owning five hundred dollars in real estate.[77]

A log schoolhouse was built on land donated by Isaac Shepard, with the cooperation of white and black neighbors. It was one of the first racially integrated schools in the state, and the school board had black and white members. Students in the early years included not only children but some of the formerly enslaved adults learning to read and write. The school building served for more than a decade as the church for a multiracial congregation.[78]

One Grant County returning veteran met a tragic end only a few years after the war. Albert Hamlet (Forty-Ninth USCI) and his wife, Millie, had two children and lived in Lancaster in 1870. Hamlet worked as a farmer and reported owning $1,800 in real estate. Accounts from that time stated that he did not have much success in farming, so he found himself working as a farm laborer in April 1871 in Watterstown Township. On April 27, he and another black laborer, James Brooks, argued about cleaning a barn. The dispute turned violent, with Brooks armed with a shotgun and Hamlet with a pitchfork. Brooks shot and killed Hamlet. Brooks was arrested and tried, pleading self-defense; the jury could not agree so Brooks was discharged. Hamlet's estate included "no real estate that he had title to" and more debts than the value of the estate. Millie was left destitute with three children under the age of six, but she remarried in March 1872.[79]

Prescott, Pierce County

Prescott offered the greatest welcome to African American settlers and veterans after the war. Located at the junction of the St. Croix and Mississippi Rivers, Prescott was an important port town. In times of low water, it was the last port accessible to large river boats. Cargo bound for St. Paul had to be offloaded at Prescott and shifted to smaller boats for transport farther upriver.[80] In the months following the war when soldiers were arriving back home, the port town was booming and needed laborers. "Help is scarce and wages are high," reported the *Prescott Journal*. It also noted that a local freedmen's aid society had been formed and had raised one hundred dollars to help the recently arrived black residents.[81] The paper supported the 1865 black suffrage referendum and reported more often and more positively on the local African American community than the newspapers in other communities where black veterans lived.[82]

Most of the African Americans who enlisted in Pierce County returned there after the war, along with other veterans, former army employees, and their families. The returned veterans were William Albare, Isaac Crawford, and Lewis Washington Jr., all of the Twenty-Ninth USCI; Charles Morgan of the Seventeenth USCI; Michael Brown and Joseph B. Brooks of the Third US Colored Heavy Artillery; and Andrew Bennett of the First and Twenty-First Wisconsin Infantry. Anthony and Thomas Willis (possibly father and son) enlisted in Minnesota but lived much of their postwar lives in Prescott. Alexander Strayhorn, born enslaved in North Carolina, worked for the Twelfth Wisconsin Infantry. The captain of Company A of the Twelfth Wisconsin was Orrin T. Maxson, a Prescott resident who wrote to the governor in 1863 urging him to allow African Americans to enlist. He came home to Prescott in October of 1864 in ill health after serving three years. Strayhorn may have come north with him at that time; he was the nephew of veteran William Albare, who may also have come north with Maxson.[83]

In August 1866, the African American community organized a celebration "of the Emancipation in the West Indies and the newly-acquired freedom of the colored race in the United States."[84] Lewis Washington Sr. was one of the speakers. The event included a feast in the park and an evening ball. The community as a whole was invited to attend. In another instance of interracial exchange, African American Baptists were invited by the white Baptist congregation in March 1868 to a joint service to tell the stories of their years of enslavement. The service was reported to be so moving that, a week later, the black Baptists were invited to join the white congregation, and several were baptized and joined at that time. The speakers included Alexander Strayhorn and Lewis Washington Sr.[85] Prescott was the only town in Wisconsin with a black community of any size where the residents did not build their own church.

In August 1869, African Americans in the Prescott area and from across the river in Hastings, Minnesota, held a convention, with one day in each city. "The object of the meeting," according to the *Prescott Journal*, "is to discuss such measures as will tend to elevate and benefit their people, and also to urge upon them the necessity of becoming farmers, mechanics, and tradesmen. . . . All the colored people in this and adjoining counties are specially required to attend, and an invitation is extended to their white friends to be present."[86]

Veteran Joseph B. Brooks (Third USCHA) called the Prescott meeting to order and delivered the first speech, mentioning white resistance to black progress: "There are a great many of our white citizens that are prejudiced against the black man. If any colored man shows signed of smartness, and aspires to be a man among men, the cry is started at once that the negro is getting above his business. Gentlemen, such talk and such news are like slavery; it must die beneath the hammer of Justice." Recognizing the lack of cheap lands in Pierce County by this time, he closed with a plea for what was referred to as "colonization": "We as newly made citizens, ought to move in a direction for the elevation of our people . . . that is to be united, and as many as can, go out and take up homesteads and go to farming." He spoke again later in the day and "advocated the idea of the colored people becoming farmers and mechanics more extensively. The speech was well received, eliciting hearty applause." The convention passed resolutions pledging efforts by the society to secure "an education or a trade for every man, woman, and child" and in favor of universal suffrage. Lewis Washington Sr. delivered opening and closing prayers.[87]

In 1870, forty-nine African Americans lived in Pierce County, about half of them in Prescott. All of the males gave their occupations as "farmer" or "farm laborer." As one-year volunteers, their enlistment bounties were too small to convert into farm ownership as the three-year enlistees from Vernon County were able to do.[88] Joseph Brooks listed his occupation as farmer and owned real estate valued at four hundred dollars. Several veterans, including Anthony Willis, Alex Strayhorn, and William Albare, owned property in town. Only two black-owned farms remained in Trimbelle Township, one of them belonging to veteran Andrew Bennett.[89]

Between 1866 and 1877, some single veterans married, and those already married added to their families. Lewis Washington Jr. was married before joining the army, but his wife died shortly after he returned home. In December 1868, he married Mary Jane Underhill, widow of Daniel Underhill, Company F, Twenty-Ninth USCI. The Washington and Underhill families combined and lived in Prescott.[90] Washington was a farm laborer in 1870, and by 1876, he had purchased and was operating a dray business (transporting cargo) in Prescott.[91]

In the 1870s, Prescott had black and white debating societies that held their own competitions but sometimes debated against each other and held social gatherings afterward. Alex Strayhorn was one of the African American debaters. He had educated himself after the war and became a preacher, with a congregation across the river in Minnesota. Later in life he was a member of the Prescott Methodist Congregation. In a joint debate with the white debaters in 1875, his closing speech was "a recital of slaving experiences that moved the audience to tears."[92]

BUFFALO SOLDIERS

Even after black soldiers served in Wisconsin regiments during the Civil War, the prewar whites-only rules for militia enrollment were never rescinded. African Americans did become a permanent part of the federal military after the war, though still in segregated units. While some USCT units were still serving in the occupied South in 1866, Congress authorized the creation of regiments of African American soldiers to serve along the frontier in the West as part of the force fighting against the Native American nations trying to maintain their independence, escorting settlers moving westward, and protecting railroad crews. They came to be called "Buffalo Soldiers" by Native people because their hair appeared to them to be similar to the hair of the buffalo. They included USCT veterans and younger recruits. These soldiers often encountered hostility and racism from the whites they were assigned to protect. They earned thirteen dollars a month, a steady income that was more than many of them could have earned working at the menial jobs in the North or as sharecroppers in the South.[93]

Alfred Carroll of Milwaukee, veteran of the Twenty-Ninth USCI and one of the leaders of the successful protest over burial rights, served a three-year term as a Buffalo soldier and reenlisted for five more. After his service, he lived in New Jersey, where his mother and brother lived after leaving Milwaukee.[94] Moses Nelson, veteran of the Eighteenth USCI, returned to Wisconsin and married in Beloit in 1867. He volunteered for a five-year term in Troop M, Tenth US Cavalry. Nelson deserted twice, never returning from the second desertion. He later lived in Indian Territory, which became the state of Oklahoma.[95] Following his service in the Eighteenth USCI, Caleb Hudson of La Crosse County did not come back to Wisconsin. He served a three-year term as a Buffalo Soldier in the Thirty-Eighth Infantry (1866–69). After service he lived in Tennessee, Texas, Louisiana, Arkansas, and Oklahoma.[96]

The men who became Buffalo Soldiers were only a few of the black veterans who looked westward. Many others who lived in Wisconsin before or after the war did not stay for long. They moved west toward the possibility of cheap land and opportunity.

Lloyd Bryon, the scribe of Company F, Twenty-Ninth USCI and prewar barber in Stevens Point and Berlin, never returned to Wisconsin. He left his wife, Hannah, in Oshkosh and married Mary Craig in Fulton, Illinois, in 1869; they had one child. In 1879, he filed for an invalid pension from Iowa. Shortly after this, he went west and left no trace. Mary Craig Bryon believed that he had joined the Buffalo Soldiers, and her father claimed that Bryon had been killed fighting Native people in Nevada. No evidence exists that he was ever a Buffalo Soldier.[97]

In addition to the Buffalo Soldiers, many of the Wisconsin black veterans ended up heading west in the first decade after the war. Benjamin Colder returned to the Elkhorn area and worked on a farm. In the summer of 1868, he suffered a broken collar bone and dislocated right shoulder when a team of horses ran away with a wagon while he was hauling wood. His ability to perform hard manual labor was limited after the injury. Colder moved west to Leavenworth, Kansas, and Marshall, Missouri, where he married, raised a family, and became a school teacher.[98]

Anderson Snyder (Seventeenth USCI) was the most traveled of the veterans. He returned to Black River Falls, where he married in the late 1860s. He listed Sparta, four towns in Minnesota, one in Illinois, one in Iowa, two in Colorado, and a brief period in Germany as his residences after Black River Falls. In his last years, he lived in Ontario, Canada.[99]

Henry Burden (Seventeenth USCI) lived in Milton Junction, Rock County, until 1868, when he went to Lincoln, Nebraska, for two years, and thereafter lived in Saline County, Nebraska, earning his living as a farmer. He married twice and had at least eight children.[100] John Sutfen married Maria Rosier in Columbia County in 1868. The couple had two children in Wisconsin before moving to Nebraska in the 1870s. Maria's mother and her children also moved from the Portage area to Nebraska.[101]

After his discharge, John Allen (Sixty-Fifth and Sixty-Seventh USCI) lived in Madison for six to eight years and then hopped westward across Illinois, Iowa, Missouri, and finally Kansas from 1887 on.[102] Mark Anthony (Forty-Ninth USCI) remained briefly in Madison after his service and then moved to Lawrence, Kansas, where he remained for more than twenty years. At Lawrence, he took up the barbering trade "because I could not earn a living outdoors as a common laborer."[103] He was married in Kansas, first to Matilda, who died in 1872, and then to Emma. He had four children, two with each wife, all born in Kansas. Around 1888 they moved to southern California. In August 1890, he became a registered voter in Whittier.[104]

Following the war, John Jones (Company D, Twenty-Ninth USCI) returned to his wife and children in Prescott and resumed working on the river. In 1868, they moved west, and he lived the remainder of his life in Kansas City, where he worked on the Missouri River.[105]

CHAPTER FIVE

AFTER RECONSTRUCTION

For African Americans, the late nineteenth and early twentieth centuries were decades of loss. Though slavery had been abolished, civil rights advances during the postwar years and Reconstruction were erased. In the disputed 1876 election, Republicans kept the White House by making a deal with Democrats to remove federal troops from the South, thus ending Reconstruction. Anti-black violence and intimidation by the Ku Klux Klan and similar groups was unrestrained. Black voters were disenfranchised across the South once again. Jim Crow segregation, the system of separate and unequal, became law in the former Confederate states and was approved by the US Supreme Court in the 1895 *Plessy v. Ferguson* decision. Also in 1895, Booker T. Washington gave his Atlanta Compromise speech, viewed by both his African American supporters and opponents as a recognition and acceptance of second-class status for African Americans.[1]

Racial discrimination was also on the rise in the North after Reconstruction. The African American population continued to grow, but it became increasingly urban and landless. Rural and small-town black communities shrank and disappeared. More and more legal and extralegal restrictions of rights and opportunities were put into place. This period is referred to by black historian Rayford Logan as the "Nadir"—the lowest point in racial relations and black civil rights during any period after the Civil War.[2]

At this same time, some white veterans began promoting reconciliation between the North and South. This required the exclusion of the African American veterans, whose participation and important role in the Union victory were erased from public memory and history. Slavery and freedom as cause and consequence of the war were ignored, with the focus shifted to the sacrifices and bravery of white soldiers on both sides.[3]

GOING WEST

When Reconstruction ended, many African American veterans and civilians fled the South. In spite of violent white opposition to the movement (because it diminished the pool of cheap labor), an estimated forty thousand black people from Louisiana, Mississippi, and elsewhere left for Kansas. The Exodusters, as they were called, traveled by steamboat or overland. Those who made it to Kansas did not find a land of milk and honey. The best land for homesteading had already been taken, and they were not eagerly welcomed by whites already in the state. However, many stayed because it was better than what they left behind in the Deep South. African Americans purchased nearly twenty thousand acres of Kansas farmland in the following decades.[4]

One such Exoduster was Charles "Archie" Blue, former employee of the Fourth Wisconsin Cavalry. He and his wife, Susan, left Madison Parish, Louisiana, in the late 1870s. They lived in Lyon County and later in Morris County, remaining in Kansas until their deaths in 1915.[5] In Milwaukee, the plight of Exodusters stranded in St. Louis, without funds to complete the journey, prompted a meeting at the Milwaukee AME Church "to devise a means to aid them in reaching new homes in Kansas.[6]

Lewis Washington Jr. (Prescott to Nebraska) and William P. Stewart (Cheyenne Valley and Peshtigo to Washington) were among the black veterans who moved west from Wisconsin.[7] Ferdinand Shavers, the former employee of Abraham Lincoln who pushed for black enlistment while living in Shullsburg, ended up in Colorado. At the 1909 National Encampment of the Grand Army of the Republic (GAR) in Salt Lake City, Shavers marched with the Colorado delegation.[8]

Another development in this period was the formation of all-black towns, in response to the social and legal segregation imposed on African Americans whenever they lived near whites. All-black towns formed in Kansas (Quindaro and Nicodemus), Mississippi (Mound Bayou), Oklahoma (Greenwood, Langston City, and Melvin), and California (Allensworth). Veteran Caleb Hudson/Tom Taylor (enlisted in La Crosse) lived in Melvin, Oklahoma. John Jones (veteran and former resident of Prescott) lived in Quindaro.[9]

Black colonization, within or outside the United States, was much discussed by African Americans tiring of rejection and restrictions and by whites who wanted to keep their distance from blacks. In March 1879, the Fond du Lac Colored Debating Society's topic was "Resolved: That the colored population would be more benefitted by colonization than by their present condition." On the affirmative side was Charles Coleman, possibly an army employee during the war. As Coleman argued, "If we can bring our colored citizen up into some of the Territories or Western States, they will at least absorb, and take in, and exercise, and have civil liberty, and they will be better off to go onward and improve and increase in intelligence." On the negative side was Van Spence, veteran of the Third USCHA, who argued that "[M]en who want to colonize the colored citizens know that they are not capable of self-government . . . let them remain in the land and country in which they originated . . . and they will naturally grow out of this state of things." Later, Spence described his early years in Fond du Lac: "when Mr. Rodgers first brought us to Fond du Lac, we could not walk along the street without having some one jeering at us and calling out 'Sambo, take that chalk out of your eye,' or something of that kind." One of his debate opponents said that this fact of life for black people in Fond du Lac had not improved as much as Spence seemed to believe.[10]

In 1879, a meeting was held at the Milwaukee AME Church "to consider the question of forming a colony in some western territory."[11] A "State Convention of Colored Men" met in Milwaukee in April and resolved to form a Wisconsin State Colonization Association. Logan Davis of Racine, veteran of the Twenty-Ninth USCI, was chosen to represent Wisconsin at a National Convention on the subject to be held in Nashville, but he did not attend the meeting.[12]

POLITICAL ACTIVITY

In spite of the Republican Party's abandonment of Reconstruction, most Wisconsin African Americans remained loyal Republicans. Black voters in Fond du Lac organized a "Garfield and Arthur Club" in 1880.[13] Milwaukee's first ward had a "Blaine Club" supporting the 1884 Republican candidate for president. "The colored voters of the ward are solid for Blain and Logan. All the colored employees at the Plankinton are all for Blaine except one." No veterans were listed as officers of the Blaine Club, but John Miles, veteran of the Thirty-Second USCI and the headwaiter at the hotel, was influential with his co-workers at the Plankinton. According to the *Milwaukee Sentinel*, "It is said that they wear their Blaine and Logan badges about their work."[14]

There were exceptions to Republican support among African Americans. Nathan Smith of La Crosse County, employed during the war by General Cadwallader Washburn, followed his foster son George Edwin Taylor into political activism. Taylor began his journalism career in 1879 with Brick Pomeroy at his *La Crosse Democrat*. It was an odd pairing, the formerly enslaved printer's devil tutored by the editor who had advocated the assassination of President Lincoln. What they had in common were love of the printed word and a desire to advance the interests of workers. Taylor contributed to other La Crosse newspapers and became the editor of the *La Crosse Evening Star* when the paper's owner was elected mayor. He then became publisher and editor of his own paper, the *Wisconsin Labor Advocate*.[15]

In May 1886, a strike in Milwaukee for the eight-hour workday was crushed when the state militia open fire on unarmed strikers, killing seven and wounding dozens of others. A new political party formed in the aftermath. George Edwin Taylor and Nathan Smith were delegates to the founding convention of the Wisconsin People's Party (Union Labor Party). Taylor was elected party secretary and central committee member. Their candidate for governor in November was the top vote-getter in Milwaukee County but finished a distant third statewide. One party candidate was elected to Congress and seven were elected to the state legislature.[16] In Racine County, the People's Party and the Democrats presented a fusion ticket whose candidates were elected county sheriff, treasurer, clerk, and coroner. The new coroner was Eighteenth USCI veteran Peter D. Thomas.[17] Two years later, the People's Party faded and Thomas, running as a Democrat, lost his reelection bid in a very close vote.[18] Peter D. Thomas remained politically active after leaving office. He was a Racine correspondent for the *Wisconsin Afro American*, a short-lived weekly Milwaukee newspaper, occasionally writing observations on politics.[19]

The Grand Army of the Republic (GAR)

The Grand Army of the Republic was the largest organization of Union Civil War veterans. It began immediately after the war, but many early posts faded out quickly. In the 1880s, the organization revived and membership peaked at more than 400,000 around 1890. It became the first effective grassroots lobbying organization in US history. Under GAR pressure, Congress approved new and more generous pension rules in 1890. This change helped thousands of struggling veterans and widows in their later years.[20]

All honorably discharged Union veterans, black and white, could join the GAR and all applicants for membership in a local post had to be accepted by a vote of post members. GAR national leadership successfully resisted efforts to exclude black veterans, but it did not censure local posts that excluded black applicants.[21] Wisconsin African American veterans were members of integrated posts, though few posts ever had more than one or two black members. Post 11 in Madison had at least six African American members during the 1880s and 1890s. Black veterans Aaron Roberts in Hillsboro and Baraboo, Arthur B. Lee in Milton, Peter D. Thomas in Racine, and William P. Stewart in Peshtigo were elected to leadership positions in their predominantly white posts.[22] Only one African American veteran was known to belong to a Milwaukee GAR post—John J. Miles.[23]

In Illinois, veterans of the Twenty-Ninth USCI were members of both African American and integrated posts. Missouri veterans who were credited to Wisconsin, including David Moore, helped to form and lead the all-black Henry Halleck Post 91 in Louisiana, Pike County, Missouri.[24]

Earning a Living

Lead mining, Wisconsin's leading industry in the 1820s and 1830s (open to enslaved and free African Americans) became the occupation of two black Civil War veterans in the late nineteenth century. James D. Williams came to the Village of Rewey, Iowa County, with discharged soldiers from the Thirteenth Wisconsin Infantry. He remained in this Welsh farming community for the remainder of his life and owned and operated a farm and a lead mine about three miles south of Rewey. Williams was a member of the Carmel Presbyterian Church and sang in the choir. He was buried in the congregation cemetery upon his death in 1903.[26]

In 1880, William Spiller(s) (First Wisconsin Cavalry), residing in the Pleasant Ridge farm community, gave his occupation as "lead miner" to the census takers. He began receiving an invalid pension for rheumatism in 1891 but continued to do light farm chores, prospecting, and mining. One of his fellow miners wrote an affidavit supporting his pension applications. In 1905, he and his wife, Eva, lived in Cassville in a home they owned free and clear. In the summer of 1907, at the age of about seventy-four, he went off to do prospecting or mining. Eva Spillers said in an application for a widow's pension, "When he did not return at the usual time for his appearance at home, search was made for him and he was found dead in a mineral hole," on July 31, 1907.[27]

One Milwaukee veteran became a recognized leader of the local African American community and became relatively wealthy. John J. Miles, who served for eighteen months in the Thirty-Second USCI, was wounded twice, first at Honey Hill in November 1864 and then at Camden, South Carolina, in April 1865.[28] After the war, he worked as a waiter at the Palmer House in Chicago. Miles then came to Milwaukee and became the head waiter at Milwaukee's Plankinton House Hotel in 1876 and held that position for thirty years. Starting four years earlier, all of the waiters at Plankinton House were black. Experienced waiters earned forty dollars per month at a time when pay for domestic work was four to six dollars per week. From this relatively prestigious position, Miles helped other African American men and women get jobs at hotels and stores, including Gimbels Department Store, and even helped a few to break into factory work at the Falk Corporation.[29] When Twenty-Ninth USCI veteran William Reed moved to Milwaukee in the late 1880s, he found work, with Miles' help, as a bellboy at the Plankinton House.[30] Miles was one of the most influential black men in the city. He was a member and leader of many black civic and fraternal organizations and was reported to own property worth $15,000, including a grocery store.[31]

Also working to help African Americans find employment in the state was a newspaper called the *Wisconsin Weekly Advocate*. This black-owned and edited periodical was published in Milwaukee from 1898 until around 1916. The paper also served as a recruitment and placement agency for

AFRICAN AMERICAN MEMBERS OF WISCONSIN GAR POSTS

Post 1, Milwaukee (John J. Miles)

Post 6, Delavan (Oscar McClellan, Eli Harwell)

Post 9, Baraboo (Abram Thornton, Aaron Roberts)

Post 11, Madison (Samuel Ewing, Dennis Hughes, Beverly Jefferson, Arthur B. Lee, William Reed, Howard Brooks)[25]

Post 17, Racine (Peter D. Thomas, Henry Rosier, Logan Davis)

Post 19, Waukesha (John J. Valentine)

Post 40, Stockbridge (George A. Johnson)

Post 60, Milton (Arthur B. Lee)

Post 90, Brodhead (Richard Burton [John Smith])

Post 91, De Pere (Henry Sink)

Post 130, Fond du Lac (Anderson Reese)

Post 133, Appleton (Horace Artis, Joseph Ellmore)

Post 141, Hillsboro (Aaron Roberts)

Post 145, Medford (Hayden Netter)

Post 159, Fort Atkinson (James Ellis)

Post 167, Eagle River (Henry Ashby)

Post 205, Chilton (Henry Bostwick)

Post 238, Trimbelle (Andrew Bennett)

Post 248, Peshtigo (William P. Stewart)

James Ellis, employed as a cook for Company A, Twenty-Ninth Wisconsin Infantry. COURTESY OF THE HOARD HISTORICAL MUSEUM

African Americans seeking employment, mostly as domestic workers. As the *Advocate* announced, it was "in a position to place an unlimited number of female colored cooks and general servants in the smaller cities of Wisconsin, Michigan, and Minnesota. Wages from $4 to $7 per week and comfortable homes guaranteed."[32] These were the jobs open to African Americans, not only in Milwaukee but across the state. Most of the veterans and their children worked as domestic employees. Those with factory jobs worked as janitors or firemen, not in production. In the small towns and rural areas, men who did not own farms were farm laborers, day laborers, or janitors, and women employed outside the home cooked, cleaned, and sewed.

A few black Wisconsin veterans broke through the limited employment options and racism of the times and achieved success in business. John J. Valentine returned to his wife, Louisa, and two daughters in Janesville after serving in the Seventeenth USCI. In 1870, they lived in Milton in a household shared with Louisa's sister Lavinia McGraw, her husband, William (also a veteran of the Seventeenth USCI), and their two sons. All four adults worked as cooks. The Valentines moved to Waukesha in the early 1870s, where John opened a restaurant. They had business setbacks, such as when the restaurant was one of a number of Waukesha businesses consumed in a fire. Wisely, Valentine had insured the business so he was able to start over. His diversified operation included a restaurant, bakery, and confectionary.[33]

Valentine was active in the local Prohibition Party, which nominated him for Town of Waukesha constable in 1883. In the 1890s, he added a hotel to his business interests, Valentine House, well-located near the train depot. It was listed and had advertisements in the *Wisconsin State Gazetteer and Business Directory.* The *Wisconsin Weekly Advocate* ran ads for Valentine House and listed it in its "Colored People's Directory." Beginning in 1898, "Valentine & Tiller, Proprs." indicated that his long-time cook Robert Tiller had been taken into the business. Valentine was a member of Waukesha Post 19 GAR and was one of only two African Americans with a biography in the *Soldiers and Sailors Album* of Waukesha County, which described his restaurant as "a well regulated and popular establishment."[34]

Valentine began receiving a pension in 1890 of six dollars per month

John J. Miles (Thirty-Second USCI).
COURTESY OF MILWAUKEE COUNTY
HISTORICAL SOCIETY

Miles's "Personal War Sketch," which
details his service during the war,
1865, was included in a Milwaukee
GAR post book. COURTESY OF MILWAU-
KEE COUNTY HISTORICAL SOCIETY

for rheumatism. He applied for increases in 1891 and 1893 but in 1895 said he was still receiving only six dollars. He asked to have his case transferred from the Milwaukee pension board because he felt he did not receive a fair examination. His next exam, at Waukesha, recommended an increase to twelve dollars per month, which was granted in 1897.[35] He also gave statements and testimony in the pension cases of Wing Jones (Third USCHA, Waukesha), William McGraw (Seventeenth USCI, his brother-in-law), and Henry Burden (Seventeenth USCI, then residing in Nebraska).[36] For the last fifteen months of the life of pensioner Charles Henry Taylor (Twenty-Ninth USCI), Valentine served as his legal guardian.[37] In late 1902, Valentine's health forced him to retire, and he died a few months later, at age eighty. His obituary described him as "a well known and thoroughly respected colored resident . . . noted for his charity and benevolence." His funeral was held at the family residence, under the auspices of his GAR comrades. Louisa remained in the family home with her sister Lavinia and received a widow's pension until her death in 1906.[38]

Another black veteran succeeded financially in a different way. Anthony Richardson (Forty-Second Wisconsin) was living in Evansville when he married Adeline Dixon. They raised two sons and a daughter. Richardson was one of three barbers in Evansville; Adeline was a dressmaker. Richardson owned and rode race horses and ran a side business in keeping with his birthplace of Bourbon County, Kentucky. In the dry town of Evansville, he was a bootlegger. His shop was vandalized once, and he was arrested and fined several times for breaking local dry laws and federal tax law. By 1910, Anthony and Adeline were the only black residents of the city. The Richardsons were prosperous enough to send daughter Alice to Fisk University in Nashville and son Arthur to Tuskegee Institute in Alabama. Arthur became a tailor in Evansville and later taught at vocational schools in Kansas and Texas. When Anthony Richardson died in 1916, the headline read "A Respected Old Citizen Passes Away," and the obituary made no mention of his brushes with the law.[39]

Successful tradesman, GAR leader, and civil rights advocate are labels that all apply to Arthur B. Lee of Milton. A veteran of the Fifty-Fourth Massachusetts, Lee was the town harness maker. He was a member of GAR Post 60 and, in April 1901, became the post adjutant. At the end of

1901, Lee was elected to a full-year term as the post's Junior Vice Commander. In the post's book of "Personal War Sketches," Lee notes that his closest comrade from his soldiering days was Lewis Douglass, son of Frederick Douglass.[40] Lee was a success as a craftsman and businessman. He frequently had front-page advertisements in the *Milton Journal*, and his business was listed in the *Wisconsin State Gazetteer and Business Directory* in most editions from the late 1870s until 1903–04.[41]

It is not known if Lee maintained contact with veterans of the Fifty-Fourth other than Lewis Douglass, but he was connected to other black veterans in Wisconsin. He belonged to the Madison GAR post while living there for a few years during the 1880s. In April 1903, he attended the funeral of veteran John J. Valentine in Waukesha.[42] Arthur B. Lee died on March 31, 1905, "following a long Illness"; the official cause of death was "senility."[43] The obituary noted that he "was the only colored man living in Milton," a phrase common in the obituaries of black veterans who had remained in small towns.[44] The GAR post passed a resolution in its next meeting that read in part: "The community has lost an honorable and upright citizen and this Post a worthy and respected comrade. Therefore, Resolved. That we extend our sincere sympathy to the family of the deceased in this their hour of affliction."[45] Amanda Lee outlived Arthur by decades. She was later celebrated for her fifty-one years of membership and activity in the Women's Relief Corps, the women's branch of the GAR, which provided support to Civil War veterans and their families. Her 1935 obituary made no mention of her racial background or that of her late husband, at the request of Arthur Lee Jr., who had moved to California and was passing for white.[46]

Ansel Clark was an enslaved laborer for the Confederate army before being captured by the Union and put to work for them. He escaped from this and went home to Arkansas but found conditions so bad that he went off looking for the Union army. He found the Eleventh Wisconsin and worked as a nurse in a field hospital through the siege of Vicksburg. When the Eleventh came home, Clark came along with Lieutenant Eli Mix, nursed the ailing veteran, and worked on his farm in Adams County. Two years later, on his way toward a job as a cook on the Great Lakes, he stopped in Portage and was convinced to stay by another veteran of the Eleventh named Captain Christie. Clark eventually settled in Portage. He was accepted as a member of the community, but it may have been a lonely life as the town's only permanent black resident. He was a coachman, volunteer fireman, constable, deputy sheriff, and humane officer. Eventually, he saved enough money to buy the home of the family who originally employed him as a coachman. At his death in 1932, his obituary was written by author Zona Gale Breese, and he was buried with military honors from the local National Guard Company, for which he served as cook.[47]

Unlike the relatively successful lives of John Valentine, Anthony Richardson, Arthur B. Lee, Aaron Roberts, and Ansel Clark, two men from northern Wisconsin were more typical of the poverty and hardship encountered by black Civil War veterans. The only African American soldier credited to Eau Claire County was Private Alfred Greene, and the only one credited to Chippewa County was William Brown. Both lived in Eau Claire before the war and were substitutes who served one-year terms in the Third US Colored Heavy Artillery at Fort Pickering in Memphis.[48] Both men lived in extreme poverty at the ends of their lives.

Greene was born enslaved and worked on a cotton plantation near Jackson, Mississippi. He escaped from his owner and arrived at the camp of the Second Wisconsin Cavalry, where he worked for Captain Arthur M. Sherman. In October 1864, when Captain Sherman resigned from the service, Greene asked to go with him and came to Eau Claire, where the two men lived together until January 1865.[49]

Alfred Greene met Amanda Roberts, a formerly enslaved woman, at Captain Sherman's house, and they were engaged before he enlisted. Greene came back to Eau Claire after his service, in April 1865, and married Amanda the following day. In 1870, they owned one thousand dollars in real estate and Alfred worked in a sawmill. He later worked "at various kinds of manual labor, gardening during the summer and during the winter and spring months sawing wood from door to door." Alfred's odd jobs included cleaning out privy vaults (the pits under outhouses). Several employers testified that he drank but that it never prevented him from working. Amanda said that he drank so that he could tolerate the smell and conditions while working in the privy vaults.[50]

Greene applied for an invalid pension in 1883, claiming rheumatism acquired during his service time: "I have been troubled every winter since the time of my discharge and been laid up unable to work for at least three weeks each winter." Captain Sherman and his wife and other Eau Claire residents wrote affidavits to support his claim. Three army comrades, including William Brown, stated that his leg pains started while in service. Greene never received a pension because the Pension Bureau ruled that his disability was not service related.[51]

The cause of Alfred Greene's death in 1892 at age forty-eight remains unknown. Amanda believed that he was beaten to death, but a coroner's jury ruled his death was due to an accidental fall from a wagon, and subsequent concussion, due to intoxication. His funeral was attended by the local GAR post, although he was never a member. Three years later, Amanda was granted a pension of eight dollars per month, retroactive to the date of Alfred's death.[52]

William Brown was born enslaved in Tennessee in the early 1820s. In 1860, he and his wife, Eliza (an English-born white woman), were living in Eau Claire. Brown worked as a lumber camp and riverboat cook from the 1850s until he enlisted in October 1864. Several Eau Claire residents testified that Brown was a strong and healthy man before he enlisted. He and Alfred Greene met while stationed at Fort Pickering.[53] In 1870, Brown was working again as a steamboat cook. He and Eliza had no children and owned eight hundred dollars in real estate. The year 1880 marked the end of his work as a cook due to rheumatism and eye disease.[54] He blamed the smallpox that he contracted while in the service for both problems. Brown was hired to do farm work in 1882, but the farmer "learned from observation that he could earn no wages . . . was all stiffened up and crippled so that he was practically worthless . . . he wanted to stay and I finally agreed with him to stay on the farm and gave him his board." Another Eau Claire resident who had known Brown for thirty years said that "he is so poor now that he is kept by charity."

His first pension examination was in 1888. The doctor found poor vision, cataracts, hip and ankle rheumatism, and back pain. The same physician treated Brown immediately after his service and said that he was already partly disabled then. In spite of this, the Pension Bureau did not grant him a pension, finding that the disabilities were not service related.

By this time, Eliza is no longer mentioned and Brown was boarding with white families because he had no means of support. No official record of his death exists in his pension files, only a letter sent by the Pension Bureau, which was returned unclaimed.[55]

VETERANS' PENSIONS

The pension system for Civil War veterans became the first large-scale social welfare program. At its peak in the 1890s, the Pension Bureau accounted for one-third of the annual federal budget.[56] Although the pensions seem small, they provided a steady income and security. The language of the pension laws appears color-blind, but African American veterans and widows were less likely to apply for or receive pensions and received lower pension payments than white counterparts with similar disabilities.[57]

Until 1890, the widows and children of soldiers who died of service-related injury or illness could receive pensions, and veterans could receive invalid pensions for disabilities acquired while in service. The pension files of many African American veterans and widows contain rejections of their pre-1890 pension applications because the veterans' disabilities or deaths were not judged to be service related. Following successful lobbying of the GAR, the Dependent Pension Act of 1890 raised rates and allowed invalid and widow's pensions regardless of the cause of disability or death. Later, veterans were allowed to apply for a pension based on old age. Exceptions were made for disability or death due to "vicious habits," which included alcoholism, drug addiction, or sexually transmitted diseases.[58]

To apply for an invalid pension, the veteran had to document his military service and explain his disability claim. The War Department was asked to confirm the veteran's service and to provide evidence from the veteran's military files of injuries, illnesses, and hospitalizations. Comrades and officers submitted statements about the applicant's service and disability. Medical examining boards throughout the country performed exams and issued a finding regarding the veteran's degree of disability. Widows had to provide documentation of marriage and of the death of the soldier. All of this was sent to the Pension Bureau in Washington, which made the final decision on whether a pension would be issued and in what amount.[59] Pensions were paid quarterly by check. Veterans or widows had to present the pension certificate to their local postmaster or other official in order to get their pension checks.[60]

African American veterans were less likely to apply for pensions for several reasons. Some believed that pensions were only for white veterans. In 1879, for instance, Thomas Hillman stated in an affidavit written for him by a notary that "being a colored man, he had been informed that no Pensions were granted to colored troops, and for that reason has not made application for a Pension until the present time." Hillman began receiving an invalid pension twenty-three years after his initial application and only seven years before his death. Illiteracy, poverty, lack of documents, and lack of comrades who could vouch for him all contributed to the delay in getting his pension. If he had qualified earlier, the family might not have lost the farm they bought in Illinois after leaving Rock County in the 1870s. Nancy Hillman received a widow's pension of twelve dollars per month for the last four years of her life."[61]

An estimated 70 percent of black Civil War veterans could not sign their pension applications.[62] To fill out the forms, Hillman and most other veterans needed a pension agent, who charged a fee and took a cut from the soldier's initial pension checks. Veterans needed a notary public to witness signatures, and those who could not read or write needed to pay a notary to write their declarations. For those living in rural areas, another expense involved traveling to town to find a pension agent or notary and to attend medical examinations.[63]

Finding former comrades was sometimes difficult for black veterans because they did not come from the same states or towns. Alex Gilchrist (Racine) and Jesse (Harrison) Harris (Texas) never received pensions in part for lack of supporting statements from comrades because they did not live near any of them.[64] On the other hand, some veterans maintained ties to former comrades in other states. William McKenney of Company F, Twenty-Ninth USCI, wrote from Chicago that he, Henry Rosier, Alexander Jones, Logan Davis, all veterans of the Twenty-Ninth from Racine, and "a few other men all from Wisconsin" had stayed in touch with one another ever since the war.[65] John Bowman and John Allen served in the Sixty-Seventh USCI. After service, Allen was in Madison for six years, then lived in Kansas. In 1891, Bowman, living in Fond du Lac, provided an affidavit supporting Allen's pension application. Thomas Grimes was never deployed after being wounded at Benton Barracks. His wartime comrades were the men with whom he was hospitalized, and they supported one another's pension claims, despite living in Wisconsin, Illinois, Missouri, and Iowa.[66]

A common problem for black veterans was the lack of required documentation. Almost none had birth certificates, and marriages during enslavement were not documented. The Pension Bureau accepted a family Bible as evidence, but most families did not have this either. Many veterans were separated from their families while enslaved. Caleb Hudson (enlisted in La Crosse) never knew his father, and his mother was sold away from him when he was a child. While enslaved in Tennessee, Oscar McClellan (Delavan) was sold away from his parents when he was fourteen, and his own son was sold away from him a generation later. The boy's mother died from grief, leaving McClellan alone again and still enslaved.[67] Many black veterans like McClellan had undocumented slave marriages before the war. Lewis Gaines of Fond du Lac and Thomas Hillman were among the veterans who came north with wives from their time of enslavement and married them legally once they were in Wisconsin. Henry Sink and Charles Branum came to Wisconsin with wives from their time in slavery but never married them legally.[68] Ellen Riley, widow of William Riley (Third USCHA), and Louisa Dangerfield, widow of Horace Dangerfield (Thirteenth USCHA), were legally married but official records of their marriages were destroyed in the Chicago fire of 1871, causing both of them problems with the Pension Bureau.[69]

Most formerly enslaved veterans used the last names of their owners when they enlisted. After the war, many changed their names as a way to break from their enslaved past. William Wilson, Thirteenth USCHA and postwar resident of Janesville, Columbus, and Waukesha, changed his name to John H. Brown in honor of the abolitionist martyr. Leroy Ironmonger (Grant County, Forty-Ninth USCI) became a preacher in St. Louis and changed his last name to Jackson. Benjamin Taylor (cook, Thirty-Fifth Wisconsin) enlisted under the name Benjamin Franklin out of fear that his owner would pursue him. After the war, he went back to using Taylor, his father's last name.[70] Many of the men who had recently escaped enslavement could neither read nor write, so their last names were spelled as the company clerks heard them. The last name of an artilleryman from La Crosse was spelled four different ways in his military records.[71]

Changed or misspelled names caused a host of problems for veterans. Late in his life, Caleb Hudson lived in Melvin, Oklahoma, an all-black town. A special examination of his pension claim was ordered to establish that Tom Taylor, the name he used after service, was the same man as Caleb Hudson, the veteran. The special examiner visited Melvin and wrote in his report that all of the town's residents were black and he rated the honesty of the persons he interviewed as "fair"—that their word was not to be trusted. Hudson/Taylor's request for an increase was delayed two years.[72] Similarly, because Alex Lewis Gilchrist's documents had so many variations of his name, he and his widow never received pensions because they could not convince the Pension Bureau that he was the same man who had served in the Seventeenth USCI.[73]

Fraud and conflicting claims, too, were major problems in the system. The Pension Bureau went to great expense to verify claims, especially from African American applicants. When Mathew Griffith (credited to Milwaukee) died in 1896, a notary public forged a pension voucher and robbed his last quarterly payment. His widow fought for five years before finally getting the money back from the thief.[74] Louisa, who married Adam Walker (credited to Milwaukee) while they were enslaved, claimed a widow's pension and had affidavits from several members of Company F saying that he died in service. Walker had not died but had married another woman in 1870. When he actually died in 1879, Louisa tried to revive her claim, but it was rejected because she and Walker had had no contact with each other since 1864.[75]

Thomas Burnett, who was wounded at the Crater and spent months as a POW, was married in Milwaukee in 1880 to Mary Johnson. In 1891, he was admitted to the Milwaukee Soldiers Home but stayed only three months. He went to Moberly, Missouri, where he died less than two months later. Two women claimed a widow's pension—Mary, his Milwaukee wife, and Mamie, who claimed that he married her in 1889 in Chicago. When he left the Soldiers Home, he went to live with Mamie in Missouri. Mary admitted to the investigator that Thomas left her "due to the soldier's infatuation with the claimant Mamie." Neither woman was granted a widow's pension.[76]

John Briggs of Racine (Twenty-Ninth USCI) was able to qualify for an invalid pension despite illiteracy, poverty, faded memory, and advanced age. He gave his age as forty-five when he enlisted, but all later documents suggest that he was much older than that. By the end of August 1864, chronic rheumatism landed him in the hospital, where he passed the rest of his service time. His bed card from L'Ouverture Hospital gave his age as sixty-three. He was discharged for disability and returned to Racine.[77] John and his wife, Charity, moved to Sycamore, Illinois, in the 1870s. When John applied for an invalid pension in 1883, he could not remember the names of any Company F comrades. Two Racine comrades from other companies of the Twenty-Ninth wrote affidavits attesting to his condition after the service. However, because documentation of his hospitalizations existed, Briggs qualified for a pension of six dollars per month until his death in 1887. Charity Briggs applied for a widow's pension but was initially denied because John's cause of death was listed as "old age." Under the 1890 pension law, she qualified for a pension of eight dollars per month.[78]

Widows kept their pensions only as long as they remained unmarried. Though the standard widow's pension seems small, it was a steady income that, along with labor such as cleaning, laundering, and other domestic work, allowed some widows to live independently. Widows or guardians with children under the age of sixteen also received two dollars per child until the latter's sixteenth birthday. If a widow remarried or was found to be living with a man, her pension was revoked. For instance, Louise Willis, widow of Thomas Willis (Eighteenth USCI), had her pension cancelled when a special examiner determined that she was living with another man.[79] Dora Ewing, widow of Samuel (Thirty-First Wisconsin), lost her pension because of a false accusation of adultery from the vindictive pension agent whom she had fired. She worked for years trying unsuccessfully to get her pension back, even though she had support from local officials in Waupaca and from the congressman who stated that her former pension agent was corrupt.[80]

Black men employed by Wisconsin units as cooks, teamsters, and other laborers could qualify for pensions, but only if their names appeared on official rosters. Fourth Wisconsin Cavalry African American employee William Southall received an invalid pension, and the widow of Lewis Haynes received a pension, though they never lived in Wisconsin, because they were on the roster. Charles "Archie" Blue, who served more than three years with the Fourth Wisconsin as a rostered cook and was an Exoduster in the 1870s, also received a pension.[81]

For men who worked for Wisconsin regiments but whose names were not on rosters, it was a different story. Henry Ashby was a servant to an officer of the Sixth Wisconsin Light Artillery for more than two years. Ashby fought as an armed combatant and was injured in battle at Corinth, Mississippi. After the war, he lived in Stevens Point and Eagle River, where he was accepted by local veterans as a member of the GAR post. He applied for an invalid pension, with supporting affidavits from white comrades and officers. Ashby's name was never on the roster while he served, so the Pension Bureau refused to grant him a pension.[82] This was true for all nonrostered African Americans who worked for Wisconsin officers and regiments—no matter what other documentation they provided, if their names were not on a roster, they and their widows never received pensions.

The cases of Peter Parsons (Eighteenth USCI), Henry Sink, and Charles Walden show the consistently lower pensions for black veterans when compared to white veterans with similar disabilities. Born enslaved in Pike County, Missouri, Parsons lived in Milwaukee and worked as a blacksmith before enlisting in September 1864. En route from Camp Randall to Benton Barracks, as the men were changing railcars, he fell or was bumped off a car and fractured his right arm near the elbow. He was hospitalized from November until February 1865, and again from May 4 until discharge in June 1865. Parsons stayed briefly in Madison, then spent the rest of his life in Quincy, Illinois. His injured arm prevented a return to his previous trade, so he worked as a gardener. His initial pension was eight dollars per month. In 1872, an examining doctor described his right arm as such: "joint ankylosed, forearm distorted, fingers fixed in a partially flexed position. Hand cannot be closed. Disability equivalent to loss of limb for the purposes of manual labor, entitling him to $18 per month." Nevertheless, he received a pension of fourteen dollars, while the pension for an upper extremity amputation was twenty-four dollars at that time. He received an increase to sixteen dollars in the 1890s. In 1903, his pension was reduced to ten dollars for unknown reasons, despite medical evaluations stating that he merited a pension equivalent to an amputation. At his death in

1915, Parsons' pension of $15.50 was still less than what doctors had recommended for him forty years earlier.[83]

Henry Sink suffered a gunshot wound with fractured bones around the left elbow in the Battle of the Crater. The elbow was fused at an angle of 135 degrees; his palm faced down and could not be turned up. He could not reach his mouth or the top of his head with his left hand. Muscle atrophy throughout the left arm except in the hand was also noted. Sink made multiple requests for a higher pension. In his 1888 application, the notary stated, "He thinks the rates allowed have been unreasonably low and disproportionate to the rates granted others for similar or equivalent disabilities." Doctor after doctor found Sink significantly disabled, and later in life he needed a full-time companion to help him eat and dress. Doctors also noted that his damaged arm was a source of pain and may have been a factor in his struggles with alcoholism. His pension always remained short of that granted for an amputation.[84]

Charles Walden, born enslaved in Pike County, Missouri, served with Sink in Company F, Twenty-Ninth USCI. His service was credited to Milwaukee. His gunshot wound, also in the Battle of the Crater, was described as a severe fracture of the proximal right ulna (near the elbow). South could not turn the palm of his right hand up or down and had almost no elbow motion. On his Discharge for Disability certificate, the doctor noted, "Arm nearly useless." This and subsequent examinations noted severe pain in the arm. No longer fit for farm labor, he learned to read and write and became a teacher and a medical doctor. He changed his last name from South to Walden, possibly for a doctor who helped to train him. Walden became addicted to painkillers and spent several stints in the Milwaukee Soldiers Home for the effects of age and drug addiction. Walden's invalid pension was never raised to the same level as for an amputation.[85]

Other veterans were denied pensions because they couldn't show proof of disability caused by the war. Charles Branum (Twelfth USCHA) applied for an invalid pension in 1890 but was denied because he had "no pensionable disability." He reapplied in 1893, stating that he was no longer able to perform manual labor and was supported by statements from neighbors, but no decision was made. Through 1895, the Fox Lake Village Board paid out funds for wood and flour for the Branum family. In March 1896, Branum appeared before the village board "to explain away some (*unspecified*) charges that had been made regarding his being unworthy of help."[86] When finally granted a pension two months later, it made local news: "Chas. Branum of this village has been granted an original pension, which will be pleasant news to his friends. He gets $8 per month, and $116 in back pay." His pension was raised to ten dollars per month in January 1897, due to his rheumatism, and disease of the eyes, heart and lungs.[87]

Branum died on December 14, 1897, leaving behind his widow Susan Mary and two minor children. Susan Mary was initially denied a pension because there was no documentation of their marriage. In early 1898, she said that, since her husband's death, she had "been doing washing and ironing and anything I could get to do." The village board and the Dodge County Soldiers Relief Commission provided aid for her and their children. On November 11, 1901, nearly four years after her husband's death, the Pension Bureau recognized the Branums's common law marriage of more than thirty years and awarded a widow's pension of eight dollars per month, plus four dollars per month for the children, retroactive to January 1898.[88]

Lydia Allen endured a long struggle to obtain a widow's pension for the service of Charles Allen (Company F, Twenty-Ninth USCI), who died in 1882 from complications of diabetes and kidney disease. With support of Charles's Company F comrades, Lydia claimed that he acquired both problems while in service, but his files included no record of his hospitalizations. The lack of service-related illness disqualified her for a widow's pension. As neighbors stated, "She works out for her neighbors and works hard to support herself and her children, and is helped more or less by kindly disposed neighbors who appreciate the heroic struggle the woman is making to earn a respectable living." Assistance from her adult children allowed her to hold onto a part of the family farm in Cheyenne Valley. In 1892, with the new pension law, she received a pension of eight dollars per month, plus four dollars per month for two minor children still in her care.[89]

Beginning in 1909 while living in Milwaukee, Mary Bryon tried to get a widow's pension based on the service of her husband, Lloyd. She had documentation of their marriage in 1869 but could not document Lloyd's death. She said he went out West around 1880 and she never saw him again. William Cleggett, Bryon's half-brother from Appleton, filed a statement that he also believed Bryon had died out West: "My reasons for believing him dead are that he was a hard drinker and then I heard in one indirect manner that a man by his name had died" in Nevada about ten or twelve years earlier.[90] Several others said that they heard he had died out West. Without documentation of his death, Mary Bryon was never able to get the pension.[91]

SOLDIERS HOMES

Near the end of the war, the West Side Soldiers' Aid Society, organized by a group of Milwaukee women, began raising funds for what became the first home for disabled soldiers. Some of the original buildings still remain at the VA Medical Complex in Milwaukee. It became known as the Northwest Branch, part of the government-supported National Homes for Disabled Volunteer Soldiers (NHDVS). The homes were originally for veterans with disabilities who were unable to earn a living and had no family to take care of them. In later years, they took in aging veterans with no means of support and nowhere else to go.[92]

Although African Americans were 9 percent of the Union soldiers and sailors, they made up only one percent of the residents of the NHDVS homes. In the early years of these institutions, residents were mainly men with severe injuries from combat (fewer black veterans were wounded in combat overall). Later, when admissions were allowed for old age, the shorter life expectancy of African American men meant that fewer reached the age of seventy. Another factor was the apparent preference of black veterans to stay with family rather than to reside in a government facility. Fewer black veterans applied to live in the homes, and many of them voluntarily left the homes when they had family with whom they could live.[93]

Among the veterans of the Twenty-Ninth USCI, Charles Walden (Company F) and Alex Jones (Company B) stayed at the Northwest Branch in Milwaukee. Walden voluntarily left the home as he approached the end of his life and was with family when he died.[94] Also staying at the Northwest Branch were Isaac Holden (Sixth USCHA, La Crosse), John H. Brown (Thirteenth USCHA), Louis Brown (Eighteenth USCI), Johnson Neal (Fifty-First Wisconsin), and Anthony Parks (Sixth Wisconsin Light Artillery). Parks and John Brown died at the home and are buried in the VA Cemetery. Louis Brown died at the Soldier's Home at Danville, Illinois. Holden and Neal left the home and were with family at the time of their deaths.[95] Matt James was on the roster of the Thirty-Eighth Wisconsin as an undercook. He lived in Madison before and after his service and lived the last three years of his life at the Northwest Branch in Milwaukee.[96]

Late in their lives, veterans Isaac Smith and William McKenney, Company F, Twenty-Ninth USCI, were residents of the Northwest Branch. Both men learned to read and write after the war. Smith was able to neatly sign his name to pension documents in the 1870s. In the 1890s, McKenney filled out pension documents entirely in his own handwriting.[97] From 1877 until the early 1890s, Smith and McKenney lived in Chicago. Each of them made statements in support of the other's pension applications. Smith listed jobs that McKenney had lost or been denied due to his hearing loss. In 1886, McKenney began receiving a pension. He said of Smith in 1892, "I have advised him every time to file his (*pension*) claim on account of his eye but he would never do it saying that he was afraid it would take too much

Wisconsin State Home for Veterans at King, Waupaca County. Henry Sink, Hayden Netter (Johnson), and Samuel (Bowden) and Dora Ewing spent time at the King home.
LIBRARY OF CONGRESS, HABS WI-323

time." Smith was granted a pension in December 1892, by which time he was nearly blind.[98] Shortly after this, Smith moved to the Soldiers Home in Milwaukee. As he had predicted years earlier, he and his old friend McKenney were "together til death." McKenney was admitted to the Milwaukee Soldiers Home, in July of 1902 and was there when Smith died from heart problems on April 20, 1903. His friend-for-life outlived him by two years. McKenney went home to family in Chicago for his last days.[99]

The Northwest Branch had more applicants than it could handle, and they did not accept the wives and widows of veterans. The Wisconsin GAR found that when men were admitted to the Soldiers Home, often their wives were left destitute. The GAR raised funds for a state home that would take in wives and widows as well as the veterans, and the state government made an annual appropriation to support the home. It opened in 1887 near Waupaca and was known as the King Home. It still operates as a long-term residence and rehab facility for veterans and spouses.[100]

Very few African American veterans stayed at the King Home. One who did was Henry Sink, admitted July 9, 1904, with his wife, Amanda. In addition to his mangled left arm, he had multiple health issues by this time and no resources to live independently. He remained there until the last

Studio portrait of Benjamin "Benny" Butts, an employee of the Fifth Wisconsin Infantry. UW ARCHIVES

months of his life, when he returned to his original Wisconsin hometown of Fond du Lac, cared for by friends and relatives.[101] Private Hayden Netter (Johnson), veteran of the First Wisconsin Infantry, moved into the home from Medford on August 19, 1903. He was dishonorably discharged from the home and returned to family in Medford, where he died months later.[102] Another black resident was Samuel Ewing, a cook with the Thirty-First Wisconsin Infantry. He and his wife, Dora, lived there from 1896 until his death in 1902, attributed to paralysis and dropsy (an old term for congestive heart failure).[103]

Black men who served as cooks or servants but were not on the rosters were excluded from the homes. Men like Samuel Arms, the drummer with Sherman's army in Georgia; Henry Ashby of the Sixth WI Light Artillery; and Benjamin Butts, employed in the Fifth Wisconsin Infantry, did not qualify because they were never rostered.

African American Communities after Reconstruction

Cheyenne Valley, Vernon County

The 1878 plat map of Forest Township shows that the families of the black and mixed-race Civil War veterans owned over twelve-hundred acres of farm and woodlots. Among the farm owners were Alfred Weaver (forty acres), Aaron Roberts (eighty acres), and Charles Allen (eighty acres), all veterans of Company F, Twenty-Ninth USCI.[104]

Charles and Lydia Allen had seven children living with them in 1880, including adult children William and Elizabeth and three under the age of ten. Son Harvey died in 1877 of tuberculosis at age nineteen.[105] The relative prosperity of the family was about to vanish, due to health problems that began while Charles was in service. His service documents indicate that he was in action at the Battle of the Crater on July 30, 1864. One card in his files says that he was present with his company to August 31, 1864, but also says that he was "sick in Fourth Div. Hospl" on that date. Bimonthly muster rolls list him as present for the remainder of the war, but return cards show him "absent, sick" at the end of September and October 1864 and on detailed service as a hospital attendant until the end of November. When the regiment served along the Texas border, he was listed as the company cook in June, on detached service with the quartermaster from July 25, and on detached service "mowing hay."[106] No casualty sheet from the Crater battle was found among his service records, nor any indication of the reason for or duration of his hospitalization.

Company F comrades Aaron Roberts and William Reed stated that Allen was hospitalized in service for diabetes and kidney disease. Roberts said in an affidavit in Allen's pension files that when Allen returned from the hospital in December 1864, he was unable to perform active army duties, which fits with his frequent assignments to detached service. Reed said in a pension affidavit that "upon his return to the company he [Allen] was still suffering with the above disability." He recalled Allen complaining of back pain and painful urination. Charles Allen died in August 1882 from complications of diabetes and kidney disease. "I was at [the] Allen House often during his last illness," said Aaron Roberts. "He often said it would kill him, it hurt him so. I was also Present at his House when he Died."[107]

Aaron Roberts began receiving an invalid pension for chronic diarrhea and piles (hemorrhoids) in the early 1880s. This may have contributed to his decision to sell the farm and move into town. Aaron, Martha, and five children were living in Hillsboro in 1885. In 1886, Martha died and was buried in the Forest-Burr Cemetery near her parents.[108] Two years later in Oshkosh, Aaron Roberts married Rachel Bostwick, who was of mixed black, white, and Brothertown heritage. Two of her brothers, Henry and Cyrenus, served in the USCT. In 1890, Aaron and Rachel, with one daughter, Lucy, and Aaron and Martha's youngest children, lived in Hillsboro.[109]

Roberts and a white partner, Loring B. T. Winslow, operated a factory that took advantage of the surrounding forest land to manufacture barrel components. It was said to be the largest manufacturer of barrel staves in the west and was listed in the *Wisconsin State Gazetteer and Business Directory*.[110] At some point, Roberts became the sole proprietor of the business. In Abram Thornton's pension files is a statement supporting his pension claim from Aaron Roberts, handwritten on the business's letterhead stationery.[111] Roberts was a member of Hillsboro GAR Post 141 and was elected adjutant, the second highest office, in 1891.[112]

The Panic of 1893 caused financial upheaval and loss across the whole country. One casualty of the Panic was Aaron Roberts's barrel stave mill, which closed due to the sudden drop in business. Roberts sold the factory and his timber land at a loss. After paying off his debts, he had only seven hundred dollars left.[113]

Former sergeant Alfred Weaver (Company F, Twenty-Ninth USCI) owned thirty-eight acres in 1880, twelve acres improved and twenty-six of forest land. He and his second wife, Mary, lived on the farm with four children. Their farm, however, was not prospering; they had no milk cows, no oxen, and the estimated value of all products in the previous year was fifty dollars.[114] It appears that the marriage fell apart and Weaver gave up the farm. In 1886, he filed for an invalid pension from Kokomo, Indiana. Weaver then filed additional documents from Richland County,

Wisconsin, in 1888 and had a medical exam in Richland Center in 1891. This was his last documented presence in Wisconsin. From 1892 on, he was a resident of Marion, Indiana. At least four of Weaver's sons stayed in Wisconsin after his departure: Ezra, Melvin, Al, and Bert (Bird). All four married in the state.[115]

Jefferson Craft (Croft), who had arrived in Cheyenne Valley prior to 1870, owned a forty-acre farm in 1878. By 1880, he and his young wife, Lottie, had four children. They moved to Viroqua, the county seat, "the first and, as of 1964, the last African American family to have lived in Viroqua." He was the village lamplighter, cared for horses, and did farm labor; he was also listed as a veteran of the Second Wisconsin Cavalry in the 1890 Veterans Census. His 1894 obituary indicated that he had come north with returning soldiers at end of the war.[116]

Samuel Waldron, veteran of the Thirty-Second Wisconsin, owned an eighty-acre farm in Forest in 1878. He and wife, Elizabeth Revels, married in 1854 while living in Indiana. Eight children lived with them on the farm in 1880.[117] Samuel began receiving an invalid pension in 1884. They remained in Cheyenne Valley until Samuel's death in 1897, whereupon Elizabeth received a widow's pension.[118]

The original Cheyenne Valley settlers were a multiracial group (white, black, and Native people), and many of the individuals were of mixed ancestry. Marriages among the children and grandchildren of the original settlers and later arrivals created further combinations of racial heritage. This caused little conflict within the community. The residents were successful farmers and businessmen and did not fit into the popular negative stereotypes of Native people or African Americans: as historian Jennifer Kirsten Stinson explains, their "reputation as settled farmers and solid citizens prevented whites from confusing them with 'Indians' as poor transients at best and marauding savages at worst, or with slow-witted sharecroppers. . . . They were not the 'negro' who was 'holding the South back;' they were leading the Midwest forward."[119] But the outside world was demanding more rigid definitions of and separations between the races in the 1890s and later. The Census Bureau eventually eliminated the use of the terms *colored* and *Mulatto* in labeling individuals by race. Many in the Cheyenne Valley would have self-identified by one of these labels rather than black, white, or Indian. Under these influences, light-skinned descendants of the settlers and veterans tended to marry other light-skinned or white partners. Light-skinned persons broke ties with and sometimes repudiated darker cousins, especially outside the confines of the farm settlement. Community-wide picnics ceased in the early 1900s but have been revived since the 1990s to reunite the descendants of the pioneering families.[120]

Delavan, Walworth County

Several black veterans made their postwar homes in Delavan and left their mark. Alfred Matson was employed by three Wisconsin regiments as an orderly-cook. He continued working as a cook on Mississippi River steamboats after the war. Matson learned barbering in Platteville and worked at a shop in Boscobel. He arrived in Delavan in 1880 and worked in a barbershop run by his brother. In 1885, he married Luticia Russell, who came to Brodhead with an army officer, attended school, and returned South as a teacher near where she had been enslaved. They had four children. Alfred Matson ran a barbershop in the basement of the Delavan Hotel for decades and was a founding member of the Grand United Order of Odd Fellows Black Lodge. He worked until his death in 1930.[121] For five to ten years, veteran Richard Burton (John Smith, Forty-ninth USCI) and Will Hamlet (son of Albert Hamlet, Forty-Ninth USCI) also worked as barbers in Delavan.[122]

Oscar McClellan escaped enslavement in Tennessee to the Thirteenth Wisconsin and became a cook. He came to the Town of Sharon, Walworth County, with a soldier who was discharged from the Thirteenth. A few months later, he went to Marengo, Illinois, to enlist, despite being over forty years old. He served with Company D, Twenty-Ninth USCI, through the siege of Petersburg, Lee's surrender, and duty on the Mexican border. He returned to Sharon and married Martha Lewis in Beloit in 1865. They lived in Sharon and McHenry County, Illinois, before settling in Delavan in 1879 and operating a small farm. In 1893, Oscar and Martha McClellan held a meeting in their home to organize an African Methodist Church and donated land for the church building. Then in his late seventies, McClellan did much of the work in constructing the church, which was dedicated in 1894. He was a trustee, and Martha was the treasurer. He passed away less than three years later. According to his obituary, McClellan "was quiet, always polite, and one of the most kind-hearted creatures on this earth." Martha received a widow's pension of eight dollars per month until her death in 1915.[123]

In 1902, Barney Moore, veteran of the Twentieth USCI, moved from Chicago to Delavan, where he was a day laborer. In 1910, he married Jerusha Steele Banks. He died in 1916, survived by his wife and a daughter from his first marriage, both living in Delavan. He and Jerusha are buried in Spring Grove Cemetery.[124]

Fond du Lac, Fond du Lac County

Fond du Lac's black population was 175 in 1885. In a state census of veterans taken at the same time, Ebenezer Morgan, Jackson Hill, Anderson Reese, and Alfred Patterson were listed.[125] Most of the black veterans present in the 1870s had either died or moved on. In 1877, Henry Sink pleaded guilty to a charge of stealing cigars from a small factory in Waupun and spent two years in prison. His two white codefendants fought the charges and went free. After his release, Sink received a pardon from the governor. He spent most of the rest of his life in De Pere.[126] William and Nancy Reed moved to Beloit, then Madison, and eventually Milwaukee.[127] Van Spence, the debater, and his wife, Missouri, buried their two-year-old daughter, Allie, in 1880 when she died from pneumonia. Shortly afterward, they moved to Litchfield, Minnesota, where they remained for the rest of his life.[128] Louis Brown and family moved to Faribault, Minnesota.[129]

After nearly twenty years in their wooden church on stilts, the congregation of the AME Zion Church purchased a lot on the opposite side of the Fond du Lac River in 1887. On this high and dry location, they built a more substantial structure. The church trustees included Anderson Reese and Louis Gaines Jr., the son of the deceased veteran.[130] In the 1890s, the church was active in community service. The Helping Hand Society was based in Milwaukee and guided by Richard B. Montgomery, the African American publisher of the *Wisconsin Weekly Advocate*. Among the officers of the Helping Hand Society were Fond du Lac residents, including two sons and two daughters of black veterans.[131] In 1898, the *Wisconsin Weekly Advocate* praised the thrift and economic stability of the Fond du Lac black families, claiming that a high percentage of them owned their own homes.[132]

The Fond du Lac African American community faded away, however, after the turn of the century. A few light-skinned members who married whites passed as white and withdrew from the community. Others moved to Milwaukee or Chicago searching for industrial jobs. Several adult children of Lewis and America Gaines moved to Pontiac, Michigan, and Cleveland, Ohio. When America's second husband died, she moved to Michigan and lived with one of her sons.[133]

Only two black veterans are known to be buried in Fond du Lac Cemeteries. Ebenezer Morgan (Forty-Ninth USCI) died in 1893 and was buried in the veterans' section of Rienzi Cemetery.[134] Henry Sink returned to Fond du Lac in the final months of his life and died at a home near the AME Zion Church in September 1905. Following a service at the church, he was buried near Ebenezer Morgan.[135]

In 1900, the black population of the city was 136; by 1910, it was only 47. The congregation of the AME Zion Church resolved to sell its church building and disband, but an individual member sold it first and left town with the money.[136] This final disgrace came in the midst of the heyday of the Wisconsin Ku Klux Klan, which burned crosses near the homes of the remaining black residents in 1924. Two years later, the Klan held a parade of five thousand that passed within two blocks of the church, just before its suspicious sale.[137]

Fox Lake, Dodge County

The history of the black community in Fox Lake is well documented at its local public library, but all of the sources are local newspapers and writings of white residents. The records include memoirs that reflect the condescension and prejudice faced by the veterans and their children and neighbors. Relations between the races may actually have been better in Fox Lake than in similar small towns, since this black community persisted well into the twentieth century.

The social isolation of African American residents was described in a matter of fact way by a white writer: "There was never any discrimination against the Negroes, except at social functions, to which they were never invited. They were treated as well as the Indians in the community."[138] Another memoir provided a description of aspects of community life in which African Americans were and weren't accepted: "What discrimination was shown toward those Negroes? Very little, on the surface; they were allowed to vote, buy homes, attend school and were treated courteously at the stores and shops, and were not exploited in employment. But the white residents usually held aloof in social contacts . . . they accepted the Indians and Negroes as folks, but did not want to become intimate with them."[139]

Three African American veterans and their families were living in Fox Lake by the late 1870s. Hayden Netter (Johnson) owned property in the village valued at $350 in 1879, on which he paid $4.22 in taxes.[140] Around 1883, Netter moved with his large family to Medford, Taylor County, leaving his half-brother Charles Branum and Wesley Walter as the only African American veterans in Fox Lake.[141]

After the war, Branum, a veteran of the Twelfth USCHA, returned to Kentucky and wanted to marry a woman named Susan Mary, who lived on a nearby plantation. Susan's mother and stepfather said that she (at age nineteen) was too young, so Susan and Charles ran away. They had a total of ten children, five of whom died in childhood. In 1876, they moved to Fox Lake, where son James was born. Charles Branum worked as a laborer.[142]

The difficulties faced in school by young James were described in a memoir by a white resident: "James (Branum) was one of the most typical Ethiopians imaginable, having the darkest skin of any in the family, and all Negro facial characteristics. His appearance prevented him from being accepted as a companion as the lighter-colored Mathews children were by some of their school mates, and he was generally resentful of any real or implied slight toward his race—while several of the white children were plainly discourteous to him, and it was a common event to have James and one or two white boys engage in a quarrel during recess."[143]

The struggles of Charles and Susan Mary Branum to get pensions are described in the section on veterans' pensions. Charles was unable to work in the last years of his life, and he died in 1897. Though not a member of the post, local GAR attended his funeral in uniform and he was buried with military honors.[144] A year later, their son James was the only resident of Fox Lake, white or black, to serve in the armed forces during the Spanish American War. He fought in Cuba, sent money home to his mother, and received the Fox Lake newspaper while deployed. He was suffering from typhoid fever when he returned home but established himself as an expressman in Chicago and brought his sisters and mother there to live.[145]

Walter was probably one of the Town of Trenton contrabands. After the war, he lived briefly in Beaver Dam and Chicago. In the 1870s, he married Susan Jane Branum, possibly one of Charles's sisters. In 1880, they lived in Fox Lake and had two daughters. Susan Jane died in 1883 and Wesley then married Samantha Pemmerton in 1885 in Fond du Lac. It appears that by 1898 he had only one child living—Clara Elizabeth, born in Fox Lake and a resident of Helena, Arkansas.[146]

In the 1890s, the church no longer had a resident minister; the pastor from the Fond du Lac AME Zion Church was brought in to hold services.[147] In 1900, the last three charter members of the Zion Church sold the building and disbanded the congregation. The last surviving member was invited to join the white Methodist Church. The black community of Fox Lake shrank but did not disappear entirely: some children of the original settlers married white neighbors, some of the men who remained became craftsmen and artisans, and some women worked as domestics.[148]

Madison, Dane County

By the 1880s, at least seven African American veterans were living in Madison in an enclave northeast of the Capitol. Dennis Hughes (unassigned) moved to the city from Belleville. William (Company F, Twenty-Ninth USCI) and Nancy Reed and Arthur (Fifty-Fourth Massachusetts) and Amanda Lee lived there for about three years before moving, the Reeds to Milwaukee and the Lees back to Milton. Howard Brooks (Company H, Twenty-Ninth USCI) lived his entire adult life in the city. Sam Ewing moved to Madison from La Crosse in the 1880s. All of these men were members of the Madison GAR post. Charles Henry Taylor (Company D, Twenty-Ninth USCI) also lived in this community.[149]

More is known about Benny Butts, who was a well-known figure in Madison. He came to the city in the 1870s and ran a barbershop on the Capitol Square. Among his clients were political and business figures, including Robert La Follette Sr. He often worked at social functions for politicians and university officials. In 1888, Butts married Amy (Anna) Roberts, the daughter of veteran Aaron Roberts of Cheyenne Valley. Benny and Amy had at least seven children, only four of whom were still living in 1910. While still caring for small children at home, Amy Butts was president of the Douglas Literary Society. Around 1900, Benny gave up barbering and worked at the Wisconsin Historical Society as a messenger for the next thirty years. Because he never appeared on an army roster, he never applied or qualified for a pension.[150] In January 1930, Amy Roberts Butts died, and within two months Benny also passed away. Both are buried in Forest Hill Cemetery.[151]

Milwaukee, Milwaukee County

Milwaukee's black population rose rapidly in the 1890s, but few veterans were among the new arrivals. The employment outlook for African Americans was bleak, with the majority still working as domestics. Jobs in the fast-growing production industries went to European immigrants. Because labor unions were closed to African Americans, there was little sense of class solidarity between black and white workers; indeed, the few Africans Americans who did find places in the big industries did so as strikebreakers. The *Wisconsin Weekly Advocate* editor Richard Montgomery helped to recruit African Americans to cross picket lines and work in the factories, even though they were usually put back on the streets when the strike was settled. One exception was in an 1898 strike at the Illinois Steel Company in Bay View, where black strikebreakers kept their jobs after the strike ended.[152]

The arc of veteran John Miles's life shows the deterioration of the position of African Americans in Milwaukee, in particular, and Wisconsin, in general. Miles had become relatively wealthy as the headwaiter at the Plankinton House; he and his wife, Anne Miles, had four children, all of them still alive in 1900. Anne Miles was mentioned in the news as one of the first black women to vote in a local school election.[153] John Miles was considered part of the old black elite, which pushed for integration and depended on connections to white patrons, who included some pre–Civil War abolitionists. Following a different line of advocacy were people like Richard Montgomery, who supported the development of black institutions rather than fighting for integration.[154]

In the 1890s, rights and opportunities for African Americans became more restricted. Theaters began segregating audiences, and hotels refused to accept black guests (it was during this period that John J. Valentine expanded his Waukesha restaurant business to include a hotel to serve African Americans). John J. Miles was among the leaders of the effort to pass a state civil rights law barring racial discrimination in public accommodations and amusements. The legislature passed the law in 1895 but reduced the penalty for violations to a five- to one-hundred-dollar fine and/or six months in jail. Miles brought one of the first suits under this law when he was refused service at the Schlitz Palm Garden. He won the case, but the Palm Garden was fined the minimum of five dollars and continued to refuse service to African Americans. The law's weak punishments rendered it ineffective.[155]

Growing discrimination affected all aspects of African American life. Housing segregation became more systematic and open, a problem that Milwaukee has still not overcome even a century later.[156] Segregation also impacted church life. St. Gall Irish Catholic parish accepted African Americans as members in the 1890s, but the "original number of about 140 colored Catholics dwindled until hardly a trace was left of the original flock" by 1911.[157]

When William Plankinton died in 1905, the new manager of the Plankinton House decided to fire all black waiters and other employees. John J. Miles himself was out of a job in 1906.[158] Gimbels Department Store followed suit and discharged all black employees.[159] By 1904, all of the black workers who began working as strikebreakers in 1898 at the Bay View steel mill had been replaced by whites. In 1910, African Americans were no longer working in blast furnaces or rolling mills in the city.[160] The Civil War veterans and their children never gained a foothold in production industries in Wisconsin. The factory doors would finally open to African Americans during World War I, when a new wave of migrants from the South came to Beloit, Racine, and Milwaukee.

Veteran Horace Dangerfield's family gives a stark picture of living conditions of black working-class families. He worked as a railroad porter for at least thirty years, sometimes as a sleeping car porter, among the best paid and most respected positions for black working men.[161] His relative economic stability did not prevent the family from suffering a string of tragic deaths from communicable diseases. Horace and Louisa Dangerfield had four children living with them in 1880 and had at least three more children later. Joshua, age three, died from enteritis in 1891. Sylvester, age seven, died in 1892 from meningitis. Daughter Neoma died of meningitis in 1895 at age thirteen. In 1900, William died from tuberculosis at age twenty-two. Horace himself died in 1893 at age fifty-five from Bright's disease. Horace and the four children were buried in Forest Home Cemetery. In 1900, Louisa was living in a mortgaged home with three surviving adult children. She never remarried.[162]

William Reed, veteran of Company F, Twenty-Ninth USCI, worked the final years of his life as a bellboy or porter, probably still at the Plankinton House. In 1894, a combination of hearing loss, disease of the lungs, and kidney disease forced him to retire. His wife, Nancy (Nina), gave a statement to the pension board, which had already denied her husband a pension several times: "He is now and for some time has been confined to the house on account of illness and that their sole source of income has ceased and that neither he nor she has any property whatever and now no source of income whatever."[163] Four days later, William Reed died from tuberculosis and was buried in an unmarked grave in Forest Home Cemetery. Nancy Reed eventually received a widow's pension.[164]

Pleasant Ridge, Grant County

Black farmers at Pleasant Ridge owned 588 acres of farmland in 1877. This total rose to nearly 700 acres in 1895, including the farms of veterans Thomas Grimes, Thomas Greene, and Thomas Richmond. This was the peak in land ownership for the community.[165]

In 1882, religious services were still being held in the log schoolhouse. Black and white neighbors decided it was time to build a church for their United Brethren Methodist congregation.[166] The school continued to serve black and white children for decades. Parents cooperated in providing firewood, building a privy, and cleaning and maintaining the building.[167] Sarah Greene, daughter of veteran Thomas Greene, graduated from Lancaster High School. For some years she studied and taught in a black college in Missouri before returning to Pleasant Ridge to teach at the log school until her health began to fail. Two other black teachers taught at the Pleasant Ridge School.[168]

Prior to the construction of the church, burials at Pleasant Ridge were in a private plot located on the Shepard farm. Caroline Shepard, whose father died in the Civil War, married veteran Samuel Gadlin in 1874 and had three children with him: daughters Nettie and Rina and a son who died at birth. Caroline died in 1877, leaving the widower Gadlin with two daughters. As was often the case in those days, when Gadlin did not remarry, the girls went to live with other families. Nettie lived with the family of veteran Thomas Greene, and Rina with the family of her uncle Edward Shepard.[169]

In building and operating the school and church, in labor-intensive farm chores, and in celebrations, the white and black neighbors cooperated with one another. However, unlike Cheyenne Valley, sexual and marital relations between the races were rare and a source of conflict at Pleasant Ridge. In 1883, widower Samuel Gadlin was accused of having sexual relations with a white woman who became pregnant. When confronted, Gadlin reportedly said that if when the baby was born it looked like him, then he was the father. He was shot in the back and killed by the woman's relatives. The assailants were charged and convicted but received light sentences. The Shepard family was angry at what Gadlin had done, to the point that they would not allow him to be buried next to his wife, Caroline Shepard Gadlin. Gadlin became the first person buried next to the United Brethren Church, in what became the community cemetery."[170]

There were several cases of white men fathering children with black women who worked as domestics in Lancaster. In one case in 1908, veteran

Thomas Greene in Pleasant Ridge after the war. WHI IMAGE ID 44862

Thomas Greene's daughter was paid to have the baby elsewhere and was given hush money to remain silent about the identity of the white father, which she did. She went to South Dakota and gave birth to a daughter, Mildred. The expectant mother was accompanied by her sister Sarah, the teacher. Sarah died at age thirty-seven while they were in South Dakota. Mildred's mother died young in Grant County, so she was raised by her Greene grandparents.[171]

In 1898, Thomas Greene built a hall with a wooden dance floor in an oak grove on his land, which became the location for community celebrations for decades. An annual barbeque was held in early August. The event included food, speeches, vocal and instrumental music, dancing Friday and Saturday nights, and liquid refreshments from a nearby still. It was also a reunion for those who grew up in the community but had left for Madison, Milwaukee, Chicago, Detroit, and other cities. White and black neighbors shared the dance floor.[172] The sponsor of the barbeque in later years was the Autumn Leaf Club, a group founded in 1906 by African American women for socialization and education, as well as to help maintain contact among the descendants of the pioneers. As black presence on the farms declined, this event continued to draw as many as three thousand participants annually, and organizers proudly pointed out that it came off without incident. The Autumn Leaf Club held monthly meetings rotating from house to house, which included musical performances, poetry readings, and educational speeches. A story about the club appeared in a 1930 issue of the national NAACP magazine, *The Crisis*.[173]

By 1918, fewer than 150 acres remained under black ownership; those acres included the two farms owned by veteran Thomas Greene and the descendants of veteran Thomas Grimes, who died in 1910.[174] By the 1940s, Ollie (Olive) Greene Lewis, the daughter of Thomas Greene and the granddaughter of veteran Charles Shepard, was the last remaining black landowner at Pleasant Ridge. The demise of the Pleasant Ridge African American community occurred primarily due to two factors. After a generation of marriages among the small number of black families, there were no marriageable partners left for the descendants. Furthermore, the children and grandchildren of the veterans were relatively well educated and found almost no employment or higher education possibilities in Grant County, so they left for cities or Southern locations.[175]

Group portrait of members of the Greene, Shepard, Gadlin, Grimes, and Craig families living in the Pleasant Ridge community, 1895. WHI IMAGE ID 45972

Prescott, Pierce County

In 1880, Pierce County's black population reached 69, about half of them in Prescott among 975 residents. This was to be the peak of the black population in the city and county. None of the Prescott males farmed; instead, one was a barber, one a brick mason, and the others laborers. The black farmers had either moved to Prescott or moved on; only Andrew Bennett remained, in the Town of Trimbelle.[176] Many moved to nearby St. Paul or other communities in Minnesota. Veteran Joseph B. Brooks, who spoke at the 1869 Emigration convention, left Prescott in the 1870s and became a teacher in Lafayette County, Arkansas.[177] Lewis and Mary Jane Washington Jr. and family (including Lewis's father) moved to Nebraska after 1885.[178] Veterans Michael Brown, Thomas Willis, and Andrew Bennett died in the 1880s and 1890s and were buried in Pierce County. Alex Strayhorn died in 1913.[179]

There is no evidence of efforts to drive out black residents, but in 1900 and 1920 only nine African Americans remained in all of Pierce County. There is evidence, however, that white attitudes had changed since the relatively warm welcome given to the freed people in the 1860s. In 1921, "an application from a colored comrade for membership" was received at the American Legion post in Ellsworth, the county seat. In an article laced with racially offensive language, the local paper reported a big turnout and heated debate at the post meeting considering the application. Members threatened to quit if the applicant were admitted. A ballot was taken and the application was accepted in a divided vote. It was found later that there was no black applicant, only a typographical error on the application.[180]

The last surviving black veteran, William Albare, Twenty-Ninth USCI, lived in Prescott until failing health forced him to move to the Milwaukee Soldiers Home, where he died in July 1921. He never learned to read or write, never married, and left no children behind. His entire postwar life was spent in Prescott as a laborer.[181]

—||—

The stories of how these veterans readjusted to life after the war brings us back to Aaron Roberts, the man whose life opens this book. Aaron, Rachel, and their children moved to Oshkosh around 1895. They bought a home and he worked initially in a carriage factory. In their years together in Oshkosh, Aaron and Rachel Roberts raised their daughter Lucy. At least two children from his first wife, Martha Stewart, lived nearby. Son Wilbert Roberts married Edith Myer in Oshkosh in 1899. Daughter Dora and her husband David Bowler and three children lived in Oshkosh in 1900.[182] In 1900, Aaron reported working only six of the previous twelve months.[183] By 1903, he was using his carpentry skills to become a building contractor, buying houses, fixing them, and reselling them. Dozens of real estate transactions involving Aaron (and sometimes Rachel) Roberts were published in local newspapers in the Fox Valley, indicating a thriving enterprise. In spite of health problems and racial prejudice, Roberts had survived near bankruptcy in manufacturing and reestablished himself as a successful businessman.[184] In 1910, the household of Aaron and Rachel Roberts included daughter Lucy and her new husband, William Moon, along with daughter-in-law Edith and two sons.[185]

Rachel Roberts died at age fifty-five on June 4, 1911. Aaron's last real estate transaction listed in the local newspaper was in 1913.[186] In 1915, he filed a request for an increase in his pension from La Valle, a village in Sauk County between Hillsboro and Baraboo. He took up residence in

Baraboo on a farm on the north edge of town. In 1920, he was listed as a farm operator, living in the household of daughter Lucy and her husband William Moon and their three sons. He was then over seventy years old and his health was failing, but he was still active. Aaron was a member of the Prince Hall Masonic Lodge in Madison, belonged to the Baraboo GAR Post 9, and was twice elected post adjutant, the second-highest office. He was also involved in ministry, probably with the local Wesleyan Methodist Church. He married once more, to Della Sebring, a white divorcee, in 1921. In the fall of 1922, Aaron's health took a turn for the worse, and he moved from the farm and into town. He died in November 1923. Della filed for a widow's pension but was denied because of the late date of their marriage.[187]

Epilogue

Legacy

The veterans of the Sixty-Second and Sixty-Fifth US Colored Infantry (USCI), including Wisconsin men, left a unique and hopeful legacy. As they were mustering out of the army in 1866, they donated nearly $6,400 of their army pay to help found Lincoln Institute (later Lincoln University) in Jefferson County, Missouri, which still operates as a historically black college. A statue in honor of the founding soldiers occupies a central location on campus.[1]

In the 1930s, a highway in Washington state was designated the Jefferson Davis Memorial Highway, named after the president of the Confederacy. In 2002, the Washington State House of Representatives voted, unanimously, to remove the name Jefferson Davis from the highway and rename it the William P. Stewart Memorial Highway, in honor of the veteran of Company F, Twenty-Ninth USCI, son of a founding member of the Cheyenne Valley settlement in Vernon County, who moved to Washington later in life. By the time the bill reached the state senate, the Daughters of the Confederacy and others had mobilized and the bill was killed in committee. In 2016, the proposal to change the name of the highway was revived and unanimously passed both the Washington senate and house. State Highway 99 is now officially known as the William P. Stewart Memorial Highway.[2]

Most of the religious congregations and church buildings that the veterans helped to build in the nineteenth century disappeared as their congregants died or moved away and their buildings fell into disuse and disrepair. Only three of those congregations still survive with black members: St. Mark's AME in Milwaukee, Wayman AME Church in Racine, and Wayman Chapel in Delavan.

Current home of the Wayman AME Church in Racine, which was founded in 1868–69. Some of its congregants were Civil War veterans. WISCONSIN ARCHITECTURE AND HISTORY INVENTORY 124659, STATE HISTORIC PRESERVATION OFFICE

Wayman Chapel in Delavan, built in 1991, is the current home of the Delavan AME Congregation, founded by African Americans in the 1890s, including Civil War veterans. COURTESY OF JEFF KANNEL

Children and Grandchildren

Many of the children and most of the grandchildren of the Pleasant Ridge veterans left the community in search of employment, marriageable partners, or higher education. Thomas Greene's children went on to have successful careers: his daughter Sarah taught seven years in a college in Missouri,[3] while his son Lester graduated from Western College in Macon, Missouri, and worked as a railroad porter. He became known as the "babies' porter" for his considerate treatment of his passengers. Lester lived in Chicago and was reported to have become a millionaire.[4] Victor D. Lewis, grandson of Thomas Greene and great-grandson of Charles Shepard, became an architect in Pennsylvania.[5] Dr. Howard Brent Shepard, grandson of Charles Shepard, graduated from the University of Minnesota dentistry school and was a dentist there and in Chicago.[6] Booker T. Richmond, grandson of Thomas Grimes and son of Lily Richmond, graduated from the University of Iowa law school in 1930 and achieved the highest score that year on the Iowa bar exam.[7]

Benny Butts (Fifth Wisconsin Infantry) married Amy (Anna) Roberts, the daughter of Aaron Roberts (Company F, Twenty-Ninth USCI), who trained at Camp Randall in its first incarnation as a military base. They lived to see Leo Butts, their son and grandson, respectively, triumph in school, on the gridiron, and in his profession. In November 1918, Leo became the first African American to play varsity football for the Badgers in a game at the brand-new Camp Randall Stadium. Two years later, Leo became the first African American graduate of the University of Wisconsin School of Pharmacy. After graduation, he moved to Gary, Indiana, worked as a pharmacist, married, and raised a

Leo Butts, 1918. UW MADISON SCHOOL OF PHARMACY

Standard Bearer
of
National Liberty Party
For President, U. S. A.
1904

Notice:- The only Negro who ever made the race for President.

Very Truly,
Geo. E. Taylor.

Presidential race poster for George Edwin Taylor, the first African American ticketed as a political party's nominee for president of the United States, running against Theodore Roosevelt in 1904. UNIVERSITY OF NORTH FLORIDA, THOMAS G. CARPENTER LIBRARY, SPECIAL COLLECTIONS AND ARCHIVES

family. When his pharmacy career was interrupted by the Great Depression, Leo went to work as a postman. After World War II, he returned to pharmacy.[8]

Nathan Smith, who had worked for General Cadwallader Washburn during the war and settled in West Salem/La Crosse, took in and raised a foster child named George Edwin Taylor. Around 1890, Taylor left La Crosse and settled in Oskaloosa, Iowa, where he continued his writing and political activism. In 1892, he was elected president of the National Colored Men's Protective Association. He was an Iowa delegate to the Republican National Convention in 1892 and to the Democratic National Convention in 1896. George Edwin Taylor went on to become a leader in the National Negro Democratic League, and in 1904, he was nominated for president by the National Negro Liberty Party, becoming the first African American candidate for the White House.[9]

The son of Alfred Matson (employed by the Twenty-Second, Eighth, and Forty-Second Wisconsin infantry regiments) and his wife, Luticia, Charles Matson (born in Delavan) became a New York jazz performer, arranger, and band leader, whose groups included some of the biggest names in 1920s music, including Coleman Hawkins. He played piano accompaniment for recordings by Mamie Smith and Bessie Smith, among others, and later was a stage actor.[10]

DESCENDANTS' MILITARY SERVICE

Many descendants of Wisconsin African American Civil War veterans followed their fathers' examples and served in the military. James Branum, son of Charles Branum (Twelfth USCHA), served in the Spanish-American War, though his unit (Eighth Regiment Colored Illinois Volunteers) arrived in Cuba after the most of the fighting had ended.[11] Oliver Davis, son of Logan Davis of Racine (Company C), served in the Ninth Cavalry during the Spanish-American War, one of the units that saved Teddy Roosevelt's Rough Riders from annihilation at San Juan Hill (later repudiated by Roosevelt).[12] Merle Stamper, son of Alexander, Janesville, Third USCHA, served in the 370th Infantry in World War I.[13] The 370th was one

of two black regiments that General John Pershing did not want under his command, so they fought as part of the French Army. They became one of the most decorated French units in the war.[14]

Many descendants of Civil War veterans Thomas Greene and Charles Shepard from Pleasant Ridge served their country in later wars. Henry Greene, Thomas's grandson, and Mason Richmond, nephew of Thomas Richmond (Sixty-Seventh USCI), served in World War I. George M.

Mason Richmond in his World War I uniform. WHI IMAGE ID 45971

Greene was a corporal in the Marines in World War II and Korea; in 1998, he was buried with his Civil War veteran relatives in the Pleasant Ridge Cemetery. Charles Wesley Greene served in World War II. Four of Lily Greene Richmond's children served: two in World War I and one in World War II. One of Olive Greene Lewis's adopted sons served in the navy.[15]

Like their fathers and grandfathers, up through World War II these men served in segregated units and could never become commissioned officers. Most were relegated to support roles, such as the quartermasters' corps. Despite having proven themselves in the Civil War, the military hierarchy reverted to the old prejudice that African American men would not make good soldiers. Black veterans in World War I felt more accepted in France than in their own country and returned home to some of the worst anti-black violence in US history, especially directed at the veterans.

Although the US military remained a segregated institution for generations, the service of African Americans in the Civil War produced some of the first permanent steps in the civil rights movement. The most obvious victory was the overthrow of the slave system. For these veterans, there was no debate about the causes and results of the war. The central issue of the war and the most important victory was the end of enslavement.

From the Civil War onward, African Americans were permanent participants in the US military. The Buffalo Soldiers continued until World War I and included Wisconsin men. The right to equal pay for black and white soldiers was won through the sacrifices of the Fifty-Fourth and Fifty-Fifth Massachusetts soldiers and their families. The right of black soldiers to be buried in military cemeteries along with white soldiers was permanently achieved. In Wisconsin, black servicemen and veterans

Peter D. Thomas (Fifteenth Wisconsin Infantry, Eighteenth USCI). WHI IMAGE ID 3399 pushed forward the petition for voting rights, which were won in 1866 and never rescinded. They wrote and spoke in support and defense of black civil rights, even as those rights were being restricted and lost.

Most of the African American veterans connected to Wisconsin lived in poverty during their postwar lives. Many who stayed on farms and in small towns lived in increasing isolation in their later years. None of them became wealthy, but there were some successful entrepreneurs like Aaron Roberts, Anthony Richardson, and John J. Valentine, and property owners like John J. Miles and Thomas Greene. None became a famous inventor, but there were many practical men who found ways to get by and get along with what they had and what they could make. There were no Medal of Honor winners, but Thomas Burnett showed the same bravery in trying to rescue the colors of the Twenty-Ninth Regiment at the Crater as other soldiers who were awarded the medal. They were not titans of industry, but men like Arthur B. Lee, Samuel Thompson, and Michael Brown were respected tradesmen. None of them became state or national leaders of the GAR, but some were elected to local leadership positions by their white comrades. None of them held high political office, but a few, like Andrew Bennett and Peter D. Thomas, were elected to local office, and Henry Sink and John J. Valentine were politically active. No famed orators or political leaders developed from this group, but Arthur B. Lee and John J. Miles carried the torch for advancing the status of their people throughout their lives. And though none became a renowned theologian, Leroy Jackson, Pinkney

A Civil War reenactor for Company F, Twenty-Ninth USCI, Rickey Townsell portrays a soldier whose story is very similar to that of Henry Sink.
COURTESY OF RICKEY TOWNSELL

Reenactors at Forest Home Cemetery, Memorial Day, 2016. COURTESY OF SANDRA WICKER

Taylor, and John Allen became ministers. None has a statue erected in his honor, but Grant County residents created a Civil War monument that included the names of Charles and John Shepard among their Civil War dead.

African American veterans of the Civil War are buried in at least thirty Wisconsin counties. Most of their final resting places are marked by headstones that recognize their service to their country. Some of those graves, previously unmarked, have received headstones in recent years due to the efforts of relatives, local historians and societies, and Civil War reenactors. On Memorial Day 2016, the Milwaukee-based reenactors representing Company F, Twenty-Ninth United States Colored Troops, dedicated a gravestone for William Reed, whose remains had lain in an unmarked grave in Forest Home Cemetery for over 120 years. On October 1, 2019, the Company F reenactors dedicated another military headstone at the same cemetery, this one for Thirteenth USCHA veteran Horace Dangerfield.

For the sacrifices made by these men and their families during and after their military service, they deserve respect and a dignified place of final rest. They also deserve to be remembered by being included in the state and national history that they helped make.

ENLISTED MEN

Listed here, by regiment, are all of the African American soldiers and sailors who served in the Civil War and who had a connection to Wisconsin. This includes men who lived in the state before or after the war, those who were in the state when they enlisted, and those whose service was credited to Wisconsin, whether or not they lived in the state. Shown is the highest rank attained by the soldier or sailor. "Age" is the serviceman's age at enlistment. In italics are the names of men with documentation of residence in Wisconsin; all others are men whose service was credited to Wisconsin but for whom there is no documentation of actual presence in the state. Also in italics are other references to an individual's presence in Wisconsin: place of residence, enlistment location, location to which service was credited, and date and place of death. If presence in Wisconsin is documented by service documents but a town or county of residence could not be found, "WI" is entered.

Many soldiers listed as unassigned in the *Roster of Wisconsin Volunteers, War of the Rebellion, 1861–1865* (www.wisconsinhistory.org/Records/Article/CS4267) were actually assigned to and served in regiments other than the Twenty-Ninth USCI; they are listed with their regiments in the table. There may be a few men listed as "unassigned" below who served with a regiment but for whom no record of their assignments has been found. Some of the unassigned men enlisted late in the war and were released from service when the war ended, before they left Camp Randall. Others were shipped to Missouri for assignment to a regiment but were never assigned for various reasons. A number of these men were sick or injured before being assigned, so they were discharged or assigned duties at Camp Randall or Benton Barracks. "Unassigned" men were considered veterans and qualified for pensions later in life.

"Rejected" men enlisted in the army but were found to be unfit for service. They were never deployed with a regiment and did not qualify for a pension. Blank spaces mean "not applicable."

—II—

Abbreviations used

Cav	cavalry
Co	county or Company
Cpl	corporal
First Sgt	first sergeant
hosp	hospital
Inf	infantry
KIA	killed in action
MIA	missing in action
MO	mustered out
POW	prisoner of war
Pvt	private
Sgt	sergeant
Sgt M	sergeant major
term exp	term of service expired
Twp	Township

Last, First Name	Rank	Residence Before Service	Age	Enlist Date	Location	Credited To	Left Service	Date	Location	Residence After Service	Death Year and Place	Burial Place in WI
						INFANTRY						
						Twenty-Ninth US Colored Infantry						
						Company B						
Bynam (Bynum), William	Pvt	*NC; Prescott, WI*	20	8/15/64	*Prescott, WI*	*River Falls, Pierce Co., WI*	MO (term exp)	8/31/65	Ringgold Barracks, TX	*Prescott, WI*		
Carter, Edward	Pvt	Hanover Co., VA	24	6/6/64	White House, VA	Madison, WI	discharged/released	4/23/65	POW, released, Camp Parole, MD			
Dorson, John	Pvt	VA	20	6/6/64	White House, VA	*Madison, WI*	MO	11/6/65	Brownsville, TX			
Johnson, Arthur	Pvt	Louisville, KY; possibly Racine, WI	30	3/26/64	Chicago, IL	Chicago, IL or Cicero, IL	discharged (disabled)	6/24/65	Fort Monroe, VA			
Jones, Alexander (Alex)	Cpl	Jackson Co., AL; Portage, WI	25	3/15/64	Chicago, IL	Niles, Cook Co., IL	MO	11/6/65	Brownsville, TX	*Portage, Racine, Milwaukee Soldiers Home, WI; Washington, DC*	1917, Washington, DC	
Lowe, James	Pvt	Columbus, WI; Portage, WI	26	3/25/64	Chicago, IL	Chicago, IL	deserted hospital	10/30/64	Summit Hospital, Philadelphia, PA			
Lumpkins, William	Pvt	Newport, KY; Menomonie, WI	24	8/31/64	*Menomonie, WI*	Menomonie, WI	discharged (term exp)	9/2/65	Ringgold Barracks, TX	Newport, KY; Columbus, OH	1919, Soldiers Home, Dayton, OH	

Last, First Name	Rank	Residence Before Service	Age	Enlist Date	Location	Credited To	Left Service	Date	Location	Residence After Service	Death Year and Place	Burial Place in WI
						Company C						
Bibb, James	Pvt	Logan Co., KY	34	4/2/64	Chicago, IL	Black Wolf, Winnebago Co., WI	discharged	11/23/65	hospital, Fort Monroe, VA			
Davis, Logan	Pvt	TN or KY; Chicago, IL	15	1/5/64	Chicago, IL	Chicago, IL	MO	11/6/65	Brownsville, TX	Racine, WI	1929, Racine, WI	Mound Cemetery, Racine Co.
Hampton, Wade	Pvt	Washington Co., NC	42	4/2/64	Chicago, IL	Black Wolf, Winnebago Co., WI	died	6/26/64	L'Ouverture, Alexandria, VA		1864, Alexandria, VA	
Holliday, Thomas	Pvt	Franklin Co., AL; IL; WI	24	2/26/64	Chicago, IL	Maine, Cook Co., IL	deserted	12/27/64	Summitt House Hospital, PA			
Johnson, Samuel	Pvt	King and Queen Co., VA	22	6/2/64	White House, VA	Madison, WI	died	3/13/65	Point of Rocks Hospital, VA		1865, VA	
Roberts, George	Pvt	Louisville, KY; Madison, WI	23	4/8/64	Madison, WI	Milwaukee, WI	died	4/25/64	Quincy, IL		1864, Quincy, IL	
Wilson, Henry	Pvt	Obion Co., TN; Boscobel, WI	19	1/14/64	Chicago, IL	Chicago, IL	discharged	11/11/65	L'Ouverture, Alexandria, VA			
						Company D						
Albare (Albur), William S. (Golden, Samuel)	Pvt	NC; Prescott, WI	23	8/15/64	Clifton, WI	Clifton, WI	discharged	9/2/65	Ringold Barracks, TX	Prescott, WI	1921, Milwaukee Soldiers Home	Wood National Cemetery, Milwaukee Co.
Burnett, Thomas H.	Cpl	Louisville, KY; Oshkosh, WI; Milwaukee, WI	21	1/18/64	Chicago, IL	Chicago, IL	MO	11/6/65	Brownsville, TX	Milwaukee, WI; IL; MO; Milwaukee Soldiers Home	1892, Moberly, MO	

Twenty-Ninth Colored Infantry, Company D, continued

Last, First Name	Rank	Age	Enlist Date	Residence Before Service	Location	Credited To	Left Service	Date	Location	Residence After Service	Death Year and Place	Burial Place in WI
Carroll, Alfred M.	First Sgt	20	1/2/64	Milwaukee, WI	Chicago, IL	Chicago, IL	MO	11/7/65	Brownsville, TX	Buffalo Soldier; NJ	1894, Cape May, NJ	
Crawford, Isaac	Pvt	22	8/15/64	Hagerstown, MD; Trimbelle, Pierce Co., WI	Prescott, WI	Prescott, WI	discharged	9/2/65	Ringgold Barracks, TX	Trimbelle, WI; Prescott, WI; River Falls, WI; St. Paul, MN; Minneapolis, MN	1903, MN	
Dixon, James R.	Pvt	32	8/3/64	Harrison Co., OH; Baraboo, WI	Baraboo, WI	Baraboo, WI	MO	9/25/65	hospital, Fort Monroe, VA			
Hughes, Dennis	Pvt	20	10/14/64	Tuscaloosa, AL; Madison, WI	Chicago, IL	Chicago, IL	MO	11/6/65	Brownsville, TX	Belleville, WI; Madison, WI	1928, Verona, Dane Co., WI	
Hunter, Edward	Pvt	38	2/26/64	Middlessex Co., VA; Markesan, WI; Waupaca, WI; Fond du Lac, WI	Chicago, IL	Maine, Cook Co., IL	died	6/14/64	near Kent Court House, VA		1864, VA	
Jones, John	Pvt	40	8/18/64	Abingdon, VA; Prescott, WI	Prescott, WI	Salem, Pierce Co., WI	discharged	8/31/65	Ringgold Barracks, TX	Prescott, WI; MO; KS	1882, Kansas City, KS	
Jordan, Joseph W.	Pvt	18	7/8/64	MD	Cold Harbor, VA	Madison, WI	MIA	7/30/64	Battle of the Crater			
McClellan, Oscar	Pvt	43	8/31/64	Madison Co., TN; Sharon, Walworth Co., WI	Marengo, IL	Leroy, Boone Co., IL	MO (term exp)	9/2/65	Ringgold Barracks, TX	Sharon, WI; Delavan, WI	1897, Delavan, WI	Spring Grove Cemetery, Delavan

Twenty-Ninth Colored Infantry, Company D, continued

Last, First Name	Rank	Residence Before Service	Age	Enlist Date	Location	Credited To	Left Service	Date	Location	Residence After Service	Death Year and Place	Burial Place in WI
Rosier, Henry	Cpl	Washington Co., MD; Fort Winnebago, Columbia Co., WI	30	3/24/64	Chicago, IL	Niles, Cook Co., IL	MO	11/6/65	Brownsville, TX	Fort Winnebago, WI; Racine, WI	1895, Racine Co., WI	Mound Cemetery, Racine Co.
Sullivan, William	Sgt	Philadelphia, PA	22	6/6/64	White House, VA	Madison, WI	MO	11/6/65	Brownsville, TX			
Taylor, Charles Henry	Pvt	Campbell Co., VA; Madison, WI	31	10/18/64	Madison, WI; Chicago, IL	Chicago, IL or Town of Fulton, Rock Co., WI	MO	11/6/65	Brownsville, TX	Madison, WI	1892, WI	Prairie Home Cemetery, Waukesha
Washington, Lewis	Pvt	Washington, DC; Waukesha, WI; Trimbelle, Pierce Co., WI	25	8/15/64	Prescott, WI	Prescott, Pierce Co., WI	discharged	9/2/65	Ringgold Barracks, TX	Prescott, WI; Omaha, NE	1895, Omaha, NE	
Wilson, Albert S.	Pvt	Louisville & Hannibal, MO; Quincy, IL	20	6/21/64	Quincy, IL	Milwaukee, WI	died	7/18/65	Corps d'Afrique Hospital, New Orleans, LA		1865, New Orleans, LA	
Company E												
Joy, Charles	Pvt	Gibbon Co., TN; IL	24	7/8/64	Collinsville, IL	Milwaukee, WI	MO	11/6/65	Brownsville, TX			
Martin, Thomas	Pvt	Richmond, VA; IL	26	4/2/64	Chicago, IL	Black Wolf, Winnebago Co., WI	MO	11/6/65	Brownsville, TX			
McGarthie (McGarthy), Archibald	Pvt	Hamilton Co., OH; IL	23	12/31/63	Chicago, IL	Black Wolf, Winnebago Co., WI	deserted	4/25/64	Quincy, IL			

Twenty-Ninth Colored Infantry, Company E, continued

Last, First Name	Rank	Residence Before Service	Age	Enlist Date	Location	Credited To	Left Service	Date	Location	Residence After Service	Death Year and Place	Burial Place in WI
Valentine, Julius	Pvt	*Stokes Co., NC; OH; Rutland, Dane Co., WI; Winneconne, WI*	31	4/2/64	Chicago, IL	*Black Wolf, Winnebago Co., WI*	MO	11/6/65	Brownsville, TX	*Adams Co., WI*		
Company F, "Milwaukee Company"												
Adams, John	Pvt	*AR; WI*	21	5/9/64	Madison, WI	*Sun Prairie, WI*	MO	11/6/65	Brownsville, TX	IL	1894, Aurora, IL	
Allen, Charles	Pvt	*Green Co., TN; Hamilton Co., IN; Forest, Vernon Co., WI*	33	4/22/64	Madison, WI	*Carleton, Kewaunee Co., WI*	MO	11/6/65	Forest, Vernon Co., WI	*Forest, WI*	*1883, Forest, Vernon Co., WI*	Revels Family Cemetery, Forest
Allen, Jefferson (Judson)	Pvt	*TN; IL*	19	2/11/64	Gallatin Co., IL	*Milwaukee, WI*	died (KIA)	7/30/64	Battle of the Crater		1864, Petersburg, VA	
Briggs, John	Pvt	*VA; IL; Racine, WI*	45	3/28/64	Chicago, IL	Wheeling, IL	discharged	6/26/65	Washington, DC	*Racine, WI; Sycamore, IL*	1887, Sycamore, De Kalb Co., IL	
Brown, Felix	Pvt	*Lewis Co., MO*	22	12/21/63	Quincy, IL	*Milwaukee, WI*	discharged	6/14/65	Ft. Monroe, VA	Lewis Co., MO	1867, MO	
Bryon, Lloyd T.	First Sgt	*Lancaster Co., PA; OH; Plover, WI; Berlin, WI*	32	3/31/64	Madison, WI	*Mequon, Ozaukee Co., WI*	MO	11/6/65	Brownsville, TX	IL; Camanche, IA; "out west"		
Carey (Cary, Casey), Richard	Pvt	*VA; Palmyra, WI*	21	6/25/64	Quincy, IL	*Milwaukee, WI*	MO	11/6/65	Brownsville, TX	*Palmyra, WI*		
Carter, Jonathan	Cpl	*Beaver Co., PA; Stockbridge, WI*	31	3/25/64	Madison, WI	*Milwaukee, WI*	MO	11/6/65	Brownsville, TX			

Twenty-Ninth Colored Infantry, Company F, continued

Last, First Name	Rank	Residence Before Service	Age	Enlist Date	Location	Credited To	Left Service	Date	Location	Residence After Service	Death Year and Place	Burial Place in WI
Christine (Christian), John	Pvt	Lewis Co., MO	35	6/16/64	Quincy, IL	*Milwaukee, WI*	discharged	6/26/65	Washington, DC	Lewis Co., MO	1886, La Grange, Lewis Co., MO	
Clark, Frank	Pvt	Sharpsburg, MD; WI	20	6/15/64	*Madison, WI*	*Otsego, Columbia, Co., WI*	MO	11/6/65	Brownsville, TX	PA		
Colder, Benjamin	Cpl	Danville, KY; Elkhorn, WI	19	6/22/64	*Madison, WI*	*Seven Mile Creek, Juneau Co., WI*	MO	11/6/65	Brownsville, TX	*Elkhorn, WI; Whitewater, WI; MO; KS*		
Cooley, Turner O.	Pvt	Shelby Co., MO	18	5/21/64	Quincy, IL	*Milwaukee, WI*	MO	11/6/65	Brownsville, TX	Shelby & Macon Co., MO	1925, Macon Co., MO	
Dodden, Robert	Pvt	TN; Quincy, IL	18	11/1/63	Quincy, IL	*Milwaukee, WI*	MO	11/6/65	Brownsville, TX	Quincy, IL		
Edwards, Aaron	Pvt	St. Charles, MO	28	6/27/64	Quincy, IL	*Milwaukee, WI*	deserted	8/23/64	near Petersburg, VA			
Ems (Aines, Ames), John	Pvt	Natchez, MS; Madison, WI	16	8/17/64	*Madison, WI*	*Madison, WI*	discharged (term exp)	9/2/65	Ringgold Barracks, TX			
Fielding, Jacob	Pvt	Pike Co., MO	45	6/16/64	Quincy, IL	*Milwaukee, WI*	discharged	1/17/65	New York City, NY	Pike Co., MO		
Foggey, Anthony	Pvt	Pike Co., MO	19	6/2/64	Quincy, IL	*Milwaukee, WI*	MO	11/6/65	Brownsville, TX	Quincy, IL	1905, IL	
Foggey, William	Pvt	Pike Co., MO	18	6/2/64	Quincy, IL	*Milwaukee, WI*	MO	11/6/65	Brownsville, TX	Pike Co., MO; IN; IL; MO	1937, Vandalia, MO	
Fry, Richard	Pvt	NY; Adams, Sauk Co., WI; Burke, Dane Co., WI	30	4/14/64	*Madison, WI*	*Decorah, WI*	deserted	7/30/64	near Petersburg, VA			

Twentieth-Ninth Colored Infantry, Company F, *continued*

Last, First Name	Rank	Residence Before Service	Age	Enlist Date	Location	Credited To	Left Service	Date	Location	Residence After Service	Death Year and Place	Burial Place in WI
Furman, Jacob	Pvt	Marion Co., MO	31	6/13/64	Quincy, IL	*Milwaukee, WI*	died	4/20/65	Ft. Monroe, VA		1865, VA	Estabrook Cemetery, Fond du Lac (unmarked)
Gaines, Lewis	Pvt	Essex Co., VA; AL; *Fond du Lac, WI*	41	4/25/64	*Madison, WI*	*Dunkirk, Dane Co., WI*	discharged	11/23/65	Ft. Monroe, VA	*Fond du Lac, WI*	*~1872-74, WI*	
Griffith, Matthew (Moore, Madison)	Pvt	VA; Pike Co., MO; Quincy, IL	40	6/2/64	Quincy, IL	*Milwaukee, WI*	discharged	6/26/65	Washington, DC	Pike Co., MO		
Griffith, William	Pvt	VA; Pike Co., MO	43	6/2/64	Quincy, IL	*Milwaukee, WI*	died	3/3/65	Balfour Hospital, VA		1865	
Hammons, Martin	Pvt	Lincoln Co., MO	22	6/25/64	Quincy, IL	*Milwaukee, WI*	MO	11/6/65	Brownsville, TX	Quincy, IL	1907	
Hammons, Robert (Donaldson, Hammond)	Pvt	Pike Co., MO	19	6/2/64	Quincy, IL	*Milwaukee, WI*	MO	11/6/65	Brownsville, TX	Pike Co., MO	1912	
Henry, Jackson	Cpl	Pike Co., MO	26	6/16/64	Quincy, IL	*Milwaukee, WI*	died	3/7/65	Point of Rocks Hospital, VA		1865, VA	
Hill, Henry	Pvt	Pike Co., MO	18	6/2/64	Quincy, IL	*Milwaukee, WI*	MO	11/6/65	Brownsville, TX	Henry Co., MO		
Houton, Jesse	Pvt	Pike Co., MO	45	6/16/64	Quincy, IL	*Milwaukee, WI*	died	10/5/64	hospital, Willet's Point, NY		1864, Queens, New York	
Houton, Perry	Sgt	Clark Co., KY; Pike Co., MO	29	6/16/64	Quincy, IL	*Milwaukee, WI*	MO	11/6/65	Brownsville, TX	Quincy, IL		
Jackson, John	Pvt	St. Louis, MO	18	5/16/64	Quincy, IL	*Milwaukee, WI*	died (KIA)	7/30/64	Battle of the Crater		1864, Petersburg, VA	

Twenty-Ninth Colored Infantry, Company F, continued

Last, First Name	Rank	Residence Before Service	Age	Enlist Date	Location	Credited To	Left Service	Date	Location	Residence After Service	Death Year and Place	Burial Place in WI
Johnson, Allen	Pvt	Pike Co., MO	21	6/2/64	Quincy, IL	*Milwaukee, WI*	MO	11/6/65	Brownsville, TX	Pike Co., MO	1919, Pike Co., MO	
Johnson, John	Pvt	Henry Co., KY	15	5/16/64	Quincy, IL	*Milwaukee, WI*	deserted	10/7/64	near Petersburg, VA			
Johnson, Richard E.	Cpl	Springfield, IL	18	5/14/64	Quincy, IL	*Milwaukee, WI*	deserted	8/3/64	near Petersburg, VA			
Lee, Charles	Pvt	KY	18	6/24/64	Quincy, IL	*Milwaukee, WI*	died	7/28/64	in camp, near Petersburg, VA		1864, Petersburg, VA	
Leeper, Rufus	Pvt	Saline Co. & Gallatin Co., IL	21	2/11/64	Gallatin Co., IL	*Milwaukee, WI*	died	9/23/64	City Point Hospital, VA		1864, City Point, VA	
Lucas, Daniel	Pvt	Albemarle Co., VA; Pike Co., MO	17	5/14/64	Quincy, IL	*Milwaukee, WI*	discharged	6/7/65	Ft. Monroe, VA	Pike Co., MO; Lincoln Co., MO	1928, Lincoln Co., MO	
Lyons, Martin	Pvt	Pike Co., MO	18	6/6/64	Quincy, IL	*Milwaukee, WI*	died	9/9/64	Freedmen's Hospital, Washington, DC		1864, Washington, DC	
Mackay, Henry	Pvt	Pike Co., MO	33	6/16/64	Quincy, IL	*Milwaukee, WI*	died	12/24/64	Point of Rocks Hospital, VA		1864, VA	
Mackay, Jackson	Pvt	Pike Co., MO	19	6/2/64	Louisiana, MO	*Milwaukee, WI*	died (KIA)	8/14/64	City Point Hospital, VA		1864, Petersburg, VA	
Mackay, Perry	Pvt	Pike Co., MO	35	6/16/64	Quincy, IL	*Milwaukee, WI*	died	9/25/65	Hospital, Ringgold Barracks, TX		1865, TX	
McCann, Anderson	Pvt	KY; Monroe Co., MO	29	6/2/64	Quincy, IL	*Milwaukee, WI*	died	12/16/64	Point of Rocks Hospital, VA		1864, VA	

Twenty-Ninth Colored Infantry, Company F, continued

Last, First Name	Rank	Residence Before Service	Age	Enlist Date	Location	Credited To	Left Service	Date	Location	Residence After Service	Death Year and Place	Burial Place in WI
McKenney, William	Cpl	Hinds Co., MS; LA; Madison, WI	18	4/7/64	Madison, WI	Sumpter, Sauk Co., WI	MO	11/6/65	Brownsville, TX	Madison, WI; Milwaukee, WI; Chicago, IL; Milwaukee Soldiers Home	1905, Chicago, IL	
Modley, Henry	Pvt	Lincoln Co., MO	18	6/16/64	Quincy, IL	Milwaukee, WI	died	2/4/65	Point of Rocks Hospital, VA		1865, VA	
Modley, John (Bingham, John)	Pvt	Lincoln Co., MO	18	6/16/64	Quincy, IL	Milwaukee, WI	MO	11/6/65	Brownsville, TX	IL		
Monroe, Joseph	Pvt	Lewis Co., MO	18	6/14/64	Quincy, IL	Milwaukee, WI	MO	11/6/65	Brownsville, TX	Quincy, IL; Lewis Co., MO		
Moore, David	Pvt	Pike Co., MO	19	6/14/64	Quincy, IL	Milwaukee, WI	MO	11/6/65	Brownsville, TX	Pike Co., MO		
Moore, Thomas	Pvt	Lewis Co., MO	30	6/14/64	Quincy, IL	Milwaukee, WI	MO	11/6/65	Brownsville, TX			
Morehead, York	Pvt	Pike Co., MO	18	6/9/64	Quincy, IL	Milwaukee, WI	died	9/21/64	City Point Hospital, VA		1864, VA	
Morris, Garrett	Pvt	Saline Co., MO	23	3/15/64	Alton, IL	Milwaukee, WI	MO	11/6/65	Brownsville, TX			
Norton, John	Pvt	Pike Co., MO	19	6/3/64	Louisiana, MO	Milwaukee, WI	died	9/1/65	General Hospital, Brownsville, TX		1865, TX	
Oden, Frank	Pvt	Pike Co., MO	18	6/16/64	Quincy, IL	Milwaukee, WI	MO	11/27/65	Springfield, IL	Chicago, IL		
Orr, George W.	Pvt	Pike Co., MO	22	6/1/64	Louisiana, MO	Milwaukee, WI	MO	11/6/65	Brownsville, TX	Quincy, IL	1919, IL	
Orr, James E.	Cpl	Pike Co., MO	25	6/1/64	Louisiana, MO	Milwaukee, WI	MO	11/6/65	Brownsville, TX			
Orr, Lewis	Pvt	Pike Co., MO	18	5/21/64	Louisiana, MO	Milwaukee, WI	MO	11/6/65	Brownsville, TX	Quincy, IL	1903, IL	

Twenty-Ninth Colored Infantry, Company F, continued

Last, First Name	Rank	Residence Before Service	Age	Enlist Date	Location	Credited To	Left Service	Date	Location	Residence After Service	Death Year and Place	Burial Place in WI
Paten (Payton), Louis	Cpl	Natchez, MS; Madison, WI	22	4/9/64	*Madison, WI*	*Milwaukee, WI*	MO	11/1/65	Brownsville, TX			
Price, Benjamin E.	Pvt	Madison Co., IL	29	3/14/64	Collinsville, IL	Milwaukee, WI	died (KIA)	7/30/64	Battle of the Crater		1864, Petersburg, VA	
Reed, William	Pvt	Platte Co., MO; IL; Madison, WI	21	4/7/64	Madison, WI	Milwaukee, WI	MO	11/6/65	Brownsville, TX	*Fond du Lac, WI; Beloit, WI; Madison, WI; Milwaukee, WI*	*1895, Milwaukee, WI*	Forest Home Cemetery, Milwaukee Co.
Rice, Julius	Cpl	Albemarle Co., VA; Pike Co., MO	21	6/25/64	Quincy, IL	Milwaukee, WI	deserted	11/1/64	Philadelphia, PA	Pike Co., MO; Jacksonville, IL	1921, Jacksonville, IL	
Roberts, Aaron	Pvt	Orange Co., IN; Forest, Vernon Co., WI	18	3/29/64	Madison, WI	Carlton, Kewaunee Co., WI	MO	11/6/65	Brownsville, TX	*Forest & Hills-boro, Vernon Co., WI; Oshkosh, WI; Baraboo, WI*	*1923, Baraboo, WI*	Walnut Hill Cemetery, Baraboo
Robinson, Richard	Pvt	Henry Co., VA; WI	18	5/18/64	*Madison, WI*	*Brighton, Kenosha Co., WI*	died (KIA)	7/30/64	Battle of the Crater		1864, Petersburg, VA	
Robinson, Wesley	Pvt	Lewis Co., MO	18	6/14/64	Quincy, IL	Milwaukee, WI	deserted	10/10/64	City Point, VA	Lewis Co., MO		
Ross, William C.	Pvt	CO or MO; WI	25	4/22/64	Madison, WI	Carlton, Kewaunee Co., WI	died (KIA)	7/30/64	Battle of the Crater		1864, Petersburg, VA	
Sink, Henry	Pvt	Batesville, AR; Rosendale, WI; Fond du Lac, WI	33	4/16/64	*Madison, WI*	*Milwaukee, WI*	discharged	3/20/65	Philadelphia, PA	*Fond du Lac, WI; Spaulding, MI; De Pere, WI*	*1905, Fond du Lac, WI*	Rienzi Cemetery, Fond du Lac
Smith, Henry	Pvt	KY	18	7/7/64	Quincy, IL	Milwaukee, WI	MO	11/6/65	Brownsville, TX	Lee Co., IA	1884, Keokuk, IA	

Twenty-Ninth Colored Infantry, Company F, continued

Last, First Name	Rank	Residence Before Service	Age	Enlist Date	Location	Credited To	Left Service	Date	Location	Residence After Service	Death Year and Place	Burial Place in WI
Smith, Isaac	Cpl	Charlottesville, VA; KY; Madison, WI	18	4/8/64	Madison, WI	Milwaukee, WI	MO	11/6/65	Brownsville, TX	Madison, WI; Chicago, IL	1903, Milwaukee, WI	Wood National Cemetery, Milwaukee Co.
Smith, Paten	Pvt	Lincoln Co., MO	18	6/2/64	Louisiana, MO	Milwaukee, WI	died	4/6/65	Fort Monroe, VA		1865, VA	
Smith, Phillip	Pvt	Monroe Co., MO	32	5/16/64	Quincy, IL	Milwaukee, WI	MO	11/6/65	Brownsville, TX	Marion Co., MO	1910, unknown location	
South, Collins	Cpl	Pike Co., MO	18	6/16/64	Quincy, IL	Milwaukee, WI	MO	11/6/65	Brownsville, TX	Quincy, IL; Pike Co., MO	1931, Pike Co., MO	
Stark, Peter R.	Sgt	Pittsburgh, PA	43	6/2/64	Quincy, IL	Milwaukee, WI	died (KIA)	7/30/64	Battle of the Crater		1864, Petersburg, VA	
Starrett (Benton), Thomas	Cpl	Lewis Co., MO	21	6/16/64	Quincy, IL	Milwaukee, WI	MO	11/6/65	Brownsville, TX	Lewis Co., MO; Quincy, IL	1920, Quincy, IL	
Stewart, William P.	Pvt	Sangamon Co., IL; Forest, Vernon Co., WI	25	2/1/65	Chicago, IL	Niles, Cook Co., IL	MO	11/6/65	Brownsville, TX	Forest, Vernon Co., WI; Laganville, Sauk Co., WI; Peshtigo, WI; Snohomish, WA	1907, WA	
Strauder (Strander), Sanford	Pvt	Fairfax Co., VA; MO	20	6/16/64	Quincy, IL	Milwaukee, WI	died (KIA)	7/30/64	Battle of the Crater		1864, Petersburg, VA	
Sturgeon, Turner	Pvt	Jefferson Co., KY; Pike Co., MO	43	5/24/64	Louisiana, MO	Milwaukee, WI	MO	11/6/65	Brownsville, TX	Quincy, IL	1866, unknown location	
Summers, Joseph	Pvt	KY; Pike Co., MO	32	6/2/64	Louisiana, MO	Milwaukee, WI	died	11/13/65	post hospital, Brownsville, TX		1865, TX	

Twenty-Ninth Colored Infantry, Company F, continued

Last, First Name	Rank	Residence Before Service	Age	Enlist Date	Location	Credited To	Left Service	Date	Location	Residence After Service	Death Year and Place	Burial Place in WI
Taburn, Edward	Pvt	Saline Co., IL	21	2/11/64	Gallatin Co., IL	*Milwaukee, WI*	MO	11/6/65	Brownsville, TX	Saline Co., IL	1919, Saline Co., IL	
Thornton, Abram	Pvt	Loudoun Co., VA; OH; *Loganville, Sauk Co., WI*	21	2/1/65	Chicago, IL	Niles, Cook Co., IL	MO	11/6/65	Brownsville, TX	*Loganville, WI; Baraboo, WI*	1918, Harrisonville, OH	
Thurman, Perry	Pvt	Pike Co., MO	18	1/1/64	Quincy, IL	*Ashford, Dodge Co., WI*	MO	11/6/65	Brownsville, TX	Quincy, IL	1921, Kirkwood, MO	
Tinsley, Charles	Pvt	Bedford Co., VA; Pike Co., MO	31	6/21/64	Quincy, IL	*Milwaukee, WI*	died (KIA)	7/30/64	Battle of the Crater		1864, Petersburg, VA	
Turner, Winston	Pvt	Amherst Co., VA; MO	44	6/23/64	Quincy, IL	*Milwaukee, WI*	deserted	7/30/64	Battle of the Crater		unknown	
Underhill, Daniel	Sgt	Lancaster Co., PA; *Black River Falls, WI; Sparta, WI*	44	4/11/64	Madison, WI	*Burke, Dane Co., WI*	discharged	6/26/65	VA	*Sparta, WI*	before 1870, unknown location	
Walden (South), Charles	Pvt	Pike Co., MO	18	6/28/64	Quincy, IL	*Milwaukee, WI*	discharged	1/7/65	Quincy, IL	Pike Co. & Sedalia, MO; *Milwaukee Soldiers Home*	1918, Sedalia, MO	
Walker, Adam	Pvt	Albemarle Co., VA; MO	35	5/31/64	Quincy, IL	*Milwaukee, WI*	discharged	10/11/65	Ft. Monroe VA	Quincy, IL	1879, IL	
Watson, Madison	Pvt	Albemarle Co., VA; Pike Co., MO	45	5/14/64	Quincy, IL	*Milwaukee, WI*	discharged	5/18/65	City Point, VA	Pike Co., MO; Lincoln Co., MO	1900, MO	

Last, First Name	Rank	Residence Before Service	Age	Enlist Date	Location	Credited To	Left Service	Date	Location	Residence After Service	Death Year and Place	Burial Place in WI
Weaver, Alfred	Sgt	Orange Co., NC; Forest, Vernon Co., WI; Woodland, Sauk Co., WI	33	3/25/64	*Madison, WI*	*Sumpter, Sauk Co., WI*	MO	11/6/65	Brownsville, TX	*Vernon Co., WI; Sauk Co., WI; Richland Co., WI; Marion, IN*	1913, Marion, IN	
Williams, Henry	Pvt	Pike Co., MO	34	6/2/64	Quincy, IL	Milwaukee, WI	died	9/11/64	City Point, VA		1864, VA	
Witherspoon (Weatherspoon), Anderson	Pvt	Murray Co., KY	16	6/21/64	Quincy, IL	Milwaukee, WI	died	4/25/65	Point of Rocks Hospital, VA		1865, VA	
Company G												
McGout, Floyd	Pvt	born MO or WI	22	8/17/64	Evansville, IN	not stated	MO	11/6/65	Brownsville, TX			
Company H												
Brooks, Howard	Pvt	MD; *Madison, WI*	37	9/3/64	*Madison, WI*	*Blooming Grove, Dane Co., WI*	MO	11/6/65	Brownsville, TX	*Madison, WI*	*Madison, WI*	Forest Hill Cemetery, Madison
Burrell, Stephen	Pvt	MO; *Whitewater, WI*	20	8/21/64	*Madison, WI*	*Hebron, Jefferson Co., WI*	discharged	8/31/65	Ringgold Barracks, TX	*Whitewater, WI*		
Cosley, John	Sgt	St. Louis, MO; *Delavan, WI*	26	8/24/64	*East Troy, WI*	*Elkhorn, Walworth Co., WI*	MO	11/6/65	Brownsville, TX	Randolph Co., Cook Co., IL	1926, Chicago, IL	
Company I												
Bennett, John E.	Pvt	Delaware Co., NY	31	7/24/64	*Madison, WI*	*Madison, WI*	died (anasarca)	3/16/65	City Point Hospital, VA		1865, VA	
Ellis, John	Pvt	Knox Co., TN	20	8/30/64	*Dodgeville, WI*	*Dodgeville, Iowa Co., WI*	discharged	9/30/65	Ringgold Barracks, TX			

Twenty-Ninth Colored Infantry, Company I, continued

Last, First Name	Rank	Residence Before Service	Age	Enlist Date	Location	Credited To	Left Service	Date	Location	Residence After Service	Death Year and Place	Burial Place in WI
Qualls, William	Pvt	Clarksville, TN	18	8/21/64	Madison, WI	Hebron, Jefferson Co., WI	discharged	9/12/65	Brazos de Santiago, TX hospital			
Tilford, Richard	Pvt	Jefferson Co., KY	43 or 51	11/9/64	Madison, WI	Farmington, Jefferson Co., WI	discharged	10/12/65	hospital, Portsmouth, VA			
Washington, Henry	Pvt	Spotsylvania, VA	16	9/19/64	Madison, WI	Hampden, Columbia Co., WI	MO	11/6/65	Brownsville, TX			
Third USCI												
Brown, Daniel, Co. D	*Pvt*	*Philadelphia, PA*	*18*	*4/4/63*	*Philadelphia, PA*	*Philadelphia, PA*	*MO*	*10/31/65*	*Jacksonville, FL*	*Fond du Lac, WI*		
Seventeenth USCI												
Bostwick, Calvin, Co. K	*Pvt*	*Calumet Co., WI*	*16 to 18*	*2/2/65*	*Fond du Lac, WI*	*Alta, Fond du Lac Co., WI*	*discharged (term exp)*	*2/20/66*	*Nashville, TN*	*Calumet Co., WI*		
Brady, Michael, Co. F	*Cpl*	*MO; La Crosse, WI*	*29*	*3/2/65*	*La Crosse, WI*	*Campbell, La Crosse Co., WI*	*discharged (term exp)*	*3/3/66*	*Nashville, TN*	*La Crosse, WI; Prescott, WI; MO; MN*	*1920, Minneapolis, MN*	
Burden (Barden), Henry, Co. B	*Pvt*	*Petersburg, VA; Racine, WI*	*18*	*2/13/65*	*Milwaukee, WI*	*Racine, WI*	*discharged (term exp)*	*2/17/66*	*Nashville, TN*	*Milton Junction, Rock Co., WI; NE*	*1914, Dorchester, NE*	
Hustin (Heutson), Josephus, Co. F	*Pvt*	*Lewisburg, VA; Eagle, Waukesha Co., WI*	*38*	*8/19/64*	*Janesville, WI*	*Bradford, Rock Co., WI*	*discharged (term exp)*	*8/22/65*	*Nashville, TN*	*Eagle, Waukesha Co., WI; IA*	*1881, Iowa City, IA*	

Seventeenth USCI, continued

Last, First Name	Rank	Residence Before Service	Age	Enlist Date	Location	Credited To	Left Service	Date	Location	Residence After Service	Death Year and Place	Burial Place in WI
Jackson, John W., Co. F	Pvt	SC; La Crosse, WI	22	2/10/65	*La Crosse, WI*	*Trempealeau, Trempealeau Co., WI*	discharged (term exp)	2/14/66	Nashville, TN			
Lewis (Gilchrist), Alexander, Co. I	Pvt	TN; Racine, WI	25	9/17/64	*Milwaukee, WI*	*Racine, WI*	discharged (term exp)	9/18/65	Nashville, TN	*Racine, WI*	1893, Racine, WI	
McGraw, William, Co. H	Pvt	Lancaster Co., PA; Janesville, WI	35	2/11/65	Janesville, WI	*Janesville, WI*	discharged (term exp)	2/12/66	Nashville, TN	*Janesville, WI; Milton, WI; PA, DC, NJ*	1898, Atlantic City, NJ	
Morgan, Charles A., Co. F	Pvt	OH; Trimbelle, Pierce Co., WI	16	8/15/64	*Prescott, WI*	*Cottage Grove, Dane Co., WI*	MO (term exp)	9/29/65	Nashville, TN	*Trimbelle, Pierce Co., WI; Prescott, WI; Minneapolis, MN; West Superior, WI*	1897-98, WI	
Robertson, Peter, Co. F	Pvt	MO; WI	21	2/13/65	*La Crosse, WI*	*Stark, Vernon Co., WI*	discharged (term exp)	2/14/66	Nashville, TN			
Snider (Snyder), Anderson, Co. A	Pvt	Cape Girardeau, MO; Baraboo, WI	29	2/14/65	*La Crosse, WI*	*La Crosse, WI*	discharged (term exp)	2/19/66	Nashville, TN	*Black River Falls, WI; Sparta, WI; MN; IL; CO.; Ontario, Canada*	1913, Ontario, Canada	
Thompson (Thomas), George, Co. K	Pvt	Jefferson Co., KY; Janesville, WI	43	2/6/65	*Janesville, WI*	*Magnolia, Rock Co., WI*	transferred to Forty-Second WI Inf	5/3/65				

Last, First Name	Rank	Residence Before Service	Age	Enlist Date	Location	Credited To	Left Service	Date	Location	Residence After Service	Death Year and Place	Burial Place in WI
Valentine, John I., Co. I	Pvt	Stokes Co., NC; OH; Janesville, WI	42	2/14/65	Janesville, WI	Lima, Rock Co., WI	discharged (term exp)	1/16/66	Nashville, TN	Janesville, WI; Milton, WI; Waukesha, WI	1903, Waukesha, WI	Prairie Home Cemetery, Waukesha
Webb, Alexander, Co. D	Pvt	Princeton City, KY; Janesville, WI	35	2/11/65	Janesville, WI	Janesville, WI	transferred to Forty-Second WI Inf	5/4/65				
Woods, Henry, Co. B	Pvt	KY; WI	35	3/9/65	Milwaukee, WI	Wauwatosa, Milwaukee Co., WI	discharged (term exp)	3/10/66	Nashville, TN			
Young, David, Co. G	Pvt	GA; WI	44	8/30/64	Janesville, WI	Turtle, Rock Co., WI	discharged (term exp)	9/1/65	Nashville, TN	Evansville, WI		
Eighteenth USCI												
Bailey, Gabriel, Co. E	Pvt	OH; Johnson Creek, Jefferson Co., WI	45	8/15/64	Janesville, WI	Lake Mills, WI	discharged (term exp)	8/15/65	Chattanooga, TN			
Belforn (Belhorn), William, Co. H	Pvt	MS; WI	24	9/12/64	Milwaukee, WI	Milwaukee, WI	MO	2/2/66	Huntsville, AL	AR		
Bostwick (Bartrick), Gyrenus, Co. H	Pvt	Calumet Co., WI	18	9/5/64	Fond du Lac	West Bend, WI	discharged (term exp)	9/4/65	Chattanooga, TN	Calumet Co., WI; Oshkosh, WI	1925, Oshkosh, WI	Riverside Cemetery, Oshkosh

Last, First Name	Rank	Residence Before Service	Age	Enlist Date	Location	Credited To	Left Service	Date	Location	Residence After Service	Death Year and Place	Burial Place in WI
Brown, Louis, Co. H	Pvt	*MO; WI*	18	9/7/64	*Janesville, WI*	*Portage, WI*	discharged (term exp)	9/6/65	Chattanooga, TN	*Salem, Kenosha Co., WI; Green Bay, WI; Fond du Lac, WI; Beloit, WI; MN; Milwaukee Soldiers Home; IL*	1929, Soldiers Home, Danville, IL	
Brown, William, Co. I	Cpl	*GA; WI*	18	9/26/64	*Janesville, WI*	*Blue Mounds, Dane Co., WI*	MO	2/21/66	Huntsville, AL			
Calup, Samuel, Co. F	Pvt	*VA; WI*	17	8/25/64	*Janesville, WI*	*Jefferson, WI*	discharged (term exp)	8/24/65	Chattanooga, TN			
Campbell, William, Co. H	Cpl	*born WI or MS; WI*	18	9/15/64	*Milwaukee, WI*	*Milwaukee, WI*	MO	2/21/66	Huntsville, AL	NE		
Dandridge, Clayborn, (Maiborn), Co. F	Pvt	*VA; WI*	18	8/20/64	*Janesville, WI*	*Janesville, WI*	MO	2/21/66	Huntsville, AL			
Davis, John, Co. F	Sgt	*Burlington TN; Rock Co., WI*	27	8/17/64	*Janesville, WI*	*Union, Rock Co., WI*	MO (term exp)	8/16/65	Chattanooga, TN	*Union, Rock Co., WI; Quincy, IL*		
Davis, Nelson, Co. F	Pvt	*IL; WI*	36	8/25/64	*Milwaukee, WI*	*Milwaukee, WI*	MO	2/21/66	Huntsville, AL			
Farson (Fa(e)rrison, Samuel, Co. E	Pvt	*TN; WI*	18	8/15/64	*Janesville, WI*	*Lake Mills, WI*	MO (term exp)	8/15/65	Chattanooga, TN	*IL; Dodge Co., WI*		
Fielding, John, Co. F	Pvt	*TN or VA; WI*	18	8/19/64	*La Crosse, WI*	*Greenfield, Monroe Co., WI*	died (chronic rheumatism)	8/15/65	hospital, Chattanooga, TN		1865, Chattanooga, TN	

Last, First Name	Rank	Residence Before Service	Age	Enlist Date	Location	Credited To	Left Service	Date	Location	Residence After Service	Death Year and Place	Burial Place in WI
Fitzpatrick, Andrew, Co. E	Pvt	AL; WI	23	8/26/64	Milwaukee, WI	Milwaukee, WI	deserted	8/5/64	Benton Barracks, MO			
Foster, Archy, Co. H	Pvt	TN; WI	18	8/15/64	Janesville, WI	Bradford, Rock Co., WI	discharged (per telegram)	6/12/65	Chattanooga, TN	Rolla, MO; KS	1905, KS	
Franklin, Benjamin, Co. E	Pvt	KY; WI	16	8/15/64	Janesville, WI	Janesville, WI	deserted	12/11/64	Bridgeport, AL			
Gilum (Gillum, Gillem), John, Co. F	Pvt	VA	25	8/24/64	Milwaukee, WI	Whitewater, Walworth Co., WI	died (typhoid)	12/13/64	hospital, Chattanooga, TN		1864, Chattanooga, TN	
Glaspy (Glasspy), Frank, Co. D	Pvt	MS; WI	18	8/4/64	La Crosse, WI	La Crosse, WI	MO	2/21/66	Huntsville, AL			
Goos(e)berry (Goolsberry), Henry, Co. E	Cpl	MS; WI (Waterloo?)	16	8/13/64	Janesville, WI	Janesville, WI	died (chronic diarrhea)	1/6/65	hospital, Nashville, TN		1865, Nashville, TN	
Graham, Robert, Co. I	Pvt	Nashville, TN (kidnapped to Milwaukee, WI)	21	8/26/64	Milwaukee, WI	Manitowoc, WI	deserted/ kidnapped	11/28/64	Nashville, TN	Nashville, TN		
Harris, John, Co. E	Cpl	GA; WI	25	8/15/64	Milwaukee, WI	Milwaukee, WI	MO	2/21/66	Huntsville, AL			
Hayes, John, Co. I	Pvt	AL; WI	20	8/26/64	Milwaukee, WI	Milwaukee, WI	deserted	10/5/64	Benton Barracks, MO			

Last, First Name	Rank	Residence Before Service	Age	Enlist Date	Location	Credited To	Left Service	Date	Location	Residence After Service	Death Year and Place	Burial Place in WI
Hill, Jackson, Co. D	Pvt	Columbus IN; IL; Ripon, WI	18	8/2/64	La Crosse, WI	La Crosse, WI	discharged	5/2/65	Marine hospital, St. Louis, MO	Fond du Lac, WI; Milwaukee Soldiers Home	1893, Milwaukee Soldiers Home	Wood National Cemetery, Milwaukee Co.
Hudson, Caleb (Taylor; Tom), Co. D	Pvt	Garrett Co., KY; La Crosse, WI	22	8/2/64	La Crosse, WI	La Crosse, WI	MO (term exp)	8/4/65	Chattanooga, TN	KY: Buffalo Soldier; TN;TX; LA; AR; Melvin, OK	1917, OK	
Hunter (Hunt), Henry, Co. H	Pvt	MS; WI	20	9/12/64	Milwaukee, WI	Milwaukee, WI	deserted/ escaped	9/14/65	guard house, Chattanooga, TN			
Jantry (Jentry, Gentry), Edward, Co. E	Pvt	AR; WI	27	8/15/64	Milwaukee, WI	Milwaukee, WI	MO	2/21/66	Huntsville, AL			
Johnson, Henry Loyd, Co. D	Pvt	MO; WI	18	8/8/64	Milwaukee, WI	Milwaukee, WI	MO	2/21/66	Huntsville, AL			
Johnson, John, Co. K	Pvt	Natchez, MS	25	9/21/64	St. Louis, MO	Cattaraugus Co., NY	MO	2/21/66	Huntsville, AL	La Crosse, WI		
Jones, John, Co. F	Pvt	born VA or WI; WI	18	8/24/64	Janesville, WI	Madison, WI	MO	2/21/66	Huntsville, AL			
Kane, Dick, Co. I	Pvt	Nashville (kidnapped to Milwaukee, WI)	21	8/26/64	Milwaukee, WI	Milwaukee, WI	deserted/ kidnapped	11/29/64	Nashville, TN	Nashville, TN		
Kimball, Frank, Co. D	Pvt	Cincinnati OH; La Crosse, WI	20	8/3/64	La Crosse, WI	La Crosse, WI	MO	2/21/66	Huntsville, AL			

Last, First Name	Rank	Residence Before Service	Age	Enlist Date	Location	Credited To	Left Service	Date	Location	Residence After Service	Death Year and Place	Burial Place in WI
Mabin, Edmund, Co. F	First Sgt	NC; WI	19	8/24/64	Milwaukee, WI	Lake, Milwaukee Co., WI	MO	2/21/66	Huntsville, AL			
Madingly, Bob, Co. D	Pvt	Nelson Co., KY; Hubbard, Dodge Co., WI	24	8/2/64	Fond du Lac, WI	Williamstown, Dodge Co., WI	MO (term exp)	8/4/65	Chattanooga, TN			
Malone, James, Co. D	Pvt	AL; WI	30	8/8/64	Milwaukee, WI	Milwaukee, WI	MO	2/21/66	Huntsville, AL			
Marks, Albert, Co. F	Sgt	TN; WI	29	8/26/64	Milwaukee, WI	Milwaukee, WI	deserted	11/4/64	hospital, St. Louis, MO			
Monroe, Alfred, Co. H	Pvt	NY; Bristol, Kenosha Co., WI	25	8/27/64	Milwaukee, WI	Milwaukee, WI	MO	2/21/66	Huntsville, AL			
Moore (More), Aaron, Co. I	Pvt	AL; WI	18	8/26/64	Milwaukee, WI	Whitewater, Walworth Co., WI	deserted	11/29/64	Nashville, TN			
Nelson, Jacob, Co. F	Pvt	TN	16	8/17/64	Janesville, WI	Union, Rock Co., WI	MO (term exp)	8/16/65	Chattanooga, TN			
Nelson, Moses, Co. I	Pvt	Rutherford Co., TN; Janesville, WI	18	8/6/64	Janesville, WI	Beloit, WI	MO (term exp)	8/5/65	Chattanooga, TN	Beloit, WI; Buffalo Soldier; AR; KS	1920, Leavenworth, KS	
Nelson, Thomas, Co. F	Cpl	AL; WI	26	8/17/64	Janesville, WI	Union, Rock Co., WI	MO (term exp)	8/16/65	Chattanooga, TN	Evansville, WI; Union, Rock Co., WI; MI; Prairie du Chien, WI; IL	1911, IL	
Newton, Isaac, Co. I	Pvt	TN; WI	27	9/21/64	Milwaukee, WI	Milwaukee, WI	deserted	10/6/64	Benton Barracks, MO			

Last, First Name	Rank	Residence Before Service	Age	Enlist Date	Location	Credited To	Left Service	Date	Location	Residence After Service	Death Year and Place	Burial Place in WI
Olmstead, James, Co. H	Pvt	VA; Ripon, WI	19	8/30/64	Fond du Lac, WI	Ripon, WI	MO (term exp)	8/29/65	Chattanooga, TN	Ripon, WI		
Ousley (Onsley), William, Co. F	Cpl	KY; Darien, Walworth Co., WI	27	8/17/64	Janesville, WI	Union, Rock Co., WI	MO (term exp)	8/16/65	Chattanooga, TN	Evansville, WI; Cedar Rapids, IA	1899, Marshalltown, IA	
Paine, Will, Co. I	Pvt	Nashville, TN (kidnapped to Milwaukee, WI)	20	8/26/64	Milwaukee, WI	Milwaukee, WI	deserted/ kidnapped	11/28/64	Nashville, TN	Nashville, TN		
Parsons, Peter, Co. I	Pvt	Canada or Pike Co., MO; Milwaukee, WI	19	9/20/64	Milwaukee, WI	Milwaukee, WI	discharged (disability)	5/30/65	Chattanooga, TN	Madison, WI; Quincy, IL	1915, Quincy, IL	
Reed, James, Co. I	Cpl	KY; WI	17	8/2/64	Janesville, WI	Beloit, WI	MO (term exp)	8/4/65	Chattanooga, TN			
Richmond, James, Co. F	Pvt	Jefferson Co., MO; WI	18	8/9/64	La Crosse, WI	Hudson, WI	MO (term exp)	8/8/65	Chattanooga, TN			
Robnett, John, Co. H	Pvt	AL; WI	18	9/10/64	Milwaukee, WI	Milwaukee, WI	died (chronic diarrhea)	2/29/65	Wilson, General Hospital, Nashville, TN		1865, Nashville, TN	
Ron, John, Co. D	Pvt	AL; La Crosse, WI	24	8/2/64	La Crosse, WI	La Crosse, WI	died (gunshot wound to abdomen)	2/11/65	post hospital, Huntsville, AL		1866, Huntsville, AL	
Sercy, Robert, Co. F	Pvt	TN; WI	18	8/25/64	Janesville, WI	Jefferson, WI	MO (term exp)	8/24/65	Chattanooga, TN	Fond du Lac, WI		

Eighteenth USCI, continued

Last, First Name	Rank	Residence Before Service	Age	Enlist Date	Location	Credited To	Left Service	Date	Location	Residence After Service	Death Year and Place	Burial Place in WI
Sheldon (Shelton), Shepard, Co. D	Cpl	*Giles Co., TN; Ripon, WI*	21	8/2/64	*La Crosse, WI*	*La Crosse, WI*	MO (term exp)	8/4/65	Chattanooga, TN	St. Louis, MO; Mexico; NM; Denver, CO.; Muskogee, OK	1909, Muskogee, OK	
Smith, General W., Co. H (also Sixth USCI)	Pvt	*KY; WI (Boscobel?)*	18	8/30/64	*Janesville, WI*	*Sun Prairie, WI*	died (congestive fever)	3/25/65	Chattanooga, TN		1865, Chattanooga, TN	
Spite, Thomas, Co. H	Pvt	*Jackson Co., MS or MO; WI*	18	8/26/64	*La Crosse, WI*	*Hudson, WI*	MO (term exp)	8/25/65	Chattanooga, TN	Hudson, WI		
Strothers, John, Co. I	Cpl	*VA; WI*	18	8/6/64	*Janesville, WI*	*Beloit, WI*	MO (term exp)	8/5/65	Chattanooga, TN	Beloit, WI	1927, South Beloit, IL	Oakwood Cemetery, Beloit
Thomas (Dabney), Peter D., Co. H	Pvt	*Tiptonville, TN; Rock Co., WI*	18	8/2/64	*Janesville, WI*	*Beloit, WI*	discharged (term exp)	8/5/65	Chattanooga, TN	Rock Co., WI; Chicago, IL; Racine, WI	1925, Racine, WI	Mound Cemetery, Racine Co.
Turner, Anthony, Co. F	Cpl	*KY; WI*	18	8/26/64	*Janesville, WI*	*Lima, Rock Co., WI*	died (typho-malarial fever)	2/3/66	post hospital, Huntsville, AL			
Turner, William, Co. H	Pvt	*KY or MS; WI*	25	9/12/64	*Milwaukee, WI*	*Milwaukee, WI*	discharged	5/29/65	Chattanooga, TN	Memphis, TN		
Van Buren, Edward Martin, Co. D	Cpl	*Stockland, IN; WI*	22	8/5/64	*La Crosse, WI*	*La Crosse, WI*	MO	2/21/66	Huntsville, AL			
Warner, Joseph, Co. H	Pvt	*MS or SC; WI*	21	9/9/64	*Milwaukee, WI*	*Milwaukee, WI*	MO	2/21/66	Huntsville, AL			

Eighteenth USCI, continued

Last, First Name	Rank	Residence Before Service	Age	Enlist Date	Location	Credited To	Left Service	Date	Location	Residence After Service	Death Year and Place	Burial Place in WI
Washington, Joseph, Co. F	Pvt	WI	18	8/23/64	La Crosse, WI	Hudson, WI	died	6/8/65	regimental hospital, Chattanooga, TN		1865, Chattanooga, TN	
White, William, Co. D	Pvt	VA; WI	40	8/3/64	La Crosse, WI	La Crosse, WI	discharged (disability)	1/15/66	Chattanooga, TN			
Wilkinson, Godfrey, Co. I	Pvt	NC; MS; WI	26	8/26/64	Milwaukee, WI	Milwaukee, WI	deserted	11/22/64	Benton Barracks, MO			
Williams(on), Lamus (Samus, Labner), Co. H	Pvt	MS; WI	25	9/12/64	Milwaukee, WI	Milwaukee, WI	MO	2/21/66	Huntsville, AL			
Williamson, Peter, Co. D	Pvt	MO; WI	22	7/28/64	La Crosse, WI	La Crosse, WI	MO	2/21/66	Huntsville, AL			
Willis, Anthony, no Co.	Pvt	VA; MN	44	6/5/64	Rochester, MN	Louisville, Scott Co., MN	MO	5/11/65	Fort Snelling, MN	MN; Prescott, WI		Pine Glen Cemetery, Prescott
Willis, Thomas, Co. G	Pvt	Waterford, MS; MN	18	8/23/64	Shakopee, MN	Shakopee, Scott Co., MN	MO (term exp)	8/15/65	Chattanooga, TN	Prescott, WI; Hastings, MN	1896, Hastings, MN	Pine Glen Cemetery, Prescott
Wilson, Washington, Co. D	Sgt	St. Charles MO; La Crosse, WI	18	8/1/64	La Crosse, WI	La Crosse, WI	MO	2/21/66	Huntsville, AL	Chicago, IL	1914, Charleston, OH	
Winn, Jacob, Co. D	Sgt	TN; WI	18	8/3/64	Fond du Lac, WI	Sheboygan Falls, WI	MO (term exp)	8/4/65	Chattanooga, TN			

Last, First Name	Rank	Residence Before Service	Age	Enlist Date	Location	Credited To	Left Service	Date	Location	Residence After Service	Death Year and Place	Burial Place in WI
Winn, William, Co. D	Cpl	TN; Ralls Co., MO; WI	18	8/3/64	Fond du Lac, WI	Sheboygan Falls, WI	MO (term exp)	8/4/65	Chattanooga, TN			
Twentieth USCI												
Moore, Barney, Co. B	Pvt	NY	32	1/14/64	Thirty-First district, NY	Thirty-First district, NY	MO	10/7/65	New Orleans, LA	Oswego, NY; Chicago, IL; Delavan, WI	1916, Delavan, WI	Spring Grove Cemetery, Delavan
Twenty-First USCI												
Wright, Cuffee, Co. H	Pvt	SC	18	9/2/64	Hilton Head, SC	Milwaukee, WI	died	4/10/65	Mt. Pleasant, SC		1865, SC	
Twenty-Third USCI												
Dix (Diggs), Anthony, Co. I	Pvt	Racine, WI	31	5/13/64	Greenfield, MA	Deerfield, MA	died (KIA)	7/30/64	Petersburg, VA		1864, Petersburg, VA	
Thirty-First USCI												
Artis, Horace, Co. F	Pvt	VA; DC	24	8/15/64	Washington, DC	Fourth congressional district, OH	MO	11/7/65	Brownsville, TX	Appleton, WI	1910, Appleton, WI	Riverside Cemetery, Appleton
Thirty-Second USCI												
Miles, John J., Co. I	Cpl	VA; PA	18	2/10/64	Lancaster, PA	Ninth congressional district, PA	MO	8/22/65	Hilton Head, SC	Chicago, IL; Milwaukee, WI	1926, Milwaukee, WI	Forest Home Cemetery, Milwaukee Co.

Last, First Name	Rank	Residence Before Service	Age	Enlist Date	Location	Credited To	Left Service	Date	Location	Residence After Service	Death Year and Place	Burial Place in WI
Grimes, Thomas, Co. H	Pvt	St. Francis Co., MO; Beetown, Grant Co., WI	23	8/30/64	Prairie du Chien, WI	Dodgeville, Iowa Co., WI	MO	6/28/65	St. Louis, MO	Beetown, Grant Co., WI	1910, Beetown, WI	Pleasant Ridge Cemetery, Beetown
Thompson (Thomas), George, Co. I	Pvt			5/3/65	transferred from Seventeenth USCI		MO	1/31/66	Huntsville, AL			
Webb, Alexander, Co. I	Pvt			5/4/65	transferred from Seventeenth USCI		MO	1/21/66	Huntsville, AL			
Forty-Third USCI												
Field, Alexander, Co. F	Pvt	Christian Co., KY	20	7/22/64	Boston, MA	Roxbury, MA	MO	10/20/65	Brownsville, TX	Sharon, Walworth Co., WI	1909, Walworth Co., WI	Oakwood Cemetery, Sharon
Forty-Seventh USCI												
Walter, Wesley, Co. A	Pvt	NC; Trenton, Dodge Co., WI	18	7/25/64	Fond du Lac, WI	Trenton, Dodge Co., WI	MO	1/15/66	Baton Rouge, LA	Beaver Dam, WI; Chicago, IL; Fox Lake, WI; Milwaukee Soldiers Home	1913, Milwaukee, WI	Wood National Cemetery, Milwaukee Co.
Hart, George, Co. A	Pvt	Canada; WI	29	7/29/64	Milwaukee, WI	Seventh ward, Milwaukee, WI	died (disease)	3/16/65	Blakeley, AL		1865, AL	
Forty-Ninth USCI												
Adams, Daniel B., Co. F	Pvt	MO; WI	26	9/26/64	Milwaukee, WI	Delafield, WI	discharged (disability)	2/23/65	Vicksburg, MS			

Last, First Name	Rank	Residence Before Service	Age	Enlist Date	Location	Credited To	Left Service	Date	Location	Residence After Service	Death Year and Place	Burial Place in WI
Andrews (Anderson), Elisha, Co. K	Pvt	KY; WI	28	9/14/64	Milwaukee, WI	Third ward, Racine, WI	died (pneumonia)	1/1/65	Vicksburg, MS		1865, Vicksburg, MS	
Anthony, Mark, Co. K	Cpl	Madison Co., AR; WI	19 /29	9/2/64	Janesville, WI	Blooming Grove, Dane Co., WI	discharged	7/7/65	Vicksburg, MS	Madison, WI; KS; CA	1908, Los Angeles, CA	
Barber (Barbour), Elijah, Co. F	Pvt	TN; WI	18	9/3/64	Janesville, WI	La Prairie, Rock Co., WI	discharged (term exp)	9/2/65	Vicksburg, MS			
Bradick, Richard, Co. I	Pvt	KY; Bellevue, Brown Co., WI	34	1/31/65	Janesville, WI	Center, Rock Co., WI	MO (term exp)	1/30/66	Vicksburg, MS	Janesville, WI; IN		
Burel (Burrell), Edmund, Co. F	Pvt	TN; WI	34	9/27/64	Milwaukee, WI	Waukesha, WI	discharged (disability)	2/18/65	Vicksburg, MS			
Chapman, Charles, Co. F	Pvt	NC; WI	29	10/1/64	Milwaukee, WI	Fourth ward, Milwaukee, WI	discharged (term exp)	9/30/65	Vicksburg, MS			
Elliot, William H. B., Co. F	Pvt	IN; WI	40	10/7/64	Janesville, WI	Decorra, Columbia Co., WI	MO (term exp)	10/6/65	Vicksburg, MS			
Fields, John, Co. H	Pvt	TN; WI	18	10/13/64	Janesville, WI	Pacific, Columbia Co., WI	deserted	3/13/65	Vicksburg, MS			
Foster, Edward, Co. K	Pvt	TN; WI	18	8/27/64	Fond du Lac, WI	Second ward, Ripon, WI	died (consumption)	5/21/65	regimental hospital, Vicksburg, MS		1865, Vicksburg, MS	

Forty-Ninth USCI, continued

Last, First Name	Rank	Residence Before Service	Age	Enlist Date	Location	Credited To	Left Service	Date	Location	Residence After Service	Death Year and Place	Burial Place in WI
Foster, Westley, Co. H	Cpl	OH; WI (possibly Dunkirk, Dane Co., WI)	18	12/17/64	*Green Bay, WI*	*Douglas, Marquette Co., WI*	MO (term exp)	12/16/65	Vicksburg, MS			
Freeman, Harrison, Co. K	Pvt	VA; Milwaukee, WI; Racine, WI	44	9/14/64	*Milwaukee, WI*	*Third ward, Racine, WI*	MO	3/22/66	Vicksburg, MS			
Greene, Lewis, Co. K	Pvt	MO; WI	18	8/27/64	*Fond du Lac, WI*	*Second ward, Ripon, WI*	died	1/5/65	regimental hospital, Vicksburg, MS		1865, Vicksburg, MS	
Hall, Edward, Co. K	Cpl	Middletown, PA; Ripon, WI	19	8/27/64	*Fond du Lac, WI*	*Second ward Ripon, WI*	discharged (term exp)	7/7/65	Vicksburg, MS	*Ripon, WI; Oshkosh, WI; Chicago, IL*		
Hamlet, Albert, Co. K	Pvt	MS; Grant Co., WI	25	8/31/64	*Prairie du Chien, WI*	*Lancaster, Grant Co., WI*	discharged (term exp)	7/7/65	Vicksburg, MS	*Lancaster, WI*	1871, Grant Co., WI	
Hicks, Iverson, Co. H	Pvt	KY; WI	28	12/15/64	*Green Bay, WI; Fond du Lac, WI*	*Eldorado, Fond du Lac Co., WI*	died (smallpox)	2/14/65	Vicksburg, MS		1865, Vicksburg, MS	
Hines, Charles Marion, Co. F	Cpl	Randolph Co., AR; Cape Girardeau, MO; La Crosse, WI	21	8/2/64	*La Crosse, WI*	*Fourth ward La Crosse, WI*	MO (term exp)	8/1/65	Vicksburg, MS	Cape Girardeau, MO	1899, location unknown	
Hunt, Charles, Co. K	Pvt	Montgomery Co., TN; Sharon, Walworth Co., WI	38	9/6/64	*Milwaukee, WI*	*Sharon, Walworth Co., WI*	discharged (term exp)	7/7/65	Vicksburg, MS	*Sharon, Walworth Co., WI; Marion Co., IL*	1888, Marion Co., IL	

Last, First Name	Rank	Residence Before Service	Age	Enlist Date	Location	Credited To	Left Service	Date	Location	Residence After Service	Death Year and Place	Burial Place in WI
Ironmonger (Jackson), Leroy, Co. K	Cpl	Green Co., TN; Westfield, Sauk Co., WI; Grant Co., WI	22	8/29/64	Prairie du Chien, WI	Glen Haven, Grant Co., WI	discharged (term exp)	7/1/65	Vicksburg, MS	St Louis, MO; IL	1926, Louisiana, MO	
Johnson, Josephus, Co. I	Pvt	KY; WI	18	11/28/64	Green Bay, WI	Matteson, Waupaca Co., WI	MO (term exp)	11/27/65	Vicksburg, MS			
Jones, William, Co. D	Pvt	VA; WI	23	10/10/64	Green Bay, WI	Hortonia, Outagamie Co., WI	MO (term exp)	10/9/65	Yazoo City, MS	Madison, WI; New London, WI; DC	1921, Washington, DC	
Lewis, Charles, Co. F	Sgt	New Orleans, LA; WI	19	9/3/64	Green Bay, WI	New Holstein, Calumet Co., WI	MO (term exp)	9/2/65	Vicksburg, MS			
Lockhart, Brown, Co. F	Pvt	NC; Grant Co., WI	20	10/5/64	Prairie du Chien, WI	Beetown, Grant Co., WI	MO (term exp)	10/5/65	Vicksburg, MS			
Milum (Milan), Albert, Co. K	Pvt	Lawrence Co., AL; Darien, Walworth Co., WI	25	8/19/64	Janesville, WI	Lima, Rock Co., WI	died (small pox)	5/17/65	post hospital, Vicksburg, MS,		1865, Vicksburg, MS	
Morgan, Ebenezer, Co. K	Pvt	NY; Stockbridge, WI; Rosendale, WI	29	8/27/64	Fond du Lac, WI	Fourth ward Fond du Lac, WI	discharged (term exp)	7/1/65	Vicksburg, MS	Rosendale, WI; Stockbridge, WI; Fond du Lac, WI	1893, Fond du Lac, WI	Rienzi Cemetery, Fond du Lac
Newman, Basil (Bazile), Co. K	Pvt	Harrison Co., VA; Racine, WI	44	9/1/64	Milwaukee, WI	Racine, WI	discharged (disability)	6/26/65	Vicksburg, MS	Milwaukee, WI; Racine, WI; IL, IN, MI	1881, Chicago, IL	

Last, First Name	Rank	Residence Before Service	Age	Enlist Date	Location	Credited To	Left Service	Date	Location	Residence After Service	Death Year and Place	Burial Place in WI
Richards, Freeman, Co. K	Cpl	*NY; Brothertown, Calumet Co., WI*	39	8/27/64	*Fond du Lac, WI*	*Fourth ward Fond du Lac, WI*	discharged	7/7/65	Vicksburg, MS	*Calumet Co., WI*	1866, Ontonagon, MI	
Robinson, John, Co. H	Pvt	*VA; WI*	19	10/28/64	*Milwaukee, WI*	*Oconomowoc, Waukesha Co., WI*	discharged (term exp)	10/24/65	Vicksburg, MS			
Shur (Sheer), Levi A. (Lemuel), Co. F	Pvt	*AL; WI*	30	9/2/64	*Fond du Lac, WI*	*Alto, Fond du Lac Co., WI*	MO (term exp)	9/1/65	Vicksburg, MS			
Smith, John, Co. C	Pvt	*MS; WI*	21	11/26/64	*Fond du Lac, WI*	*Lima, Sheboygan Co., WI*	deserted	8/1/65	Yazoo City, MS			
Smith, John (Burton, Richard), Co. I	Pvt	*MO; Bradford Rock Co., WI*	25	11/14/64	*Fond du Lac, WI*	*Rohm (Rhine), Sheboygan Co., WI*	MO (term exp)	11/14/65	Vicksburg, MS	*Janesville, WI; Albany, WI; Brodhead, WI; Delavan, WI; Beloit, WI*	1916, Beloit, WI	Oakwood Cemetery, Beloit
Smith, Martin, Co. F	Pvt	*VA; Milwaukee, WI*	46	10/3/64	*Milwaukee, WI*	*Second ward Milwaukee, WI*	MO	6/24/65	regimental hospital, Vicksburg, MS	*Milwaukee, WI*	possibly 1874, Milwaukee, WI	
Taylor, Chesley A., Co. F	Pvt	*MS; Grant Co., WI*	24 to 27	10/6/64	*Prairie du Chien*	*Beetown, Grant Co., WI*	MO (term exp)	10/5/65	Vicksburg, MS	*Bloomington, Grant Co., WI; IA*	1905, Quincy, IL Soldiers Home	
Taylor, Enoch, Co. F	Cpl	*Hines Co., MS; Rock Co., WI*	20	9/2/64	*Janesville, WI*	*La Prairie, Rock Co., WI*	MO (term exp)	9/1/65	Vicksburg, MS	*Janesville, WI; MI*	1920, Detroit, MI	Oak Hill Cemetery, Janesville

Forty-Ninth USCI, continued

Last, First Name	Rank	Residence Before Service	Age	Enlist Date	Location	Credited To	Left Service	Date	Location	Residence After Service	Death Year and Place	Burial Place in WI
Taylor, Jerry, Co. F	Pvt	VA; Grant Co., WI	33	8/31/64	Prairie du Chien, WI	Lancaster, Grant Co., WI	MO	6/24/65	regimental hospital, Vicksburg, MS	Clinton, IA	1905, Clinton, IA	
Taylor, John, Co. I	Pvt	MO; Grant Co., WI	19	10/24/64	Prairie du Chien, WI	Beetown, Grant Co., WI	discharged (term exp)	10/23/65	Vicksburg, MS			
Tillman, Abraham, Co. F	Pvt	TN; WI	20	8/24/64	Milwaukee, WI	Sharon, Walworth Co., WI	MO	3/22/66	Vicksburg, MS			
Warren, James, Co. D	Pvt	MD; WI	24	10/5/64	Prairie du Chien, WI	Wilson, Richland Co., WI	MO	10/4/65	Vicksburg, MS			
Washington, George, Co. F	Pvt	TN; WI	45	9/14/64	Milwaukee, WI	Third ward Racine, WI	MO	6/24/65	regimental hospital, Vicksburg, MS			
Williams, John, Co. F	Pvt	VA; Patch Grove, Grant Co., WI	24	9/1/64	Prairie du Chien, WI	Mifflin, Iowa Co., WI	died (dysentery)	6/23/65	Yazoo City, MS		1865, Yazoo City MS	
Williams, Nathan, Co. H	Pvt	TN; WI	38	11/18/64	Milwaukee, WI	Pewaukee, Waukesha Co., WI	discharged (term exp)	11/12/65	Vicksburg, MS			
Wilson, Joseph, Co. C	Pvt	Canada; WI	19	12/24/64	Milwaukee, WI	Summitt, Waukesha Co., WI	died (disease)	6/29/65	regimental hospital, Vicksburg, MS		1865, Vicksburg, MS	
Fiftieth USCI												
Davis, Jeff, Co. E	Pvt	Richmond, VA; MS	18	9/9/64	Vicksburg, MS	Oakland, Jefferson Co., WI	died (disease)	12/22/64	hospital, Vicksburg, MS		1864, Vicksburg, MS	

Fiftieth USCI, continued

Last, First Name	Rank	Residence Before Service	Age	Enlist Date	Location	Credited To	Left Service	Date	Location	Residence After Service	Death Year and Place	Burial Place in WI
Ford, Henry, Co. K	Pvt	Milliken's Bend, LA: *Rock Co., WI*	37	8/19/64	*Janesville, WI*	*Johnstown, Rock Co., WI*	discharged (term exp)	8/19/65	Vicksburg, MS			
Shepard, Charles, Co. K	Pvt	Fauquier Co., VA; *Beetown, Grant Co., WI*	42	8/30/64	*Prairie du Chien*	*Dodgeville, Iowa Co., WI*	died (anemia)	8/26/65	hospital, Vicksburg, MS		1865, Vicksburg, MS	
Fifty-Fourth Massachusetts Vol Infantry												
Lee, Arthur B., Co. A	Sgt	Charleston SC; MA	29	2/13/63	Boston, MA		MO	8/20/65	Charleston, SC	*MO, IL; Janesville, WI; Milton, WI; Madison, WI; WI; Milton, WI*	1905, Milton, WI	Milton Cemetery, Rock Co.
Tucker, John, Co. F	Pvt	OH or IN; *Racine, WI*	21	4/8/63	Readville, MA		deserted	7/21/65	Charleston, SC			
Fifty-Fifth Massachusetts Vol Infantry												
Bowdry, William, Co. B	Pvt	*Milwaukee, WI; Prairie du Chien, WI*	24	6/15/63			discharged (disability)	7/16/65	Beaufort Island, SC	*Milwaukee, WI*		
Caldwell, William, Co. B	Pvt	Milwaukee, WI	38	6/15/63			discharged (disability)	7/28/64	Folly Island, SC	*Milwaukee, WI*		
Cross, David, Co. K	Pvt	*Waukesha, WI; Oconomowoc, WI; Janesville, WI*	18	6/11/63		*Oconomowoc, WI*	MO	8/29/65	Charleston, SC	*Oconomowoc, WI; MO; Cairo, IL*	1911, location unknown	

Fifty-Fifth Massachusetts Vol Infantry, continued

Last, First Name	Rank	Residence Before Service	Age	Enlist Date	Location	Credited To	Left Service	Date	Location	Residence After Service	Death Year and Place	Burial Place in WI
Cross, Edwin, Co. K	Pvt	Oconomowoc, WI; Janesville, WI	19	6/16/63			MO	8/29/65	Charleston, SC	Oconomowoc, WI		
Diggs, Edward, Co. D	Pvt	Hagerstown, MD; Racine, WI; Caledonia, WI	18	5/23/63	Readville, MA	Racine, WI	POW or MIA	12/18/63	Sandy Hook, VA or NC		unknown (MIA)	
Dodge, Henry, Co. H	Pvt	Mineral Point, WI	20			Mineral Point, WI	MO	8/29/65	Charleston, SC	Mineral Point, WI; St. Louis, MO	1901, MO	
Golden, Augustus H., Co. B	Sgt	Milwaukee, WI	41	6/15/63	Readville, MA		MO	8/29/65	Charleston, SC	Milwaukee, WI		
Sutfen, John, Co. B (F & S)	Pvt	NY or Milwaukee, WI; Eagle, Waukesha Co, WI	23	6/15/63	Boston, MA		MO	8/29/65	Charleston, SC	Milwaukee, WI; Portage, WI; Omaha, NE; Milwaukee Soldiers Home; Council Bluffs, IA	1920, Council Bluffs, IA	
Thomas, Richard, Co. I	Pvt	KY; Evansville, WI	23	6/23/64	Boston, MA	Roxbury, MA	discharged	9/1/65	hospital, New York City, NY	Evansville, WI; Brodhead, Monroe, WI (Green Co. Poor House)	1866, Monroe, WI	Green Co. Poor House (unmarked)

Last, First Name	Rank	Residence Before Service	Age	Enlist Date	Location	Credited To	Left Service	Date	Location	Residence After Service	Death Year and Place	Burial Place in WI
Fifty-Fifth USCI												
Newsom, David, Co. A	teamster	Northampton Co., NC, MS	44	5/1/63	Corinth, MS	none stated	MO	12/31/65	Baton Rouge, LA	*Fond du Lac, WI*		
Patterson, Alfred, Co. I	Pvt	Lawrence Co., AL; MS	28	2/1/63	Corinth, MS	none stated	MO	12/31/65	Baton Rouge, LA	*Fond du Lac, WI; Chicago, IL; MI; Milwaukee Soldiers Home*	*1915, Milwaukee, WI*	Wood National Cemetery, Milwaukee Co.
Sixty-Fifth USCI												
Allen John, Co. C	Pvt			8/15/65	transferred from Sixty-Seventh USCI 8/65		MO	1/8/67	Baton Rouge, LA	*Madison, WI; IL, IA, MO, KS*	1917, Johnson Co., KS	
Battice (Battis), John, Co. D	Pvt			8/25/65	transferred from Sixty-Seventh USCI 8/65		discharged (term exp)	8/31/65	Baton Rouge, LA	*Fairwater, Fond du Lac Co., WI; Milwaukee Soldiers Home*	*1901, Milwaukee, WI*	Wood National Cemetery, Milwaukee Co.
Jenkins, Jerard C., Co. C	Sgt Maj			8/15/65	transferred from Sixty-Seventh USCI 8/65		discharged (term exp)	2/24/66	New Orleans, LA			
Kneley (Kneeley), William, Co. C	Pvt			8/15/65	transferred from Sixty-Seventh USCI 8/65		died (consumption)	4/4/66	Baton Rouge, LA		1866, Baton Rouge, LA	

Last, First Name	Rank	Residence Before Service	Age	Enlist Date	Location	Credited To	Left Service	Date	Location	Residence After Service	Death Year and Place	Burial Place in WI
Primess, Stephen, Co. D	Pvt			8/15/65	transferred from Sixty-Seventh USCI 8/65		discharged (term exp)	9/28/65	Baton Rouge, LA			
Rankin, Edward, Co. E	Pvt			8/15/65	transferred from Sixty-Seventh USCI 8/65		discharged (term exp)	9/21/65	Baton Rouge, LA			
Thompson, William, Co. C	Pvt			8/15/65	transferred from Sixty-Seventh USCI 8/65		discharged (term exp)	2/7/66	Baton Rouge, LA			
Thompson, William J., Co. C	Pvt			8/15/65	transferred from Sixty-Seventh USCI 8/65		MO (term exp)	9/8/65	Baton Rouge, LA	Brothertown, Calumet Co., WI; Little Rapids, Brown Co., WI	1881, Brown Co., WI	
Sixty-Seventh USCI (reg Consolidated into Sixty-Fifth USCI, 7/12/65)												
Adams, George H., Co. K	Pvt	Brookfield, WI; Milwaukee, WI; MN	21	1/18/65	Boscobel, WI	Henrietta, Richland Co., WI	transferred to Ninety-Second USCI					
Allen, John, Co. H	Pvt	NC; WI	25	2/13/65	Milwaukee, WI	Brookfield, Waukesha Co., WI;	transferred to Sixty-Fifth USCI					

Sixty-Seventh USCI, continued

Last, First Name	Rank	Residence Before Service	Age	Enlist Date	Location	Credited To	Left Service	Date	Location	Residence After Service	Death Year and Place	Burial Place in WI
Bailey, Thomas, Co. K	Pvt	NY	19	11/15/64	*Fond du Lac, WI*	*Herman, Sheboygan Co., WI*	discharged (disability)	7/28/65	Baton Rouge, LA			
Battice (Battis), John, Co. E	Pvt	LA; *Fairwater (Metomen), Fond du Lac Co., WI*	25	9/1/64	*Fond du Lac, WI*	*Metomen, Fond du Lac Co., WI*	transferred to Sixty-Fifth USCI					Wood National Cemetery, Milwaukee Co.
Bowman, John, Co. H	Pvt	VA; Cass Co., MI; WI	28	1/11/65	*Milwaukee, WI*	*Granville, Milwaukee Co., WI*	discharged (disability)	7/26/65	Baton Rouge, LA	*Oshkosh, WI; Fond du Lac, WI*	*1912, WI*	
Campbell, William, Co. I	Sgt	PA; IL	18	12/17/64	Quincy, IL	Durham, Hancock Co., IL	MO	8/15/65	Baton Rouge, LA	*Green Bay, WI; WI Veterans Home, King, WI*	*1898, WI Veterans Home, King, WI*	WI Veterans Memorial Cemetery, King
Crawford, Milton, Co. K	Pvt	KY; WI	26	10/14/64	*Fond du Lac, WI*	*Osceola, Fond du Lac Co., WI*	died (malaria)	8/2/65	hospital, Baton Rouge, LA		1865, Baton Rouge, LA	
Curtis, William, Co. E	Pvt	WI	17	11/10/64	*Janesville, WI*	*Vermont, Dane Co., WI*	discharged (disability)	7/28/65	hospital, Baton Rouge, LA			
Dodge, Antoine (Anthony), Co. K	Pvt	MO; WI	24	1/9/65	*Milwaukee, WI*	*First Ward Kenosha, WI*	transferred to Ninety-Second USCI					Green Ridge Cemetery, Kenosha
Howard, Henry, Co. E	Pvt	MD; WI	18	10/6/64	*Janesville, WI*	*Roxbury, Dane Co., WI*	discharged (disability)	7/28/65	Baton Rouge, LA	*Madison, WI*		

Last, First Name	Rank	Residence Before Service	Age	Enlist Date	Location	Credited To	Left Service	Date	Location	Residence After Service	Death Year and Place	Burial Place in WI
Jackson, Abraham, Co. E	Pvt	VA; OH; *Wash-ington, Sauk Co., WI*	44	10/24/64	*Washington, Sauk Co., WI*	none stated	died (dysentery)	5/20/65	Bayou Sara, LA		1865, Bayou Sara, LA	
Jenkins, Jerard C., Co. H	Pvt	OH	25	1/25/65	Milwaukee, WI	Milwaukee, WI	transferred to Sixty-Fifth USCI					
Johnson, James A., Co. E	Pvt	Clarksville, TN	18	12/7/64	Madison, WI	none stated	discharged (disability, underage)	7/28/65	Baton Rouge, LA	Milwaukee, WI	1930, Milwaukee, WI	
Kneley (Kneeley, Kaeley), William, Co. H	Pvt	MS	21	2/14/65	Milwaukee, WI	Richmond, Wal-worth Co., WI	transferred to Sixty-Fifth USCI					
Lacksy (Lackey), Samuel, Co. H	Pvt	GA	22	1/4/65	Milwaukee, WI	Milwaukee, WI	died (pneumonia)	5/22/65	hospital, Bayou Sara, LA		1865, Bayou Sara, LA	
Newson (Nusom, Nuson), George W., Co. H	Pvt	IN; *Dodge Co.; Metomen, Fond du Lac Co., WI*	23	12/15/64	Leroy, WI	Leroy, Dodge Co., WI *(drafted)*	died (typho-malarial fever)	4/4/65 or 4/7/65	hospital, Morganza, LA		1865, Morganza, LA	
Priness, Stephen, Co. E	Pvt	TN	26	9/22/64	Summit, WI	Summit, Waukesha Co., WI	transferred to Sixty-Fifth USCI					
Randolph, Henry, Co. E	Pvt	Ashtabula, OH; WI	18 (16)	2/2/65	Milwaukee, WI	Sharon, Walworth Co., WI	discharged (disability, underage)	7/26/65	Baton Rouge, LA	Pittsburgh, PA		
Rankin, Edward, Co. E	Pvt	MO; WI	21	9/21/64	Milwaukee, WI	Bloomfield, Walworth Co., WI	transferred to Sixty-Fifth USCI					

Last, First Name	Rank	Residence Before Service	Age	Enlist Date	Location	Credited To	Left Service	Date	Location	Residence After Service	Death Year and Place	Burial Place in WI
Richmond, Thomas, Co. I	Pvt	Randolph Co., MO	25	1/31/64	Macon, MO	Randolph Co., MO	discharged (convalescent)	6/14/65	Benton Barracks, MO	MO; Beetown, Grant Co., WI	1909, WI	Pleasant Ridge Cemetery, Beetown
Shaw, Allen, Co. K	Pvt	MN	18	1/19/65	Milwaukee, WI	Fourth ward Milwaukee, WI	transferred to Ninety-Second USCI					
Thompson, William, Co. H	Pvt	NC	40	2/8/65	Fond du Lac, WI	Polk [no further information]	transferred to Sixty-Fifth USCI					
Thompson, William J., Co. H	Pvt	NY; Brothertown, WI; Stockbridge, WI	29	9/9/64	Fond du Lac, WI	Empire, Fond du Lac Co., WI	transferred to Sixty-Fifth USCI					
Sixty-Eighth USCI												
Babcock, William, Co. I	Sgt	Charleston, RI; WI	21	3/21/64	Green Bay, WI	Morrison, Brown Co., WI	discharged	5/29/65	Webster General Hospital, Memphis, TN	Green Bay, WI; Neenah, WI	1899, WI	Brown Co., Greenwood Cemetery, De Pere
Bell, Alexander, Co. I	Cpl	MI; WI	24	3/15/64	Green Bay, WI	Liberty Grove, Door Co., WI	MO	2/5/66	Camp Parapet, LA	LA		
Bland, James (Williams, James; Johnson, Charles), Co. I	Pvt	Lincoln, MO	18	3/29/64	Louisiana, MO	none stated	MO	2/5/66	Camp Parapet, LA	Green Bay, WI		
Flows, Major, Co. I	Cpl	Montgomery Co., TN; WI	20	3/17/64	Green Bay, WI	Greenville, Outagamie Co., WI	MO	2/5/66	Camp Parapet, LA			

Last, First Name	Rank	Residence Before Service	Age	Enlist Date	Location	Credited To	Left Service	Date	Location	Residence After Service	Death Year and Place	Burial Place in WI
Franklin, Benjamin, Co. I	Pvt	MO or KY	21	4/6/64	Green Bay, WI	First ward Oshkosh, WI	MO	2/5/66	Camp Parapet, LA			
Freeman, John, Co. I	Pvt	NC; WI	28	3/21/64	Green Bay, WI	Greenville, Outagamie Co., WI	MO	2/5/66	Camp Parapet, LA			
Grace, Albert, Co. I	Cpl	Lexington Co., KY; WI	35	3/22/64	Green Bay, WI	Morrison, Brown Co., WI	MO	2/5/66	Camp Parapet, LA			
Harness, Edward, Co. G	Pvt	Mackinac, MI; WI	24	4/8/64	Green Bay, WI	Woodville, Calumet Co., WI	died	10/29/64	Regimental Hospital, Memphis, TN		1864, Memphis, TN	
Harrison (Harris), Jesse, Co. I	Pvt	Pemberton Co., AR; Watertown, WI	28	3/17/64	Green Bay, WI	Greenville, Outagamie Co., WI	MO	2/5/66	Camp Parapet, LA	Vicksburg, MS; Palestine, TX		
Heddy, Norban, Co. I	Pvt	Jefferson Co., KY; WI	24	3/17/64	Green Bay, WI	Greenville, Outagamie Co., WI	died	10/25/64	Regt Hospital, Memphis, TN		1864, Memphis, TN	
Jacob, Sanford, Co. I	Pvt	McCracken Co., KY; WI	18	3/17/64	Green Bay, WI	Greenville, Outagamie Co., WI	MO	2/5/66	Camp Parapet, LA	KY		
Jones, William N., Co. I	Pvt	Todd Co., KY; WI	21	3/17/64	Green Bay, WI	Greenville, Outagamie Co., WI	died	7/22/64	St. Louis, MO US General Hospital		1864, St. Louis, MO	
McDonald, Jasper, Co. I	Pvt	Murray Co., TN; Oshkosh, WI	24	3/17/64	Green Bay, WI	Greenville, Outagamie Co., WI	discharged (disability)	8/1/65	New Orleans, LA	Chicago, IL; Sycamore, IL	1891, IL	

Last, First Name	Rank	Residence Before Service	Age	Enlist Date	Location	Credited To	Left Service	Date	Location	Residence After Service	Death Year and Place	Burial Place in WI
Nusom (Newsom), John Q., Co. I	Sgt	IN; Waupun, WI	20	3/17/64	Green Bay, WI	Greenville, Outagamie Co., WI	MO	2/5/66	Camp Parapet, LA			
Phillips, Henry P., Co. I	Pvt	KY; Neenah, WI	21	3/21/64	Green Bay, WI	Greenville, Outagamie Co., WI	deserted	8/24/65	General Hospital, MO			
Rollins, Charles, Co. I	Cpl	Racine, WI; Oshkosh, WI	19	3/16/64	Green Bay, WI	Greenville, Outagamie Co., WI	MO	2/5/66	Camp Parapet, LA	New Orleans, LA		
Thomas, William, Co. I	Pvt	Franklin Co., AL; WI	20	3/21/64	Green Bay, WI	Greenville, Outagamie Co., WI	died	4/12/64	Benton Barracks, MO		1864, St. Louis	
Thomas, William R., Co. I	First Sgt	Cincinnati, OH; Oshkosh, WI	22	3/16/64	Green Bay, WI	Greenville, Outagamie Co., WI	MO	2/5/66	Camp Parapet, LA	Oshkosh, WI; Marinette, WI; Green Bay, WI;	1894, Fort Howard, Brown Co., WI	
Williams, Benjamin, Co. I	Pvt	Lewis Co., MO; WI	29	3/21/64	Green Bay, WI	Greenville, Outagamie Co., WI	deserted	10/23/64	camp at Memphis, TN			
Ninety-Second USCI												
Adams, George H., Co. H	Pvt			7/12/65	transferred from Sixty-Seventh USCI		MO	12/31/65	New Orleans, LA	Milwaukee, WI; Chicago, IL; Minneapolis, MN	1911, MN	

Last, First Name	Rank	Residence Before Service	Age	Enlist Date	Location	Credited To	Left Service	Date	Location	Residence After Service	Death Year and Place	Burial Place in WI
Dodge, Antoine (Anthony), Co. E	Pvt			7/12/65	transferred from Sixty-Seventh USCI		MO	12/31/65	New Orleans, LA	*Kenosha, WI*	*1889, Kenosha, WI*	Green Ridge Cemetery, Kenosha
Shaw, Allen, Co. I	Pvt			7/12/65	transferred from Sixty-Seventh USCI		MO	12/31/65	New Orleans, LA			
One Hundredth USCI												
Tyre, Abraham, Co. E	Pvt	TN	34	10/1/64	Cincinnati, OH		MO (term exp)	10/21/65	Nashville, TN	*Milwaukee, WI; Milwaukee Soldiers Home*		
One Hundred Second USCI												
Valentine, Shadrick, no Co.	Pvt	NC; OH; *Dane Co., WI; Adams Co., WI; Pierce Co., WI*	32	9/2/64	Grand Rapids, MI	Sparta, Kent Co., MI	died (typhoid)	11/1/64	Camp Casey, VA		1864, Camp Casey, VA	
One Hundred Sixth USCI												
Fitch, Willis, Co. C	Pvt	Green Co., AL	21	8/22/64	Athens, AL	German, Chenango Co., NY	MO	11/7/65	Bridgeport, AL	*Appleton, WI*	*1910, WI*	Wood National Cemetery, Milwaukee Co.

ARTILLERY

Third USCHA

Last, First Name	Rank	Residence Before Service	Age	Enlist Date	Location	Credited To	Left Service	Date	Location	Residence After Service	Death Year and Place	Burial Place in WI
Bostwick, Henry, no Co.	Pvt	*Brothertown, Calumet Co., WI*	20	8/30/64	*Fond du Lac, WI*	*Calumet, Fond du Lac Co., WI*	MO	5/30/65	Benton Barracks, MO	*Brothertown, WI; Chilton, WI; Oshkosh, WI; Soldiers Home; Waupaca, WI*	1933, WI Veterans Home, King, WI	Riverside Cemetery, Oshkosh
Brookfield, William, no Co.	Pvt	*AR; Koshkonong, Jefferson Co., WI*	22	8/16/64	*Janesville, WI*	*Koshkonong, Jefferson Co., WI*	MO	5/30/65	Benton Barracks, MO	Janesville, WI		
Brooks (Brook), Joseph B., no Co.	Pvt	*MO or IL; Prescott, WI*	24	8/22/64	*Prescott, WI*	*Pierce Co., WI*	MO	5/30/65	Benton Barracks, MO	Prescott, WI; LaFayette Co., AR		
Brown, Michael, no Co.	Pvt	*PA; Prescott, WI*	42	3/27/65	*La Crosse, WI*	*Clifton, Pierce Co., WI*	MO	5/30/65	Benton Barracks, MO	Prescott, WI	1894, WI	Pine Glen Cemetery, Prescott
Brown, William, Co. F	Pvt	*TN; Milwaukee, WI; Eau Claire, WI*	41	10/6/64	*La Crosse, WI*	*Chippewa Falls, WI*	MO (term exp)	10/6/65	Memphis, TN	Eau Claire, WI		
Douglas(s), John, Co. M	Pvt	*TN; WI*	22	1/30/65	*Milwaukee, WI*	*Wheatland, Kenosha Co., WI*	deserted	2/24/66	Fort Pickering, TN			
Edmunds (Edwards), Robert, no Co.	Pvt	*TN; WI*	23	3/14/65	*La Crosse, WI*	*First ward, La Crosse, WI*	MO	5/30/65	Benton Barracks, MO	La Crosse, WI		

Last, First Name	Rank	Residence Before Service	Age	Enlist Date	Location	Credited To	Left Service	Date	Location	Residence After Service	Death Year and Place	Burial Place in WI
Green, Alfred, Co. M	Pvt	Richmond, VA; MS; Eau Claire, WI	18	3/6/65	La Crosse, WI	N. Eau Claire, WI	MO (term exp)	3/7/66	Memphis, TN	Eau Claire, WI	1892, Eau Claire, WI	Forest Hill Cemetery, Eau Claire
Green, William, Co. F	Pvt	TN; MN or WI	18	1/21/65	La Crosse, WI	Washington Co., WI (or MN)	MO (term exp)	1/23/66	Memphis, TN			
Harris, Henry, no Co.	Pvt	VA; WI	18	8/29/64	Milwaukee, WI	Somers, Kenosha Co., WI	MO	5/30/65	Benton Barracks, MO			
Harrison, William, Co. F	Pvt	TN; WI	19	2/14/65	La Crosse, WI	Lillian, Goodhue Co., MN	MO	2/14/66	Memphis, TN			
Howard, Willis, no Co.	Pvt	IA; WI	18	3/27/65	La Crosse, WI	Clifton, Pierce Co., WI	MO	5/30/65	Benton Barracks, MO			
Johnson, Henry, Co. F	Pvt	Washington, DC; WI	21	2/1/65	La Crosse, WI	Neshonoc, La Crosse Co., WI	discharged (disability)	7/10/65	Memphis, TN	Woodstock, IL		
Johnson, John, no Co.	Pvt	VA; WI	30	2/16/65	La Crosse, WI	Second ward La Crosse, WI	MO	5/30/65	Benton Barracks, MO			
Johnson, Samuel, no Co.	Pvt	IL; La Crosse, WI	18	3/14/65	La Crosse, WI	Third ward La Crosse, WI	MO	5/30/65	Benton Barracks, MO	La Crosse, WI	1880, La Crosse, WI	
Jones, Wing, Co. M	Pvt	KY; WI	35	10/31/64	Milwaukee, WI	Summitt, Waukesha Co., WI	MO (term exp)	10/23/65	Memphis, TN	Waukesha, WI	1903, Waukesha, WI	Prairie Home Cemetery, Waukesha
Konye (Konge, Kenge, Konke) Frank, no Co.	Pvt	MO; WI	30	3/13/65	La Crosse, WI	Second ward La Crosse, WI	MO	5/30/65	Benton Barracks, MO			

Artillery, Third USCHA, continued

Last, First Name	Rank	Residence Before Service	Age	Enlist Date	Location	Credited To	Left Service	Date	Location	Residence After Service	Death Year and Place	Burial Place in WI
Lampkins, John, Co. F	Pvt	GA; WI	19	2/14/65	La Crosse, WI	Second district, MN or Second district, WI	MO (term exp)	2/17/66	Memphis, TN			
Lay, James, Co. F	Pvt	Nashville, TN; Racine, WI	30	9/19/64	Milwaukee, WI	Third ward, Racine, WI	discharged (term exp)	9/18/65	Memphis, TN	Racine, WI		
Nelson, Jerrett, Co. M	Pvt	TN; WI	18	2/18/65	Janesville, WI	Newport, Columbia Co., WI	MO	4/30/66	Memphis, TN			
Pindar (Pender, Pinder, Ponder), Jack, no Co.	Pvt	AR; WI	19	2/23/65	Milwaukee, WI	Holland, Sheboygan Co., WI	MO	5/30/65	Benton Barracks, MO			
Rankins, Edward, Co. F	Pvt	St. Louis, MO; Racine, WI	21	9/21/64	Milwaukee, WI	Bloomfield, Walworth Co., WI	discharge (disability)	8/4/65	Memphis, TN	Racine, WI		
Reynolds, Manuel, no Co.	Pvt	MO; WI	19	4/10/65	Fond du Lac, WI	Auburn, Fond du Lac Co., WI	MO	5/30/65	Benton Barracks, MO	1870, Waupun, WI (state prison)		
Rice, William H., no Co.	Pvt	Oxford, OH; WI	22	1/26/65	Milwaukee, WI	Pleasant Prairie, Kenosha Co., WI	MO	5/30/65	Benton Barracks, MO			
Riley, William, Co. M	Pvt	Pike Co., MO; Milwaukee, WI (possibly Watertown)	23	12/27/64	Milwaukee, WI	First ward, Milwaukee, WI	MO (term exp)	12/26/65	Memphis, TN	Chicago, IL	1906, Chicago, IL	

Last, First Name	Rank	Residence Before Service	Age	Enlist Date	Location	Credited To	Left Service	Date	Location	Residence After Service	Death Year and Place	Burial Place in WI
Spence, Van(ce), Co. M	Pvt	AL; GA; Fond du Lac, WI	27	2/24/65	Milwaukee, WI	Second ward, Milwaukee, WI	MO (term exp)	2/23/66	Memphis, TN	Leroy, Dodge Co., WI; Fond du Lac, WI; Litchfield & Minneapolis; MN	1910, Minneapolis, MN	
Stamper, Alexander, unassigned	Pvt	TN; Albany, Green Co., WI; Janesville, WI	24	8/17/64	Janesville, WI	Union, Rock Co., WI	MO (term exp)	5/30/65	Benton Barracks, MO	Janesville, WI; Chicago, IL; Janesville, WI	1922, Janesville, WI	Oak Hill Cemetery, Janesville
Taylor, Pinkney, Co. G	Pvt	Lincoln or Frances Co., MO; Beetown, Grant Co., WI	18	10/18/64	Prairie du Chien, WI	Beetown, Grant Co., WI	discharged (term exp)	8/17/65	Memphis, TN	Beetown, Grant Co., WI; Clinton, IA	1935, IA	
Thomas, John, Co. M	Cpl	IN; WI	19	2/7/65	Milwaukee, WI	First ward, Milwaukee, WI	MO (term exp)	2/8/66	Memphis, TN			
Thompson, Samuel W., no Co.	Pvt	VA; La Crosse, WI	22	2/10/65	La Crosse, WI	Second ward, La Crosse, WI	MO (term exp)	5/30/65	Benton Barracks, MO	La Crosse, WI		
Wayne, Monroe, Co. M	Sgt	VA; Beetown, Grant Co., WI	32	3/8/65	Milwaukee, WI	Muskego, Waukesha Co., WI	MO (term exp)	3/7/66	Benton Barracks, MO	Beetown, Grant Co., WI; Dubuque, IA; Leavenworth, KS	1892, Leavenworth, KS	
Williams, Joseph, Co. M	Pvt	McNary or Madison Co., TN; WI	23	12/12/64	Fond du Lac, WI	Eldorado, Fond du Lac Co., WI	MO (term exp)	12/11/65	Fort Pickering, TN (Memphis)	Madison Co., TN; DeSoto & Bolivar Co., MS	1905, probably MS	

Last, First Name	Rank	Residence Before Service	Age	Enlist Date	Location	Credited To	Left Service	Date	Location	Residence After Service	Death Year and Place	Burial Place in WI
Yates, William, Co. M	Pvt	NC; WI	34	12/22/64	Milwaukee, WI	Lake, Milwaukee Co., WI	deserted	10/8/65	Fort Pickering, TN			
Fourth USCHA												
Harwell (Howell), Eli	Pvt	Giles Co., TN; KY	18	10/26/63	Cairo, IL		MO	2/25/66	Pine Bluff, AR	Columbus, KY; Delavan, WI	1917 or 18, Delavan, WI	Eagle River Cemetery, Vilas Co.
Sixth USCHA												
Holden, Isaac, Co. K	Pvt	MS	32	3/1/64	Natchez, MS	not stated	MO	5/13/66	Natchez, MS	KS; IA; Watertown, WI; Oshkosh, WI; Onalaska, WI; Milwaukee Soldiers Home; La Crosse, WI	1889, Onalaska, WI	Campbell Cemetery, North La Crosse
Twelfth USCHA												
Branum (Brannon, Brannum), Charles, Co. F	Cpl	Scott Co., KY	21	8/3/64	Camp Nelson, KY	Scott Co., KY	MO	4/24/66	Louisville, KY	KY; OH; Fox Lake, WI	1897, Dodge Co., WI	Riverside Cemetery, Fox Lake
Tucker, Daniel	Pvt	Hardin Co., KY	25	1/15/65	Fort Boyle, KY	Spring Prairie, Walworth Co., WI	MO	4/24/66	Louisville, KY	KY		
Thirteenth USCHA												
Dangerfield, Horace, Co. F	Sgt	MO; Milwaukee, WI	28	9/21/64	Milwaukee, WI	Fourth ward, Milwaukee, WI	MO (term exp)	8/18/65	Lexington, KY	Milwaukee, WI	1893, Milwaukee, WI	Forest Home Cemetery, Milwaukee Co.

Last, First Name	Rank	Residence Before Service	Age	Enlist Date	Location	Credited To	Left Service	Date	Location	Residence After Service	Death Year and Place	Burial Place in WI
Greene, Thomas, Co. F	Pvt	*MO; Beetown, Grant Co., WI*	23	10/1/64	*Prairie du Chien, WI*	First district, MO or Third district, WI	MO	11/18/65	Louisville, KY	*Beetown, Grant Co., WI*	*1937, WI*	Pleasant Ridge Cemetery, Beetown
Wilson, William (Brown, John H.), Co. F	Pvt	TN	19	3/13/65	Chicago, IL	First district, Chicago, IL	MO	11/18/65	Louisville, KY	*Chicago, IL; Janesville, WI; Fond du Lac, WI, WI; Columbus, WI; Waukesha, WI; Racine, WI*	*1922, Milwaukee Soldiers Home*	Wood National Cemetery, Milwaukee Co.
CAVALRY												
Martin, Frank U., QM Sgt., Co. F, Third USC Cav	First Sgt	Chenango Co., NY	25	5/7/64	Vicksburg, MS		discharged	10/28/65	Memphis, TN	*Eau Claire Co., WI; Merrillan, Jackson Co., WI*	*1910, WI*	Merillan Cemetery, Jackson Co.
Peebles, Dennis R., Pvt, Co. K, First USC Cav	Pvt	Bristol, VT; NY	36	9/19/64	Troy, NY	Fifteenth district, NY	MO	2/4/66	Brazos de Santiago, TX	*Oakdale, Monroe Co., WI; Menasha, WI; Plover, WI*	*1912, Portage Co., WI*	McDill Cemetery, Portage Co.
UNASSIGNED												
Anthony, James	Pvt	TN; WI	28	9/24/64	Vernon, Waukesha Co., WI	First district, WI						
Barnum, James	Pvt	Hawkins Co., TN	33	9/13/64	Madison, WI	Cortland, Columbia Co., WI						
Barnum, William	Pvt	Wake Co., NC	26	8/15/64	Prescott, WI	Cottage Grove, Dane Co., WI						

Unassigned, continued

Last, First Name	Rank	Residence Before Service	Age	Enlist Date	Location	Credited To	Left Service	Date	Location	Residence After Service	Death Year and Place	Burial Place in WI
Barton, Felix		Monroe Co., IL; Forest, Vernon Co., WI	18	10/8/64	La Crosse, WI	Forest, Vernon Co., WI	died (lung inflammation)	2/4/65	Memphis, TN		1865, Memphis, TN	
Bond, William	Pvt	IN; WI	28	10/25/64	Milwaukee, WI	Caledonia, Racine Co., WI						
Brown, Chris				10/?/64	Janesville, WI							
Brown, James			19	1/9/65		Dover, WI						
Bryon, Willis		WI	28	1/25/65	Boscobel, WI	Waterloo, Grant Co., WI						
Caleb, John	Pvt				unassigned							
Call, William	Pvt			12/23/64	unassigned	Fond du Lac, WI	MO	5/3/65	Madison, WI			
Cardwell, Frank	Pvt	Jackson, TN; WI	28	9/19/64	Milwaukee, WI	Third ward, Racine, WI						
Ellmore, Joseph	Pvt	IL; WI	19	2/28/65	Milwaukee, WI	Pewaukee, Waukesha Co., WI	MO	3/3/65	Madison, WI	La Crosse, WI; Appleton, WI	1913, Appleton, WI	Riverside Cemetery, Appleton
Ford, Harry (Henry)	Pvt	Milliken's Bend, LA; Lima, Rock Co., WI	37	8/19/64	Janesville, WI	Johnstown, Rock Co., WI						
Foster, Edward	Pvt	Cape Girardeau Co., MO	18	9/23/64	Utica, WI	Utica, Winnebago Co., WI						
Green, James		Canada; WI	23	10/29/64	Milwaukee, WI	Oak Creek, Milwaukee Co., WI						

Last, First Name	Rank	Residence Before Service	Age	Enlist Date	Location	Credited To	Left Service	Date	Location	Residence After Service	Death Year and Place	Burial Place in WI
Hall, William		MO; WI	23	3/31/64	Madison, WI	Mequon, Ozaukee Co., WI	discharged (disability)	6/28/65	Quincy, IL	Quincy, IL		
Hall, William H.	Pvt	Baltimore, MD	22	4/16/64	Madison, WI	Third ward, Milwaukee, WI						
Harris, John				4/15/64		Milwaukee, WI						
Hillman, Thomas	Pvt	TN; Rock Co., WI	29	8/18/64	Janesville, WI	La Prairie, Rock Co., WI	discharged	5/25/65	Marine Hospital, St. Louis, MO	Rock Co.; Champaign Co., IL; Walnut Hill, IL		
Holstein (Holster), Joseph	Pvt	NY; Milwaukee, WI	37	10/19/64	Milwaukee, WI	Lake, Milwaukee Co., WI	discharged	5/26/65	St. Louis, MO			
Hughes, Dennis			19	2/23/65	Milwaukee, WI	Holland, Sheboygan Co., WI						Forest Hill Cemetery, Madison
Jackson, William	Pvt	MS; WI	24	9/20/64	Milwaukee, WI	Rochester, Racine Co., WI						
Johnson, David L.	Pvt	TN; WI	25	8/19/64	Janesville, WI	Union, Rock Co., WI						
Johnson, Henry			45	10/12/64	Milwaukee, WI	Summit, Waukesha Co., WI						
Johnson, James	Pvt	Clarksville, TN; WI	18	12/7/64	Madison, WI	Kendall, Lafayette Co., WI						
Mason, William			18	12/7/64	Galesburg, KY	East Troy, Walworth Co., WI						

Unassigned, continued

Last, First Name	Rank	Residence Before Service	Age	Enlist Date	Location	Credited To	Left Service	Date	Location	Residence After Service	Death Year and Place	Burial Place in WI
McDonald, Jerry (Derry)			18	9/25/64	Galesburg, KY	East Troy, Walworth Co., WI						
Nelson, James	Pvt	GA; WI	22	11/30/64	Fond du Lac, WI	Holland, Sheboygan Co., WI						
Nelson, Willie			18	10/28/64	Janesville, WI	Sun Prairie, Jefferson Co., WI						
Newton, Jasper	Pvt	SC; WI	18	9/30/64	Janesville, WI	unknown	died (disease)	11/24/64	Harvey Hospital, Madison, WI		1864, Madison, WI	
Owens, James			18	11/21/64	Fort Boyle, KY	East Troy, Walworth Co., WI						
Ross, Samuel			24	9/29/64	Milwaukee, WI	Fourth ward, Milwaukee, WI						
Scott, Henry			28	8/5/64	La Crosse, WI	First ward La Crosse, WI						
Searls (Seares), James	Pvt	Decatur, SC; Milwaukee, WI; Racine, WI	37	9/1/64	Milwaukee, WI	Merton, Waukesha Co., WI				IL; Atchison & Leavenworth, KS	1907, Soldiers Home, Topeka, KS	
Sennett, John E.	Pvt	Delaware Co., NY	31	7/24/64	Madison, WI	First ward, Madison, WI						
Sercer, Robert	Pvt	Memphis, TN	22	6/6/64	Madison, WI	Delavan, Walworth Co., WI						
Smith, Andrew	Pvt	Oakland, TN; WI	20	9/20/64	Milwaukee, WI	Bloomfield, Walworth Co., WI						

Unassigned, continued

Last, First Name	Rank	Residence Before Service	Age	Enlist Date	Location	Credited To	Left Service	Date	Location	Residence After Service	Death Year and Place	Burial Place in WI
Smith, Richard		*Racine, WI*	40	9/22/64	*Milwaukee, WI*	*Third ward, Racine, WI*						
Turner, Dennis	Pvt	*Woodville, KY*	24	4/7/64	*Madison, WI*	*Sumpter, Sauk Co., WI*						
Thompson, Reuben	Pvt	*OH; Sauk Co., WI; Adams Co., WI*	37	10/3/64	*Washington, Sauk Co., WI*	*Third district, WI*	MO 5/26/65	*Wash-ington, Sauk Co., WI, 1860 census*		*Westfield and Baraboo, Sauk Co., WI; Wash-ington, DC*	1911, Washington, DC	
Toney, Gabriel	Pvt	*MS; Boscobel, Grant Co., WI*	18	2/21/65	*Boscobel, WI*	*Monroe, Green Co., WI*	MO	5/3/65		*Collinsville and Greenville, IL*		
Walker, Edmund (Edward) H.	Pvt	*KY; Fond du Lac, WI*	29	10/12/64	*Chicago, IL*	*First district, Chicago, IL*	MO	5/23/65	Springfield, IL	*Fond du Lac, WI*		
Warren, Nelson			18	10/3/64		*Vermont, Dane Co., WI*		from archive muster roll				
Washington, George				8/2/64		*Milwaukee, WI*						
Washington, George				1/6/65		*Milwaukee, WI*						
Washington, George	Pvt	*TN; WI*	19	9/30/64	*Milwaukee, WI*	*First ward, Milwaukee, WI*						

Unassigned, continued

Last, First Name	Rank	Residence Before Service	Age	Enlist Date	Location	Credited To	Left Service	Date	Location	Residence After Service	Death Year and Place	Burial Place in WI
Williams, Bill	Pvt		18	9/2/64	Fond du Lac, WI	Metomen, Fond du Lac, Co. WI	died (disease)	2/10/65	Benton Barracks, MO		1865, St. Louis, MO	
Wilson, Albert C.				9/21/64		Wauwatosa, WI						
Wilson, Carter		Natchez, MS	18	4/11/64	Madison, WI	Leeds, Columbia Co., WI						
Wilson, Willie				10/28/64		Sun Prairie, WI						
Young, William	Pvt	MO; WI	21	10/9/64	Fond du Lac, WI	Fredonia, Ozaukee Co., WI						
NAVY												
Barber, Jonathan	landsman	WI	19	10/7/64	Cairo, IL							
Lewis, Major General Lyon	landsman	WI	28	9/8/64	Chicago, IL							
Mason, Henry Forest Rose, Huntress	landsman	WI	18	9/10/64	Cairo, IL							
Mitchell, James K. Lackwanna	landsman	WI	23	11/24/64	New York [uncertain if city or state]							
WISCONSIN REGIMENTS												
Barton, Leonard, Co. B, Thirty-Second WI Inf	Pvt	IL; Forest, Vernon Co., WI	20	9/21/64	drafted—Vernon Co., WI	Forest, Vernon Co., WI	MO	6/12/65	Milwaukee, WI	Forest, Vernon Co., WI; Shreveport, LA		

Last, First Name	Rank	Residence Before Service	Age	Enlist Date	Location	Credited To	Left Service	Date	Location	Residence After Service	Death Year and Place	Burial Place in WI
Bennett, Andrew, Co. B First, Co. H Twenty-First, Co. H Third WI Inf	Pvt	NY; Trimbelle, Pierce Co., WI	26	11/20/63	Trimbelle, WI	Trimbelle, Pierce Co., WI	MO	7/18/65		Trimbelle, Pierce Co., WI	1896, Pierce Co., WI	Trimbelle Cemetery, Pierce Co.
Bowman, John, Co. H Thirty-Ninth WI Inf	Pvt	VA; MI; Marinette, WI	23	5/23/64	Marinette, WI		MO	9/22/64	Camp Washburn, WI	Oshkosh, WI; Fond du Lac, WI	1912, WI	WI Veterans Memorial Cemetery, King
Butler, Cornelius, Co. C Thirty-Ninth WI Inf	Pvt	VA; Kenosha, WI	41	5/17/64	Kenosha, WI		MO	9/22/64	Camp Washburn, WI	Kenosha, WI; Pleasant Prairie, WI; Evanston, IL	1892, Evanston, IL	
Donaldson, Henry, Co. I Thirty-Seventh WI Inf	Pvt	KY; Lancaster, Grant Co., WI	32	11/19/63	Prairie du Chien, WI	Lancaster, Grant Co., WI	MO	7/27/65		Lancaster, WI		
Fiddler, Jefferson, Co. A Third WI Inf	Pvt	Stockbridge, WI; Neenah, WI	21	6/15/61	Fond du Lac, WI		discharged (disability)	11/11/62	Baltimore, MD			
Fiddler, Jefferson (re-enlistment)	Pvt	Stockbridge, WI; Neenah, WI	24	3/11/64	Fond du Lac, WI	Sheboygan, WI	died (KIA)	5/25/64	Dallas, GA		1864, Dallas, GA	
Jefferson, Beverly, Co. E First WI Inf	Pvt	VA; OH; Madison, WI	22	4/?/61	Madison, WI		term exp	8/?/61		Madison, WI	1908, buried Madison, WI	Forest Hill Cemetery, Madison
Jefferson, John Wayles, Eighth WI Inf	Pvt	VA; OH; Madison, WI		8/26/61	Madison, WI		MO	10/11/64	Madison, WI	Memphis, TN	1892, TN	Forest Hill Cemetery, Madison

Wisconsin Regiments, continued

Last, First Name	Rank	Residence Before Service	Age	Enlist Date	Location	Credited To	Left Service	Date	Location	Residence After Service	Death Year and Place	Burial Place in WI
Johnson, George A., Co. K Fourth WI Cav.	Pvt	NY; WI	27	4/27/61						Stockbridge, WI	1917, Stockbridge, WI	Lakeside Cemetery, Stockbridge
Johnson, Nathaniel H., Co. K, Fourth WI Cav.	Pvt	NY; Stockbridge, WI	39	4/27/61	Chilton, WI		discharged (disability)	1/4/62	Baltimore, MD	Stockbridge, WI	1884, Calumet Co., WI	Lakeside Cemetery, Stockbridge
Nash (Reese), Anderson, Co. H Thirty-Seventh WI Inf	Pvt	KY; Spring Valley, Rock Co., WI		11/27/63	Spring Valley, WI	Spring Valley, Rock Co., WI	MO	7/27/65		Fond du Lac, WI	1904, , Fond du Lac, WI	Rienzi Cemetery, Fond du Lac
Neal, Johnson, Co. C Fifty-First WI Inf	Pvt	GA; Columbus, WI		3/1/65	Columbus, WI		MO	8/19/65	Camp Randall, WI	TN; Milwaukee Soldiers Home; Pine Bluff, AR	1912, Pine Bluff, AR	
Johnson (Netter), Hayden, Co. E First, Co. G Twenty-First, Co. I Twenty-First WI Inf	Pvt	KY; Trenton, Dodge Co., WI	27	11/20/63	Trenton, WI	Trenton, Dodge Co., WI	MO	7/18/65		Fox Lake, WI; Medford, WI; WI Soldiers Home, Waupaca, WI	1904, Medford, Taylor Co., WI	
Pendleton, Jerome, Co. I Twenty-First WI Inf.	Pvt	WI		8/12/62		Menasha, WI	died (wounds)	1/29/63	New Albany, IN		1863, New Albany, IN	

Last, First Name	Rank	Residence Before Service	Age	Enlist Date	Location	Credited To	Left Service	Date	Location	Residence After Service	Death Year and Place	Burial Place in WI
Pendleton, John, Co. C Thirty-Eighth WI Inf	Pvt	WI		8/24/64		Brothertown, WI	discharged (disability)	1/5/65		Stockbridge, WI	1894, Stockbridge, WI	
Revels, Aaron, Co. G First WI Cav	Pvt	NC; Forest, Vernon Co., WI	24	3/25/64	Forest, Vernon Co., WI	Farmington, Washington Co., WI	MO	6/14/65	Madison, WI	Forest, Vernon Co., WI	1903, Forest, Vernon Co., WI	
Revels, Henry, Co. K Sixth WI Inf	Pvt	GA; Forest, Vernon Co., WI	24	2/27/62	Sparta, WI	Sparta, Monroe Co., WI	MO	7/22/65		Forest, Vernon Co., WI	1909, Forest, Vernon Co., WI	
Revels, John W., Co. A and Co. K Third WI Cav	Pvt	IN; Forest, Vernon Co., WI	18	11/5/63	Madison, WI		discharged (disability)	3/23/65		Forest, Vernon Co., WI	1912 or 14, MO	
Revels, William J., Co. K Sixth WI Inf	Cpl	IN; Forest, Vernon Co., WI	19	2/17/62	Sparta, WI	Sparta, Monroe Co., WI	died (KIA)	8/19/64	Weldon Railroad, VA		1864, Weldon Railroad, VA	
Richardson, Anthony, Co. H Forty-Second WI Inf	Pvt	KY; Beetown, Grant Co., WI	19	8/25/64	Prairie du Chien, WI	Lancaster, Grant Co., WI	MO	6/20/65	With company, Madison, WI	Beetown, WI; Janesville, WI; Evansville, WI	1916, Evansville, WI	Maple Hill Cemetery, Evansville
Roseman, Henry G., Co. I Thirty-Seventh WI Inf	Pvt	AR; Beaver Dam, WI	21	11/20/63	Fond du Lac, WI		MO	5/24/65	Whitehall Hospital, Philadelphia, PA	Beaver Dam, WI; AR	1922, Phillips Co., AR	
Rosier, John, Co. E Fifth WI Inf	Pvt	VA; Fort Winnebago, Columbia Co., WI	39	9/19/64	Portage City, WI	Ft. Winnebago, Columbia Co., WI	MO	6/20/65	Hull's Hill, VA	Fort Winnebago, WI	1869, T Fort Winnebago, Columbia Co., WI	

Wisconsin Regiments, continued

Last, First Name	Rank	Residence Before Service	Age	Enlist Date	Location	Credited To	Left Service	Date	Location	Residence After Service	Death Year and Place	Burial Place in WI
Shepard, John N., Co. D Forty-Second WI Inf	Pvt	VA; Beetown, Grant Co., WI	17	8/25/64	Lancaster, WI	Lancaster, Grant Co., WI	died (disease)	3/28/65	Cairo, IL		1865, Cairo, IL	
	Pvt	TN; Beetown & Millville, Grant Co., WI	28	11/16/63	Prairie du Chien, WI	Prairie du Chien, Crawford Co., WI	MO	7/19/65	Edgefield, TN	Millville, WI; Little Grant, WI; Beetown, WI; Cassville, Grant Co., WI	1907, WI	Cassville Cemetery, Cassville
Stanton, August "Zach," new Co. D Sixteenth WI	Pvt	Chilton, WI	17	8/31/64		Chilton, Calumet Co., WI	MO	6/2/65		Chilton, WI	1878, Chilton, WI	Hillside Cemetery, Chilton
Stanton, Cato, Co. G Fourteenth WI, Co. E Twenty-First WI	Pvt	RI; Chilton, WI	28	9/23/61	Chilton, WI		discharged (disability)	6/26/65	Louisville, KY	Chilton, WI; Marinette, WI	1902, Calumet Co., WI	Quinney Cemetery, Calumet Co.
Stanton, William, new Co. D Sixteenth WI	Pvt	Chilton, WI	15	9/1/64		Chilton, Calumet Co., WI	MO	6/2/65		Chilton, WI	1900, Chilton, WI	Hillside Cemetery, Chilton
Waldron (Waldon), Samuel, Co. C Thirty-Second WI Inf	Pvt	NC; Forest, Vernon Co., WI	40	9/21/64	drafted, La Crosse, WI	Forest, Vernon Co., WI	MO	6/12/65		Forest, Vernon Co., WI	1897, Forest, Vernon Co., WI	Revels Family Cemetery, Forest
REJECTED												
Fields, Henry		VA	44	5/24/64	Quincy, IL	Eighth ward, Milwaukee, WI						

Rejected, continued

Last, First Name	Rank	Residence Before Service	Age	Enlist Date	Location	Credited To	Left Service	Date	Location	Residence After Service	Death Year and Place	Burial Place in WI
Griffie, Levi		KY; MO	43	3/12/64	Quincy, IL	*Fifth ward, Milwaukee, WI*						
Johnson, Henry		DC; WI	44	4/15/64	Waukesha, WI	*Germantown, Washington Co., WI*						
Parsons, Peter		KY	21	4/25/64	Quincy, IL	*Eighth ward, Milwaukee, WI*						
Scott, William D., Co. F		SC	23	3/5/64	Ridge Prairie, IL	*Fifth ward, Milwaukee, WI*						
Stark, Peter		Pike Co., MO	27	6/23/64	Quincy, IL	*Fifth ward, Milwaukee, WI*						
Taylor, James, Co. F		MO	32	12/4/63	Quincy, IL	*Third ward, Milwaukee, WI*						
Tolbert, William		MA; WI	40	4/11/64	Madison, WI	*Burke Twp, Dane Co., WI*				IL		
Turner, Dennis		KY; WI	24	4/7/64	Madison, WI	*Sumpter, Sauk Co., WI*						

EMPLOYEES

Listed below are two groups of non-enlisted African American men who were employed by Wisconsin regiments or officers during the Civil War. The first group includes 181 men whose names appeared on official rosters of Wisconsin regiments from the *Roster of Wisconsin Volunteers, War of the Rebellion, 1861–1865* (www.wisconsinhistory.org/Records/Article/CS4267, or from original muster rolls in the Wisconsin Historical Society Archives). Almost all of them were listed as cooks or undercooks; one was listed as a cook and musician, and three were wagoners. For all of these men, I was able to find clear documentation that indicates their race. Included on official rosters are several dozen other cooks whose race I couldn't confirm and who were therefore not included. Shown in the table are the unit(s) with which these individuals served, the date and location when they joined the regiment, how and when they left the service, later service as an enlisted soldier, and documented residence in Wisconsin. In italics are the names of men with documentation of residence in Wisconsin. Also in italics are enlistment locations in Wisconsin and, for nine men, the location in Wisconsin to which their service was credited (thereby reducing the local draft quota). This list reflects a small percentage of the African American men who were actually employed by Wisconsin regiments. Most companies and regiments never placed the names of employees on official rosters, and other units included them inconsistently. Note that sixteen of these men died while in service and one is documented to have suffered a catastrophic injury.

The second list includes men who were employed by Wisconsin regiments or officers during the war but whose names never appear on official muster rolls. The initial sources for information on these men is provided in the right hand column. Also shown are the units with which they worked, their job or their employer, the date and location when they began working (if known), how they left the service, later service as an enlisted soldier, and residence in Wisconsin after the war. I believe that this is only a tiny fraction of the non-rostered African Americans who worked with Wisconsin regiments and officers. In italics are the names of men who lived in Wisconsin before or after their service and Wisconsin locations where they began working with the regiment or where they lived after the war. Blank spaces mean "not applicable."

Those men whose names appeared on official rosters as cooks, musicians, wagoners, and other occupations were eligible later in life for pensions and admission to soldiers homes. Those whose names never appeared on official rosters were denied both of those, even when documents and statements were provided by former officers and soldiers to support their claims.

Abbreviations used

Batt	battery
Capt	captain
Cav	cavalry
Co	Company
Col	colonel
Gen	general
HA	heavy artillery
Inf	infantry
LA	light artillery
Lt	lieutenant
Lt Col	lieutenant colonel
MO	mustered out
term exp	term of service expired
USCI	United States Colored Infantry
USCHA	United States Colored Heavy Artillery

Employees

*cook and musician **wagoner

On Regimental Rosters	Worked With	Later Worked With	Date Joined	Location Where Joined	Left Service	Later Service as Enlisted Soldier	WI Residence After the War	Burial Place in WI
Alexander, William	Co. H, Thirty-Fifth WI Inf		6/2/64	Port Hudson, LA	deserted 8/14/64			
Allston, Isaac	Co. F, Fourth WI Cav		9/1/63	Baton Rouge, LA	deserted 4/25/65			
Anglen, Jared	Co. G, Thirteenth WI Inf		5/1/63	none listed	MO 11/24/65			
Bailey, Francis	Co. C, Fourth WI Cav		10/1/63	Baton Rouge, LA	died 2/20/64, Baton Rouge, LA (disease)			
Ball, Alexander	Co. D, Thirty-First WI Inf		no date	none listed	unknown			
Bell, Robert	Co. F, Seventeenth WI Inf		12/18/63	Vicksburg, MS	absent sick at MO of regiment			
Bentley, Benjamin	Co. K, Fourth WI Cav		12/5/63	Baton Rouge, LA	unknown			
Blue, Archie	Co. G, Fourth WI Cav		8/1/62	Vicksburg, MS	MO 8/22/65			
Bonner, Billy	Co. K, Thirty-Third WI Inf	Co. B, Eleventh WI Inf; Co. K, Thirty-Third WI Inf	2/20/64	Enterprise, MS	MO 9/4/65			
Boullin, Abraham	Co. G, Seventeenth WI Inf		9/28/63	Vicksburg, MS	MO 7/14/65			
Bowden (Ewing), Samuel	Co. C, Thirty-First WI Inf		10/31/63	Murfreesboro, TN	MO 6/20/65		La Crosse, Madison, Waupaca, Soldiers Home	

On Regimental Rosters	Worked With	Later Worked With	Date Joined	Location Where Joined	Left Service	Later Service as Enlisted Soldier	WI Residence After the War	Burial Place in WI
Bradley, Albert	Co. C, Twenty-Seventh WI Inf		4/26/64	none listed	deserted 5/2/64			
Bradley, Andrew J.	Co. C, Thirteenth WI Inf		10/15/63	none listed	deserted 2/10/65			
Brem, Major	Co. K, Thirty-Fifth WI Inf		5/9/64	Port Hudson, LA	MO 3/15/66			
Bridges (Bryder, Brydes), Mac	Co. F, Fourth WI Cav		11/15/63	Baton Rouge, LA	MO 5/28/66			
Brimm, Robert	Co. H, Twentieth WI Inf		11/23/63	Brownsville, TX	MO 7/14/65			
Brown, Charles	Co. C, Thirty-Fifth WI Inf		6/4/63	Port Hudson, LA	deserted 2/25/65			
Brown, William	Co. B, Fourth WI Cav		7/1/63	Baton Rouge, LA	unknown			
Butler, Joseph	Co. E, Fourth WI Cav		9/5/63	Baton Rouge, LA	died 4/16/66, Ft. McIntosh, TX			
Campbell, Spencer	Co. I, Seventeenth WI Inf		7/1/63	Vicksburg, MS	deserted 1/1/65			
Carey, Richard	Co. E, Thirty-Eighth WI Inf		3/18/64	Porter [no further information]	deserted	enlisted in Co. F, Twenty-Ninth USCI	*Palmyra before and after service*	
Carter, Chas.	Co. A, Fourth WI Cav		7/13/63	Baton Rouge, LA	MO 5/28/66			
Carter, Tom	Co. D, Thirty-First WI Inf		10/30/63	La Vergne, TN	MO 6/20/65			

On Regimental Rosters	Worked With	Later Worked With	Date Joined	Location Where Joined	Left Service	Later Service as Enlisted Soldier	WI Residence After the War	Burial Place in WI
Casey, Elias	Co. B, Seventeenth WI Inf		5/1/63	none listed	MO 7/14/65			
Cate, Nicholas	Co. C, Fourth WI Cav		7/1/63	Port Hudson, LA	MO 5/28/66			
Cheatham, Robert	Co. K and Co. H, Fifteenth WI Inf	Co. I, Thirteenth WI Inf	8/1/63	Winchester, TN	MO 11/24/65			
Clark, John (York)	Co. A, Fourth WI Cav		7/15/63	Baton Rouge, LA	MO 5/28/66			
Clay, Henry	Co. F, Thirty-First WI Inf		10/31/63	Murfreesboro, TN	MO 7/20/65			
Clifton, Lindsay	Co. K, Fourth WI Cav		12/1/63	Plaquemines, LA	unknown			
Coates (Coats), John	Co. H, Twelfth WI Inf		11/8/63	Natchez, MS	died, 1/24/64, Natchez, MS (disease)			
Collins, George	Co. D, Twentieth WI Inf		11/27/63	Brownsville, TX	MO 7/14/65			
Collins, Isaac	Co. H, Thirty-Eighth WI Inf		8/6/64	Friendship, WI	MO 6/2/65			
Collins, Joseph	Co. M and Co. B, Fourth WI Cav		9/3/64	Clinton, LA			credited to Ripon but not resident	
Comer, Charles	Co. A, Thirteenth WI Inf		3/17/63	none listed	MO 11/24/65			
Cotton, Albert	Co. C, Thirteenth WI Inf		3/17/63	none listed	deserted 5/26/64			

On Regimental Rosters	Worked With	Later Worked With	Date Joined	Location Where Joined	Left Service	Later Service as Enlisted Soldier	WI Residence After the War	Burial Place in WI
Conway, George	Co. L, Third WI Cav	Co. D reorganized Third WI Cav	1/6/64	Ft. Smith, AR	deserted 8/27/65			
Cowan, Henry	Co. I, Thirty-First WI Inf		10/31/63	Murfreesboro, TN	deserted 7/16/64			
Crockett, David	Co. E and Co. H, Fifteenth WI Inf		10/10/62	none listed	unknown			
Cunningham, Samuel	Co. E, Thirty-First WI Inf		10/28/63	Murfreesboro, TN	MO 6/20/65			
Dallas, George M	Co. C, Twenty-Seventh WI Inf		3/21/64	Little Rock, AR	MO 8/29/65			
Davis, Stephen	Co. B, Thirty-First WI Inf		10/1/63	La Vergne, TN	MO 6/20/65			
Davis, Thomas Jefferson	Co. H and Co. A, Fifteenth WI Inf	Co. K Thirteenth WI Inf	3/10/63	none listed	MO 11/24/65			
Dixon, Joseph	Co. F Twentieth WI Inf		11/25/63	Brownsville, TX	MO 7/14/65			
Dobbs, Henry	Co. A, Thirty-Third WI Inf	Co. F Eleventh WI Inf.	3/5/64	Memphis, TN	MO 9/4/65			
Dodge, Peter	Co. K, Thirteenth WI Inf		7/1/63	none listed	deserted 7/12/65			
Dodget, Archibald	Co. L and Co. E, Fourth WI Cav		8/25/64	Baton Rouge, LA	deserted 11/5/65			

On Regimental Rosters	Worked With	Later Worked With	Date Joined	Location Where Joined	Left Service	Later Service as Enlisted Soldier	WI Residence After the War	Burial Place in WI
Doyle, Alex	Co. F, Fourth WI Cav		11/20/63	Baton Rouge, LA	deserted 6/27/64			
Drake, Edward	Co. M and Co. B, Fourth WI Cav		8/18/64	Baton Rouge, LA	MO 5/28/66		credited to Ripon but not resident	
Edwards, Samuel	Co. D, Seventeenth WI Inf		12/1/63	none listed	no information			
Ellis, James	Co. A, Twenty-Ninth WI Inf		4/14/64	Grand Encore, LA	MO 6/22/65		Fort Atkinson	
Emmett (Emil), Robert	Co. K, Fourth WI Cav		12/1/63	Baton Rouge, LA	MO 5/28/66			
Ennis, Chas.	Co. I, Fourth WI Cav		6/30/63	Port Hudson, LA	unknown			
Francis, Peter	Co. D, Fourth WI Cav		6/10/63	Port Hudson, LA	MO 5/28/66			
Franklin, Benjamin	Co. C, Thirty-Fifth WI Inf		6/4/63	Port Hudson, LA	MO 3/15/66			
Friday, Mac	Co. H, Thirty-Fifth WI Inf		6/2/64	Port Hudson, LA	absent sick when regiment MO			
Fugua (Faqua), Richard	Co. K, Twentieth WI Inf		10/1/64	Carrolton LA,	MO 7/14/65			
Furlong, Geo. W.	[Co. unknown], Thirty-First WI Inf		9/5/63	none listed	unknown			
Gale, Sam	Co. G, Fourth WI Cav		10/30/63	Baton Rouge LA	deserted 11/22/63			
Gaskins, Richard	Co. D Twenty-Ninth WI Inf		4/20/64	Grand Encore, LA	MO 6/22/65			
Gayton, Peter	Co. G, Fourth WI Cav		10/31/63	Baton Rouge, LA	MO 5/28/66			

On Regimental Rosters	Worked With	Later Worked With	Date Joined	Location Where Joined	Left Service	Later Service as Enlisted Soldier	WI Residence After the War	Burial Place in WI
Germany, John	Co. G, Fourth WI Cav		7/1/63	Carronton, LA	MO 5/28/66			
Gibson, Joseph	[Co. unknown], Thirty-First WI Inf		6/26/63	none listed	unknown			
Graham, Antonio (Antoine)	Co. E, Fourth WI Cav		9/5/63	Baton Rouge, LA	MO 5/28/66			
Graves, William	Co. C, Thirty-Fifth WI Inf		6/4/63	Port Hudson, LA	MO 3/15/66			
Gray, Gabriel	Co. F, Twenty-Eighth WI Inf		7/7/63	Pine Bluff, AR	died 8/1/64, Pine Bluff (disease)			
Green, Joseph	Co. H, Twenty-Seventh WI Inf		3/14/64	Little Rock, AR	deserted 3/16/64			
Griffin, Thomas	Co. E, Seventeenth WI Inf		9/28/63	Vicksburg, MS	MO 7/14/65			
Griffin, Giles	Co. E, Seventeenth WI Inf		1/1/64	Vicksburg, MS	MO 7/14/65			
Haines, James	Co. F, Thirteenth WI Inf		9/1/63	none listed	MO 11/25/65			
Hamilton, Jerry	Co. G, Seventeenth WI Inf		9/28/63	Vicksburg, MS	MO 7/14/65			
Harris, Calvin	Co. G, Twenty-Ninth WI Inf		4/15/63	Grand Ecore, LA	MO 6/22/65			

Employees, continued

On Regimental Rosters	Worked With	Later Worked With	Date Joined	Location Where Joined	Left Service	Later Service as Enlisted Soldier	WI Residence After the War	Burial Place in WI
Harris, George*	Co. C and Co. H, Thirty-First WI Inf		10/31/63	Murfreesboro, TN	MO 7/8/65			
Hartshorn (Hawthorne), Charles	Co. C, Twenty-Ninth WI Inf		12/31/63	Algiers, LA	MO 7/22/65			
Haynes, Lewis	Co. B, Thirty-First WI Inf		10/20/63	Murfreesboro, TN	MO 7/20/65			
Henry	Co. F, Thirty-Third WI Inf		not listed	none listed	both legs shot off, 3/30/65, Spanish Fort, AL			
Hicks, Willis	Co. K, Thirty-Third WI Inf		1/10/64	Memphis, TN	died 10/10/64, White River, AR (disease)			
Holmes, Dan'l	Co. I and Co. A, Fourth WI Cav		6/30/63	Baton Rouge, LA	MO 5/28/66			
Holstein, D. (Hall, David)**	Co. H, Thirty-First WI Inf		10/31/63	Murfreesboro, TN	died 11/20/63, Murfreesboro TN			
Howard, Henry	Co. K, Thirty First WI Inf		10/30/63	Murfreesboro, TN	absent sick at MO of regt.			
Hughes, Benjamin	Co. I, Thirteenth WI Inf		8/1/64	none listed	deserted 10/15/64			
Hunter, Edward	Co. H, Thirty-Fifth WI Inf		6/6/64	Port Hudson, LA	MO 3/15/66			

On Regimental Rosters	Worked With	Later Worked With	Date Joined	Location Where Joined	Left Service	Later Service as Enlisted Soldier	WI Residence After the War	Burial Place in WI
Hustin, Allen	Co. H, Thirty-First WI Inf		10/28/63	Murfreesboro, TN	MO 7/8/65			
Jack, Nora	Co. B, Fourth WI Cav		7/1/63	Baton Rouge, LA	not with regiment at MO			
Jackson, Andrew	Co. K, Twenty-Seventh WI Inf		12/1/63	Little Rock, AR	MO 8/29/65			
Jackson, Charles	Co. F, Thirty-Third WI Inf		12/22/63	Hebron, MS	unknown			
Jackson, Henry	Co. H, Twenty-Seventh WI Inf		2/16/64	Little Rock, AR	died 1/22/65, Little Rock (disease)			
Jackson, John	Co. D, Twenty-Seventh WI Inf		3/23/64	Little Rock, AR	MO 7/31/65			
Jackson, Wesley	Co. H, Twenty-Seventh WI Inf		3/4/64	Little Rock, AR	absent sick at MO of regiment			
Jacobs, Marshall	Co. D, First WI HA		4/25/64	Ft. Jackson, LA	MO 8/18/65		*credited to Jefferson, Green Co. but not resident*	
James, Matt	Co. E, Thirty-Eighth WI Inf		5/11/64	*Madison, WI*	MO 7/26/65		*Madison; Milwaukee Soldiers Home (1887–90)*	
Jefferson, James	Co. F, Thirty-First WI Inf		1031/63	Murfreesboro, TN	MO 6/20/65			

Employees, continued

On Regimental Rosters	Worked With	Later Worked With	Date Joined	Location Where Joined	Left Service	Later Service as Enlisted Soldier	WI Residence After the War	Burial Place in WI
Jefferson, Thomas	Co. D, Fourth WI Cav		9/1/63	Baton Rouge, LA	MO 5/28/66			
Jefferson, Thomas	Co. I, Thirteenth WI Inf		10/5/62	none listed	died 7/63, Ft. Donelson, TN			
Jenkins, Abraham	Co. F, Seventeenth WI Inf		12/1/63	Vicksburg, MS	deserted 5/5/64			
Jenkins, Emanuel	[Co. unknown], Thirty-First WI Inf		no date	none listed	unknown			
Johnson, Spencer	Co. H, Fourth WI Cav		9/1/63	Baton Rouge, LA	deserted 3/28/65			
Joiner, John	Co. H, Thirty-Eighth WI Inf		9/2/64	*Friendship, WI*	MO 6/2/65			
Jones, Daniel	Co. F, Thirty-Third WI Inf		12/22/63	Hebron, MS	unknown		*son lived in Delavan*	
Jones, Spencer	Co. A, Fourth WI Cav		9/1/64	Baton Rouge, LA	unknown			
Jordan, Jerry	Co. F, Twenty-Ninth WI Inf		8/25/64	Clinton, LA	MO 6/22/65			
Kelly, William	Co. C, Fourth WI Cav		7/1/63	Port Hudson, LA	MO 8/22/65			
King, John	Co. K, Twenty-Seventh WI Inf		12/7/63	Little Rock, AR	MO 8/29/65			
Kirk, Buck	Co. I, Thirteenth WI Inf		9/16/63	none listed	MO 11/24/65			

On Regimental Rosters	Worked With	Later Worked With	Date Joined	Location Where Joined	Left Service	Later Service as Enlisted Soldier	WI Residence After the War	Burial Place in WI
La Vier, Thomas	Co. A, Twenty-Ninth WI Inf		4/14/64	Grand Ecore, LA	died 8/1/64, Thibodaux, LA (disease)			
Love (Gove), Wadkins	Co. C, Twenty-Eighth WI Inf		11/20/63	Pine Bluff, AR	deserted 5/31/65			
Mack, James	Co. L, Fourth WI Cav		8/25/64	Baton Rouge, LA	deserted		*credited to Tomah but not resident*	
Manchester, Henry	Co. B and Co. K, Thirty-First WI Inf		10/31/63	Murfreesboro, TN	MO 7/8/65			
Manley, Lemuel	Co. K, Thirty-Eighth WI Inf		8/25/64	*Friendship, WI*	MO 6/2/65			
Mays, Samuel	Co. B, Thirteenth WI Inf		11/1/63	none listed	deserted 6/25/65			
McAlroy, William P.	Co. H, Twenty-Seventh WI Inf		3/20/62	Little Rock, AR	MO 8/29/65			
McCrary (McClary), Wiley	Co. E, Thirty-First WI Inf		10/28/63	Murfreesboro, TN	MO 7/20/65			
McDade, James	Co. F, Fourth WI Cav		3/3/63	Baton Rouge, LA	MO 8/22/65			
McKillop, Caleb	Co. E, Seventeenth WI Inf		9/28/63	Vicksburg, MS	unknown			
Mitchell, John	Co. D, Twenty-Eighth WI Inf		7/7/63	Pine Bluff, AR	MO 8/23/65			

Employees, continued

On Regimental Rosters	Worked With	Later Worked With	Date Joined	Location Where Joined	Left Service	Later Service as Enlisted Soldier	WI Residence After the War	Burial Place in WI
Monger, Lem	Co. D, Thirty-Fifth WI Inf		5/5/65	Mobile, AL	deserted 5/23/65			
Moore, Frank	Co. I and Co. E, Fourth WI Cav		9/3/64	Baton Rouge, LA	deserted 11/5/65		*credited to Tomah but not resident*	
Murray, Robert	Co. M, Fourth WI Cav		8/18/64	Baton Rouge, LA	deserted 4/4/65			
Nelson, Isham	Co. F, Thirteenth WI Inf		9/8/63	none listed	deserted 6/16/65			
Nolan, Alexander**	Thirty-First WI Inf, not on Co. roll		10/30/63	Murfreesboro, TN	MO 7/8/65			
Oglesby, George	Co. C, Thirty-First WI Inf		10/31/63	Murfreesboro, TN	MO 7/20/65			
Owens, Moses	Co. A, Thirty-First WI Inf		10/30/63	Murfreesboro, TN	MO 6/20/65			
Palton, Andrew	Co. G, Thirty-First WI Inf		10/31/63	Stone River, TN	MO 7/8/65			
Parks, Anthony	Sixth Battery, WI LA		1/1/64	Huntsville, AL	MO 7/3/65, Madison, WI		*Racine; Milwaukee*	Wood National Cemetery, Milwaukee Co., WI
Patten, Lewis	Co. A, Seventeenth WI Inf		10/10/63	Natchez, MS	MO with regiment, early 1864	enlisted, Co. F, Twenty-Ninth USCI	*Madison before enlistment*	
Perry, Commodore	Co. G, Fourth WI Cav		8/24/64	Baton Rouge, LA	died, Centerville, TX (no date given)			

On Regimental Rosters	Worked With	Later Worked With	Date Joined	Location Where Joined	Left Service	Later Service as Enlisted Soldier	WI Residence After the War	Burial Place in WI
Phoenix, George	Co. D, Twentieth WI Inf		11/27/63	Brownsville, TX	MO 7/14/65			
Picton, William M.	Co. G, Twenty-Ninth WI Inf		4/1/64	Natchitoches, LA	MO 6/22/65			
Pitman, Wiley	Co. A, Thirty-First WI Inf		11/14/64	Atlanta, GA	MO 6/20/65			
Preston, Lewis	Co. A, Twentieth WI Inf		11/29/63	Brownsville, TX	MO 7/14/65			
Price, John	Co. I, Twenty-Seventh WI Inf		2/1/64	Little Rock, AR	MO 8/29/65			
Ranolds, Calvin	Co. B, Seventeenth WI Inf		5/1/63	Smith's Plantation, LA	MO 7/14/65			
Richardson, Peter	Co. E, Twenty-Seventh WI Inf		9/1/63	Duvall's Bluff	MO 8/29/65			
Rob, Tom	Co. K, Thirteenth WI Inf		10/1/63	none listed	died 4/17/65, Bull's Gap, TN (disease)			
Rogers, Benjamin	Co. A, Thirty-Third WI Inf	Co. F 11th WI Inf.	12/30/63	Memphis, TN	MO 9/4/65			
Rollins, Jack	Co. H, Twentieth WI Inf		11/23/63	Brownsville, TX	MO 7/14/65			
Roshell, David	Co. C, Twenty-Ninth WI Inf		12/1/63	New Iberia, LA	MO 7/22/65			

Employees, continued

On Regimental Rosters	Worked With	Later Worked With	Date Joined	Location Where Joined	Left Service	Later Service as Enlisted Soldier	WI Residence After the War	Burial Place in WI
Runnells, James	Co. C, Thirty-Fifth WI Inf		5/17/64	Port Hudson, LA	absent sick at MO			
Satterfield, Louis	Co. B and Co. H, Fourth WI Cav		11/1/63	Baton Rouge, LA	MO 5/28/66			
Seymour, Anton	Co. I, Fourth WI Cav		6/30/63	Port Hudson, LA	died 6/19/64, Baton Rouge, LA (disease)			
Smith, Isaac	Co. C, Fourth WI Cav		3/30/64	Baton Rouge, LA	MO 5/28/66			
Smith, John	Co. E, Twenty-Seventh WI Inf		1/4/64	Pulaski, AR	MO 8/29/65			
Smith, Solesta	Co. F, Twenty-Ninth WI Inf		11/24/63	New Iberia, LA	MO 6/22/65			
Smith, Thomas	Co. I, Fourth WI Cav		8/1/64	Baton Rouge, LA	deserted 3/26/65		*credited to Sparta but not resident*	
Southall, Wm.	Co. M and Co. H, Fourth WI Cav		6/30/63	Port Hudson, LA	MO 8/21/65			
Stansfield, Lewis	Co. I, Twenty-Eighth WI Inf		11/29/63	Pine Bluff, AR	died 8/8/65, Clarksville, TX (disease)			
Stansfield, Richard	Co. D, Twenty-Eighth WI Inf		7/7/63	Pine Bluff, AR	MO 8/23/65			
Steward, John	Co. D, First WI HA		4/25/64	*Jefferson, WI*	deserted 7/15/65			

On Regimental Rosters	Worked With	Later Worked With	Date Joined	Location Where Joined	Left Service	Later Service as Enlisted Soldier	WI Residence After the War	Burial Place in WI
Strange, Isaac	Co. E, Fourth WI Cav		9/5/63	Baton Rouge, LA	MO 8/22/65			
Taylor, Clark	Co. H, Thirteenth WI Inf		11/1/63	none listed	MO 11/24/65			
Taylor, Clayborn	Co. K, Thirty-Fifth WI Inf		5/9/64	Port Hudson, LA	MO 3/15/66			
Thomas, Alexander	Co. H, Fourth WI Cav		9/1/63	Baton Rouge, LA	died 11/26/64, Baton Rouge, LA (disease)			
Thomas, Edmund	Co. I, Fourth WI Cav		6/30/63	Baton Rouge, LA	unknown			
Thomas, John	Co. C, Fourth WI Cav		10/1/63	Baton Rouge, LA	MO 5/28/66			
Thomason, John	Co. H, Thirty-First WI Inf		10/28/63	Murfreesboro, TN	MO 7/8/65			
Thomison, Matt**	Co. I, Thirty-First WI Inf		10/31/63	Murfreesboro, TN	deserted 7/16/64			
Thompson, John	Co. G, Thirty-Third WI Inf		12/31/63	Vicksburg, MS	unknown			
Thompson, Moses	Co. K, Fourth WI Cav		12/5/63	Baton Rouge, LA	MO 5/28/66			
Tremeleau, Joseph	Co. H, Fourth WI Cav		9/1/63	Baton Rouge, LA	deserted 7/23/65			
Turner, Dennis	Co. H, Seventeenth WI Inf		9/1/63	Natchez, MS	deserted 3/20/64			
Turner, Manuel	Co. D, Twenty-Ninth WI Inf		4/20/64	Grand Ecore, LA	MO 6/22/65			

On Regimental Rosters	Worked With	Later Worked With	Date Joined	Location Where Joined	Left Service	Later Service as Enlisted Soldier	WI Residence After the War	Burial Place in WI
Turner, Moses	Co. I, Seventeenth WI Inf		4/1/63	Lake Providence, LA	MO 7/14/65			
Valentine, John	Co. K, Thirty-Eighth WI Inf		8/31/64	*Newark Valley, Adams Co., WI*	MO 6/2/65			
Walker, Alexander	Co. A, Seventeenth WI Inf		10/1/3	Vicksburg, MS	MO 7/14/65			
Walker, Henry	Co. B, Fourth WI Cav		11/1/63	Baton Rouge LA	MO 5/28/66			
Warren, James	Co. F, Forty-First WI Inf		5/17/64	*Richland Center, WI*	MO 9/23/64, (term exp)			
Washington, George	Co. A, Thirty-First WI Inf		10/30/63	Murfreesboro, TN	died 8/1/64, Atlanta, GA (disease)			
Watson, Abraham	Co. C, Twenty-Eighth WI Inf		11/20/63	Pine Bluff, AR	died 9/19/64, Pine Bluff, AR (disease)			
Watson, Fred	Co. E, Fourth WI Cav		9/5/63	Baton Rouge, LA	deserted 3/25/65			
Weimms, Henderson	Co. B, Thirteenth WI Inf		11/14/63	none listed	deserted 6/23/65			
Wells, Robert	Co. I, Twenty-Eighth WI Inf		7/7/63	Pine Bluff, AR	MO 8/23/65			
West, Tom	Co. D, Thirty-First WI Inf		10/7/63	La Vergne, TN	MO 6/20/65			
Wheat, Jerry	Co. D, Thirty-Fifth WI Inf		5/7/65	Mobile, AL	MO 3/15/66			

On Regimental Rosters	Worked With	Later Worked With	Date Joined	Location Where Joined	Left Service	Later Service as Enlisted Soldier	WI Residence After the War	Burial Place in WI
White, Frank	Co. D, Twenty-Seventh WI Inf		11/1/63	Little Rock, AR	absent sick at MO of regiment			
White, Peter	Co. F, Twentieth WI Inf		11/25/63	Brownsville, TX	MO 7/14/65			
White, Thomas	Co. L, Fourth WI Cav		8/10/64	Baton Rouge, LA	unknown			
White, Wilson	Co. D, Fourth WI Cav		7/10/63	Port Hudson, LA	MO 5/28/66			
Wiley, Henry	Co. H, Thirteenth WI Inf		12/1/63	none listed	deserted 6/24/65			
Williams, Albert	Co. D, Fourth WI Cav		6/30/63	Port Hudson, LA	MO 5/28/66			
Wilson, Carter	Co. H, Seventeenth WI Inf		9/1/63	Natchez, MS	MO 7/14/65		*credited to Leeds but not resident*	
Woodfall, Peter	Co. A, Twentieth WI Inf		3/23/64	Brownsville, TX	MO 7/14/65			
Young, Stephen	Co. L, Third WI Cav	Co. D, reorganized Third WI Cav	6/12/63	Rolla, MO	MO 9/8/65			

Employees, continued

Non-Roster, Other Sources	Unit	Job or Employer	Date Joined	Location Where Joined	Left Service	Later Service as Enlisted Soldier	Wisconsin Residence after the War	Source	Burial Place in Wisconsin
Allen, George Washington	[Co. unknown], Sixth WI Inf	Gen Bragg	unknown	unknown	unknown			Beudot & Herdegen—Mickey Sullivan memoir	
Allen, David	Co. A, Eighth WI Inf	cook	unknown	unknown	unknown			Fold3 WI index card, Co. A, Eighth WI Inf	
Allen, Joseph	Co. C, Sixth WI Inf	cook	unknown	unknown	deserted			Mickey Sullivan memoir; Dawes autobiography	
Anderson, William	Co. E, Thirteenth WI Inf	under cook	11/23/63	TN	MO 7/14/65		Madison	Capital Times, May 17, 1979	
Arms, Samuel	PA regiment	drummer	Fall 64	GA	went to PA with officer		Cheyenne Valley	Vernon Co. Historical Museum	Forest-Burr Cemetery, Forest
Ashby, Henry	Batt C, Sixth Independent WI LA	Lt Col Samuel Clark	7/1/61	Huntsville, TN	discharged 10/64		Eagle River	Documents from WI Veterans Museum	Eagle River Cemetery, Forest
Bernard, Matt	Sixth WI Inf	servant, cook	unknown	unknown	unknown			Lance Herdegen papers, Civil War Museum	
Butts, Benjamin	Fifth WI Inf	Col Thomas Allen	unknown	Petersburg, VA	came to WI with officer		Richland Center, Madison	newspapers article, Madison	Forest Hill Cemetery, Madison

Non-Roster, Other Sources	Unit	Job or Employer	Date Joined	Location Where Joined	Left Service	Later Service as Enlisted Soldier	Wisconsin Residence after the War	Source	Burial Place in Wisconsin
Clark, Ansel	Eleventh WI Inf	Capt Christie	unknown	AR	MO with regiment		*Adams Co., Portage*	newspapers articles, Portage	Silver Lake Cemetery, Portage
Cleggett, William	Eighth Batt, WI LA	Cook	11/28/61	*Racine, WI*	discharged 5/62		*Plover, Appleton*	pension files, Lloyd Bryon (half-brother)	Riverside Cemetery, Appleton
Cowen, Gus	Co. G, Twenty-First WI Inf	Capt James Randall	unknown	GA	came to WI with officer		*Mukwonago*	Jack Holzhueter files, WHS archives	Oak Knoll Cemetery, Mukwonago
Custis, Peter	Thirty-Sixth WI Inf	Col Warner	unknown	VA	came to WI with officer		*Dane Co., Green Bay, Sturgeon Bay*	article by Victoria Tashjian	Bayside Cemetery, Sturgeon Bay
Epps, Richard	Co. E, Sixth WI Inf	Lt Col Watrous	unknown	VA	came to WI with officer			J. Watrous, biographical sketch of Epps	
Fortune, George	First WI Cav	Col Daniels	unknown	unknown	unknown		*Madison*	noted on his draft registration	
Green, Alfred	Co. F Twenty-Eighth WI Inf	Capt Arthur Sherman	unknown	TN	unknown	Co. M, Third USCHA	*Eau Claire*	pension files	
Harris, Jessie	First WI Inf	Capt Skinner	unknown	unknown	3 months with First WI Inf	Co. I, Sixty-Eighth USCI	*Watertown*	pension files	
Hughes, Dennis	Co. H, Eighth WI Inf	Lt Lafayette Munsel	unknown	AL	came to WI with regiment	Co. D, Twenty-Ninth USCI	*Belleville, Madison*	pension files; newspaper clippings, Madison	

Employees, continued

Non-Roster, Other Sources	Unit	Job or Employer	Date Joined	Location Where Joined	Left Service	Later Service as Enlisted Soldier	Wisconsin Residence after the War	Source	Burial Place in Wisconsin
Jackson, William	Sixth WI Inf	Gen Rufus Dawes	unknown	VA	went to Ohio with Gen. Dawes after the war			Dawes autobiography	
Matson, Alfred	Eighth, Twenty-Second, Forty-Second WI Inf	servant, cook	unknown	unknown	unknown		*Prairie du Chien, Platteville, Boscobel, Delavan*	newspaper articles; family members	Spring Grove Cemetery, Delavan
McClennan, Oscar	Co. K, Thirteenth WI Inf	cook	unknown	Humboldt, TN	unknown	Co. D, Twenty-Ninth USCI	*Sharon, Delavan*	Joseph Holzhueter files, WHS archives	
McKenney, William	Eleventh WI Inf	Lt Col Chas. Wood	unknown	Helena, AR	came to WI with officer	Co. F, Twenty-Ninth USCI	*Madison, Milwaukee*	pension files	
Reese, Arthur Arlington	Co. G, Twelfth WI Inf	Lt Frank Putney	unknown	SC	came to WI with officer		*Waukesha*	family members	
Riley, John (Jack)	Sixth WI Inf	barber	unknown	*Fond du Lac, WI*	unknown		*Fond du Lac*	Beaudot & Herdegen, Sullivan memoir	
Robinson, Nelson	Co. B, Eleventh WI Inf	Capt McDonald	unknown	VA	came to WI with officer		*La Crosse*	obituary, *La Crosse Tribune*	
Rolett, Shandy	Co. I, Sixty-Eighth USCI	servant, cook	unknown	unknown	unknown		*Green Bay before and after the war*	pension file of Wm. R. Thomas, Sixty-Eighth USCI	
Roseman, Henry	Co. I, Sixteenth WI Inf	cook	unknown	unknown	unknown	Co. I, Thirty-Seventh WI Inf	*Beaver Dam*	pension file	

Non-Roster, Other Sources	Unit	Job or Employer	Date Joined	Location Where Joined	Left Service	Later Service as Enlisted Soldier	Wisconsin Residence after the War	Source	Burial Place in Wisconsin
Smith, Isaac	Co. E, Twenty-Seventh WI Inf	Col Charles Harris	unknown	Helena, AR	came to WI with officer	Co. F, Twenty-Ninth USCI	*Madison, Milwaukee*	pension file	
Smith, Nathan	Co. F, Twenty-Ninth WI Inf	Gen Cadwallader Washburn	unknown	unknown	came to WI with officer		*La Crosse, West Salem*	Mouser, *Black La Crosse*, 2002	
Strayhorn, Alexander	Co. H, Thirteenth WI Inf	Capt O. T. Maxson	unknown	unknown	came to WI with officer		*Prescott*	Prescott history by Ahlgren & Beeler	
Stubblefield, George W.	Fiftieth WI Inf	unknown	unknown	WI	left at MO of regiment		*Rock Co., Butternut, Ashland Co.*	family member	Union Cemetery, Butternut
Taylor, Enoch	Co. G, Fifteenth WI Inf	unknown	unknown	unknown	unknown	Co. F, Forty-Ninth USC	*Janesville*	Cunningham Museum, Lancaster; pension file	
Thomas (Dabney), Peter D.	Co. H, Thirty-First WI Inf	Capt Chas. Nelson	unknown	TN	came to WI with officer	Co. H, Eighteenth USCI	*Beloit, Racine*	pension file; newspaper articles, Racine	
Thompson, Samuel A.	Co. D, Fourteenth WI Inf	barber	unknown	MS	unknown	unassigned, Third USCHA	*La Crosse*	Mouser, *Black La Crosse*, 2002	
Williams, Elisha	Twelfth WI Inf	unknown	unknown	GA	unknown		*Madison*	article, historicmadison.org	
Williams, James D.	Thirteenth WI Inf	unknown	unknown	unknown	came to WI with soldiers		*Rewey*	Jack Holzhueter files, WHS archives	Carmel Cemetery, Rewey

Acknowledgments

Many thanks to the Wisconsin Historical Society for its interest in publishing this work and for its library and archives, whose resources and assistance made it possible. The library's collection of microfilmed newspapers was invaluable. The National Archives and Records Administration houses the pension files of the Civil War veterans and records of the United States Colored Troops. Its knowledgeable and helpful staff made my limited time in Washington always productive.

I also wish to thank the libraries, historical societies, and museums that provided vital pieces in the assembly of a more complete picture of African Americans in pre- and postwar Wisconsin. These libraries include: Black River Falls, Fond du Lac, Fox Lake, La Crosse, Milwaukee, Wauwatosa, and Marquette University. The following museums and historical societies provided important information: Fond du Lac Historical Society, Galloway House, Fond du Lac; Vernon County Historical Museum, Viroqua; Cunningham Museum, Grant County Historical Society, Lancaster; Milwaukee County Historical Museum; Civil War Museum, Kenosha; Milton Historical Museum; Cheyenne Valley Settlers Association, Hillsboro; Wisconsin Veterans Museum, Madison; Evansville Historical Society; Wisconsin Black Historical Society/Museum, Milwaukee; Delavan Historical Society; Rock County Historical Society, Janesville; Southwest Wisconsin Room, UW Platteville; and the Wisconsin Historical Society Area Research Centers in River Falls, Milwaukee, and La Crosse.

Thanks to Vicky Tashjian, with whom I co-authored an article for the Winter 2018–2019 issue of the *Wisconsin Magazine of History* about Henry Sink, a black Civil War veteran from the Fox Valley. This book might never have been created if we hadn't met.

Notes

Abbreviations

CMSR: Combined Military Service Records

NARA: National Archives and Records Administration

OR: *The War of the Rebellion: A Compilation of the Official Records of the Union and Confederate Armies*

PF: Pension File (NARA)

RDR: Regimental Descriptive Rolls (Blue Book)

RPMGB: Records of the Provost Marshall General's Bureau

RWV: *Roster of Wisconsin Volunteers, War of the Rebellion, 1861–1865*

WHS: Wisconsin Historical Society

Preface

1. *New York Anglo African*, May 11, 1861.

Introduction

1. David W. Blight, *Race and Reunion: The Civil War in American Memory* (Cambridge, MA: Harvard University Press, 2001), 309.

2. Blight, *Race and Reunion*, 60, 205, 209.

3. Maurice McKenna, *Fond du Lac County, Wisconsin, Past and Present* (Chicago: S. J. Clarke Co., 1912), 159–178.

4. Blight, *Race and Reunion*, 175.

5. Blight, *Race and Reunion*, 180.

6. Michael Stevens, ed., *As If It Were Glory: Robert Beecham's Civil War from the Iron Brigade to the Black Regiments* (Madison: Madison House Publishers, 1998), xviii.

7. Stevens, ed., *As If It Were Glory*, xvii.

8. Blight, *Race and Reunion*, 174.

9. *Milwaukee Sentinel*, January 1, 1867.

10. William H. Wiggins, *O Freedom: Afro-American Emancipation Celebrations* (Knoxville, TN: University of Tennessee Press: 1987), 25–36.

11. *Delavan Enterprise*, August 8, 1888.

12. *Milwaukee Sentinel*, August 2, 1889.

13. "Juneteenth Day—Milwaukee," www.juneteenthdaymilwaukee.com.

14. Lancaster Historic Preservation Commission, "Lancaster's Historic Courthouse Square" pamphlet, 2006.

15. George Washington Williams, *A History of the Negro Troops in the War of the Rebellion, 1861–1865*, reprint (New York: Negro Universities Press, 1969), 328–331, 332.

16. Blight, *Race and Reunion*, 338.

17. *Sedalia Weekly Conservator*, September 14, 1908.

18. Richard Slotkin, *No Quarter: The Battle of the Crater, 1864* (New York: Random House 2009), 353.

19. The following are the numbers of Wisconsin African American soldiers listed by different authors: 155 in William Gladstone's *United States Colored Troops, 1863–1867* (Gettysburg, PA: Thomas Publications, 1990), 120; 363 in Richard Current's *The History of Wisconsin: The Civil War Era, 1848–1873* (Madison: State Historical Society of Wisconsin, 1976), 330; 250 in E. B. Quiner's *The Military History of Wisconsin* (Chicago: Clarke & Co., 1866), 162; 353 in Frank Klement's *Wisconsin in the Civil War: The Home Front and the Battle Front, 1861–1865* (Madison: State Historical Society of Wisconsin, 1997), 97; H. Russell Austin's *The Building of a Vanguard State* (Milwaukee: Milwaukee Journal, 1976) and Robert C. Nesbitt's *Wisconsin: A History* (Madison: University of Wisconsin Press, 1977) make no mention of black soldiers from Wisconsin.

Chapter One

1. Aaron Roberts obituaries, *Baraboo Daily News*, November 26 and 28, 1923.

2. Paul Heinegg, "Free African Americans of Virginia, North Carolina, and South Carolina," www.freeafricanamericans.com/; "Sheppherd, Abraham," NCpedia, www.ncpedia.org/biography/sheppard-abraham.

3. Cory D. Robbins, *Forgotten Hoosiers* (Bowie, MD: Heritage Books, 1994), 136–139; Heinegg, "Free African Americans."

4. Wes Smith, "'Reverse Underground Railroad' is Touted for Preservation," *Chicago Tribune*, May 25, 1997.

5. Zachary Cooper, *Black Settlers in Rural Wisconsin* (Madison: State Historical Society of Wisconsin, 1977), 5; Robbins, *Forgotten Hoosiers*, 136–139;

1860 US Census: Town of Forest, Bad Ax County and Town of Westfield, Sauk County, Wisconsin (the name of Bad Ax County was changed to Vernon County in 1862).

6. "Has K. K. K. Organized Here? Flaming Cross Looms in West," *Baraboo Daily News*, November 21, 1923.

7. "Black History in Wisconsin: Fur Trade Era," Wisconsin Historical Society (hereafter WHS) website, www.wisconsinhistory.org/Records /Article/CS502#fur.

8. Cooper, *Black Settlers*, 3–5; "Black History in Wisconsin: Early 19th Century," WHS website, www.wisconsinhistory.org/Records/Article /CS502#fur; Dodge Manumission Papers, 1838, Iowa Series 16, No. 20– 21, University of Wisconsin–Platteville Archives; "An Abolitionist in Territorial Wisconsin: The Journal of Reverend Edward Mathews, Part I," *Wisconsin Magazine of History* 59 (Autumn 1968): 10–12.

9. 1840 Wisconsin Territorial Census, "Slavery in Wisconsin," WHS website, www.wisconsinhistory.org/Records/Article/CS1784.

10. V. Jacques Voegeli, *Free But Not Equal* (Chicago: University of Chicago Press, 1967), 1–4; Leslie A. Schwalm, *Emancipation's Diaspora: Race and Reconstruction in the Upper Midwest* (Chapel Hill: University of North Carolina Press, 2009), 3.

11. Joe William Trotter Jr., *Black Milwaukee: The Making of an Industrial Proletariat, 1915–1945*, 2nd ed. (Champaign: University of Illinois Press, 2007), xxxv; "Race in Wisconsin," Slavery in the North website, http:// slavenorth.com/wisconsin.htm; William Vollmar, "The Negro in a Midwest Frontier City, 1835–1870" (master's thesis, Marquette University, 1968), 676.

12. "Statistics of Wisconsin," 1850 US Census, 917, www2.census.gov /library/publications/decennial/1850/1850a/1850a-45.pdf?#.

13. Cooper, *Black Settlers*, 21–22; Olive Green Lewis, "History of the Negro Pioneer Settlers," (unpublished memoir), Grant County Historical Museum.

14. Cooper, *Black Settlers*, 23; 1860 US Census: Beetown Township, Grant County, Wisconsin; Shawn Godwin, *Pleasant Ridge: A Rural African American Community in Grant County, Wisconsin*, report prepared for Old World Wisconsin, State Historical Society of Wisconsin, Madison, 1998.

15. Ruby West Jackson and Walter T. McDonald, *Oral History Research Report*

for Old World Wisconsin, Pleasant Ridge African-American Exhibit, 1998, 3, Cunningham Museum.

16. Vollmar, "The Negro in a Midwest Frontier City," 11–13; "Quarlls, Caroline (1824–1892), Fugitive Slave," WHS website, www.wisconsinhistory .org/Records/Article/CS1729; John Henry Davidson, *Negro Slavery in Wisconsin and the Underground Railroad* (Milwaukee, WI: Parkman Club Publications, 1897), 48–51.

17. "Stockbridge-Munsee: Early Historical Background," Milwaukee Public Museum website, www.mpm.edu/content/wirp/ICW-159; "The Underground Railroad in Wisconsin," WHS website, www.wisconsinhistory .org/Records/Article/CS566; Doug Welch, "The Milton House and the Underground Railroad," *Wisconsin Magazine of History* 103 (Fall 2019): 19–20.

18. Chauncey Olin, "Reminiscences of the busy life of Chauncey C. Olin," XLII–LII, in *A Complete Record of the John Olin Family* (Indianapolis: Baker-Randolph Co., 1893), online facsimile at www.wisconsinhistory .org/turningpoints/search.asp?id=1557.

19. Maurice McKenna, *Fond du Lac County, Wisconsin, Past and Present* (Chicago: S. J. Clarke Co., 1912), 143–144.

20. Olin, "Reminiscences," LII; 1850 US Census: Town of Waukesha, Waukesha County; 1860 US Census: Town of Trimbelle, Pierce County.

21. "A Journey from Slavery to Freedom: A Brief Biography of Joshua Glover," WHS website, www.wisconsinhistory.org/Records/Article /CS4368; Olin, "Reminiscences," LIII–LXI.

22. Vollmar, "The Negro in a Midwest Frontier City," 42–44.

23. "The Illinois Slave Law," *Frederick Douglass Paper*, September 2, 1853, www.accessible-archives.com/2013/09/new-illinois-slave-law-action -1853; Edward A. Miller Jr., *The Black Civil War Soldiers of Illinois: The Story of the Twenty-Ninth U.S. Colored Infantry* (Columbia: University of South Carolina Press, 1998), 7–8.

24. Schwalm, *Emancipation's Diaspora*, 102; Richard Current, *The History of Wisconsin: The Civil War Era, 1848–1873* (Madison: State Historical Society of Wisconsin, 1976), 283; "American Colonization Society," http:// slavenorth.com/colonize.htm.

25. *Waupaca Register*, July 9, 1858; Edward Hunter minor pension certificate 184545, Pension File, Civil War and Later Survivors' Certificates, 1861–

1934, Records of the Department of Veterans Affairs, Record Group 15, National Archives and Records Administration (hereafter PF).

26. Vollmar, "The Negro in a Midwest Frontier City," 15, 54; Carroll mother's application 598904, PF; A. Bailey, Milwaukee City Directory of 1862 (Milwaukee: Stark & Son Publishers, 1862), 58–59; Alfred Carroll, Compiled Military Service Records, NARA website, www.nps.gov/civilwar/search-soldiers.htm (hereafter CMSR).

27. While her name is spelled multiple different ways in the historical record, the Valentine family confirms that her name was spelled "Lavinia."

28. 1850 US Census: Towns of Rutland and Oregon, Dane County; and Janesville, Rock County; 1860 US Census: Janesville, Rock County and Town of Trimbelle, Pierce County; Record Group 110, Records of the Provost Marshall General's Bureau (Civil War), Enrollment Lists and Corrections to Enrollment Lists, 1863–1865, Consolidated Draft Lists, NM 65, E-172, Class 1, Fifth District, Wisconsin, vol. 2, 588, NARA (hereafter RPMGB); Record Group 110, Original Draft Lists, NM 65, Entry 172-A, Class 1, Fifth District, Wisconsin, vol. 2, 588, RPMGB; Wisconsin Sixth Congressional District, Box 1, Folder 2; John Valentine invalid certificate 557884, PF.

29. 1860 US Census: Fort Winnebago Township, Columbia County; H. Rosier widow's certificate 829372 and J. Rosier widow's certificate 346223, PF.

30. 1840 US Census: Oneida, New York; 1860 US Census: Town of Eagle, Waukesha County; John Sutfen, marriage certificates: Milwaukee County Marriage Records, 1836–1848, vol. 3, 110, WHS Library, and Columbia County Marriage Records, vol. 1, 454, WHS Library; Wisconsin First Congressional District, Class 1, vol. 2, Consolidated Draft Lists, RPMGB.

31. Carolyn Andler, Brothertown Tribal Genealogist, email message to author, December 12, 2012.

32. 1860 US Census: Town of Westfield, Sauk County; 1860 US Census of Agriculture: Town of Westfield, Sauk County.

33. Cooper, *Black Settlers*, 5; 1855 WI State Census: Town of Viroqua, Bad Ax County; 1860 US Census: Forest Township, Bad Ax County.

34. Wisconsin Fourth Congressional District, Box 3, Original Draft Lists (RPMGB).

35. Vol. 1, 171, Record of Marriages (1850–1853) and Ministers' Credentials, 1836–1962: Wisconsin, Circuit Court (Kenosha County), WHS Library; 1860 US Census: First Ward, City of Kenosha, Kenosha County.

36. 1855 WI State Census: Town of Albion, Jackson County; 1860 US Census: Town of Albion, Jackson County; Lawrence Eaton Jones, Jean Hagen Anderson, and Jo Ann Gordon Dougherty, "History of the Black River Falls, Wisconsin, Business District, 1839 to 1977," 98, unpublished, Black River Falls Public Library; Jackson County Grantee and Grantor Indexes, Black River Falls Public Library (Deeds: vol. 3, 65, 346; vol. 4, 45–46; vol. 6, 184; and vol. 7, 238), microfilm; US Federal Census Mortality Schedules, 1850–1885, Jackson County, www.ancestry.com/search /collections/8756/.

37. *Population of the United States in 1860; Compiled from the Original Returns of the Eighth Census.* (Washington, DC: Government Printing Office, 1864), 528–531.

38. "How Does a City Choose to Remember Its Past?" America's Black Holocaust Museum, https://abhmuseum.org/rememberance/; "A Journey from Slavery to Freedom: A Brief Biography of Joshua Glover," WHS website, www.wisconsinhistory.org/Records/Article/CS4368.

39. "Missouri State Archives: Missouri's Dred Scott Case, 1846–1857," Missouri Digital Heritage website, www.sos.mo.gov/archives/resources /africanamerican/scott/scott.asp; "Chief Justice Taney," American History from Revolution to Reconstruction and Beyond, University of Groningen website, www.let.rug.nl/usa/documents/1826-1850/dred -scott-case/chief-justice-taney.php.

40. John H. Warren and John S. Dean, eds., *The Legislative Manual of the State of Wisconsin, First Annual Edition* (Madison: Smith & Cullaton, State Printers—Argus Office, 1862), 155.

Chapter Two

1. James M. McPherson, *Battle Cry of Freedom: The Civil War Era* (New York: Oxford University Press, 1988), 562; Richard N. Current, *The History of Wisconsin, Volume 2: The Civil War Era, 1843–1873* (Madison: State Historical Society of Wisconsin, 1976), 146.

2. McPherson, *Battle Cry of Freedom*, 352–353.

3. McPherson, *Battle Cry of Freedom*, 274–275, 317.

4. "Recruiting African American soldiers for the Union Army," Frederick Douglass Heritage website, www.frederick-douglass-heritage.org /african-american-civil-war/.

5. "Delany, Martin Robinson, 1812–1885," BlackPast.org, www.blackpast .org/aah/delany-major-martin-robison-1812-1885.

6. W. H. Noland to Governor Randall, April 18, 1861, Military Correspondence, 1837–1910, Series 49, Box 43, Wisconsin Historical Society (hereafter WHS) Archives.

7. Cornelius Butler to Governor Salomon, July 29, 1862, Military Correspondence, 1837–1910, Series 49, Box 14, WHS Archives.

8. Stephen Engle, *Gathering to Save a Nation: Lincoln and the Union's War Governors* (Chapel Hill: University of North Carolina Press, 2016), 222.

9. Ferdinand D. Shavers to Governor Salomon, August 12, 1862, Military Correspondence, 1837–1910, Series 49, Box 14, WHS Archives.

10. Arnold P. Powers, *Devour Us Not: Short Stories of African-American Struggles, Triumphs, and Defeats* (Xlibris Corp., 2013), 27.

11. Thomas Holmes to Governor Salomon, August 6, 1862, Military Correspondence, 1837–1910, Series 49, Box 14, WHS Archives.

12. George Washington Williams, *A History of the Negro Troops in the War of the Rebellion, 1861–1865*, reprint (New York: Negro University Press, 1969), 88.

13. The Twenty-Eighth Wisconsin Volunteer Infantry website, www .28thwisconsin.com/service/riots.html; Frank Abiel Flower, *History of Milwaukee* (Chicago: Western Publishing Co., 1881), 721–723.

14. Maurice McKenna, *Fond du Lac County, Wisconsin, Past and Present* (Chicago: S. J. Clarke Co., 1912), 153.

15. Ira Berlin, Barbara J. Fields, Steven F. Miller, Joseph P. Reidy, and Leslie S. Rowland, *Free at Last: A Documentary History of Slavery, Emancipation, and the Civil War* (New York: New Press, 1992), 27–28.

16. McPherson, *Battle Cry of Freedom*, 355.

17. "Living Contraband—Former Slaves in the Nation's Capital During the Civil War," National Park Service website, www.nps.gov/articles/living -contraband-former-slaves-in-the-nation-s-capital-during-the-civil -war.htm; John David Smith, "Let Us All Be Grateful That We Have Col-

ored Troops That Will Fight" in *Black Soldiers in Blue: African American Troops in the Civil War Era*, ed. John David Smith (Chapel Hill: University of North Carolina Press, 2002), 11–12.

18. Chandra Manning, *Troubled Refuge: Struggling for Freedom in the Civil War* (New York: Vintage Books, 2016), 185.

19. E. B. Quiner, *Military History of Wisconsin* (Chicago: Clarke & Co., 1866), 698; "Wisconsin Union Soldiers and Runaway Freedwoman," Jubilo! The Emancipation Century website, https://jubiloemancipationcentury .wordpress.com/2013/02/19/wisconsin-union-men-and-runaway -freedwoman/.

20. "Contrabands in Kentucky," *Fond du Lac Weekly Commonwealth*, November 29, 1862; Richard H. Groves, *Blooding the Regiment: An Account of the Twenty-Second Wisconsin's Long and Difficult Apprenticeship*, 37–40, 58, D1–3 (self-pub., 2002).

21. "22nd Wisconsin Infantry History," WHS website, www.wisconsin history.org/Records/Article/CS2306; Groves, *Blooding the Regiment*, 104–115.

22. Manning, *Troubled Refuge*, 185–186; Halbert Eleazer Paine, *A Wisconsin Yankee in Confederate Bayou Country: The Civil War Reminiscences of a Union General*, ed. Samuel C. Hyde (Baton Rouge, LA: LSU Press, 2009), 75, 77–78.

23. Manning, *Troubled Refuge*, 209; "Paine, Col. Halbert E., 1826–1905," WHS website, www.wisconsinhistory.org/Records/Article/CS1618.

24. Christopher C. Wehner, *The Eleventh Wisconsin in the Civil War: A Regimental History* (Jefferson, NC: McFarland & Company, Inc., 2008), 61.

25. Wehner, *The Eleventh Wisconsin*, 63–65.

26. See James B. Rogers, *War Pictures: Experiences and Observations of a Chaplain in the U.S. Army in the War of Southern Rebellion* (Chicago: Church & Goodman, 1863).

27. Rogers, *War Pictures*, 211–226.

28. V. Jacques Voegeli, *Free but Not Equal: The Midwest and the Negro during the Civil War* (Chicago: University of Chicago Press, 1967), 60.

29. Voegeli, *Free but Not Equal*, 5–7, 86–88.

30. Frank L. Klement, *Wisconsin in the Civil War* (Madison: State Historical Society of Wisconsin, 1997), 94–95; "Clark, Satterlee Jr., 1816–1881," WHS website, www.wisconsinhistory.org/Records/Article/CS6463;

Edward Noyes, "White Opposition to Black Migration into Civil-War Wisconsin," *Lincoln Herald*, 73 (1971): 182–183.

31. *Journal of the Assembly of the State of Wisconsin. Annual Session, A.D. 1863* (Madison: 1863), 105, 694–696; Klement, *Wisconsin in the Civil War*, 95; Noyes, "White Opposition," 185–186.

32. *Fond du Lac Commonwealth*, October 22 and 29, 1862; McKenna, *Fond Du Lac County*, 156.

33. Zona Gale Breese, "Noted Author Visits City, Writes of Experiences in Tracing Family's History," *Fond du Lac Commonwealth Reporter*, October 13, 1933.

34. *Racine Weekly Advocate*, October 8, 1862.

35. "Free Labor in Racine," *Milwaukee See Bote*, November 3, 1862 (extract published in *Journal of the Assembly of Wisconsin, Annual Session 1863* [Madison: State Printer, 1863], 971).

36. Voegeli, *Free but Not Equal*, 60–62; *Fond du Lac Weekly Commonwealth*, November 5 and 12, 1862; *Racine Weekly Journal*, November 12, 1862.

37. "An Experiment," *Dodge County Citizen*, April 16, 1863.

38. Gregory Bond, "The Freedmen of Wisconsin," *Civil War Monitor* (Spring 2014): 20–21, 74; *History of Dodge County, Wisconsin* (Chicago: Western Publishing Co., 1880), 711–712; "Black Republicans," *Beaver Dam Argus*, April 15, 1863.

39. Manning, *Troubled Refuge*, 113.

40. William Cleggett, deposition in pension file of Lloyd Bryon, widow's pension application 908954, PF.

41. William J. K. Beaudot and Lance J. Herdegen, *An Irishman in the Iron Brigade: The Civil War Memoirs of James P. (Mickey) Sullivan, Sergt., Company K, Sixth Wisconsin Volunteers* (New York: Fordham University Press, 1993), 39; A. T. Glaze, *History of Business in the City and County of Fond du Lac from Early Times to the Present* (Fond du Lac, WI: Haber Printing, 1905), 309.

42. Lance Herdegen and Sherry Murphy, eds., *Four Years with the Iron Brigade: The Civil War Journal of William Ray, Company F, Seventh Wisconsin Volunteers* (Cambridge, MA: Da Capo Press, 2002), 35.

43. Rufus R. Dawes, *Service with the Sixth Wisconsin Volunteers* (Marietta, OH: 1890), 55, 200, 238.

44. "Fourth Regiment Cavalry," *Roster of Wisconsin Volunteers, War of the*

Rebellion, 1861–1865 Volume I (Madison: Democrat Printing Company), 1886, 156–201 (hereafter *RWV Vol. I*), WHS website, http://content .wisconsinhistory.org/cdm/ref/collection/quiner/id/49822; McAlroy enlistment in the Twenty-Seventh, *Roster of Wisconsin Volunteers, War of the Rebellion, 1861–1865 Volume II* (Madison: Democrat Printing Company), 1886 (hereafter *RWV Vol. II*), http://content.wisconsinhistory .org/cdm/ref/collection/quiner/id/47843.

45. Quiner, *Military History of Wisconsin*, 498–507.

46. Paine, *A Wisconsin Yankee*, 86; "Fourth Regiment Cavalry," *RWV Vol. I*, 182.

47. E. B. Quiner, *Correspondence of the Wisconsin Volunteers, 1861–1863, Volume 8*, 229, WHS website, http://digital.library.wisc.edu/1711.dl /wiarchives.uw-whs-mss00600; Michael J. Martin, *A History of the 4th Wisconsin Infantry and Cavalry in the Civil War* (New York: Savas Beatie LLC, 2006), 196; *Prescott Journal*, July 11, 1863.

48. "Fourth Regiment Cavalry," *RWV Vol. I*, 156–201; Archie Blue, Company G, Fourth Wisconsin Cavalry, *Regimental Descriptive Rolls (Blue Book*, hereafter referred to as *RDR*); "Book of Local Credits," Wisconsin Adjutant General Draft Records, 1862–1865, Series 1137, Box 8, vol. 1, 290–292, WHS Archives; Juanita Patience Moss, *The Forgotten Black Soldiers in White Regiments during the Civil War*, revised ed. (Westminster, MD: Heritage Books, 2008), 152–153.

49. "Fourth Regiment Cavalry," *RWV Vol. I*, 156–201; Moss, *The Forgotten Black Soldiers*, 152–153.

50. See *RWV Vol. II*, (Madison: Democrat Printing Company), 1886, http:// content.wisconsinhistory.org/cdm/ref/collection/quiner/id/49823.

51. "Twenty-Second Regiment Infantry," *RWV Vol. II*, 201–230.

52. *Delavan Enterprise*, July 22, 1998.

53. "Thirty-Eighth Wisconsin Infantry," *RDR*.

54. Henry Ashby invalid application 620204, PF; Wisconsin Veterans Museum website, https://wisvetsmuseum.pastperfectonline.com /byperson?keyword=Ashby%2C+Henry.

55. Letter from S. E. Clark, October 21, 1893, found in Ashby invalid application 620204, PF; Battle of Rienzi information at www.rienzihills.com /Rienzi/History/CivilWar/warears1861.htm.

56. Albert Hamlet, Compiled Military Service Records, NARA website (hereafter CMSR), www.nps.gov/civilwar/search-soldiers-detail.htm?

soldierId=9EFEBCA4-DC7A-DF11-BF36-B8AC6F5D926A; biographical
sheet and photo on Albert Hamlet, Cunningham Museum.

57. McKenney invalid certificate 295601, Pension File, Civil War and Later
    Survivors' Certificates, 1861–1934, Records of the Department of Veter-
    ans Affairs, Record Group 15, National Archives and Records Adminis-
    tration (hereafter PF).

58. McKenney and Isaac Smith invalid certificate 832548, PF; McKenney
    and Smith, CMSR; Eleventh Wisconsin Infantry: Charles Wood and
    Charles Harris, RDR.

59. Hughes invalid certificate 666988, PF; Hughes, CMSR; Historic Madison
    Inc. of Wisconsin, "Slaves," www.historicmadison.org/Madison's%20
    Past/connectingwithourpast/slaves.html.

60. Thomas invalid certificate 1141153, PF; Dabney/Thomas, CMSR; E.W.
    Leach, Racine County Militant (Racine: E.W. Leach, 1915), 134–136; Ra-
    cine Journal-News, February 22, 1922.

61. Perine to Governor Salomon, July 18, 1863, Military Correspondence,
    1837–1910, Series 49, Box 42, WHS Archives.

62. Orrin T. Maxson to William Watson, Secretary to the Governor, July 29,
    1863, Military Correspondence, 1837–1910, Series 49, Box 22, WHS
    Archives.

63. Edward Noyes, "The Negro in Wisconsin's Civil War Effort," Lincoln Her-
    ald, 69 (1967), 75; letter from Assistant Adjutant General C. W. Foster to
    Governor Salomon, July 31, 1863, Military Correspondence, 1837–1910,
    Series 49, Box 23, WHS Archives.

64. Orrin T. Maxson to Governor Salomon, October 19, 1863, Military Cor-
    respondence, 1837–1910, Series 49, Box 22, WHS Archives.

65. Noyes, "The Negro in Wisconsin's Civil War Effort," 75; original found
    in "Annual Report of the Adjutant General" in Messages of the Governor of
    Wisconsin, Together with the Annual Reports of the Officers of the State, for
    the Year A.D. 1864 (Madison, 1865), 450.

66. Birney to van Steenwyk, van Steenwyk to Salomon, October 29, 1863,
    Military Correspondence, 1837–1910, Series 49, Box 22, WHS Archives.

67. McPherson, Battle Cry of Freedom, 505.

68. Lincoln, open letter to Greeley, in Life and Works of Abraham Lincoln
    Volume 8, ed. Marion Mills Miller (New York: Current Literature Pub-
    lishing Co., 1907), 44–45.

69. McPherson, *Battle Cry of Freedom*, 557–559.

70. *Douglass' Monthly*, 721, quoted in McPherson, *Battle Cry of Freedom*, 558.

71. The Emancipation Proclamation, NARA website, www.archives.gov /exhibits/featured-documents/emancipation-proclamation.

72. See Chandra Manning, *What this Cruel War was Over: Soldiers, Slavery, and the Civil War* (New York: Vintage Books, 2007).

73. Frederick Douglass, April 6, 1863, Smithsonian National Museum of American History, "Changing America, 1863," https://americanhistory .si.edu/changing-america-emancipation-proclamation-1863-and -march-washington-1963/1863/military-service.

74. Frank R. Rollin, *Life and Public Services of Martin R. Delany, Sub-assistant Commissioner Bureau Relief of Refugees, Freedmen, and of abandoned lands, and late Major 104th U.S. Colored Troops* (Boston: Lee & Shepard, 1883), 145–147, 153.

75. Noah Andre Trudeau, *Like Men of War: Black Troops in the Civil War, 1862–1865* (Boston: Little, Brown, 1998), 91–93; War Department, Adjutant General's Office, General Orders No. 323, Washington, September 28, 1863.

76. Smith, "Let Us All Be Grateful," 36.

77. Smith, "Let Us All Be Grateful," 40.

78. Williams, *History of the Negro Troops*, 180.

79. Berlin, Fields, et al., *Free at Last*, 447–448; James W. Hollandsworth Jr., "The Execution of White Officers in Black Units by Confederate Forces during the Civil War," in *Louisiana History* 35, no. 4 (Fall 1994): 484.

80. Ella Lonn, *Desertion During the Civil War* (Gloucester, MA: Peter Smith, 1966; original published in 1928), 149–150.

81. Wisconsin First Congressional District, Class 1, 246, 254, 501, Consolidated Draft Lists, RPMGB; Wisconsin Second Congressional District, Class 1, 190, Consolidated Draft Lists, RPMGB; Wisconsin Third Congressional District, Class 1, 108, Consolidated Draft Lists, RPMGB.

82. Wisconsin Third Congressional District, Class 1, vols.1 and 2, Consolidated Draft Lists, RPMGB.

83. H. Russell Austin, *The Wisconsin Story: The Building of a Vanguard State* (Milwaukee: Milwaukee Journal, 1973), 141–142.

84. Flower, *History of Milwaukee*, 725–726.

85. McKenna, *Fond Du Lac County*, 154.

86. Flower, *History of Milwaukee*, 725–726.

87. Andrew Pratt to Governor Salomon, November 22, 1863, Military Correspondence, 1837–1910, Series 49, Box 23, WHS Archives.

88. Salomon answer to Pratt, November 27, 1863, Military Correspondence, Series 33, vol. XI, 84, WHS Archives.

89. First WI Infantry, First WI Cavalry, Thirty-Seventh WI Infantry, *RDR*.

90. "Black Towns Wisconsin," Soul of America, http://legacy.soulofamerica .com/black-towns-wisconsin.phtml; Caroline K. Andler, Ancestry of Catherine Ross, at Genealogy.com, www.genealogy.com/ftm/a/n/d /Caroline-K-Andler-Dousman/FILE/0041page.html; 1860 US Census: Chilton, Calumet County; *RWV Vol. I*, 793 and "Sixteenth Regiment, New Companies, Company F," *RWV Vol. II*, 41.

91. David Silverman, *The Brothertown and Stockbridge Indians and the Problem of Race in Early America* (Ithaca, NY: Cornell University Press, 2010), 100–105; History Cooperative, "New Guinea: Racial Identity and Inclusion in the Stockbridge Indian Communities of New York," https:// historycooperative.org/journal/new-guinea-racial-identity-and -inclusion-in-the-stockbridge-and-brothertown-indian-communities -of-new-york/.

92. "Diary of the Revels Family since 1747 to 1908," Vernon County Historical Society; Beaudot & Herdegen, *An Irishman in the Iron Brigade*, 60–61; 1860 US Census: Forest Township, Bad Ax County; Sixth WI Infantry, Henry & William Revels (*RDR*); First WI Cavalry, Aaron Revels; Third WI Cavalry, John W. Revels; Company K, Sixth WI Infantry, 535, *RWV Vol. I*.

93. First Wisconsin Infantry and Eighth Wisconsin Infantry, *RDR*; Thomas Jefferson Foundation Inc., "John Wayles Jefferson," www.monticello .org/getting-word/people/john-wayles-jefferson; "Col. Jefferson Dies in Chicago," *Madison Democrat*, March 19, 1908.

94. The Thomas Jefferson Foundation Inc., "Report of the Research Committee on Thomas Jefferson and Sally Hemings, VI. Conclusions": www .monticello.org/site/plantation-and-slavery/vi-conclusions, and "Eston Hemings Jefferson," www.monticello.org/getting-word/people /eston-hemings-jefferson; Annette Gordon-Reed, *Thomas Jefferson and Sally Hemings: An American Controversy* (Charlottesville: University of Virginia Press, 1997), 1–2, 17–18, 38–40.

95. Edward A. Miller Jr., *The Black Civil War Soldiers of Illinois: The Story of the Twenty-Ninth U.S. Colored Infantry* (Columbia: University of South Carolina Press, 1998), 9.

96. Miller, *The Black Civil War Soldiers of Illinois*, 13.

97. Wisconsin Adjutant General's Office, Special Order No. 13, April 7, 1864, Kenosha Civil War Museum Archives.

98. Alfred Weaver, Twenty-Ninth USCI, CMSR.

99. 1860 US Census: John Q. Nusom, Waupun, and Charles Rollins, Oshkosh; Fifth Congressional District, 393, 443, Consolidated Draft Lists (RPMGB); Sixty-Eighth US Colored Infantry, CMSR.

100. Bell invalid certificate 1081956, PF.

101. Spelled either "Paten" or "Payton."

102. Twenty-Ninth USCI: Roberts, Allen, Sink, Gaines, Underhill, Carter, Bryon, Colder, McKenney, Isaac Smith, Briggs, CMSR; Muster and Descriptive Roll, Company F, Twenty-Ninth United States Colored Infantry, Series 1200, Box 255, folders 2 and 6, WHS Archives.

103. Muster and Descriptive Roll, Company F, Twenty-Ninth United States Colored Infantry, Series 1200, Box 255, folder 2, WHS Archives; Roberts invalid certificate 336574, PF; Robinson, Ross, Roberts, CMSR.

104. Muster and Descriptive Roll, Company F, Twenty-Ninth United States Colored Infantry, Series 1200, Box 255, folder 2, WHS Archives; Wisconsin Fourth Congressional District, Box 3, Original Draft Lists and Wisconsin Sixth Congressional District, Box 2, folder 3, Original Draft Lists (RPMGB); Isaac Smith, invalid certificate 832548, PF.

105. Muster and Descriptive Roll, Company F, Twenty-Ninth United States Colored Infantry, Series 1200, Box 255, folder 2, WHS Archives.

106. Berlin, Fields, et al., *Free at Last*, 345, 359; *The War of the Rebellion: A Compilation of the Official Records of the Union and Confederate Armies*, Series III, vol. 2, 883–897.

107. Berlin, Fields, et al., *Free at Last*, 359–360.

108. Berlin, Fields, et al., *Free at Last*, 363–365.

109. M. Griffith widow's certificate 552981, PF. The letter appears to have been written by the soldier himself or another soldier on his behalf.

110. The Civil War page, National Park Service: www.nps.gov/civilwar/search-battle-units-detail.htm?battleUnitCode=UWI0039RI and www.nps.gov/civilwar/search-battles-detail.htm?battleCode=tn031; "Thirty-Ninth WI Infantry," *RDR*.

111. Bruce Mouser, *Black La Crosse, Wisconsin, 1850–1906: Settlers, Entrepreneurs & Exodusters* (La Crosse, WI: La Crosse County Historical Society, 2002), 37–38; University of Wisconsin La Crosse, Murphy Library Digital Collections.

112. Noyes, "The Negro in Wisconsin's Civil War Effort," 77; *Milwaukee Sentinel* editorial, "Important Order Respecting Substitutes," July 21, 1864.

113. Muster-in Rolls, United States Colored Infantry, Series 1200, Box 255, folders 2 and 6, WHS Archives; Third USCHA, all Wisconsin recruits, CMSR.

114. Military Correspondence: Series 49, Box 24, WHS Archives.

115. *Jackson County Banner*, republished in *Milwaukee Sentinel*, September 1, 1864.

116. Flower, *History of Milwaukee*, 731.

117. Eighteenth USCI: Graham, Kane, Paine, CMSR.

118. Graham, Kane, Paine, CMSR.

119. "Lincoln Unimpressed with Kentucky's Impressment of African-Americans," The History Engine, https://historyengine.richmond.edu /episodes/view/6518.

120. Johnson, Riley, Burrell, Howard, Turner, CMSR; Funding Universe, "Marshall and Ilsley Corporation History", www.fundinguniverse.com /company-histories/marshall-ilsley-corporation-history/; James W. Low, *Low's Railway Directory for 1862* (New York: Wynkoop, Hallenbeck & Thomas, Printers, 1862).

121. *Annual Report of the Adjutant General of the State of Wisconsin, for the Year Ending December 31, 1864* (Madison: Atlee and Rublee, 1865), 10, accessed at https://babel.hathitrust.org/cgi/pt?id=wu.89070036934 ;view=1up;seq=20.

122. Flower, *History of Milwaukee*, 734–735; *AG Report 1865*, 23–24; Third USCHA: Reynolds, CMSR.

Chapter Three

1. The following sections are ordered based on when the units went into service with Wisconsin African American men on their rosters.

2. Frank R. Rollin, *Life and Public Services of Martin R. Delany, Sub-assistant Commissioner Bureau Relief of Refugees, Freedmen, and of abandoned lands, and late Major 104th U.S. Colored Troops* (Boston: Lee & Shepard, 1883 {c1868}), 145–154; Luis F. *Emilio, History of the Fifty-Fourth Regiment of*

Massachusetts Volunteer Infantry, 1863–1865 (Boston: Boston Book, 1894), 9–12, 19–20, 35–36, 339, 367; Charles Barnard Fox and Fifty-Fifth Regimental Association. *Record of Service of the Fifty-Fifth Regiment of Massachusetts Volunteer Infantry* (Cambridge, MA: John Wilson & Son, 1868), 1–6.

3. Emilio, *History of the Fifty-Fourth Regiment*, 24; Fox, *Record of Service of the Fifty-Fifth Regiment*, 112, 118, 120, 124, 136, 141, 142; pension card, Richard Thomas, at Fold 3, www.fold3.com/image/249/2982487; Noah Andre Trudeau, *Voices of the 55th: Letters from the 55th Massachusetts Volunteers, 1861–1865* (Dayton, Ohio: Morningside, 1996), 11–14.

4. E. Diggs, Compiled Military Service Records, NARA website (hereafter CMSR); Fox, *Record of Service of the Fifty-Fifth Regiment*, 124.

5. Annual Return of Alterations and Casualties incident to the Fifty-fourth Regiment of Massachusetts Volunteers. Morris Island, January 6, 1864; Tucker, CMSR.

6. The 1989 film *Glory* presents the history of the Fifty-Fourth from its creation through the Battle of Fort Wagner.

7. Arthur W. Bergeron Jr., "The Battle of Olustee," in *Black Soldiers in Blue: African American Troops in the Civil War Era*, ed. John David Smith (Chapel Hill: University of North Carolina Press, 2002), 136–149.

8. Trudeau, *Voices of the 55th*, 18.

9. Bergeron, "The Battle of Olustee," 137–151, 467.

10. *The War of the Rebellion: A Compilation of the Official Records of the Union and Confederate Armies* (hereafter *OR*), Series I, vol. 35, Part 1, "Reports" (Washington, DC: Government Printing Office, 1892), 298, 315.

11. Tucker, CMSR.

12. Fifty-Fourth Massachusetts Infantry muster rolls, April 30, 1864, Fold 3 database: Lee, Field and Staff, www.fold3.com/image/249/296975657; Tucker, Company F, www.fold3.com/image/249/296976150.

13. Trudeau, *Voices of the 55th*, 116–118.

14. Trudeau, *Voices of the 55th*, 23.

15. John David Smith, "Let Us All Be Grateful That We Have Colored Troops That Will Fight" in *Black Soldiers in Blue: African American Troops in the Civil War Era*, ed. John David Smith (Chapel Hill: University of North Carolina Press, 2002), 51.

16. Fox, *Record of Service of the Fifty-Fifth Regiment*, 111.

17. Noah Andre Trudeau, *Like Men of War: Black Troops in the Civil War,*
    1862–1865 (Boston: Little, Brown, 1998), 254; members of Twenty-
    Ninth USCI, CMSR.
18. Fox, *Record of Service of the Fifty-Fifth Regiment,* 35–37.
19. Trudeau, *Like Men of War,* 319–330.
20. Bowdry, E. Cross, CMSR; Trudeau, *Voices of the 55th,* 163, says that the
    regimental roster indicates that Cross was not injured. However, Cross's
    muster out roll gives the details of his wound at Honey Hill.
21. National Park Service, The Civil War, Battle Unit Details: Fifty-Fourth
    and Fifty-Fifth Massachusetts Regiments, www.nps.gov/civilwar
    /search-battle-units.htm#fq%5B%5D=State%3A%22Massachusetts
    %22&fq%5B%5D=Battle_Unit_Function%3A%22Infantry%22.
22. The Civil War; Battle Unit Details, National Parks Service website, www
    .nps.gov/civilwar/search-battle-units-detail.htm?battleUnitCode=UUS
    0067RI00C; descriptive rolls and muster rolls for all members of the
    Sixty-Eighth USCI, www.fold3.com, CMSR.
23. William R. Thomas, Babcock, Bell, Flows, Grace, Nusom, Rollins, CMSR.
24. Series I, Vol 39, Part I—Reports, *OR,* 255, 300–303; all Wisconsin mem-
    bers of the Sixty-Eighth USCI, CMSR.
25. Morning reports book, Eighteenth USCI, NARA; Babcock, Phillips, Roll-
    ins, CMSR.
26. Series I, Vol. 49, Part I—Reports, Correspondence, etc. 287–288, Report
    No. 81, Brigadier General John P. Hawkins, commanding First Division,
    US Colored Troops, *OR.*
27. Series I, Vol. 49, Part 1—"Reports," Correspondence, etc. casualties, 102,
    114, *OR;* McDonald, CMSR.
28. Series I, Vol. 49, Part 1— "Reports," 102, 103, 114, *OR;* Forty-Seventh
    USCI Walter, Fiftieth USCI Shepard and Ford, CMSR.
29. Infantry Regiments 31 (444–470) and 33 (501–524), *Roster of Wisconsin*
    Volunteers, War of the Rebellion, 1861–1865 Volume II (Madison: Democrat
    Printing Company), 1886 (hereafter *RWV Vol. II*), http://content
    .wisconsinhistory.org/cdm/ref/collection/quiner/id/49823.
30. Burnett, Carroll, Rosier, CMSR; Burnett invalid certificate 349601,
    Pension File, Civil War and Later Survivors Certificates, 1861–1934,
    Records of the Department of Veterans Affairs, Record Group 15, NARA
    (hereafter PF); Rosier widow's certificate 829372, PF; Wisconsin Second

Congressional District, Class 1, 321, Consolidated Draft Lists, RPMGB and Wisconsin First Congressional District, 253, Consolidated Draft Lists, RPMGB.

31. Julius Valentine (Twenty-Ninth USCI), John Valentine (Seventeenth USCI), Shadrach Valentine (One Hundred Second USCI), CMSR; Wisconsin Fifth Congressional District, 588, Consolidated Draft Lists, RPMGB.

32. Edward A. Miller Jr., *The Black Civil War Soldiers of Illinois: The Story of the Twenty-Ninth U.S. Colored Infantry* (Columbia: University of South Carolina Press, 1998), 36.

33. *Memorial of Colonel John A. Bross, Twenty-Ninth U.S. Colored Troops, who fell leading the assault on Petersburgh, July 30, 1864: together with a sermon by his pastor, Rev. Arthur Swazey* (Chicago: Tribune Book and Job Office, 1865), 10–11, accessed at http://content.wisconsinhistory.org/cdm/ref /collection/quiner/id/30271 (hereafter *Bross Memorial*).

34. Miller, *The Black Civil War Soldiers of Illinois*, 38–41, 46–52; Morning Reports, Twenty-Ninth Regiment USCI, NARA.

35. Twenty-Ninth USCI: Edward Carter, John Dorson, Samuel Johnson, Joseph Jordan, William Sullivan, CMSR.

36. Twenty-Ninth USCI: Edward Hunter, CMSR.

37. Twenty-Ninth USCI: Wade Hampton, CMSR.

38. Muster and Descriptive Roll, Company F, Twenty-Ninth United States Colored Infantry, Series 1200, Box 255, folder 2, Wisconsin Historical Society (hereafter WHS) Archives; Miller, *The Black Civil War Soldiers of Illinois*, 32, 34, 44.

39. Lewis Orr invalid certificate 708239, PF.

40. Lewis Orr invalid certificate 708239, PF; Twenty-Ninth USCI: A. Foggey, J. Henry, H. Hill, J. Houton, P. Houton, H. Mackay, P. Mackay, J. Monroe, D. Moore, J. Norton, G. Orr, J. Orr, L. Or, J. Rice, T. Starrett. P. Thurman—Claims for Compensation for Enlisted Slaves, CMSR.

41. "Guide to Civil War Slave Compensation Claims from Compiled Military Service Records," St. Louis (MO) County Library website, www.slcl.org /content/guide-civil-war-slave-compensation-claims-compiled-military -service-records.

42. Muster rolls, Wisconsin USCT volunteers, WHS Archives.

43. Morning Reports, Company F, Twenty-Ninth USCT, NARA; Muster and

Descriptive Roll, Company F, Twenty-Ninth USCI, Series 1200, Box 255, folder 2, WHS Archives.

44. Twenty-Ninth USCI: Muster and Descriptive Roll, Company F, Twenty-ninth USCI, Series 1200, Box 255, folders 2 and 6, WHS Archives; Morning Reports, Twenty-Ninth USCI, NARA.

45. Richard Slotkin, *No Quarter: The Battle of the Crater, 1864* (New York: Random House, 2009), 132–134.

46. Slotkin, *No Quarter*, 128–134, 147; Miller, *The Black Civil War Soldiers of Illinois*, 59–60.

47. Series I, vol. 40, Part I, "Reports," 246–250, OR; Twenty-Third USCI: Diggs, CMSR; Thirty-Seventh Wisconsin Infantry: Roseman, Nash, Donaldson, CMSR.

48. *Bross Memorial*, 79; General Henry Goddard Thomas, "The Colored Troops at Petersburg," in *Battles and Leaders of the Civil War*, vol. IV (New York: Century Co., 1888), 563–567.

49. Thomas, "The Colored Troops at Petersburg," 563; Joseph T. Wilson, *The Black Phalanx: A History of the Negro Soldiers of the United States in the War of 1775–1812, 1861–'65* (Hartford, CT: American Publishing Company, 1888), 413, 426; George Washington Williams, *A History of the Negro Troops in the War of the Rebellion, 1861–1865*, reprint (New York: Negro University Press, 1969), 341; Edwin Bearss, *The Petersburg Campaign: Volume 1, the Eastern Front Battles, June–August 1864* (El Dorado Hills, CA: Savas Beatie LLC, 2012), 216.

50. Slotkin, *No Quarter*, 203, 266; Bearss, *The Petersburg Campaign*, 219.

51. James W. Guthrie, *Camp-Fires of the Afro-American; or, the Colored Man as Patriot* (Philadelphia: Afro-American Publishing Company, 1899), 528–529 (reprinted testimony of Henry Reese).

52. Wilson, *The Black Phalanx*, 427; Williams, *A History of the Negro Troops*, 342; Slotkin, *No Quarter*, 93–94.

53. Slotkin, *No Quarter*, 289–294; Bearss, *The Petersburg Campaign*, 234–235.

54. Series I, vol. 40, Part 1, "Reports," OR, 248. Company F figures are modified based on CMSR.

55. Twenty-Ninth USCI: Jordan, Allen, J. Jackson, J. Mackay, Price, Robinson, Ross, Stark, Strauder, C. Tinsley, CMSR; Twenty-Third USCI, A. Diggs, CMSR.

56. *Bross Memorial*, 75, address by H. G. Spafford, Esq., to the Circuit Court

of Cook County, IL. WHS website, http://content.wisconsinhistory.org /cdm/ref/collection/quiner/id/30271.

57. Twenty-Ninth USCI: Maxon, Stevens, Bailey, Burnett, Brockwa, CMSR.

58. Twenty-Ninth USCI: Bross, CMSR; *Bross Memorial*, 75; Slotkin, *No Quarter*, 252–253.

59. Slotkin, *No Quarter*, 253.

60. Thomas, "The Colored Troops at Petersburg," 564.

61. Grant's testimony to the Congressional inquiry, quoted in Guthrie, *Camp-Fires of the Afro-American*, 512.

62. Twenty-Ninth USCI: Bibb, Oden, CMSR.

63. Twenty-Ninth USCI: Henry Sink and Charles South, CMSR; Henry Sink invalid certificate 101361, PF; Charles South/Walden invalid pension certificate 68350, PF.

64. Twenty-Ninth USCI: Weaver, CMSR; Alfred Weaver invalid certificate 442418, PF.

65. Twenty-Ninth USCI: Sink, South, Weaver, CMSR; Sink, South, and Weaver, PF.

66. The Friends of Freedmen's Cemetery: "Convalescent Soldiers in L'Ouverture Hospital "Express Our Views" on Burial Location," www.freedmens cemetery.org/resources/documents/louverture.shtml, *includes list of petition signers*. Original petition is located in *NARA Record Group 92, Records of the Office of the Quartermaster General, Entry 576, General Correspondence and Reports Related to National and Post Cemeteries*.

67. African American Historic Sites, www.aahistoricsitesva.org/items /show/237; City of Alexandria website, www.alexandriava.gov/historic /civilwar/default.aspx?id=73499; *Friends of Freedmen's Cemetery*, www .freedmenscemetery.org/resources/documents/louverture.shtml; *Carroll and Christian (Christine)*, CMSR; Burial list: Friends of Freedmen's Cemetery, www.freedmenscemetery.org/burials/burials.pdf and copied from plaque in Freedmen's Cemetery, December 8, 18.

68. Arlington National Cemetery brochure, March 2015, www .arlingtoncemetery.mil/Portals/0/Web%20Final%20PDF%20of%20 Brochure%20March%202015.pdf; Martin Lyons, Co. F, Twenty-Ninth USCI, buried in section 27, grave 2165, https://ancexplorer.army.mil /publicwmv/#/arlington-national/search/results/1 CgVMeW9ucxIGTW FydGlu/.

69. 1850 US Census: Oregon, Dane County, and 1860 US Census: Newark
    Valley, Adams County; Original Draft Lists, WI: Sixth Congressional
    District, Box 2, Folder 2; S. Valentine, CMSR; Find a Grave: www
    .findagrave.com/memorial/47010607.

70. Twenty-Ninth USCI: Underhill, Carter, Colder, CMSR.

71. Miller, *The Black Civil War Soldiers of Illinois*, 106–139; Twenty-Ninth
    USCI: L. Washington Jr., Wm. Albare, Crawford, Bynum, J. Jones, Bar-
    num, Lumpkin, Brooks, S. Burrell, and Cosley, CMSR.

72. Special Orders No. 116. In Records Group 94, Entry # 112–115, PI–17,
    Twenty-Ninth Regiment USCI, Order Book, volume 1; Twenty-Ninth
    USCI: Wm. P. Stewart, Thornton, CMSR.

73. Twenty-Ninth USCI: Underhill, Lumpkins, Paten, CMSR.

74. Morning Reports, Twenty-Ninth USCI, April 1865, 18, NARA.

75. Miller, *The Black Civil War Soldiers of Illinois*, 145–150; National Parks
    Service Battle Unit Details, Twenty-Ninth USCI, www.nps.gov/civilwar
    /search-battle-units-detail.htm?battleUnitCode=UUS0029RI00C.

76. George Washington Williams, *History of the Negro Race in America from
    1619 to 1880: Negroes as Slaves, as Soldiers, and as Citizens* (New York: G.
    P. Putnam and Sons, Knickerbocker Press, 1883), 546.

77. Morning Reports, Twenty-Ninth USCI, April 1865, NARA.

78. Twenty-Ninth USCI: Bennett, S. Johnson, Furman, Wm. Griffith, Henry,
    J. Houton, Leeper, Lyons, H. Mackay, A. McCann, H. Modley, Morehead,
    Paten Smith, H. Williams, Witherspoon, CMSR.

79. Eighteenth USCI: Willis, Sheldon, Ousley, C. Bostwick, CMSR; Ousley
    widow's certificate 505286, PF; Wisconsin First Congressional District,
    Class 1, vol. 2, Ousley, Consolidated Draft Lists, RPMGB; email from
    Caroline Andler to the author, December 12, 2012.

80. Eighteenth USCI: all men credited to or enlisted in Wisconsin, CMSR.

81. Eighteenth USCI: Hudson, CMSR; Hudson invalid certificate 1161617, PF.

82. *Regimental Books, Eighteenth U.S. Colored Infantry*, Records Group 94,
    Entry # 112–115, PI–17, vol. 5, Companies A–D, Company D Morning
    Reports, October 16–30, 1864, NARA.

83. *Regimental Books, Eighteenth U.S. Colored Infantry*, Records Group 94,
    Entry # 112–115, PI–17. Vol. 5, Companies A–D. Vol. 6, Companies E–K,
    November and December, 1864, NARA.

84. Sheldon invalid certificate 835970, PF.

85. W. E. B. Du Bois, *Black Reconstruction in America, 1860–1880*, reprint (Cleveland: World Publishing Co., 1964), 110.

86. *Regimental Books, Eighteenth U.S. Colored Infantry*, Records Group 94, Entry # 112–115, PI–17: Vol. 5, Companies A–D. and Vol. 6, Companies E–K, NARA.

87. Hudson invalid certificate 1161617, PF.

88. Eighteenth USCI: all Wisconsin men, CMSR.

89. Smith, "Let Us All Be Grateful," 41.

90. Richard Wheeler, *Sherman's March* (New York: Thomas Y. Crowell Publishers, 1978), 17–18.

91. Wheeler, *Sherman's March*, 17–18.

92. First WI Infantry, Eighth WI Infantry, *RDR*; Thos. Jefferson's Monticello, "Getting Word: African American Families of Monticello," www.monticello.org/getting-word/people/beverly-frederick-jefferson.

93. Carole Emberton, "A Hungry Belly and Freedom," We're History webpage, http://werehistory.org/hungry-belly-and-freedom/.

94. Anna Sarah Rubin, "Sherman's March in American History and Cultural Memory," Oxford Research Encyclopedias, http://oxfordre.com/americanhistory/view/10.1093/acrefore/9780199329175.001.0001/acrefore-9780199329175-e-204; Civil War Library, www.civilwarlibrary.org/sherman-s-march-chronology.html.

95. "African Americans and Sherman's March," Civil War Emancipation webpage, https://cwemancipation.wordpress.com/2014/12/07/african-americans-and-shermans-march/; Wheeler, *Sherman's March*, 108.

96. Julia Pferdehirt, *Freedom Train North: Stories of the Underground Railroad in Wisconsin* (Madison: Wisconsin Historical Society Press, 2014), 89–90.

97. National Parks Service, The Civil War; Battle Unit Details, www.nps.gov/civilwar/search-battle-units-detailhtm?battleUnitCode=UUS0049RI00C.

98. *Regimental Records, Forty-Ninth USCI, Descriptive Book*, vol. 1 (Wisconsin volunteers appear beginning on page 52 through page 58), original volume viewed at NARA, Washington, DC; Forty-Ninth USCI: all Wisconsin men, notably Edward Hall, Hines, Hunt, Ironmonger, F. Richards, Milum, Jerry Taylor, Chesley Taylor, Enoch Taylor, John Taylor, CMSR.

99. Forty-Ninth USCI: M. Smith, Hall, Ironmonger, C. Taylor, E. Taylor, Je. Taylor, Jo. Taylor, Hines, Milum, Richards, CMSR; Richards-Simons

marriage certificate, Calumet County marriages, vol. 1, 136, WHS Library.

100. Forty-Ninth USCI: all Wisconsin men, notably Milum, Hicks, Foster, CMSR.

101. Morning Reports, Forty-Ninth USCI, vols. 1–8, NARA.

102. Forty-Ninth USCI: comments are from the muster roll cards of Delia Carter, Lizzie Dixon, Martha Freeman, CMSR.

103. Forty-Ninth USCI: Lucinda Beard, Adam Beard, CMSR; Adam Beard, widow's certificate 773045, PF.

104. Forty-Ninth USCI: all members credited to Wisconsin towns, CMSR.

105. Sarah Anderson, *"Quite Unhealthy": Deadly Disease Among Albemarle-born Black Soldiers*, University of Virginia John L. Nau Center for Civil War History, http://naucenter.as.virginia.edu/blog-page/541.

106. Grimes, CMSR; Grimes widow's certificate 726926, PF.

107. Grimes invalid certificate 348944, PF; Hillman, invalid certificate 1117795, PF; R. Thompson invalid certificate 166248, PF.

108. Sixty-Eighth USCI: Jones, Thomas, CMSR; unassigned: Williams, CMSR.

109. Sixty-Seventh USCI: Adams, Dodge, Newsom, Jackson, Campbell, Battise, Kneley, CMSR.

110. Smith, "Let Us All Be Grateful," 42.

111. The Civil War: Battle Unit Details, National Parks Service website, www.nps.gov/civilwar/search-battle-units-detail.htm?battleUnitCode=UUS0067RI00C.

112. Sixty-Fifth USCI: Thompson, Battise, CMSR.

113. The Civil War, Battle Unit Details, National Parks Service website, www.nps.gov/civilwar/search-battle-units-detail.htm?battleUnitCode=UUS0067RI00C; Abraham Jackson, David Newsom, Milton Crawford, Samuel Lackey, William Kneley.

114. Seventeenth USCI: all WI volunteers, notably Valentine, Morgan, CMSR; 1850 US Census: Town of Rutland and Town of Oregon, Dane County; 1860 US Census: Town of Trimbelle, Pierce County, City of Janesville, Rock County, and Town of Newark Valley, Adams County.

115. The Civil War, Battle Unit Details, National Parks Service website, www.nps.gov/civilwar/search-battle-units-detail.htm?battleUnitCode=UUS0067RI00C; CMSR: all WI men in Seventeenth USCI.

116. David L. Valuska, *The African American in the Union Navy: 1861–1865*

(New York: Garland Publishing Inc., 1993), 19; Michael J. Bennett, *Union Jacks: Yankee Sailors in the Civil War* (Chapel Hill: University of North Carolina Press, 2004), 157–158.

117. Valuska, *The African American in the Union Navy*, 67.

118. *Official Records of the Union and Confederate Navies in the War of the Rebellion* (Washington, DC: Government Printing Office, 1897; reprinted 1987), Series I, vol. 6, 252.

119. Valuska, *The African American in the Union Navy*, 20–23; Bennett, *Union Jacks*, 158.

120. Valuska, *The African American in the Union Navy*, 3.

121. James L. Mooney, ed., *Dictionary of American Naval Fighting Ships* (Washington, DC: Naval History Division: Government Printing Office, 1969), vol. 2, 429; vol. 4, 10; Navy Rendezvous Index Cards: Barber, Lewis, Mason, Mitchell; Valuska, 161, 242, 279, 282.

122. The Civil War, Battle Unit Details, Third Regiment, United States Colored Heavy Artillery, National Parks Service website, www.nps.gov/civilwar /search-battle-units-detail.htm?battleUnitCode=UUS0003RAH0C; Stephen V. Ash, *A Massacre in Memphis: The Race Riot that Shook the Nation One Year after the Civil War* (New York: Hill and Wang, 2013), 76.

123. Third USCHA, CMSR: soldiers who enlisted in Wisconsin; Billy Brookfield, CMSR.

124. Williams, Brown, Douglas, Yates, CMSR.

125. Alfred Green, Henry Johnson, James Lay, Jerret Nelson, William Green, William Riley, Van Spence, Pinckney Taylor, John Thomas, and Monroe Wayne, CMSR.

126. Dangerfield, Green, Wilson, CMSR.

127. Branum, Holden, CMSR. Holden, widow's certificate 523781, PF; 1880 US Census: Fox Lake, Dodge County; 1900 and 1910 US Census: La Crosse; 1885 WI Veterans Census: Milwaukee. Isaac Holden's wife Julia said late in her life that she had served as a cook for General Franz Sigel of the Twenty-Sixth WI Infantry before and during the war.

128. "USCT History," African American Civil War Memorial and Museum, www.afroamcivilwar.org/about-us/usct-history.html. It is unclear if this quote comes from a speech, letter, or conversation.

129. Trudeau, *Like Men of War*, 458.

130. *Series I, Vol. 47, Part I, Serial 98, OR, 1028, 1042–1043*; Emilio, *History of the Fifty-Fourth Regiment, 293.*

131. Trudeau, *Like Men of War*, 395.

132. Robert J. Zalimas Jr., "A Disturbance in the City," in *Black Soldiers in Blue*, John David Smith, ed., 372–379.

133. Tucker, CMSR. The charge of desertion was officially removed from his military record in 1889.

134. Fifty-Fifth Massachusetts: all Wisconsin members, CMSR.

135. "The Grand Review of Armies: 1865 and 2015," Jubilo! The Emancipation Century: African Americans in the 19th Century: Slavery, Resistance, Abolition, the Civil War, Emancipation, Reconstruction, and the Nadir, https://jubiloemancipationcentury.wordpress.com/2015/08/17 /the-unions-grand-review-1865-and-2015/.

136. Miller, *The Black Civil War Soldiers of Illinois*, 152–153.

137. Morning Reports, Twenty-Ninth USCI, April–May 1865, p. 20, NARA.

138. Miller, *The Black Civil War Soldiers of Illinois*, 157–158.

139. Juneteenth Day—Milwaukee, www.juneteenthdaymilwaukee.com /juneteenth-day-history.

140. Miller, *The Black Civil War Soldiers of Illinois*, 158–159; Twenty-Ninth USCI: Wilson, Summers, Norton, P. Mackay, Bryon, CMSR.

141. Charles Henry Taylor invalid certificate 340413, PF.

142. Miller, *The Black Civil War Soldiers of Illinois*, 160–169; Morning Reports, Twenty-Ninth USCI, April 1865, NARA.

143. Sixty-Eighth USCI: all Wisconsin men, CMSR.

144. Seventeenth and Eighteenth USCI, CMSR.

145. Forty-Ninth USCI: notably Freeman, Tillman, CMSR.

146. Ash, *A Massacre in Memphis*, 84.

147. Ash, *A Massacre in Memphis*, 77.

148. "Memphis Riot, 1866," at BlackPast.org, https://blackpast.org/aah /memphis-riot-1866; Donald R. Shaffer, *After the Glory: The Struggles of Black Civil War Veterans* (Lawrence: University Press of Kansas, 2004), 25–26, 33–34; Ash, 93–158; Report of the Select Committee on the Memphis Riots (Washington, DC: Government Printing Office, 1866), 35.

149. Sixty-Fifth USCI: Allen, CMSR; Allen widow's certificate 856149, PF.

150. 1860 US Census: Town of Forest, Vernon County: Barton, Stewart, Roberts; Sauk County: Woodland Township—Weaver, Westfield Township—Thornton; Columbia County Fort Winnebago Township—Rosier; Waukesha County Town of Eagle—Sutfen.

151. Company B, Thirty-second WI Infantry, *RDR*; unassigned: F. Barton, CMSR.

152. Unassigned USCI: Felix Barton, CMSR.

153. Seventeenth USCI, Huston, CMSR; Letter from Wisconsin Acting Assistant Provost Marshal General's Office to the Commander of the Twenty-Ninth Regiment USCT, May 30, 1865, Series 1200, Box 255, WHS Archives.

154. Letter from Hannah Rosier to Governor Lewis, February 3, 1865.

155. Fifth WI Infantry: Rosier, *RDR*.

156. Edward Noyes, "The Negro in Wisconsin's Civil War Effort," *Lincoln Herald* 69 (1967), 77–78; *Journal of the Wisconsin Senate*, 1864, p. 53, 68.

Chapter Four

1. Doug Welch, "The Milton House and the Underground Railroad," *Wisconsin Magazine of History* 103 (Fall 2019): 20–22.

2. Letter from Andrew Pratt to Governor Salomon, November 22, 1863, Military Correspondence: Series 49, Box 23, WHS Archives; Salomon's answer to Pratt, November 27, 1863, Military Correspondence: Series 33, vol. XI, p. 84, WHS Archives.

3. Ezra Goodrich, *The Negro Imbroglio in the Milton Lodge of the Good Templars* (self-pub., 1865), Milton Historical Society Museum; 1880 US Census: Wells, Faribault County, MN.

4. A. B. Lee obituary, *Milton Journal*, April 6, 1905.

5. 1870 US Census Mortality Schedule: Milton, Rock County.

6. Rock County Marriages, vol. 4, 343, WHS Library. Interracial marriages were rare before and after the war, but at least eight black veterans living in Wisconsin were married to white women.

7. Dane County Marriages, vol. 3, 300, WHS Library; letter from Jennie Drew to Milton Historical Society, February 26, 1979, Milton Historical Society.

8. *Dodge County Citizen*, June 22, 1865.

9. *Beaver Dam Argus*, June 21, 1865.

10. *Beaver Dam Argus*, September 13, 1865.

11. 1870 US Census: City of Beaver Dam, Dodge County; 1875 Wisconsin State Census: City of Beaver Dam, Dodge County.

12. *Chilton Times*, August 26, September 2 and 9, 1865 and May 26, July 7, and August 18, 1866.

13. "Thomas, R.," Compiled Military Service Records, National Archives website (hereafter CMSR); Anderson Nash invalid certificate 411734, Pension File, Civil War and Later Survivors' Certificates, 1861–1934, Records of the Department of Veterans Affairs, Record Group 15, National Archives and Records Administration (hereafter PF); John Smith (Richard Burton) widow's certificate 860818, PF. Anderson Nash was Thomas's nephew, and Thomas's ex-wife married John Smith, veteran of the Forty-Ninth USCI.

14. "The Story of Gus Cowen," *Mukwonago Chief*, November 14, 1984; Find a Grave, www.findagrave.com/memorial/183162689/augustus-cohen.

15. Wisconsin Legislature, Petitions, remonstrances, and resolutions, 1836–1997, Series 180, Box 27, WHS Archives.

16. *Milwaukee Sentinel*, October 10, 1865.

17. *Wisconsin Legislative Reference Bureau, State of Wisconsin 2011–2012 Blue Book* (Madison, 2011), 223.

18. John Holzhueter, "Ezekiel Gillespie, Lost and Found," *Wisconsin Magazine of History* 60, no. 3 (Spring 1977): 178–184.

19. Holzhueter, "Ezekiel Gillespie," 179; Governor's proclamation, published in *Prescott Journal*, April 28, 1866.

20. *Prescott Journal*, April 21, 1866.

21. *Dodge County Citizen*, April 5, 1866.

22. *Milwaukee Sentinel*, April 5 and 6, 1866.

23. La Crosse County Poll Lists, 1859–1868, 1891–1903, Series 11, Box 1, folder 1, UW–La Crosse Area Research Center.

24. *Fond du Lac Weekly Commonwealth*, September 16, October 7, and October 14, 1868.

25. *Fond du Lac Daily Commonwealth*, September 9, 11, 21, and 28, and October 8, 1872.

26. *Fond du Lac Daily Commonwealth*, September 3 and 4, 1872.

27. *Janesville Gazette*, August 19, 1872.

28. *Fox Lake Representative*, undated scrapbook entry, L-99-5-1, Harriet O'Connell Historical Room, Fox Lake Public Library.

29. *Janesville Gazette*, October 2, 1872.

30. 1870 US Census: City of Fond du Lac, Fond du Lac County: Sink, Gaines, Newsom, Reed, Patterson; Village of Rosendale: Patterson.

31. 1870 US Census: Fond du Lac County.

32. 1870 US Census: Wisconsin, for towns noted after each veteran's name.

33. 1870 US Census: City of Eau Claire.

34. 1860 US Census: Third Ward, Racine; 1870 US Census: Sixth Ward, Racine.

35. Isaac Smith invalid certificate 832548, PF; McKenney, invalid certificate 295601, PF.

36. Bruce L. Mouser, *For Labor, Race, and Liberty: George Edwin Taylor, His Historic Run for the White House, and the Making of Independent Black Politics* (Madison: University of Wisconsin Press, 2011), 22.

37. *Milwaukee Sentinel*, September 2, 1872.

38. Census Bureau, US Department of the Interior, *Statistics of the Population of the United States at the 10th Census* (June 1, 1880) (Washington, DC: Government Printing Office, 1883), 414–415.

39. Ruby West Jackson and Walter T. McDonald, *Oral History Research Report for Old World Wisconsin, Pleasant Ridge African-American Exhibit*, 1998, 6, Cunningham Museum.

40. William Thomas widow's certificate 420944, PF.

41. Lee invalid certificate 751637, PF; Jones invalid certificate 586111, PF.

42. Thomas Buchanan, "Black Milwaukee: 1890–1915" (master's thesis, University of Wisconsin–Milwaukee, 1974), 128.

43. Sally Albertz, "Fond du Lac's Black Community and Their Church: 1865–1943," in *Source of the Lake: 150 Years of History in Fond du Lac*, Clarence B. Davis, ed. (Fond du Lac, WI: Action Printing, 2002), 38–39; Western Historical Company, History of Dodge County, Wisconsin (Chicago: Western Historical Co., 1880), 473.

44. Zachary Cooper, *Black Settlers in Rural Wisconsin* (Madison: State Historical Society of Wisconsin, 1977), 8.

45. Dorothy Eaton Ahlgren and Mary Cotter Beeler, *A History of Prescott, WI: A River City and Farming Community on the St. Croix and Mississippi* (Prescott Area Historical Society, 1996), 323; Prescott Methodist Church

records, 1860–1879, Church and Cemetery Records, Genealogical Society of Utah Project: Pierce County, Wisconsin, 1844–1980, reel 10, item 1, Micro 24, UW–River Falls.

46. Sometimes spelled "Artist."

47. Parsons invalid certificate 127207, PF.

48. 1870 US Census of Agriculture: Town of Forest, Vernon County.

49. Twenty-Ninth USCI: Charles Allen, CMSR; Vernon County Deeds, vol. R, 239, WHS Library; 1870 US Census: Town of Forest, Vernon County.

50. 1870 US Census of Agriculture: Town of Forest, Vernon County.

51. 1870 US Census: Town of Forest, Vernon County; Vernon County marriages, vol. 1, 300.

52. 1870 US Census: Town of Westfield, Sauk County; Stewart widow's certificate 648648, PF.

53. 1870 US Census: Town of Westfield, Sauk County; Thornton invalid certificate 321030, PF.

54. 1870 US Census: Town of Woodland, Sauk County.

55. 1870 US Census: Woodland Township, Sauk County; Weaver divorce, Grant County, IN, Order Book M, 97, Ancestry.com; Cass County, IN, Cass County Circuit Court, marriage certificate vol. 6, 199, Ancestry.com; 1878 plat map, Town of Forest, Vernon County; 1880 US Census: Town of Forest, Vernon County.

56. 1870 US Census: Town of Forest, Vernon County; 1870 US Census of Agriculture: Town of Forest, Vernon County; Howard Sherpe, "Vernon County (Bad Ax), Wisconsin, Post Offices," 1978, Vernon County History Museum.

57. Cooper, *Black Settlers in Rural Wisconsin*, 8, 20.

58. 1870 US Census: Rosendale, Fond du Lac County; 1880 US Census: Fond du Lac; Caroline Andler, email to the author, June 25, 2012.

59. Sink invalid pension certificate 101361, PF; Reed widow's certificate 430676, PF; 1870 US Census: Fond du Lac; J. G. Griffith Co. expense book, original document held by Fond du Lac Historical Society.

60. 1870 US Census: Fond du Lac.

61. 1870 and 1880 US Census: Fond du Lac.

62. Albertz, "Fond du Lac's Black Community and Their Church," 38–39.

63. "Glimpses of Fox Lake's Negro Colony," held at Fox Lake Public Library History Room, M2003-26-92, 3.

64. 1870 US census, *The Blue Book of the State of Wisconsin*, 1872, http://digicoll.library.wisc.edu/cgi-bin/WI/WI-idx?type=turn&entity=WI.WIBlueBk1872.p0277&id=WI.WIBlueBk1872&isize=M.

65. Author unknown, "The Negro Colony" (3 pages), held at Fox Lake Library History Room, M2003-26-92, 1; Harriet R. O'Connell, "Fox Lake Negro Colony," Fox Lake Public Library History Room, M99-4-1, 2; Gregory Bond, "The Freedmen of Wisconsin," in *Civil War Monitor*, Spring 2014, 21, 74.

66. O'Connell, "Fox Lake Negro Colony," 3.

67. *History of Dodge County, Wisconsin* (Chicago: Chicago Western Publishing Co., 1880), 473; author unknown, "The Fox Lake Negro Colony," M2003-26-92.

68. Brady invalid certificate 746093, PF.

69. 1870 US Census: First Ward, La Crosse; Bruce Mouser, *Black La Crosse, Wisconsin, 1850–1906: Settlers, Entrepreneurs & Exodusters* (La Crosse, WI: La Crosse County Historical Society, 2002), 10–12, 41–42.

70. 1870 US Census: Town of Campbell, La Crosse County.

71. Washburn was elected Congressman in 1867 and Governor of Wisconsin in 1871.

72. Mouser, *For Labor, Race, and Liberty*, 3–4, 15–18.

73. Shawn Godwin, *Pleasant Ridge: A Rural African American Community in Grant County, Wisconsin*, prepared for Old World Wisconsin (Madison: State Historical Society of Wisconsin, 1998, last revised, 2000), 37.

74. Olive Green Lewis, "History of the Negro Pioneer Settlers of Grant County," 2, Cunningham Museum.

75. Lewis, "History of the Negro Pioneer Settlers," 2.

76. 1870 Census: Clinton, IA, Taylor; 1870 Census: Janesville, Richardson.

77. Warren Gray and G. Delevan Pattengill, *New Map of Grant County, Wisconsin, Compiled from Official Records and Actual Surveys*, 1868; Grant County plat book, 1877; 1870 US Census: Lancaster, Grant County.

78. Jackson and McDonald, *Oral History Research Report for Old World Wisconsin*, 3, Cunningham Museum; Cooper, *Black Settlers in Rural Wisconsin*, 26.

79. Castello N. Holford, *History of Grant County, Wisconsin*, reprint (Marceline, MO: Walsworth Publishing Co., 1900), 775; 1870 US Census: Lancaster, Grant County; Grant County Probate, Box 66, Albert Hamlet,

held by Register in Probate, Grant County Courthouse, Lancaster; "William Hamlet," biography and picture, Grant County Historical Society.

80. Ahlgren and Beeler, *A History of Prescott, WI*, 73.

81. *Prescott Journal*, April 28, 1866, and November 25, 1865.

82. *Prescott Journal*, January 7, 1863, and November 4 and 6, 1865.

83. Ahlgren and Beeler, *A History of Prescott, WI*, 568; Samuel Golden (William Albare) obituary, *Prescott Tribune*, July 22, 1921.

84. *Prescott Journal*, July 16 and August 4, 1866.

85. Ahlgren and Beeler, *A History of Prescott, WI*, 323.

86. *Prescott Journal*, July 9 and August 6, 1869.

87. *Prescott Journal*, August 6, 1869.

88. 1870 US Census: Pierce County.

89. 1870 US Census: Prescott and Trimbelle, Pierce County.

90. 1870 US Census: Prescott.

91. 1870 US Census: Prescott; Ahlgren and Beeler, *A History of Prescott, WI*, 581.

92. Ahlgren and Beeler, *A History of Prescott, WI*, 383.

93. "Charles Young Buffalo Soldiers national Monument," National Park Service, www.nps.gov/chyo/learn/historyculture/buffalo-soldiers.htm; "Who are the Buffalo Soldiers?," National Buffalo Soldier Museum, www.buffalosoldiermuseum.com/who-are-the-buffalo-soldiers.

94. Pension index card, Alfred Carroll, Co. D, Twenty-Ninth USCI; Carroll pension application for mother 598904, PF.

95. Rock County marriages, vol. 2, 4; pension index card, Moses Nelson, Co. I, Eighteenth USCI; Nelson invalid pension certificate 1126970, PF.

96. Pension index card, Caleb Hudson (Tom Taylor), Company D, Eighteenth USCI; Hudson invalid pension certificate 1161617, PF.

97. Lloyd T. Bryon's widow's pension application 908954, PF.

98. Benjamin Colder invalid certificate 659813, PF; 1880 US Census: Leavenworth, KS; 1900 and 1910 US Census: Marshall, Saline County, MO.

99. Jackson County Marriages, vol. 1, 62, WHS Library; Snyder (Snider) invalid certificate 520605, PF.

100. Burden invalid certificate 532171, PF.

101. 1880 and 1900 US Census: Lincoln, NE.

102. J. Allen widow's certificate 856149, PF.

103. Letter, Anthony to Pension Bureau, September 15, 1887, in Anthony widow's certificate 656853, PF.

104. Anthony widow's certificate 656853, PF; Great Register, Los Angeles County CA, 1888–1890, 101, on "California Great Registers, 1866–1910," database, *FamilySearch*, https://familysearch.org/ark:/61903/1:1:VY -DQ-NYH, Mark Anthony, August 1, 1890; Voter Registration, Whittier, Los Angeles, California, FHL microfilm 977,994. Film # 005030133, Image 226 of 308, Family History Library, Salt Lake City, UT.

105. John Jones's widow's certificate 287241, PF.

Chapter Five

1. Rayford W. Logan, *The Negro in American Life and Thought: The Nadir, 1877–1901* (New York: Colliers Books, 1954), 275–280.

2. Logan, *The Negro in American Life and Thought*, 52–53, 79–96.

3. David W. Blight, *Race and Reunion: The Civil War in American Memory* (Cambridge, MA: Belknap Press of Harvard University Press, 2001), 3–5.

4. Nell Irvin Painter, *Exodusters: Black Migration to Kansas after Reconstruction* (New York: Knopf, 1976); Raymond Gavins, *The Cambridge Guide to African American History* (New York: Cambridge University Press, 2016), 93–94.

5. Blue invalid certificate 645431, Pension File, Civil War and Later Survivors' Certificates, 1861–1934, Records of the Department of Veterans Affairs, Record Group 15, NARA (hereafter PF); 1880 US Census: Agnes City, Lyon County, KS.

6. *Milwaukee Sentinel*, April 5, 1879.

7. John Jones, PF; Washington invalid certificate 531583, PF; Stewart, PF.

8. Ardis E. Parshall, "This Splendid Outpouring of Welcome," in *Civil War Saints*, ed. Kenneth L. Alford (Provo, UT: Religious Studies Center, Brigham Young University, and Salt Lake City: Deseret Books, 2012), 341, 363, https://rsc.byu.edu/sites/default/files/pubs/pdf/chaps /CWS%2019%20Parshall.pdf.

9. DeNeen L. Brown, "All-black towns across America: Life was hard but full of promise," *Washington Post*, March 27, 2015; Encyclopedia of African-American Culture and History, "Black Towns," www.encyclopedia .com/history/encyclopedias-almanacs-transcripts-and-maps/black -towns; Quindaro, www.civilwaronthewesternborder.org/encyclopedia /quindaro-kansas; Hudson/Taylor, PF; John Jones, PF.

10. *Fond du Lac Daily Commonwealth*, March 29, 1879.

11. *Milwaukee Sentinel*, March 3, 1879.

12. *Milwaukee Sentinel*, April 3, 1879.

13. *Milwaukee Sentinel*, September 3, 1880.

14. *Milwaukee Sentinel*, September 11, 1884.

15. Bruce Mouser, *Black La Crosse, Wisconsin, 1850–1906: Settlers, Entrepreneurs & Exodusters* (La Crosse, WI: La Crosse County Historical Society, 2002), 39–41.

16. Bruce L. Mouser, *For Labor, Race, and Liberty: George Edwin Taylor, His Historic Run for the White House, and the Making of Independent Black Politics* (Madison: University of Wisconsin Press, 2011), 39–43; *The Blue Book of the State of Wisconsin* (1887), 434, 450, 465–468.

17. *Racine Journal*, October 6, November 3, and November 10, 1886; E. W. Leach, *Racine County Militant: An Illustrated Narrative of War Times and a Soldiers Roster* (Racine: E. W. Leach, 1915), 136.

18. *Racine Journal*, November 7, 1888.

19. *Wisconsin Afro American*, October 8 and November 19, 1892.

20. Larry M. Logue and Peter Blanck, "'Benefit of the Doubt': African-American Civil War Veterans and Pensions," *Journal of Interdisciplinary History* 38 (2008): 381–382.

21. Donald R. Shaffer, *After the Glory: The Struggles of Black Civil War Veterans* (Lawrence: University Press of Kansas, 2004), 7; Barbara Gannon, *The Won Cause: Black and White Comradeship in the Grand Army of the Republic* (Chapel Hill: University of North Carolina Press, 2014), 2, 3, 24–26.

22. *Roster of Posts of the Grand Army of the Republic, Department of Wisconsin*, Madison: Post 9, Baraboo, 1921, 1922, 1923, Pam 01-3165, WHS Library; GAR Post No. 60 (Milton) Meeting Minute Books, 1896–1902 (folder 4), and 1902–1905 (folder 5), Mss1: Box 25; Leach, 136, Wisconsin Veterans Museum Archives; Thomas J. McCrory, *Grand Army of the Republic: Department of Wisconsin* (Black Earth, WI: Trails Books, 2005), 269.

23. *Roster of Posts of the Grand Army of the Republic, Department of Wisconsin*, annual reports: Wisconsin Historical Library, pamphlet 01-3165; Wolcott post member book; Milton post member book.

24. Sons of Union Veterans of the Civil War, Department of Missouri,

"Missouri GAR Records," Henry Halleck Post #91, www.suvcwmo.org /missouri-gar-records.html.

25. GAR Post 11, Madison, Constitution, by-laws and complete roll of members, 1866–1926, WVM Mss1, Box 15, Folder 6, Wisconsin Veterans Museum.

26. University of Wisconsin System: All in Wisconsin, Campus Stories, "UW–Platteville students to present research at Posters on the Hill," www.wisconsin.edu/all-in-wisconsin/story/uw-platteville-students -to-present-research-at-posters-on-the-hill/, posted March 27, 2018; The Mining and Rollo Jamison Museums, "African American Lead Miners in Wisconsin," http://mining.jamison.museum/african-american -lead-miners-in-wisconsin; 1880 US Census: Belmont, Lafayette County; John-Brian Paprock and Teresa Peneguy Paprock, *Sacred Sites of Wisconsin* (Black Earth, WI: Trails Books, 2001), 167.

27. 1880 US Census: Beetown, Grant County; 1905 WI State Census: Cassville, Grant County; Spillers, PF.

28. Miles, Compiled Military Service Records, National Archives website (hereafter CMSR), www.nps.gov/civilwar/search-soldiers-detail .htm?soldierId=4005D0BA-DC7A-DF11-BF36-B8AC6F5D926A.

29. *Milwaukee Sentinel*, September 2, 1872; Thomas Buchanan, "Black Milwaukee: 1890–1915" (master's thesis, University of Wisconsin–Milwaukee, 1974), 5–10; Joe William Trotter Jr., *Black Milwaukee: The Making of an Industrial Proletariat, 1915–1945*, 2nd edition (Champaign: University of Illinois Press, 2007), 12.

30. Buchanan, "Black Milwaukee: 1890–1915," 5; 1900 US Census: Fourth ward, City of Milwaukee; Milwaukee City Directory 1891, 719.

31. Buchanan, "Black Milwaukee: 1890–1915," 41; *Cleveland Gazette*, November 12, 1887; Trotter, *Black Milwaukee*, 26, 32.

32. *Milwaukee Weekly Advocate*, January 12, 1899.

33. 1870 US Census: Milton, Rock County; *Milwaukee Sentinel*, November 25, 1876; *WI State Gazetteer and Business Directory*, Waukesha: 1876– 1877, 1879, 1882.

34. *WI State Gazetteer and Business Directory*, Waukesha: 1882, 1888–1889, 1893–1894, 1897–1898, 1903–1904; *Wisconsin Weekly Advocate*, January 12 and August 3, 1899; *Soldiers and Citizens Album of Biographical Record of Army Men and Citizens* (Chicago: Grand Army Publishing Co., 1890), 505.

35. John J. Valentine invalid certificate 557884, PF.

36. Valentine, PF.

37. C. H. Taylor invalid certificate 340413, PF.

38. Valentine, PF; Valentine obituary, *Waukesha Dispatch*, April 16, 1903.

39. Rock County marriages, vol. 1, 122, and vol. 3, 57, WHS Library; Ruth Ann Montgomery, "Evansville Barbers," www.evansvillehistory.net; 1910 US Census: Evansville, IN; *Evansville Review*, July 29, 1899, April 29, 1909, July 24, 1913, August 6, 1914, September 28, 1916.

40. GAR Post 60 Meeting Minute Books, 1896–1902 (folder 4), and 1902–1905 (folder 5), Mss1: Box 25, Wisconsin Veterans Museum Archives.

41. *Wisconsin State Gazetteer and Business Directory*, 1897–1898, 605.

42. *Milton Journal*, April 16, 1903; 1870 US Census: Milton, Rock County.

43. Rock County Deaths, vol. 5, 332, WHS Library.

44. *Milton Journal*, April 6, 1905.

45. GAR Post No. 60 Meeting Minute Book, 1902–1905, Mss1: Box 25, folder 5, 73–74, Wisconsin Veterans Museum Archives.

46. Letter, Jennie Drew to Milton Historical Society, February 26, 1979; Amanda Lee obituary, *Janesville Gazette*, 1935 (undated copy held in Milton History Museum).

47. Dorothy G, McCarthy, "Tales of Old Portage: Ansel Clark—From slave to Respected Citizen," *Portage Register-Democrat*, April 19, 1932; *Milwaukee Journal*, April 21, 1932.

48. A. Green, W. Brown, CMSR; 1860 US Census: North Eau Claire.

49. Green widow's certificate 360058, PF.

50. Green, PF; 1870 and 1880 US Census: City of Eau Claire.

51. Green, PF.

52. Green, PF; Eau Claire County death records, vol. 1, p. 252, WHS Library.

53. 1860 census: Village of Eau Claire, Eau Claire County; W. Brown, CMSR; W. Brown invalid application 641621, PF.

54. 1870 and 1880 US Census: Eau Claire.

55. W. Brown, PF.

56. Erin Blakemore, "Pensions for Veterans Were Once Viewed as Government Handouts," History.com, www.history.com/news/veterans-affairs-history-va-pension-facts.

57. Logue and Blanck, "'Benefit of the Doubt,'" 377–379; Shaffer, *After the Glory*, 122.

58. Shaffer, *After the Glory*, 121–122; Logue and Blanck, "'Benefit of the Doubt,'" 372, 388.

59. Logue and Blanck, "'Benefit of the Doubt,'" 380–381.

60. Shaffer, *After the Glory*, 135.

61. Hillman invalid certificate 1117795, PF.

62. Shaffer, *After the Glory*, 234, note 8.

63. Shaffer, *After the Glory*, 123–126.

64. Gilchrist invalid application 861159, PF; Harris/Harrison invalid application 509688, PF.

65. Rosier widow's certificate 829372, PF.

66. John Allen, PF; Grimes widow's certificate 726926, PF.

67. Hudson/Taylor, PF; *Delavan Enterprise*, October 6, 1993.

68. Gaines, Fond du Lac County Marriages, vol. 1, 253, WHS Library; Hillman, Sink, Branum, PF.

69. Riley widow's certificate 673279, PF; Dangerfield widow's certificate 398253, PF.

70. Brown/Wilson file number C2539152, PF; Ironmonger file number C256374, PF; Franklin/Taylor invalid certificate 1109675, PF.

71. Unassigned Third USCHA: Frank Kenge, CMSR.

72. Hudson, PF.

73. Lewis/Gilchrist, PF.

74. Griffith widow's certificate 552981, PF.

75. Twenty-Ninth USCI: Adam Walker, CMSR; Walker widow's application 172517, PF.

76. Burnett: widow's application 547584 & 979243, PF.

77. Briggs, CMSR.

78. Briggs widow's certificate 294859, PF.

79. Thomas Willis widow's certificate 467238, PF.

80. Ewing/Bowden widow's certificate 589605, PF.

81. Southall invalid certificate 1154038, PF; Haynes widow's certificate 740098, PF; Blue, PF.

82. Ashby invalid application 620204, PF.

83. Parsons, CMSR; Parsons, PF; "How much is a disability worth?" Vermont in the Civil War, https://vermontcivilwar.org/pw/pensions/howmuch.php.

84. Sink, PF.

85. Charles South/Walden invalid pension certificate 68350, PF.

86. Fox Lake Village Board minutes book, March 4, 1896, Fox Lake Library History Room, L95-1-1.

87. Branum, PF; *Fox Lake Representative*, May 22, 1896.

88. Branum, PF; Fox Lake Village Board minutes, October 5, 1898, Fox Lake Library; *Fox Lake Representative*, undated clipping in file at Fox Lake Library Local History Room.

89. Charles Allen, PF.

90. Bryon, PF.

91. Bryon, PF.

92. Shaffer, *After the Glory,* 137; National Trust for Historic Preservation, "Women in Preservation: How the West Side Soldier's Aid Society Paved the Way for the Milwaukee VA Soldiers Home," https://savingplaces.org/stories/women-in-preservation-how-the-west-side-soldiers-aid-society-paved-the-way-for-the-milwaukee-va-soldiers-home#.XYwtNlVKipo.

93. Shaffer, *After the Glory,* 137–138.

94. US National Home for Disabled Veteran Soldiers, 1866–1938, Milwaukee, Northwest Branch Admit book: Jones, Register No. 13240; South/Walden, Alex Jones invalid certificate 586111, PF.

95. US National Home for Disabled Veteran Soldiers, 1866–1938, Milwaukee, Northwest Branch Admit book: Holden register no. 13274, Brown/Wilson register no. 22449, Louis Brown register no. 11737, Neal register no. 15704, and Parks register no. 12381; Holden, PF; Brown/Wilson, PF; Louis Brown, PF; Neal invalid certificate 882287, PF; Parks widow's certificate 352321, PF.

96. James invalid certificate 614567, PF.

97. Isaac Smith, PF; McKenney, PF.

98. Isaac Smith, PF; McKenney, PF.

99. Smith, PF; McKenney, PF; National Soldiers' Home, Milwaukee, Northwest Branch Admit book, register no. 3265 and 13864; Milwaukee County Deaths, vol. 30, p. 31, WHS Library.

100. Hosea W. Rood and E. B. Earle, *History of Wisconsin Veterans' Home, 1886–1926* (Madison: Democrat Printing Company, 1926), 13–16.

101. WI Veterans Home at King, Records and Photographs, 1866–1986: Numerical Index, 1887–1937, Mss33, vol. 14, Box 8, folder 10, 83–84, Wisconsin Veterans Museum Archives; Sink obituary, *Fond du Lac Daily Commonwealth*, September 25, 1905.

102. WI Veterans Home at King, Records and Photographs, 1866–1986: Numerical Index, 1887–1937, Mss33, vol. 14, Box 8, folder 10, p. 78, Wisconsin Veterans Museum Archives; Death Certificate, Taylor County, vol. 1, p. 179, WHS Library.

103. Wisconsin Veterans Home at King, Records and Photographs, 1866–1986: Numerical Index, 1887–1937, Mss33, vol. 14, Box 8, folder 10, p. 36, Wisconsin Veterans Museum Archives; Ewing/Bowen, PF.

104. 1878 Plat Map, Vernon County, on display in Vernon County Museum, Viroqua.

105. 1880 US Census: Town of Forest, Vernon County; Vernon County death records, vol. 1, 11, WHS Library.

106. Charles Allen, CMSR.

107. Charles Allen widow's certificate 354849, PF.

108. 1885 Wisconsin State Census: Hillsboro, Vernon County; Forest Burr Cemetery Records, held at Vernon County Museum, Viroqua.

109. Roberts invalid certificate 336574, PF; Rachel R. Roberts obituary, *Oshkosh Northwestern*, June 5, 1911.

110. Iva May (Roberts) Storey, *Ancestry and Relatives of Harriet Jennett (Roberts) Roberts* (self-published, June 1985), 37; Polk & Co., *Wisconsin State Gazetteer and Business Directory*, 1893–1894, 395–396.

111. Thornton, PF.

112. *Roster, Department of Wisconsin, Grand Army of the Republic* (Milwaukee: Burdick, Armitage, and Allen, 1891), Post 141, Hillsboro.

113. Storey, *Ancestry and Relatives of Harriet Jennett (Roberts) Roberts*, 37.

114. 1880 US Census: Town of Forest, Vernon County; 1880 US Census of Agriculture: Town of Forest, Vernon County.

115. Weaver invalid certificate 442418, PF; Clark County Marriages, vol. 2, 132, WHS Library; Waupaca County Marriages, vol. 3, 479, WHS Library; Eau Claire County Marriages, vol. 3, 482 (Ezra) and vol. 4, 108 (Al), WHS Library.

116. 1870 and 1880 US Census: Forest Township, Vernon County; 1890 US Census of Veterans: Vernon County, Viroqua; Kristen Parrott, "Vernon County Museum Notes," *Vernon County Broadcaster*, February 9 and 16, 2018; *Vernon County Censor*, November 7, 1894.

117. 1880 US Census: Forest Township, Vernon County; 1890 US Veterans Census: Vernon County, Forest Township.

118. Waldron widow's certificate 474938, PF.

119. Jennifer Kirsten Stinson, "Becoming Black, White, and Indian in Wisconsin Farm Country, 1850s–1910s," *Middle West Review* 2 (Spring 2016): 66.

120. Stinson, "Becoming Black, White, and Indian," 53–84.

121. *Delavan Enterprise*, July 22, 1998.

122. Smith/Burton widow's certificate 560818, PF; *Delavan Enterprise*, August 8, 1888.

123. *Delavan Enterprise*, October 6, 1993; McClellan widow's certificate 483790, PF.

124. Moore invalid certificate 664641, PF; *Delavan Republican*, July 27, 1916.

125. 1885 Wisconsin State Census and Census of Veterans: Fond du Lac.

126. *Dodge County Democrat* (Juneau), August 8 and 15, September 5, 1877; *Dodge County Pionier* (Mayville), August 3 and 10, 1877; *Juneau Telephone*, October 24, 1877; *Mayville Telephone*, March 13, 1878; Pardon of Henry Sink, Wisconsin Governor Pardon Papers, 1837–1986, Series 98, Box 30, WHS Archives.

127. Reed invalid application 690624, PF.

128. 1880 US Census Mortality Schedules: Town of Fond du Lac; 1885 MN State Census: Litchfield, Meeker County; Spence widow's certificate 708261, PF. In Litchfield, Spence was a member of the GAR post, while in Fond du Lac no USCT veteran ever became a member.

129. Louis Brown invalid certificate 627205, PF.

130. Sally Albertz, "Fond du Lac's Black Community and Their Church: 1865–1943," *Source of the Lake: 150 Years of History in Fond du Lac*, Clarence B. Davis, ed. (Fond du Lac, WI: Action Printing, 2002), 39–40; Fond du Lac Register of Deeds, vol. 96, p. 291.

131. *Wisconsin Weekly Advocate*, May 21, 1898 and January 12, 1899.

132. *Wisconsin Weekly Advocate*, May 21, 1898.

133. *Wisconsin Weekly Advocate*, January 12, 1899.

134. Morgan, widow's certificate 404643, PF.

135. Sink death certificate; Sink obituary, *Fond du Lac Daily Commonwealth*, September 25, 1905, PF.

136. Albertz, "Fond du Lac's Black Community and Their Church," 42–43.

137. Albertz, "Fond du Lac's Black Community and Their Church," 49–50.

138. Unknown author, "The Negro Colony," original document held at Harriet O'Connell Historical Room, Fox Lake Library, M2003-26-92, 4.

139. O'Connell, "Fox Lake Negro Colony," M99-4-1, 4.

140. Tax Roll, Village of Fox Lake, 1879, L2005-11-1, L2005-3-1, Harriet O'Connell Historical Room, Fox Lake Public Library.

141. 1880 US Census: Fox Lake, Dodge County.

142. 1880 US Census: Fox Lake; Branum, Twelfth USCHA, CMSR; Branum widow's certificate 523259, PF.

143. Author unknown, "Negro Colony—Part 2 (Glimpses of the Branum Family)," M2003-26-92, 1, Harriet O'Connell Historical Room, Fox Lake Library.

144. "Negro Colony—Part 2," 1(a).

145. "Negro Colony—Part 2," 2–3.

146. "Negro Colony—Part 2," 2–3.

147. *Wisconsin Weekly Advocate*, December 9, 1898.

148. O'Connell, "Fox Lake Negro Colony," M99-4-1, 8.

149. Grand Army of the Republic, Department of Wisconsin Records: Post No. 11, Lucius Fairchild Post, Madison, WVM Mss1, Box 15, folder 6, Constitution, by-laws and complete roll of members, 1866–1926; Charles Henry Taylor, PF.

150. Butts obituary, *Wisconsin State Journal*, March 7 and 8, 1930; 1900, 1910, 1920 US Census: Second Ward, Madison; *Wisconsin Weekly Advocate*, June 4, 1898.

151. *Wisconsin State Journal*, March 7 and 8, 1930; *Capital Times*, April 2, 1930.

152. Trotter, *Black Milwaukee*, 13–14.

153. Milwaukee County Marriages, vol. 14, 450, WHS Library; *Wisconsin Weekly Advocate*, October 30, 1902.

154. Buchanan, "Black Milwaukee: 1890–1915," 105, 118; Trotter, *Black Milwaukee*, 27–28.

155. Trotter, *Black Milwaukee*, 22–26.

156. Trotter, *Black Milwaukee*, 22–25.

157. Buchanan, "Black Milwaukee: 1890–1915," 125–126.

158. Buchanan, "Black Milwaukee: 1890–1915," 51.

159. Trotter, *Black Milwaukee*, 13.

160. Trotter, *Black Milwaukee*, 13, 14.

161. Milwaukee City Directories, Dangerfield: 1868, 84; 1878, 143; 1885, 181; 1891, 224, WHS Library.

162. Milwaukee City Directories, 1863–1892, WHS Library; 1880 US Census, Milwaukee: ED110, 19; 1900 US Census: ED 75, sheet 20; Milwaukee County Death Records: vol. 15, 178 (Joshua), vol. 16, 268 (Sylvester), vol. 20, 66 (Neoma), vol. 25, 521 (William), and vol. 19, 51 (Horace), WHS Library; Forest Home Cemetery Records, Dangerfield, WHS Library.

163. Reed, PF.

164. Forest Home Cemetery records, Reed; Reed, PF.

165. Plat maps, Grant County: 1877, 1895.

166. Zachary Cooper, *Black Settlers in Rural Wisconsin* (Madison: State Historical Society of Wisconsin, 1977), 27; "Pleasant Ridge," WHS website, www.wisconsinhistory.org/Records/Article/CS11855. In 1998, this building was moved and reconstructed at Old World Wisconsin, the outdoor historical museum in Waukesha County.

167. Ruby West Jackson and Walter T. McDonald, *Oral History Research Report for Old World Wisconsin, Pleasant Ridge African-American Exhibit*, 1998, 3, Cunningham Museum.

168. 1880 US Census: Beetown Township, Grant County; Sarah Greene obituary, *Grant County Herald*, April 25, 1908; Sarah Greene tombstone, Pleasant Ridge Cemetery.

169. Shepard family genealogy, Grant County Historical Museum; 1880 US Census: Beetown Township, Grant County.

170. Shawn Godwin, *Pleasant Ridge: A Rural African American Community in Grant County, Wisconsin* (paper prepared for Old World Wisconsin, Madison: State Historical Society of Wisconsin, 1998, revised 2000), 81.

171. Jackson and McDonald, *Oral History Research Report*, 5–6, 17; *Grant County Herald*, April 25, 1908.

172. Jackson and McDonald, *Oral History Research Report*, 7–8.

173. Everett W. Grimes, "The Autumn Leaf Club," in *The Crisis*, April 1930, 119; Autumn Leaf Club annual program, Cunningham Museum.

174. Grant County Plat Maps, 1895, 1918.

175. Godwin, *Pleasant Ridge*, 76–77; Cooper, *Black Settlers*, 28–29.

176. 1880, 1900, 1910 US Census: Pierce County.

177. 1880 US Census: La Grange Township, Lafayette County, AR.

178. 1885 WI State Census: Prescott, Pierce County; Washington, PF.

179. Dorothy Eaton Ahlgren and Mary Cotter Beeler, *A History of Prescott,*

WI: A River City and Farming Community on the St. Croix and Mississippi (Prescott Area Historical Society, 1996), 410, 568; Willis widow's certificate 467238, PF; *Pierce County Herald*, January 16, 1896.

180. 1900, 1910, 1920 US Census, Pierce County; *Pierce County Herald*, April 14, 1921.

181. Albare (Golden), invalid certificate 1041204, PF; 1880, 1900, 1910, 1920 US Census: Pierce County, Prescott.

182. 1900 US Census: Fourth Ward, Oshkosh; Marriage of Wilbert Roberts and Edith Myer, Winnebago County Marriages, vol. 6, 317, WHS Library.

83. 1895 Wisconsin Census of Veterans: Oshkosh; 1900 Oshkosh City Directory; 1900 US Census: Tenth Ward, Oshkosh.

184. *Oshkosh Northwestern*: November 2, 1907, December 3, 1910, April 11, 1911, August 7, 1912, and January 15, 1913.

185. 1910 US Census: Tenth Ward, Oshkosh.

186. Rachel Roberts obituary, *Oshkosh Northwestern*, June 5, 1911 and January 15, 1913.

187. 1920 US Census: Baraboo, Sauk County; *Roster of Posts of the Grand Army of the Republic, Department of Wisconsin*, Madison: Post 9 Baraboo, 1921, 1922, 1923—held at Wisconsin Historical Library, Pam 01-3165; Aaron Roberts obituaries, *Baraboo Daily News*, November 26 and 28, 1923; Roberts, PF. Census takers continued to have trouble fitting the descendants of Aaron Roberts and others of the Cheyenne Valley community into their racial categories. William and Lucy Roberts Moon were noted as "black" in 1910, "Mulatto" in 1920, "white" in 1930, and "Indian" in 1940.

Epilogue

1. Donald R. Shaffer, *After the Glory: The Struggles of Black Civil War Veterans* (Lawrence: University Press of Kansas, 2004), 33.

2. *Seattle Times*, February 15, 2016; "Highway 99 renamed in honor of Snohomish settler William P. Stewart," *Everett HeraldNet*, May 21, 2016, www.heraldnet.com/news/highway-99-renamed-in-honor-of -snohomish-settler-william-p-stewart.

3. Sarah Greene obituary, *Grant County Herald*, April 25, 1908.

4. *The Exponent*, February 6, 1975; 1900 US Census: Beetown Township, Grant County.

5. Victor D. Lewis obituary, *Philadelphia Inquirer*, February 11, 1999.

6. *Dubuque Telegraph Herald*, "Pleasant Ridge still rekindles memories," and "We were taught to love," undated clippings (ca. 1995), Grant County Museum Archives.

7. "Aunt Lillie Returns to Old Lancaster Home," *Wisconsin State Journal*, undated clipping, Cunningham Museum.

8. University of Wisconsin, Athletic Department: "Camp Randall 100," www.camprandall100.com/2017/05/30/leo-butts/; 1930 and 1940 US Census: Gary, IN.

9 Bruce L. Mouser, *For Labor, Race, and Liberty: George Edwin Taylor, His Historic Run for the White House, and the Making of Independent Black Politics* (Madison: University of Wisconsin Press, 2011), 29, 35–46, 55–57, 71, 87, 89, 114–119.

10. 20sJazz.com, www.20sjazz.com/tag/Charles+Matson.

11. *Fox Lake Representative*, "Fifty Years Ago," April 29, 1948.

12. E. W. Leach, *Racine County Militant: An Illustrated Narrative of War Times and a Soldiers Roster* (Racine: E. W. Leach, 1915), 134; Oliver Davis, Ninth US Cavalry, Spanish American War, on Fold3, www.fold3.com/image /304/308694070, CMSR.

13. Stamper widow's certificate 916214, Pension File, Civil War and Later Survivors' Certificates, 1861–1934, Records of the Department of Veterans Affairs, Record Group 15, NARA.

14. American Battle Monuments Commission, "370th Infantry Regiment, U.S. Army, 'Black Devils,'" www.arcgis.com/apps/MapJournal/index .html?appid=cf9b8ef96cba452dbad5a86fb20e1152.

15. Loose documents in files, "Pleasant Ridge," Cunningham Museum; newspaper clipping, unnamed paper, 1947, "Ex Slave Tells of Flight to Grant Co. in 1860s," Cunningham Museum.

INDEX

Page numbers in italics refer to illustrations.

Abolitionism, 12–15, 21, 24–25

Adams, George, 74

Adams County, WI, 31, 66, 125

African Americans

    all-black towns, 116–117, 131

    arrival in Wisconsin, 4, 7–20

    colonization, 15, 22, 111, 116–117

    exclusion from history, 1–2, 4–5, 9, 115

    infant mortality, 100

    names, 130–131

    population, 10, 14, 19, 99–100, 106, 110, 115, 143, 144, 152

    protests, 54–55, 66

    westward movement, 111–113, 116–117

    Wisconsin communities, 8, 9, 28, 103–111, 139–154

Albare, William (Sanuel Golden), 67, 109, 111, 153

Alexandria National Military Cemetery, 66

Allen, Charles, 44, 46, 85, 103, 104, 135, 139–140

Allen, Delbert, 103

Allen, Elizabeth, 139

Allen, Harvey, 139

Allen, Jefferson, 62

Allen, John, 84, 113, 129–130, 162

Allen, Lizzie Arms, 103

Allen, Lydia, 104, 135, 139

Allen, William, 139

Allensworth, CA, 116

American Indians, 9–10, 13, 17–18, 41–42, 111, 141, 144–145

Anthony, Emma, 113

Anthony, Mark, 113

Anthony, Matilda, 113

Appleton, WI, 121, 135

Arlington National Cemetery, 66

Arms, Mary Ellen Roberts, 101

Arms, Samuel, 71–72, 81, 101, 103, 139

Artis, Carrie Reese, 103

Artis, Horace, 103, *103*, 121

Artis, Oliver, 103

Ashby, Henry, 31–32, 71, 121, 133, 139

Autumn Leaf Club, 151

Avon (township), WI, 39

Babcock, William, 56

Bailey, Frederick, 63

Baraboo, WI, 7, 9, 119, 121, 154

Barber, Jonathan, 77, 78

Barron, Quartus H., 28

Bartlett, Leon C., 30

Barton, Candace Revels, 102, 105

Barton, Felix, 86, 104

Barton, Leonard, 71, 85–86, 102, 105

Barton, Martha, 85–86

Barton, Wesley, 8, 85–86

Battise, John, 74, 75

Battle of Antietam, 35

Battle of Honey Hill, 55, 120

Battle of Milliken's Bend, 72

Battle of Mobile Bay, 78

Battle of Nashville, 69

Battle of the Crater, 2, 4, 60–68, 131, 134, 139, 161

Beard, Adam, 73

Beard, Lucinda, 73

Beaver Dam, WI, 28, 41, 91, 95, 146

Beecham, Robert, 2

Beetown (township), WI, 10, 73, 108

Bell, Alexander, 43, 56

Belleville, WI, 146

Beloit, WI, 3, 33, 49, 103, 112, 143, 148

Bennett, Andrew, 16, 41, 71, 109, 111, 121, 152, 161

Benton Barracks, 43, 68, 73, 74, 75, 78, 130

Berlin, WI, 44, 60, 112

Bibb, James, 63–64

Birney, John W., 34, 34, 93, 95

Black River Falls, WI, 19, 49, 113

Black Wolf (township), WI, 63

Blue, Charles "Archie," 30, 31, 116, 133

Blue, Susan, 116

Boscobel, WI, 39, 74, 142

Bostwick, Calvin, 17, 20

Bostwick, Cyrenus, 17, 20, 68, 96, 101, 140

Bostwick, Henry, Jr., 17, 20, 101, 121, 140

Bostwick, Henry, Sr., 17

Bostwick, Lucy Caesar Cochagen, 17

Bostwick, Rachel, 17

Bowden, Samuel. See Ewing, Samuel

Bowdry, William, 55, 81

Bowler, David, 153

Bowler, Dora Roberts, 153

Bowman, John, 48, 129–130

Bradick, Anna Tousey Hunter, 102

Bradick, Richard, 102

Brady, Michael, 76, 93, 103, 107

Branum, Charles, 79, 102, 130, 134–135, 145, 146, 159

Branum, James, 145, 159

Branum, Susan Mary, 135, 145

Breese, Zona Gale, 27, 126

Briggs, Charity, 97, 132

Briggs, John, 44, 97, 132

Brighton, WI, 62

Bristol, WI, 14

Brockway, E. L., 49

Brockway, James, 63

Brodhead, WI, 93, 121, 142

Brookfield, William, 78, 97

Brooks, Howard, 67, 97, 121, 146

Brooks, James, 108

Brooks, Joseph B., 109, 110, 111, 152

Bross, John, 58, 63

Brothertown, WI, 17, 41, 68, 72, 92

Brown, Eliza, 97, 127, 128

Brown, John H. (William Wilson), 74, 79, 130, 136–137

Brown, Louis, 97, 103, 105, 136–137, 143

Brown, Michael, 94, 97, 109, 152, 161

Brown, William, 97, 126, 127–128

Brown County, WI, 99, 101

Bryon, Hannah, 112

Bryon, Lloyd, 44, 60, 67–68, 82, 112, 135–136

Bryon, Mary Craig, 112, 135–136

Buffalo Soldiers, 111–112, 160

Burden, Henry, 113, 124

Burks, Lindsley, 106

Burlington, WI, 14

Burnett, Mamie, 131

Burnett, Mary Johnson, 131

Burnett, Thomas, 57, 63, 131, 161

Burnside, Ambrose, 60, 61, 63

Burr, WI, 105

Burrell, Edmund, 51

Burrell, Stephen, 67

Burton, Julia Cattron, 102

Burton, Richard (John Smith), 102, 121, 142

Butler, Barbara Blankenheim, 18

Butler, Benjamin, 24

Butler, Cornelius, 18–19, 22, 48

Butts, Amy (Anna) Roberts, 101, 146, 157

Butts, Benjamin "Benny," 101, 138, 139, 146–147, 157

Butts, Leo, 157–158, 157

Cady, Edson P., 28

Caldwell, William, 81

Calumet County, WI, 13, 15, 17–18, 41, 92, 101

Camp Casey, 59

Camp Quincy, 46, 58, 59

Camp Randall, 72, 74, 157

Campbell, William J., 74

Campbell (township), WI, 107

Carey, Richard, 64

Carlton, WI, 62

Carney, George, 19

Carroll, Alfred, 16, 20, 57, 66, 112

Carroll, Sarah, 16

Carroll, Walter, 16

Carter, Aurora Fiddler, 101

Carter, Jonathan, 44, 67, 101

Cassville, WI, 120

Cheyenne Valley, 3, 12, 100, 103, 116, 135

    African American community, 8, 104–105, 139–142

    residents, 8, 18, 42, 44, 67, 71, 72, 85

Chilton, WI, 41, 51, 71, 92, 121

Chippewa County, WI, 126

Christine, John (John Christian), 64, 66

churches, 100, 105, 106, 108, 109–110, 111, 120, 142, 143, 144, 146, 148, 149, 154, 155, 156

civil rights, 9, 20, 115, 148, 160–161

Civil War. See also military service and individual battles

    casualties, 25, 30, 32, 33, 42, 54, 55, 56, 57, 62–64, 69, 104, 107, 120, 131, 133, 134, 136

    causes, 1, 20, 21, 115–116, 160

    combat, 54–57, 60–64, 67–68, 69, 72, 77, 78

    commemorations, 3–4, 81

    contrabands, 24–29, 32, 39, 43, 71, 77, 80, 105, 106, 146

    disease, 31, 39, 56, 57, 59, 66, 68, 69, 70, 71, 72, 73, 74, 75,

82–83, 92–93, 127, 132, 139
Grand Review of the Armies, 81
homefront, 85–87
monuments, 3–4, 155, 162
postwar, 89–113
prisoners of war, 25, 39, 48, 54, 62, 63–64
reenactors, 3, 4, *161*, 162, *162*
refugees, 8, 24–28, 71
Clark, Ansel, 25–26, 125–126
Clark, Marshall, 19
Clark, Samuel, 31–32
Clark, Satterlee, 26–27, 28
Cleggett, William, 29, 135–136
Colder, Benjamin, 44, 67, 112–113
Coleman, Charles, 117
Collins, Isaac, 31
Columbia County, WI, 16–17, 57, 85, 101, 102, 113
Columbus, WI, 51, 78, 79, 130
Confederate States of America, 1, 20, 35, 39
contrabands, 24–29, 32, 39, 43, 71, 77, 80, 105, 106, 146
Cosley, John, 67
Cowen, Gus, 71, 93
Craft, Jefferson, 141
Craft, Lottie, 141
Craig family, *152*
Craven, Bank, 39
Crawford, Ida Morgan, 102
Crawford, Isaac, 67, 102, 109
Crawford, Milton, 75
crime, 143, 144, 150
Cross, David, 81
Cross, Edwin, 55, 81

Dabney, Peter. *See* Thomas, Peter D.
Dane County, WI, 16, 19, 66, 146–147
Dangerfield, Horace, 79, 93, 96, 130, 148–149, 162
Dangerfield, Joshua, 148
Dangerfield, Louisa, 130, 148, 149
Dangerfield, Neoma, 148–149
Dangerfield, Sylvester, 148
Dangerfield, William, 149
Darien, WI, 68
Darlington, WI, 49
Davis, John, 97, 103
Davis, Logan, 117, 121, 129, 159
Davis, Oliver, 159
Dawes, Rufus, 29
Delany, Martin, 22, 36, 53
Delavan, WI, 3, 121, 155, 156, 159
African American community, 142–143
residents, 31, 102, 130
Democratic Party, 115, 118, 158
Dependent Pension Act of 1890, 128, 132, 135
De Pere, WI, 121, 143
Diggs, Anthony, 61, 62
Diggs, Edward, 53–54
Dodge, Antoine, 74
Dodge, Henry, 10, 81
Dodge County, WI, 26–27, 28, 41, 71, 74, 91–92, 94–95, 102, 106, 135. *See also* Fox Lake, WI
Donaldson, Henry, 40, 41, 61, 102, 107, 108
Donaldson, Martha Grimes, 102
Doolittle, James, 15, 28
Douglass, Frederick, 21–22, 36, 125

Douglass, John, 78
Douglass, Lewis, 125

Eagle River, WI, 121, 133
Eagle (township), WI, 17, 85, 93
Eastman, John, 100
Eau Claire, WI, 49, 97, 126–128
Eau Claire County, WI, 126
Edmunds, Robert, 93, 95, 97
Eleventh Louisiana Infantry, 72
Elkhorn, WI, 44, 67, 112
Ellenboro, WI, 32
Ellis, James, 121, *121*
Ellmore, Joseph M., 107, *107*, 121
Ellsworth, Lemuel, 97
Emancipation Day, 3, 4, 109–110
Emancipation Proclamation, 2,
    35–36, 80
employment, 15, 16, 18–20,
    27–28, 50, 96–99, 105, 106, 107,
    110, 119–128, 130, 142, 146–147,
    148, 149, 152, 153, 157
    barbers, 15–16, 19, 22, 29, 34,
    107, 112, 113, 124, 142, 146, 152
    cooks, 15, 18, 24, 29, 30, 31, 36,
    57, 64, 71, 73, 76, 97, 98, 121,
    122, 126, 127, 130, 133, 138, 139,
    142
    domestic workers, 120, 122, 132,
    135, 146, 147, 150–151
    factory work, 97, 120, 122, 140,
    144, 147, 148
    labor shortages, 26–28, 50, 109
    mining, 10, 119–120
    strikebreakers, 147
    strikes, 99, 118

war employment, 5–6, 8, 23, 24,
    25–26, 29–33, 39, 51, 70–71,
    72–73, *76*, 125, 132–133, 139,
    221–242
entrepreneurs, 16, 22, 111, 119, 122,
    125, 140, 146, 153, 161
Evansville, WI, 93, 124
Ewing, Dora, 132, 137, 138
Ewing, Samuel (Samuel Bowden),
    121, 132, 137, 138, 146
exclusion laws, 15, 26–27
Exodusters, 116, 133

farmers, 10–12, 14, 16–18, 58, 85,
    104, 107, 108, 110–111, 119, 139–
    142, 149, 151, 154
Ferguson, Nimrod, 59
Fiddler, Jefferson, 71, 101
Flows, Major, 56
Fond du Lac, WI, 3, 14, 24, 26, 40, 41,
    51, 99, 100, 117, 121
    African American community,
    27, 28, 105–106, 143–144
    employment, 96
    enlistments, 45, 48, 68, 72, 78
    political activity, 95, 117
    residents, 28, 29, 44, 46, 64, 74,
    96, 103, 117, 129, 130, 138
Fond du Lac County, WI, 18, 19, 86,
    96, 99, 100
Ford, Henry, 57
Forest (township), WI, 101, 102, 105.
    See also Cheyenne Valley
Forrest, Nathan Bedford, 48, 58
Fort Atkinson, WI, 121
Fort Pillow massacre, 48, 58, 83–84

Fort Sumter, 20
Fort Winnebago (township), WI, 16
Fortune, George, 39
Foster, Edward, 72
Fox Lake, WI, 100, 134–135
    African American community,
    28, 106, 144–146
    employment, 97
    political activity, 96
    residents, 79
Frame, Henry M., 51
Franklin, Benjamin, 130
freedmen's aid societies, 109
Freedmen's Cemetery, 66
Freeman, Harrison, 83
Fugitive Slave Act, 7, 12, 14–15, 24

Gadlin, Caroline Shepard, 102,
    149–150
Gadlin, Nettie, 150
Gadlin, Rina, 150
Gadlin, Samuel, 102, 108, 149–150
Gadlin family, 152
Gaines, America (Mary), 105–106,
    144
Gaines, Lewis, 28, 44, 86, 96, 105–
    106, 130, 144
Gaines, Lewis, Jr., 143
Gambel, Alonzo, 30
Garnett, Henry Hyland, 93
Gilchrist, Alex, 129, 131
Gillespie, Ezekiel, 93, 94, 100
Gimbels Department Store, 120, 148
Glover, Joshua, 14–15, 72
Golden, Augustus, 81, 93
Golden, Samuel. See Albare, William

Goodrich, Ezra, 90
Grace, Albert, 56
Graham, Robert, 50
Grand Army of the Republic, 2, 7,
    116, 119, 121, 122, 123, 124–125,
    127, 128, 133, 138, 140, 145, 146,
    154, 161
Grant, Ulysses S., 61, 63, 81, 95–96
Grant County, WI, 10–12, 32, 40, 41,
    43, 51, 72, 73, 79, 100, 102, 103,
    107–108, 130, 149–152, 162
Green, Alfred, 78, 126–127
Green, Amanda Roberts, 126, 127
Green Bay, WI, 43, 48, 68, 100, 101,
    103
Green County, WI, 93
Greene, Charles Wesley, 160
Greene, George M., 159–160
Greene, Hattie Shepard, 102
Greene, Henry, 159
Greene, John, 13
Greene, Lester, 157
Greene, Lillie, 11
Greene, Lily, 75
Greene, Mildred, 150–151
Greene, Sarah, 12, 149, 151, 157
Greene, Thomas, 11, 12, 75, 79, 102,
    107, 149, 150–151, 150, 157, 159,
    161
Greene, William, 12
Greene family, 152
Greenwood, OK, 116
Griffith, Matilda, 47
Griffith, Matthew, 47, 131
Grimes, Amy Greene, 102
Grimes, Joseph, 40

Grimes, Nancy, 11
Grimes, Thomas, 40, 73–74, 102,
    107, 108, 130, 149, 151, 157
Grimes family, 152

Hall, Edward, 72
Hamlet, Albert, 32, 74, 107, 108, 142
Hamlet, Millie, 108
Hamlet, Will, 142
Hampton, Wade, 59, 66
Harris, Charles, 32, 39
Harris, Jessie, 39
Harris, Jesse, 129
Harrison, Jesse, 129
Hartford, WI, 49
Harwell, Eli, 3, 121
Hastings, Samuel, 97
Haynes, Lewis, 132
Hemings, Eston. See Jefferson, Eston
Hemings, Madison, 42
Hemings, Sally, 42
Helping Hand Society, 143
Heuston, Anna Hanson, 86–87
Heuston, Josephus, 33, 86–87
Hicks, Iverson, 72
Hill, Henry, 60
Hill, Jackson, 74, 105, 143
Hillman, Nancy, 129
Hillman, Thomas, 74, 129, 130
Hillsboro, WI, 119, 121, 140
Hines, Charles Marion, 72
Holden, Isaac, 79, 136–137
Holmes, Thomas, 23
Holsey, Samuel, 39
Holstein, Joseph, 93
Horner, William, 10–11

Hovey, Charles E., 26
Howard, Henry, 51
Hudson, Caleb (Tom Taylor), 68–69,
    112, 116–117, 130, 131
Hudson, WI, 97
Hughes, Dennis, 33, 121, 146
Hunter, Edward, 15–16, 20, 59, 102
Hunter, Nancy Ann Toucey, 15

Illinois, 119
    exclusion law, 15
    recruitment, 43, 59
Illinois Steel Company, 147, 148
Ilsley, Charles, 51
Ilsley, Frederick, 51
Iowa County, WI, 119
Iron Brigade, 29, 42
Ironmonger, Leroy. See Jackson,
    Leroy
Isbell, Lewis, 43, 45

Jackson, Abraham, 74, 75, 102
Jackson, John, 62
Jackson, Leroy (Leroy Ironmonger),
    72, 130, 161–162
Jackson, Susan Thompson, 75, 102
Jackson, William, 29
James, Matt, 31, 137
Janesville, WI
    employment, 90, 97
    enlistments, 33, 48, 68, 83
    residents, 16, 43, 76, 79, 90–91,
    103, 108, 122, 130, 159
Jefferson, Beverly, 42, 121
Jefferson, Eston (Eston Hemings), 42
Jefferson, John Wayles, 42

Jefferson, Julia Isaacs, 42

Jefferson, Thomas, 42

Jefferson County, WI, 67

Johnson, Andrew, 81, 83

Johnson, George A., 121

Johnson, Hayden. *See* Netter, Hayden

Johnson, Henry, 78

Johnson, Henry Loyd, 51

Johnstown, WI, 39

Joiner, John, 31

Jones, Alexander, 100, 102, 129, 136

Jones, John, 113, 117

Jones, Maria Rosier, 100, 102

Jones, William N., 74

Jones, Wing, 124

Jorden, Joseph, 62

Juneteenth Day, 3, 82

Kane, Dick, 50

Kansas, 116

Kenosha, WI, 14, 18–19, 22, 48, 74

Kenosha County, WI, 62, 97

Kewaunee County, WI, 62

King Home, *137*, 138

Kneley, William, 74, 75

Korean War, 160

Ku Klux Klan, 9, 115, 144

La Crosse, WI, 3
    African American community,
        106–107
    employment, 34, 50, 97, 99
    enlistments, 48, 68, 70, 86, 130
    political activity, 93, 95
    residents, 34, *34*, 43, 48, 72, 76,
        79, 99, 103, 116, 136, 146, 158

La Crosse County, WI, 112, 118

Lackey, Samuel, 75

Lafayette County, WI, 40

Lake Mills, WI, 3

Lancaster, WI, 3, 108, 150

Langston City, OK, 116

La Valle, WI, 153

Lay, James, 78

Lee, Amanda Jane Barker, 91, 125,
    146

Lee, Arthur B., 3–4, 53, 54, 80, 89,
    90–91, *91*, 96, 100, 119, 121,
    124–125, 146, 161

Lee, Arthur, Jr., 91, 125

Lee, Mary Hagney, 91, 100

Lee, Robert E., 66, 67–68

Lee, Rose, 90

Lewis, Major, 77, 78

Lewis, Ollie (Olive) Greene, *12*, 151,
    160

Lewis, Victor D., 157

Lincoln, Abraham, 15, 20, 21, 22, 23,
    35–36, 54, 80, 94

Lincoln University, 155

literacy, 5, 26, 50, 56, 105, 108, 129,
    130, 134, 137

Loganville, WI, 101

L'Ouverture Hospital, 64–66, 132

Lumpkin, William, 67

Lyons, Martin, 66

Mackay, David, 61, 64, 82

Mackay, Jackson, 62

Mackay, Perry, 82

Madison, WI, 3, 119, 121, 125

African American community, 146–147
credited to, 59, 62
employment, 97
enlistments, 45, 46, 57, 67
residents, 22, 31, 32, 40, 42, 44, 46, 60, 67, 103, 113, 129, 133, 137, 143, 146–147
training, 72, 74, 86, 157
Manley, Lemuel, 31
Markesan, WI, 16
Mason, Henry, 77, 78
Massachusetts
Fifty-Fifth Massachusetts Infantry, 2, 4, 53–55, 70, 80–81, 85, 160
Fifty-Fourth Massachusetts Infantry, 2, 3–4, 53–55, 70, 80–81, 160
Mather, Jesse, 26
Matson, Alfred, 3, 31, 142, 159
Matson, Charles, 159
Matson, Luticia Russell, 142, 159
Mauston, WI, 46
Maxon, John, 63
Maxson, Orrin T., 33–35, 109
McAlroy, William P., 29
McCann, Anderson, 64
McClellan, Martha Lewis, 142–143
McClellan, Oscar, 3, 121, 130, 142–143
McDonald, Jasper, 57
McGraw, Lavinia, 16, 17, 122, 124
McGraw, William, 16, 103, 122, 124
McKenney, William "Pitt," 25, 32, 44, 60, 95–96, 97, 98, 129, 137–138

Medford, WI, 121, 138, 145
Melvin, OK, 116, 117, 131
Menominee, WI, 61, 67
Miles, Anne, 147
Miles, John J., 98, 118, 119, 120, 121, 123, 147–148, 161
military service, 1–6, 9, 20–23, 33–51, 53–84, 84, 159–162, 163–220. See also United States Army; United States Navy; Wisconsin militia
bounties, 40, 49, 59, 85, 104, 110–111
draft, 6, 23, 33, 39–41, 48–51
draft associations, 40, 49–50, 59
noncommissioned officers, 33, 35, 38, 56, 60, 67, 76, 79
recruitment, 33–39, 37, 43–51, 53
substitutes, 40, 48–51, 72, 86, 126
Milton, WI, 3, 13, 40, 90–91, 96, 119, 121, 122, 124–125, 146
Milton House, 13, 14, 89–90
Milton Junction, WI, 113
Milum, Albert, 72
Milwaukee, WI, 2–3, 49, 51, 59, 98, 100, 116, 117, 119, 121, 124, 143, 155, 162
African American community, 147–149
credited to, 4, 46–47, 50, 57, 59, 60, 62, 64, 66, 82, 131, 134
employment, 50, 96, 98, 99, 120, 122
enlistments, 48, 68, 78

lynching, 19
political activity, 94, 95, 118
residents, 16, 17, 19, 55, 57, 66,
  72, 74, 78, 79, 93, 97, 99, 103,
  112, 120, 123, 131, 133, 135, 143,
  146, 147–149
Soldiers Home, 4, 79, 131, 134,
  136, 137, 138, 153
Underground Railroad, 12–13,
  14–15
Milwaukee County, WI, 19, 40, 99,
  100, 147–149
Missouri, 8, 11, 14, 35, 57, 60, 89,
  119, 155
commemorations, 4
recruitment, 44, 46, 59, 68, 69
Mitchell, Aaron, 46–47
Mitchell, James, 77–78
Mix, Eli, 125
Monroe County, WI, 19
Montgomery, Richard B., 143, 147
Moon, Lucy Roberts, 140, 153, 154
Moon, William, 153, 154
Moore, Barney, 143
Moore, David, 119
Moore, Jerusha Steele Banks, 143
Morgan, Charles, 16, 76, 94, 102, 109
Morgan, Ebenezer, 18, 86, 105, 143,
  144
Morgan, Moses, 76, 94
Morgan, Nancy, 94, 105
Mound Bayou, MS, 116
Mukwonago, WI, 93
multiracial families, 7, 13, 15, 17–18,
  41–42, 68, 91, 97, 105, 127, 140,
  141, 144, 150–151, 154

Munsel, Lafayette, 33
Nash, Anderson. *See* Reese, Anderson
National Colored Men's Protective
  Association, 158
National Homes for Disabled Volun-
  teer Soldiers. *See* Soldiers Homes
National Negro Democratic League,
  159
National Negro Liberty Party, 159
Neal, Johnson, 51, 136–137
Nelson, Charles, 33
Nelson, Jerret, 78, 83
Nelson, Moses, 112
Nelson, Thomas, 97
Netter, Hayden (Hayden Johnson),
  28, 41, 71, 96, 97, 102, 121, 137,
  138, 145
Netter, Seressa Newsom, 102
Newsom, David, 75, 105
Newsom, George, 74, 102
Newsom, John Q., 56
Nicodemus, KS, 116
Noland, William H., 22
Norton, John, 82
Nusom, John Q., 56

Oden, Frank, 64
Old Colored Soldiers Re-Union, 4
Oregon, WI, 16
Orr, James, 59
Orr, Lewis, 59
Orr, Lucy, 59–60
Oshkosh, WI, 3, 57, 79, 96, 97, 101,
  112, 153
Ousley, William, 68, 103
Ozaukee County, WI, 23–24

Paine, Halbert, 25, 29–31
Paine, Will, 50
Palmyra, WI, 64
Paris, WI, 14
Parks, Anthony, 71, 136–137
Parsons, Peter, 103, 133–134
Paten, Lewis, 44, 60, 67
Patterson, Alfred, 96, 105, 143
Pendleton, Jerome, 41
Pendleton, John, 41
Pendleton, Peter, 41
pensions, 103, 112, 119, 120, 122–
    124, 126–136, 137–138, 139–140,
    141, 143, 147, 149, 153, 154
    agents, 129, 132
    discrimination, 133–134
    fraud, 131
Perine, James, 33
Pershing, John, 159
Peshtigo, WI, 116, 119, 121
Phillips, Henry, 56
Pierce County, WI, 14, 16, 41, 66, 67,
    71, 76, 102. See also Prescott, WI
Plankinton House, 98, 99, 118, 120,
    147, 148, 149
Platteville, WI, 142
Pleasant Ridge, WI, 100, 157, 160
    African American community,
    10–12, 107–108, 149–152
    residents, 13, 73, 79, 120, 152
Plover, WI, 29
political activity, 93–96, 117–118,
    122, 158–159, 161. See also
    suffrage
Port Washington, WI, 23–24

Portage, WI, 17, 49, 51, 97, 113,
    125–126
Potter, Edward E., 80
Potter, John F., 28
poverty, 96, 97, 100, 108, 126–128,
    134–135, 161
Prairie du Chien, WI, 43, 48, 49, 73
Pratt, Andrew, 40–41, 89–90
Prescott, WI, 3, 100
    African American community,
    43, 109–111, 152–153
    employment, 50, 97
    political activity, 94
    residents, 68, 76, 103, 113, 116,
    117
Price, Benjamin, 62
Price, Warrick, 51
Prohibition Party, 122

Quarlls, Caroline, 12, 16
Quindaro, KS, 116, 117

Racine, WI, 3, 14, 29, 60, 119, 121,
    155, 156
    African American community,
    27–28
    employment, 148
    political activity, 117
    residents, 43, 44, 53, 54, 61, 62,
    81, 83, 97, 99, 103, 117, 129, 132,
    159
Racine County, WI, 19, 99, 118
racism, 1–2, 4, 9, 10, 16, 19, 27, 36,
    38–39, 43, 62, 70, 77, 80, 83–84,
    90, 91–92, 95, 110, 112, 115, 131,
    144, 152–153, 159, 160

Randall, J. M., 93
Ray, William, 29
Raymond, WI, 13–14
Reconstruction, 1, 9, 89–113, 115, 117
Reed, Nancy (Nina), 103, 143, 146, 149
Reed, William, 64, 82, 98, 103, 105, 120, 121, 139–140, 143, 146, 149, 162
Reedsburg, WI, 49
Reese, Anderson (Anderson Nash), 41, 61, 103, 105, 121, 143
Reese, Arthur Arlington, 102
Reese, Henry, 61–62
Reese, Orcia Valentine, 102
Republican Party, 1, 20, 28, 93–94, 115, 117–118, 158
Revels, Aaron, 42, 101, 102, 104
Revels, Henry, 42, 101, 102, 104
Revels, John, 42, 101, 102, 104
Revels, Mark, 100
Revels, William, 42, 101, 102, 104
Rewey, WI, 119–120
Reynolds, Manuel, 51
Richards, Charlotte Simons, 72, 92
Richards, Freeman, 72, 92, 101
Richardson, Adeline Dixon, 124
Richardson, Alice, 124
Richardson, Anthony, 51, 103, 107, 108, 124, 161
Richardson, Arthur, 124
Richland Center, WI, 141
Richland County, WI, 140
Richmond, Booker T., 157
Richmond, Lily Greene, 157, 160
Richmond, Mason, 159, *159*

Richmond, Thomas, 74, 108, 149, 159
Riley, Ellen, 130
Riley, John, 29
Riley, William, 51, 78, 130
riots, 23–24, 81, 83–84
Ripon, WI, 68, 72
Roberts, Aaron, 7–8, 9, 20, 44, 46, 64, 101, 102, 104, 119, 121, 139–140, 146, 153–154, 161
Roberts, Della Sebring, 154
Roberts, Edith Myer, 153
Roberts, George, 57
Roberts, Ishmael, 7
Roberts, Martha Stewart, 101, 104, 140, 153
Roberts, Rachel Bostwick, 101, 140, 153
Roberts, Wilbert, 153
Robinson, Richard, 44, 62
Rochester, WI, 14
Rock County, WI, 13, 19, 23, 39, 41, 55, 72, 78, 93, 97, 99, 103, 113, 129
Rogers, James B., 26, 27
Rollins, Charles, 43, 56
Ron, John, 70
Roseman, Henry, 41, 61, 89, 91–92
Rosendale, WI, 18, 105
Rosier, Hannah Bruce, 16, 85, 87
Rosier, Henry, 17, 57, 101, 102, 121, 129
Rosier, John, 16–17, 51, 85, 87, 101, 102
Ross, William, 11, 44, 62
Russell, Calvin, 39
Rutland (township), WI, 16

St. Mark's African Methodist Episco-
pal Church, 100, 155
Salem (township), WI, 97
Salomon, Edward, 22, 33, 34, 40–41
Sauk County, WI, 8, 18, 43, 46, 60,
67, 74, 75, 101, 104, 153
Schlitz, Joseph, 51
schools, 10, 26, 100, 105, 106, 108,
145, 149
Scott, Dred, 19–20
secession, 1, 2, 20
sectional reconciliation, 1, 2, 9,
115–116
segregation, 9, 10, 14, 20, 64–66,
111, 115, 119, 147–148, 160
Sharon (township), WI, 83, 142
Shavers, Ferdinand, 22–23, 40, 116
Shaw, Robert, 3
Sheldon, Shepard, 68, 69
Shelton, James, 19
Shepard, Caroline, 10
Shepard, Charles Edward, 11
Shepard, Charles P., 3, 10–11, 20, 40,
57, 74, 102, 107, 151, 157, 159,
162
Shepard, Edward, 150
Shepard, Eliza, 11
Shepard, Ella, 11
Shepard, Emily, 11
Shepard, Howard Brent, 157
Shepard, Isaac, 10, 11, 40, 107, 108
Shepard, John, 3, 10, 20, 51, 107, 162
Shepard, Sarah, 10
Shepard family, 152
Sherman, Arthur M., 126, 127

Sherman, William Tecumseh, 70–71,
81
Shirley, Frances, 27
Shopiere, WI, 23
Showalter, John, 32
Shullsburg, WI, 22, 116
Sink, Amanda Bostwick, 101, 138
Sink, Charlotte Simmons Richards,
101
Sink, Henry, 18, 18, 44, 45, 46, 64,
65, 86, 95, 101, 105, 121, 130,
133, 134, 137, 138, 143, 144, 161
slavery, 1–8, 10–15, 19–21, 24–25,
32, 35–36, 42, 46–47, 55, 59–60,
77, 82, 94, 96, 110, 111, 115–116,
130, 160
Emancipation Proclamation, 2,
35–36, 80
Fugitive Slave Act, 7, 12, 14–15,
24
Slavery Abolition Act (Great Brit-
ain), 3, 109
Smith, Isaac, 25, 32, 44, 46, 60, 97,
137–138
Smith, John. See Burton, Richard
Smith, Martin, 15, 72
Smith, Nathan, 48, 107, 118, 158
Smith, Phillip, 64
Smith, Sarah, 107
Snyder, Anderson, 113
Soldiers Homes
King, 137, 138
Milwaukee, 4, 79, 131, 134, 136–
138, 153
South, Charles. See Walden, Charles

Southall, William, 132

Spafford, H. C., 63

Spanish-American War, 145, 159

Sparta, WI, 44, 67, 113

Spence, Allie, 143

Spence, Missouri, 143

Spence, Van, 28, 78, 105, 117, 143

Spillers, Eva, 120

Spillers, William, 40, 41, 107, 120

Spite, Thomas, 97

Stamper, Alexander, 97, 159

Stamper, Merle, 159

Stanton, Catherine, 41

Stanton, Cato, 41, 71

Stanton, Maria, 41

Stanton, Moses, 41

Stanton, William, 41, 71

Stanton, Zack, 41

Stantonville, WI, 41

Stark, Peter, 62

Stevens, Isaac, 63

Stevens Point, WI, 112, 133

Stewart, Eliza Thornton, 18, 101, 104

Stewart, Hettie, 18

Stewart, Martha, 18

Stewart, Walden, 8, 18

Stewart, William P., 18, 40, 67, 101,
    104, 116, 119, 121, 155

Stockbridge, WI, 13, 15, 44, 67, 121

Strauder, Sanford, 62

Strayhorn, Alexander, 109, 110, 111,
    152

suffrage, 10, 20, 27, 93–95, 109, 110,
    115, 147, 160–161

Sullivan, Mickey, 29

Summers, Joseph, 82

Sun Prairie, WI, 2

Sutfen, Averline, 17

Sutfen, John, 17, 81, 85, 93, 97, 101,
    113

Sutfen, Maria Rosier, 17, 101, 113

Sutfen, Sarah, 17

Sutfen, Titus, 17, 85

Taylor, Andrew, 94–95

Taylor, Benjamin (Benjamin Frank-
    lin), 130

Taylor, Charles Henry, 82, 124, 146

Taylor, Chesley, 40, 107, 108

Taylor, Enoch, 97

Taylor, George Edwin, 107, 118,
    158–159, 158

Taylor, Henry, 40

Taylor, Jerry, 74

Taylor, Pinckney, 78, 107, 162

Taylor, Tom. See Hudson, Caleb

Taylor County, WI, 145

Thomas, George, 69, 70

Thomas, Henry Goddard, 2

Thomas, John, 78

Thomas, Lorenzo, 34

Thomas, Nora, 100

Thomas, Peter D. (Peter Dabney), 33,
    118, 119, 121, 160, 161

Thomas, Richard, 81, 92–93, 102

Thomas, William R., 43, 56, 74, 97,
    100

Thompson, Delany Revels Roberts,
    101

Thompson, George, 76

Thompson, Reuben, 18, 74, 75, 101,
    102, 104

Thompson, Samuel, 93, 95, 107, 161

Thompson, Sarah Ann Thornton, 18, 101, 104

Thornton, Abram, Jr., 18, 67, 101, 104, 121, 140

Thornton, Abram, Sr., 18

Thornton, Ellen, 18

Tiller, Robert, 122

Tillman, Abraham, 83

Tinsley, Charles, 62

Titball, Robert, 12, 16

Trenton (township), WI, 41, 106, 146

Trimbelle (township) WI, 14, 16, 41, 76, 111, 121, 152

Tucker, John, 53, 54, 81

Turner, William H., 51

Underground Railroad, 8, 12–13, 89–90

Underhill, Daniel, 19, 20, 44, 67, 102, 111

Underhill, Harriet, 19

Union Labor Party, 118

Union (township), WI, 97

United States
Bureau of Colored Troops, 36
Congress, 3, 19, 23, 24, 28, 54–55, 60, 63, 111, 119
Pension Bureau, 127, 128–129, 130, 131, 133, 135
Supreme Court, 19, 115
War Department, 36, 48, 49, 128

United States Army
100-day regiments, 48
African Americans, 1–6, 9, 20, 21–23, 111. *See also* United States Colored Troops

Buffalo Soldiers, 111–112, 160
desertions, 39, 43, 50, 56, 68, 70, 78, 81, 112
discrimination, 36, 38–39, 40–41, 54–55, 66, 81, 128–129, 133, 160
enlistment form, *45*
flags, *38, 79*
muster roll, *44*
recruitment poster, *37*

United States Colored Heavy Artillery
Sixth Regiment, 79
Third Regiment, 51, 78, 83–84
Thirteenth Regiment, 79, 162
Twelfth Regiment, 79

United States Colored Heavy Infantry
Third Regiment, 49

United States Colored Infantry
Eighteenth Regiment, 33, 50, 68–70, 73, 83
Fiftieth Regiment, 57
Forty-Ninth Regiment, 32, 72–73, 83
Forty-Second Regiment, 73, 76
Forty-Seventh Regiment, 57
One Hundred Second Regiment, 66
Seventeenth Regiment, 76, 83, 86
Sixty-Eighth Regiment, 43, 55–57, 70, 73, 83
Sixty-Fifth Regiment, 73–75, 84, 155
Sixty-Second Regiment, 74, 155
Sixty-Seventh Regiment, 73–75, 84
Twenty-Fourth Regiment, 38

Twenty-Ninth Regiment, 3, 7, 15, 32, 33, 43–47, 55, 57–68, 81–83, 86–87, 89, 112, 119, 153, 155, 161, 162

Twenty-Third Regiment, 2, 61, 62

United States Colored Troops, 32, 33, 35–39, 43–47, 51, *58*, 80, 81–82, *84*, 111

United States Navy, 36, 77–78, 160

Utley, William, 24–25

Valentine, John, 16, 20, 31, 58

Valentine, John J., 16, *17*, 20, 58, 76, 102, 103, 121, 122–124, 125, 147, 161

Valentine, Julius, 16, 17, 20, 57–58

Valentine, Louisa, 16, *17*, 122, 124

Valentine, Shadrach, 16, 20, 58, 66

Valentine House, 122

Van Steenwyk, Gysbert, 34–35

Vernon County, WI, 40, 43, 46, 99, 100, 101, 102. *See also* Cheyenne Valley

Viroqua, WI, 141

Walden, Charles (Charles South), 4, 64, 133, 134, 136

Waldon, Samuel. *See* Waldron, Samuel

Waldron, Elizabeth Revels, 102, 141

Waldron, Samuel, 71, 85, 102, 141

Walker, Adam, 131

Walker, Louisa, 131

Walter, Clara Elizabeth, 146

Walter, Samantha Pemmerton, 146

Walter, Susan Jane Branum, 102, 146

Walter, Wesley, 28, 57, 102, 145, 146

Walworth County, WI, 19, 67, 68, 83, 99, 102, 142–143

Washburn, Cadwallader, 48, 107, 118, 158

Washington, Booker T., 115

Washington, George, 71

Washington, Lewis, Jr., 13, 16, 20, 67, 102, 109, 111, 116, 152

Washington, Lewis, Sr., 13–14, *13*, 94, 109, 110, 152

Washington, Mary Jane Underhill, 19, 102, 111, 152

Watertown, WI, 39

Watterstown (township), WI, 108

Waukesha, WI, 13, 14, 51, 79, 121, 122, 124, 125, 130, 147

Waukesha County, WI, 17, 85, 86, 102

Waupaca, WI, 15–16, 132, 138

Waupaca County, WI, 137

Wayman African Methodist Episcopal Church (Racine), 155, *156*

Wayman Chapel (Delavan), 155, 156

Wayne, Monroe, 78

Weaver, Al, 141

Weaver, Alfred, 43, 44, 46, 60, 64, 85, 101, 104–105, 139, 140–141

Weaver, Bert (Bird), 141

Weaver, Charity Revels, 101, 104

Weaver, Ezra, 141

Weaver, Mary Serton, 105, 140

Weaver, Melvin, 141

Webb, Alexander, 76

West Bend, WI, 49

West Salem, WI, 107, 158

West Side Soldiers' Aid Society, 136

Westfield (township), WI, 18, 104

white supremacy, 1, 2, 19, 115

Wilkins, Charles F., 93, 95

William P. Stewart Memorial Highway, 155

Williams, Bill, 74

Williams, George Washington, 2, 3,
39, 67

Williams, James D., 119

Williams, Joseph, 78

Williams, Thomas, 25

Willis, Anthony, 109, 111

Willis, Louise, 132

Willis, Thomas, 68, 109, 132, 152

Wilson, Albert, 82

Wilson, William. *See* Brown, John H.

Winnebago County, WI, 16, 19, 63,
99, 101

Winneconne, WI, 16

Winslow, Loring B. T., 140

Wisconsin
African American communities,
8, 9, 28, 103–111, 139–154
arrival of African Americans, 4,
7–20
attitudes, 9, 15, 16, 26–28, 51,
89–93, 110, 141–142, 144–145,
152–153
exclusion law, 15, 26–27
lynchings, 19
slavery in, 10

Wisconsin Afro American (newspaper), 118

Wisconsin Labor Advocate (newspaper), 118

Wisconsin militia, 6, 10, 20, 21, 22,
41–42, 48, 111, 118

Eighth Wisconsin Infantry, 31,
33, 42

Eighth Wisconsin Light Artillery,
29

Eleventh Wisconsin Infantry,
25–26, 32, 125

Fifteenth Wisconsin Infantry, 33

Fifth Wisconsin Infantry, 87

Fifty-First Wisconsin Infantry, 51

First Wisconsin Cavalry, 41

First Wisconsin Infantry, 41, 42

Fortieth Wisconsin Infantry, 48

Forty-Second Wisconsin Infantry,
31

Fourteenth Wisconsin Infantry,
26, 41

Fourth Wisconsin Cavalry, 31,
132–133

Fourth Wisconsin Infantry, 25,
29–31

Iron Brigade, 29, 42

Second Wisconsin Cavalry, 32,
126

Second Wisconsin Infantry, 76

Seventeenth Wisconsin Infantry,
31, 71

Seventh Wisconsin Infantry, 29,
30

Sixteenth Wisconsin Infantry, 71

Sixth Independent Wisconsin
Light Artillery, 31–32, 71

Sixth Wisconsin Infantry, 29, 42

Third Wisconsin Infantry, 71

Thirteenth Wisconsin Infantry, 31

Thirty-Eighth Wisconsin Infantry, 31
Thirty-Fifth Wisconsin Infantry, 31
Thirty-First Wisconsin Infantry, 31, 57, 71
Thirty-Ninth Wisconsin Infantry, 48
Thirty-Second Wisconsin Infantry, 71, 85
Thirty-Seventh Wisconsin Infantry, 41, 61
Thirty-Third Wisconsin Infantry, 57
Twelfth Wisconsin Infantry, 33
Twenty-Eighth Wisconsin Infantry, 23–24
Twenty-First Wisconsin Infantry, 71, 93
Twenty-Second Wisconsin Infantry, 24–25, 31
Twenty-Seventh Wisconsin Infantry, 29, 31
Wisconsin People's Party, 118
Wisconsin State Colonization Association, 117
Wisconsin Weekly Advocate (newspaper), 120–122, 143, 147
women
    employment, 96, 106, 122, 124, 132, 135, 146
    entrepreneurs, 16
    refugees, 26
    war employment, 8, 29, 31, 32, 72–73
Women's Relief Corps, 125

Wood, Charles, 32
Woodland (township), WI, 104
World War I, 148, 159, 160
World War II, 159–160

Yates, William, 78

Zion African Methodist Episcoal Church (Fond du Lac), 100, 106, 143, 144, 146
Zion Methodist Church (Fox Lake), 100, 106, 146

About the Author

Jeff Kannel has been a volunteer and tour guide at the Civil War Museum in Kenosha, Wisconsin since 2012. He has been researching the Twenty-Ninth United States Colored Troops and other Wisconsin African American servicemen since 2011. An active speaker on these topics, Kannel is also co-author (with Professor Victoria Tashjian) of "Henry Sink: Settler, Soldier, Citizen" for the *Wisconsin Magazine of History.*